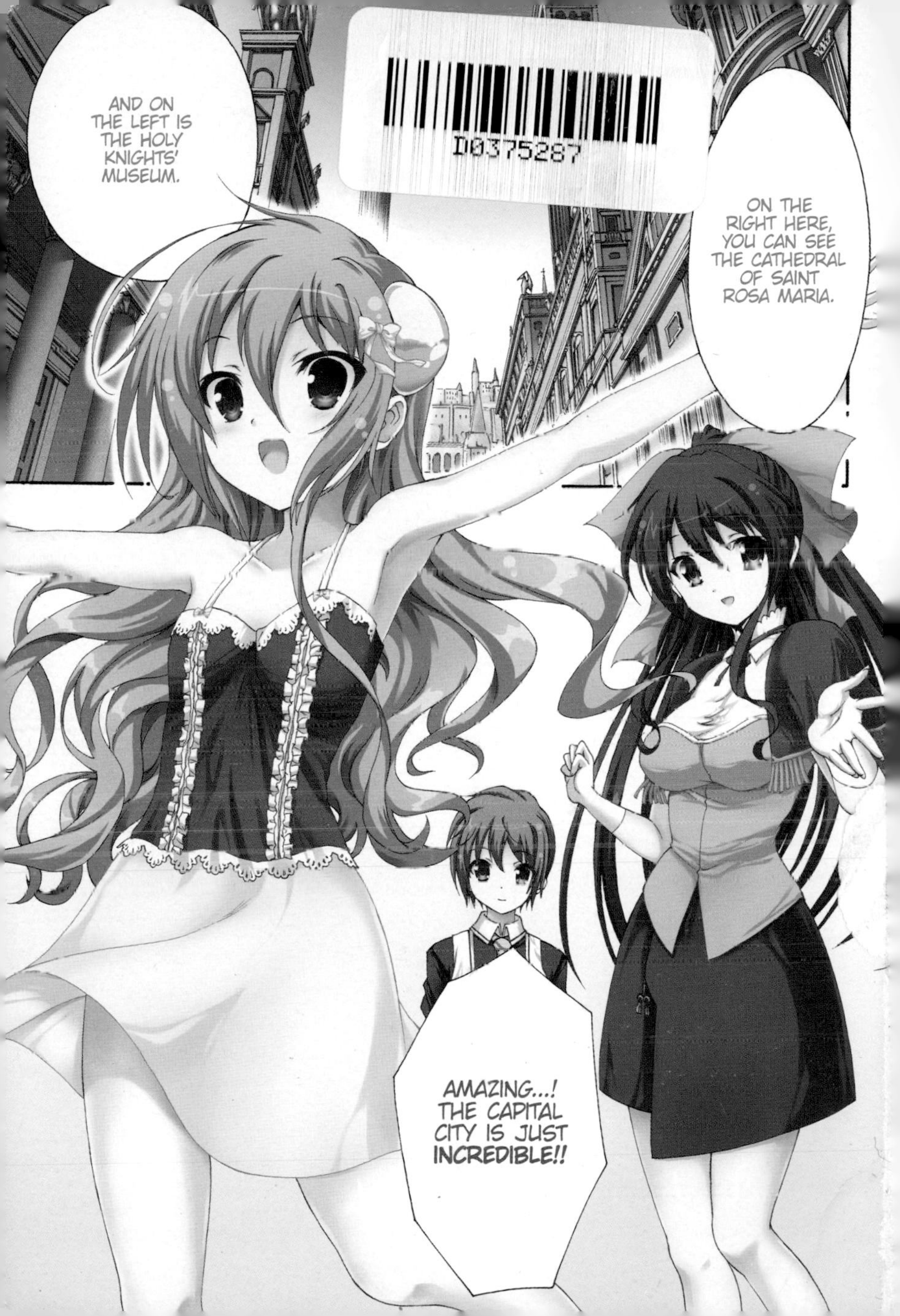
ON THE RIGHT HERE, YOU CAN SEE THE CATHEDRAL OF SAINT ROSA MARIA.
AND ON THE LEFT IS THE HOLY KNIGHTS' MUSEUM.
AMAZING...! THE CAPITAL CITY IS JUST INCREDIBLE!!

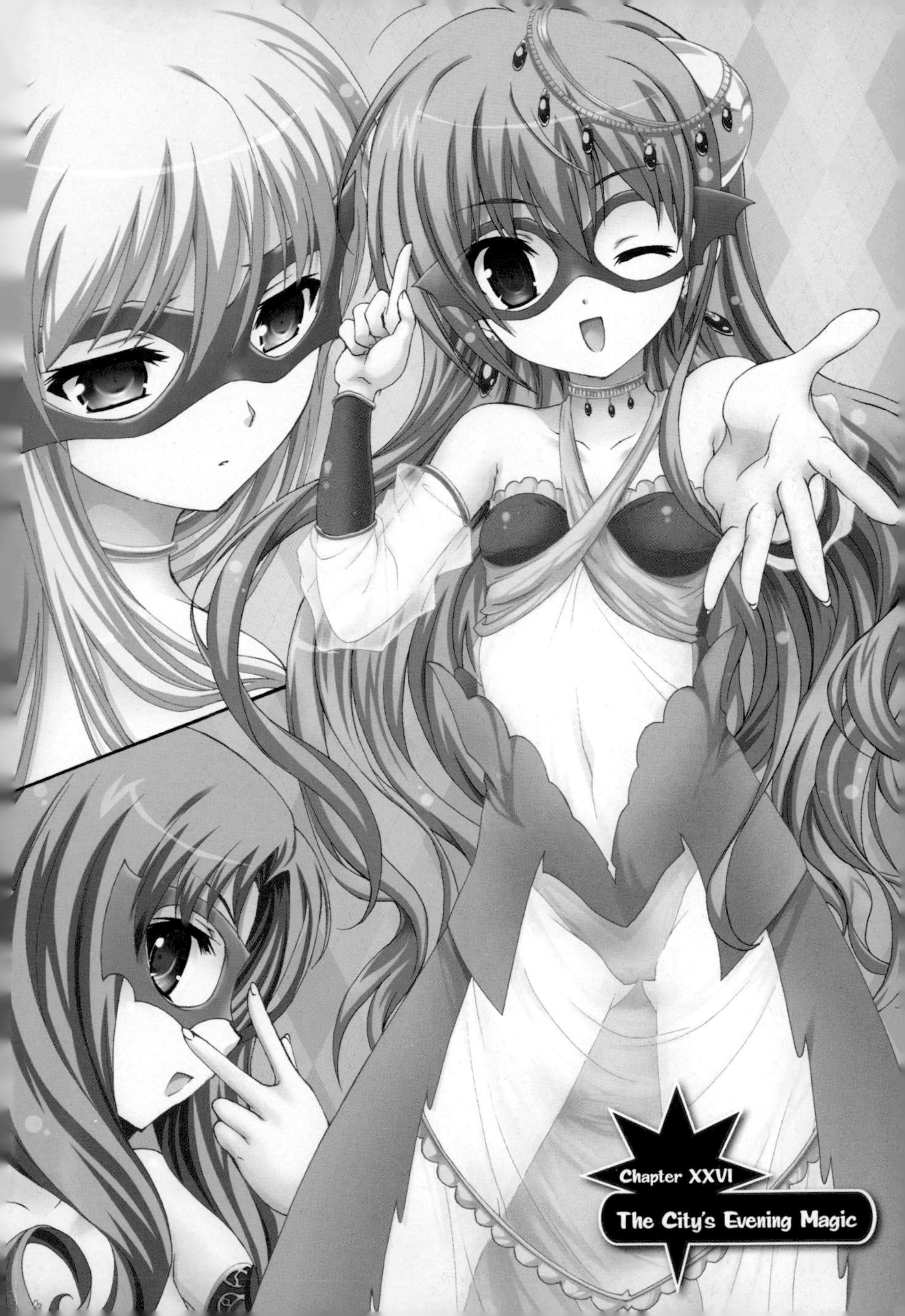
Chapter XXVI
The City's Evening Magic

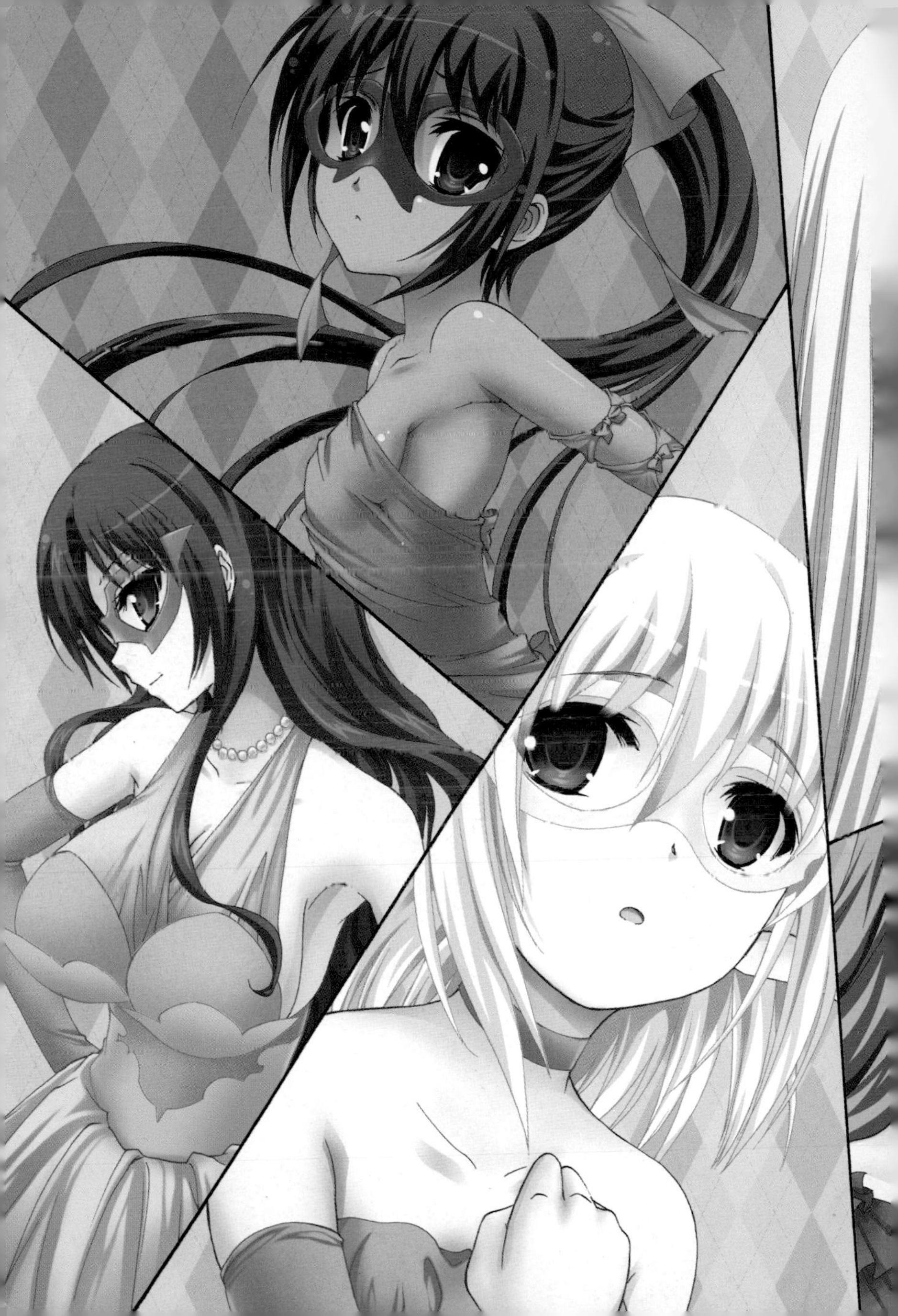

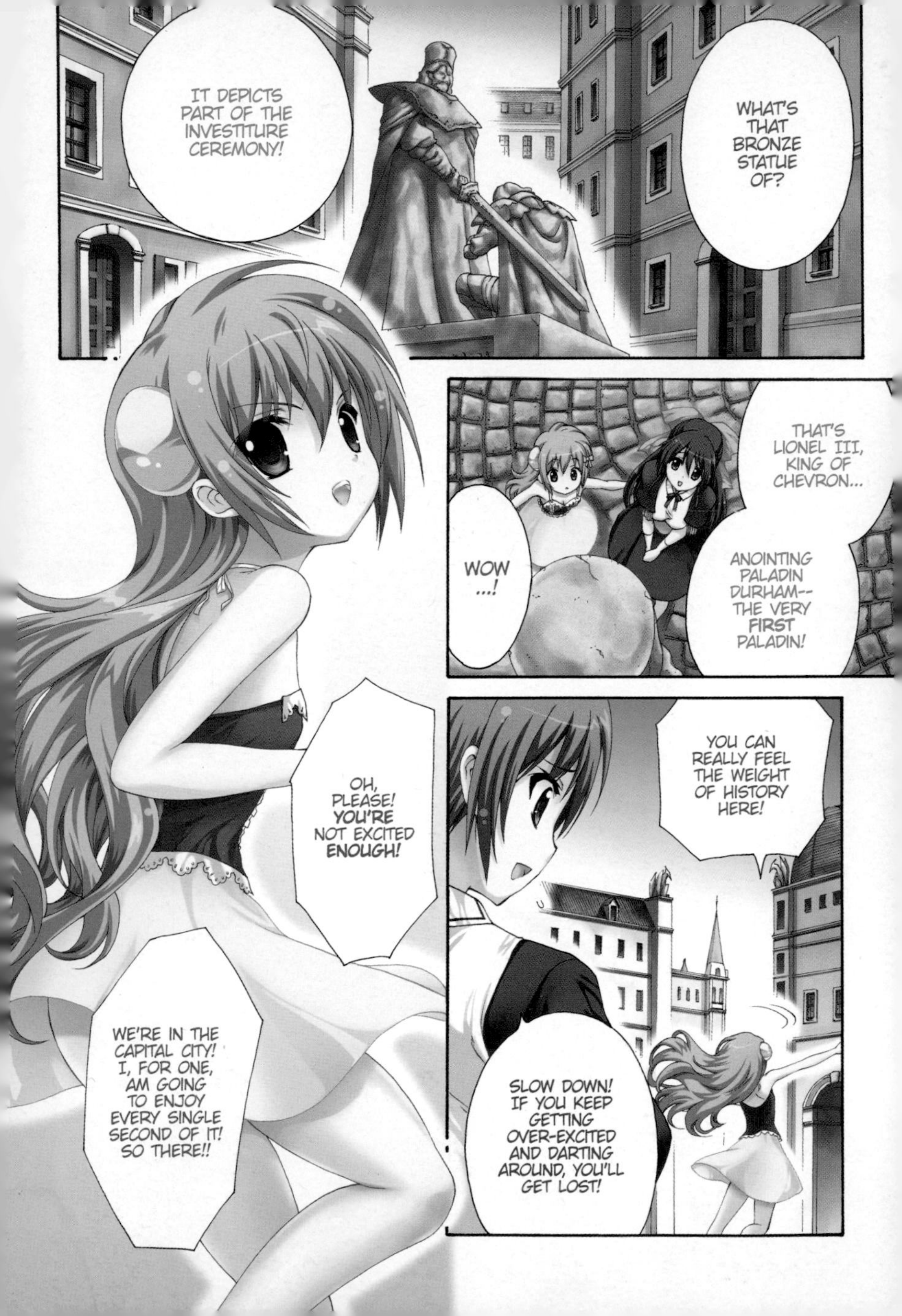
WHAT'S THAT BRONZE STATUE OF?
IT DEPICTS PART OF THE INVESTITURE CEREMONY!
THAT'S LIONEL III, KING OF CHEVRON...
ANOINTING PALADIN DURHAM-- THE VERY **FIRST** PALADIN!
WOW ...!
YOU CAN REALLY FEEL THE WEIGHT OF HISTORY HERE!
SLOW DOWN! IF YOU KEEP GETTING OVER-EXCITED AND DARTING AROUND, YOU'LL GET LOST!
OH, PLEASE! **YOU'RE** NOT EXCITED **ENOUGH!**
WE'RE IN THE CAPITAL CITY! I, FOR ONE, AM GOING TO ENJOY EVERY SINGLE SECOND OF IT! SO THERE!!

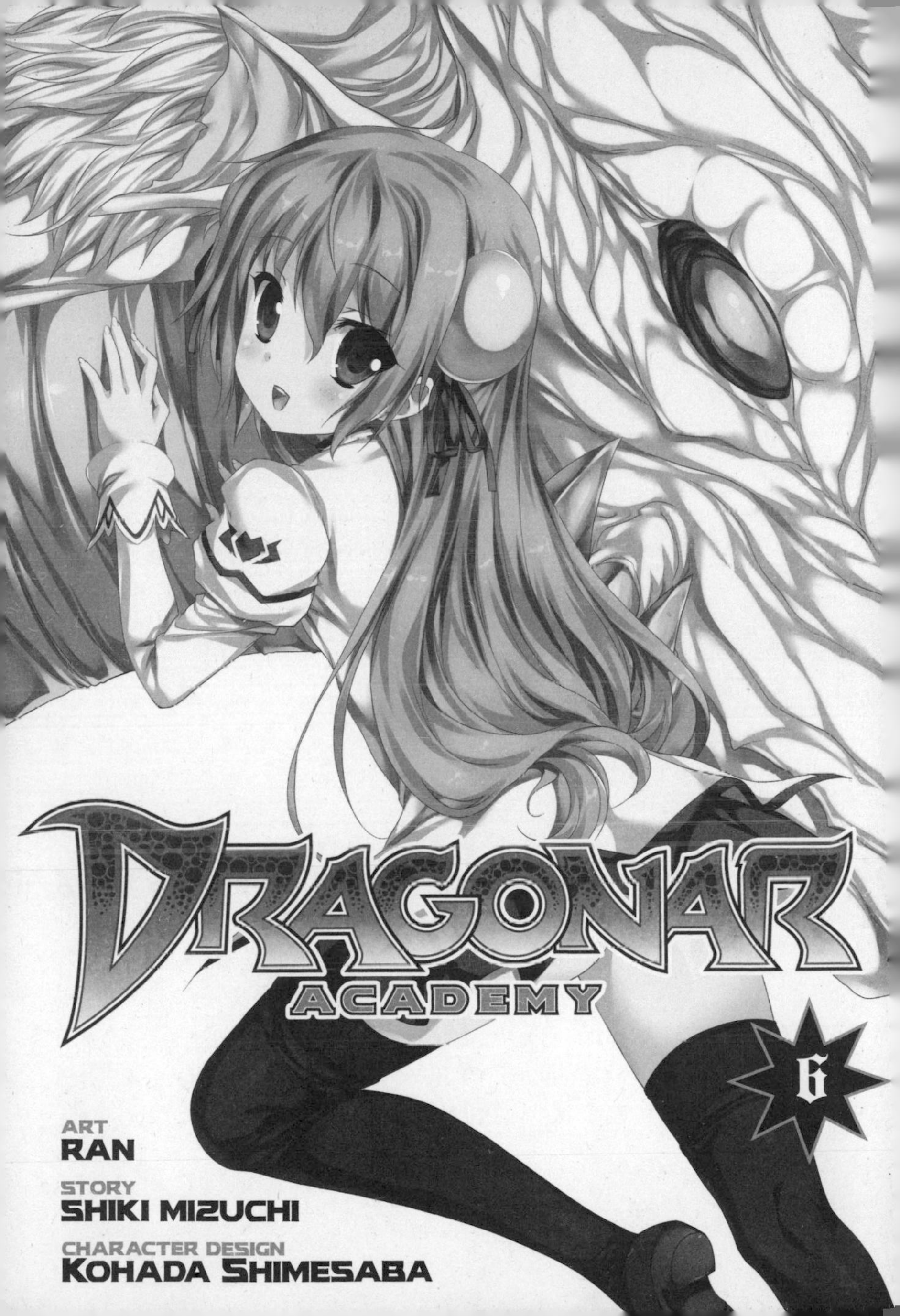

DRAGONAR ACADEMY

6

ART
RAN

STORY
SHIKI MIZUCHI

CHARACTER DESIGN
KOHADA SHIMESABA

SEVEN SEAS ENTERTAINMENT PRESENTS

DRAGONAR ACADEMY
VOLUME 6

art by **RAN** / story by **SHIKI MIZUCHI** / character design by **KOHADA SHIMESABA**

TRANSLATION
Nan Rymer

ADAPTATION
Libby Mitchell

LETTERING AND LAYOUT
Paweł Szczęszek

COVER DESIGN
Nicky Lim

PROOFREADER
Lee Otter

MANAGING EDITOR
Adam Arnold

PUBLISHER
Jason DeAngelis

DRAGONAR ACADEMY VOL. 6
© Ran 2013, © Shiki Mizuchi 2013
Edited by MEDIA FACTORY.
First published in Japan in 2013 by KADOKAWA CORPORATION, Tokyo.
English translation rights reserved by Seven Seas Entertainment, LLC.
under the license from KADOKAWA CORPORATION, Tokyo.

Seven Seas books may be purchased in bulk for educational, business, or
promotional use. For information on bulk purchases, please contact Macmillan
Corporate & Premium Sales Department at 1-800-221-7945 (ext 5442)
or write specialmarkets@macmillan.com.

Seven Seas and the Seven Seas logo are trademarks of
Seven Seas Entertainment, LLC. All rights reserved.

ISBN: 978-1-626921-29-0

Printed in Canada

First Printing: May 2015

10 9 8 7 6 5 4 3 2 1

FOLLOW US ONLINE: *www.gomanga.com*

READING DIRECTIONS

This book reads from *right to left*, Japanese style.
If this is your first time reading manga, you start
reading from the top right panel on each page and
take it from there. If you get lost, just follow the
numbered diagram here. It may seem backwards at
first, but you'll get the hang of it! Have fun!!

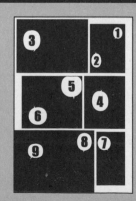

DRAGONAR ACADEMY CAST OF CHARACTERS

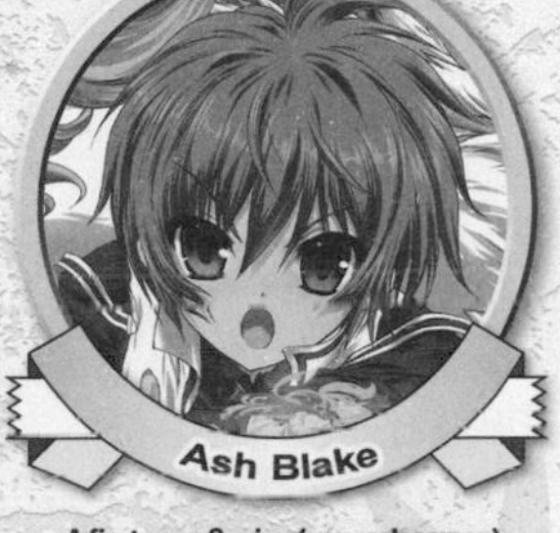
Ash Blake

A first-year Senios (upperclassman) at Ansullivan Dragonar Academy. He has the gift of riding any dragon. He's partnered with the young dragon Eco.

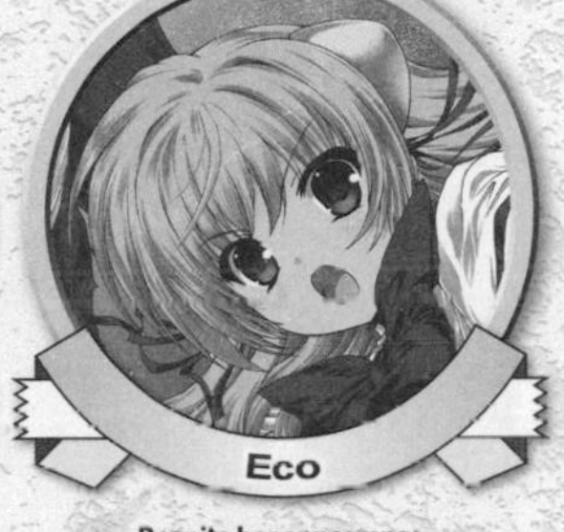
Eco

Despite her appearance, Eco is a dragon--and Ash's Steed! She's young and inexperienced, but was still able to craft an Ark for him.

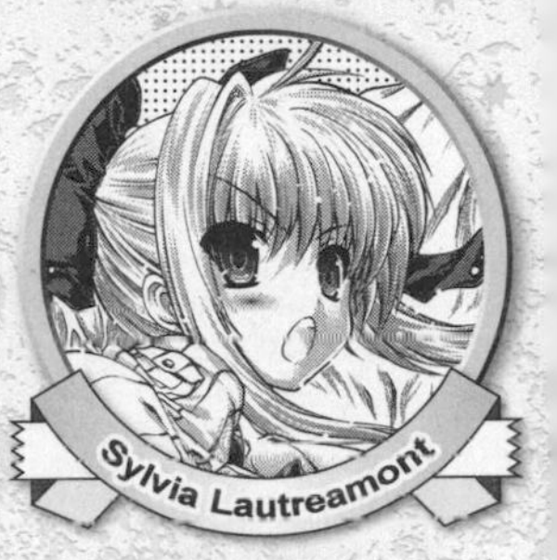
Sylvia Lautreamont

The fourth princess of the Knightdom of Lautreamont. Known as the Ice Blue Princess, she is partnered to the Maestro dragon Lancelot.

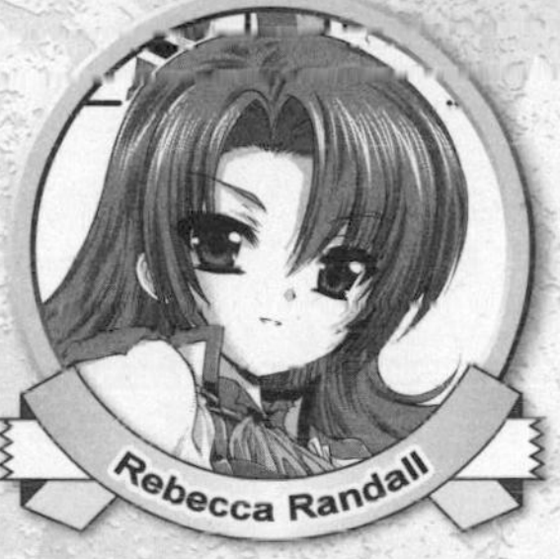
Rebecca Randall

A third-year student at Ansullivan Dragonar Academy and president of the student council. She's the school's most gifted Dragonar, and rides the Maestro dragon Cúchulainn. She's called the Scarlet Empress.

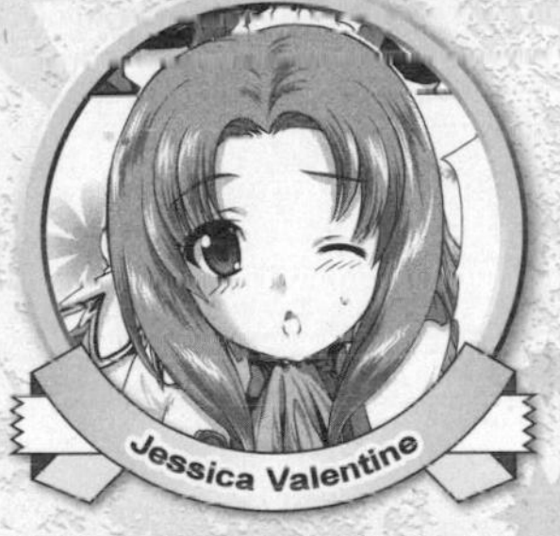
Jessica Valentine

A first-year Senios at Ansullivan Dragonar Academy and a childhood friend of Rebecca's. Since discovering Ash's identity as the Silver Knight, she's been trying everything she can think of to get close enough to him to bear his offspring.

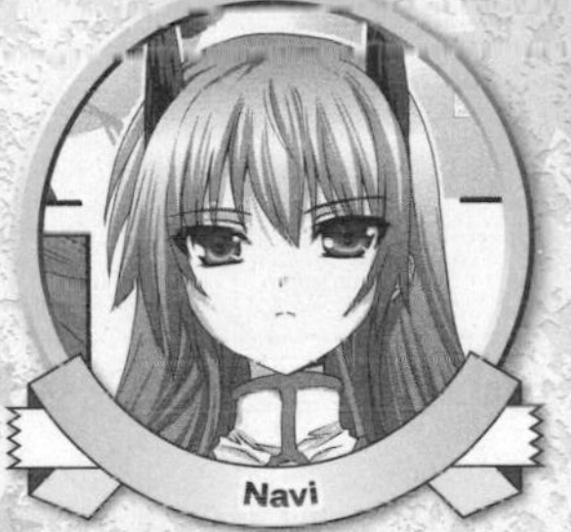
Navi

A mysterious entity who appears in the Dragon's Workshop, a shared space constructed by the Holy Dragons long ago. Navi helps Eco build an Ark, and has been appearing in Ash's dreams.

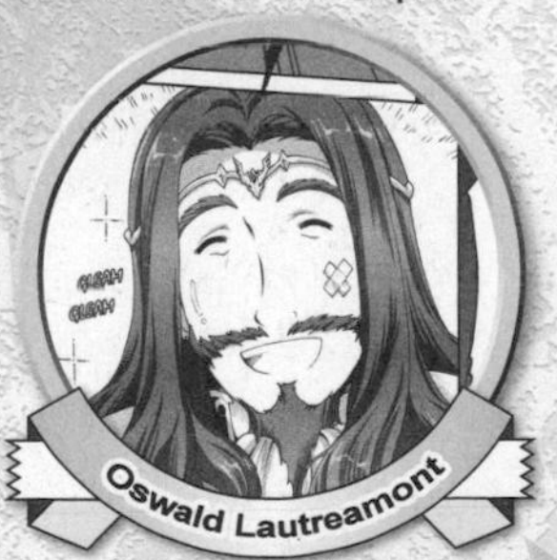
Oswald Lautreamont

The king of Lautreamont Knightdom. He holds the title of Paladin, but the truth is, he's never bonded with a dragon. He's a doting parent, blinded by his love for his children.

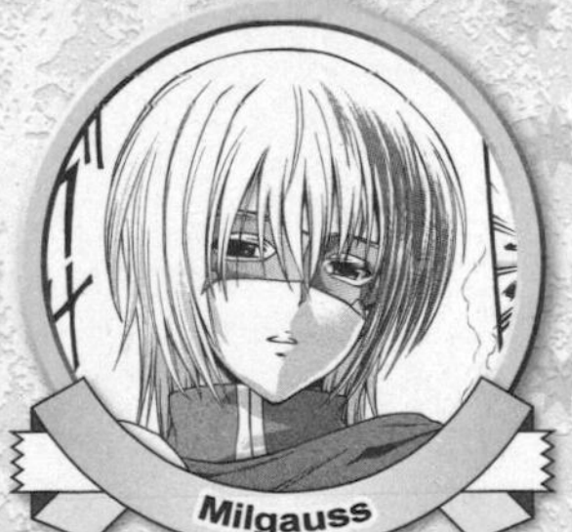
Milgauss

A soldier from the Zepharos Empire, Milgauss attacked Ash during the Dragonar Festival of Aries. His true identity and motivations are shrouded in mystery.

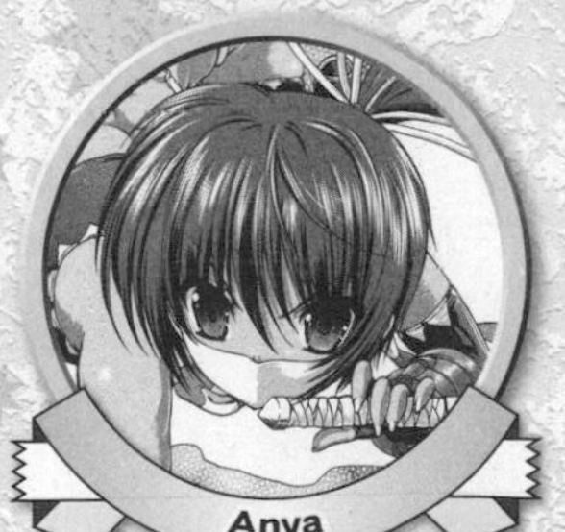
Anya

A girl who works alongside Milgauss. As an operative for the Empire's intelligence service, she is currently undercover in the knightdom.

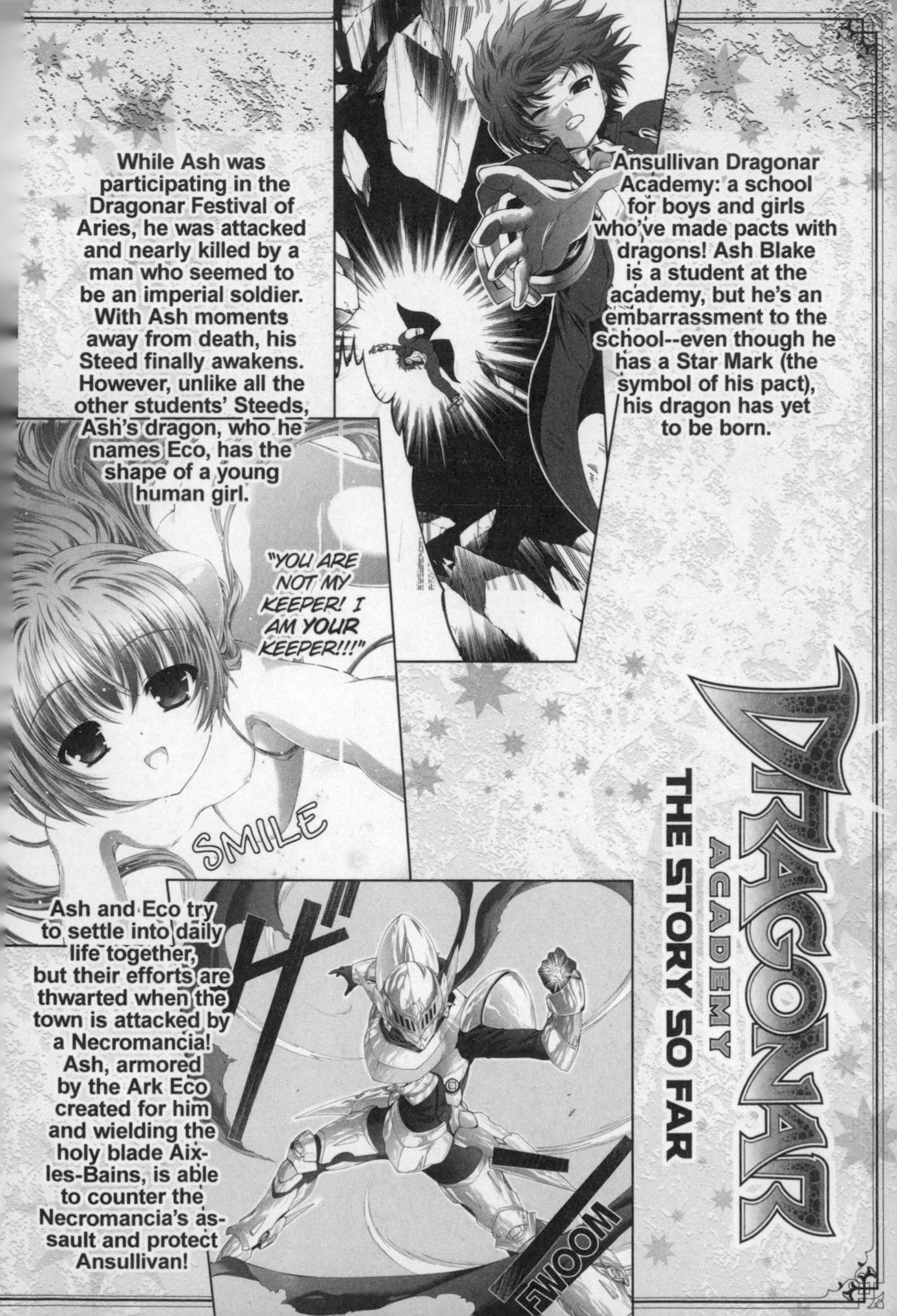
DRAGONAR ACADEMY
THE STORY SO FAR
Ansullivan Dragonar Academy: a school for boys and girls who've made pacts with dragons! Ash Blake is a student at the academy, but he's an embarrassment to the school--even though he has a Star Mark (the symbol of his pact), his dragon has yet to be born.
While Ash was participating in the Dragonar Festival of Aries, he was attacked and nearly killed by a man who seemed to be an imperial soldier. With Ash moments away from death, his Steed finally awakens. However, unlike all the other students' Steeds, Ash's dragon, who he names Eco, has the shape of a young human girl.
"YOU ARE NOT MY KEEPER! I AM YOUR KEEPER!!!"
SMILE
Ash and Eco try to settle into daily life together, but their efforts are thwarted when the town is attacked by a Necromancia! Ash, armored by the Ark Eco created for him and wielding the holy blade Aix-les-Bains, is able to counter the Necromancia's assault and protect Ansullivan!
FWOOM

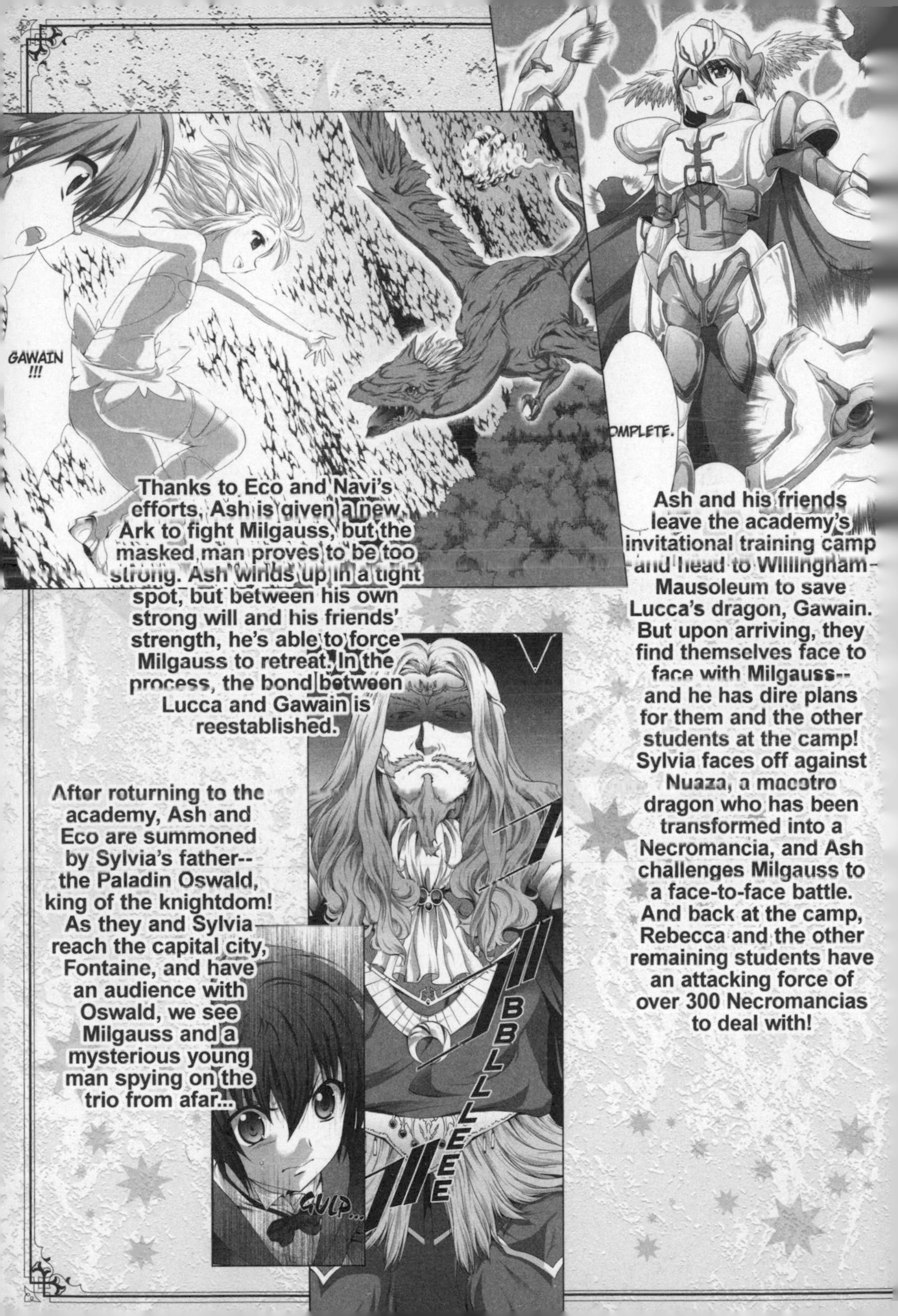
OMPLETE.
Ash and his friends leave the academy's invitational training camp and head to Willingham Mausoleum to save Lucca's dragon, Gawain. But upon arriving, they find themselves face to face with Milgauss--and he has dire plans for them and the other students at the camp! Sylvia faces off against Nuaza, a maestro dragon who has been transformed into a Necromancia, and Ash challenges Milgauss to a face-to-face battle. And back at the camp, Rebecca and the other remaining students have an attacking force of over 300 Necromancias to deal with!
GAWAIN!!!
Thanks to Eco and Navi's efforts, Ash is given a new Ark to fight Milgauss, but the masked man proves to be too strong. Ash winds up in a tight spot, but between his own strong will and his friends' strength, he's able to force Milgauss to retreat. In the process, the bond between Lucca and Gawain is reestablished.
BBLLLEEE
GULP...
After returning to the academy, Ash and Eco are summoned by Sylvia's father--the Paladin Oswald, king of the knightdom! As they and Sylvia reach the capital city, Fontaine, and have an audience with Oswald, we see Milgauss and a mysterious young man spying on the trio from afar...

星刻の竜騎士

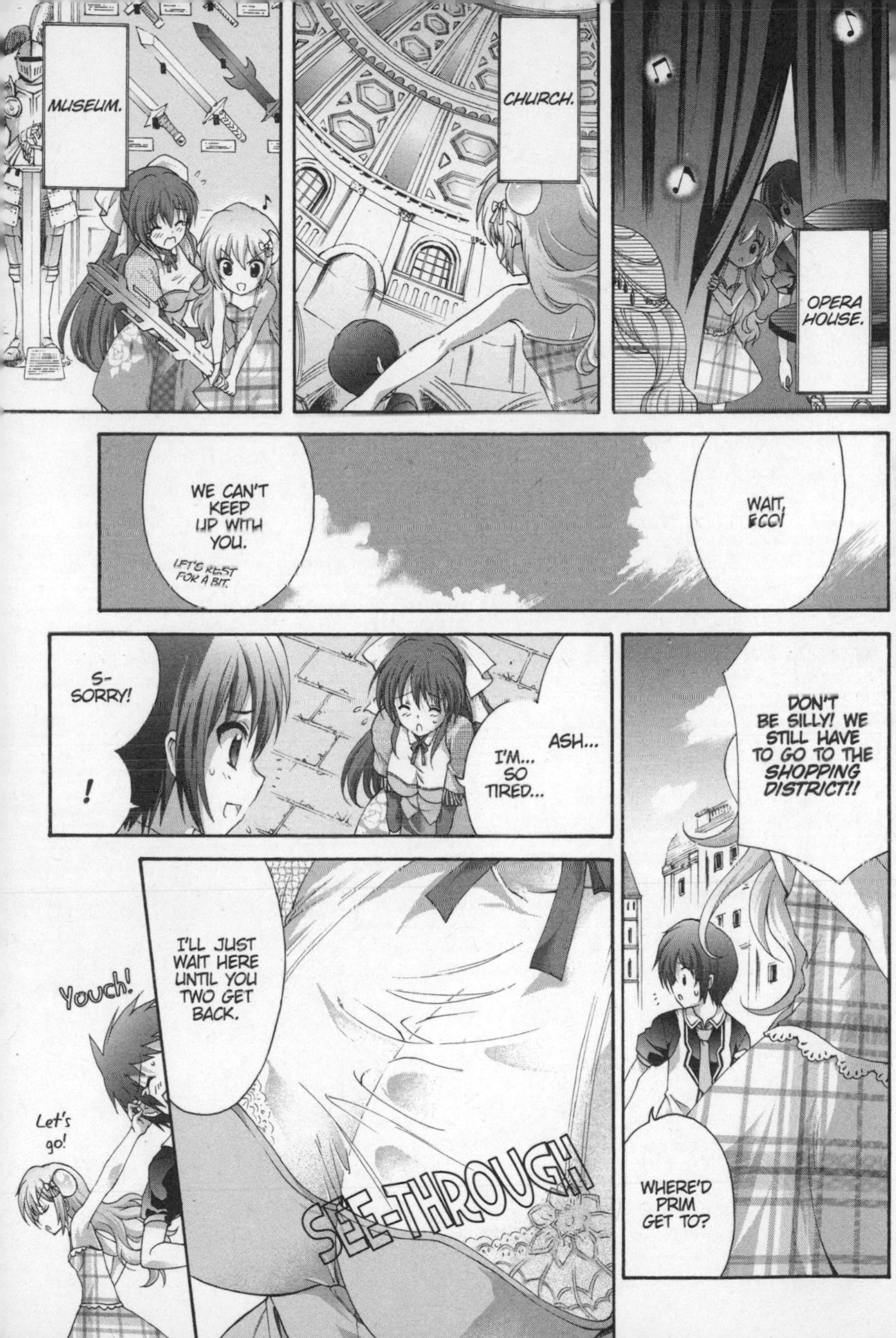
OPERA HOUSE.
CHURCH.
MUSEUM.
WAIT, ECO!
WE CAN'T KEEP UP WITH YOU.
LET'S REST FOR A BIT.
DON'T BE SILLY! WE STILL HAVE TO GO TO THE SHOPPING DISTRICT!!
WHERE'D PRIM GET TO?
ASH... I'M... SO TIRED...
S-SORRY!
!
I'LL JUST WAIT HERE UNTIL YOU TWO GET BACK.
SEE-THROUGH!
Youch!
Let's go!

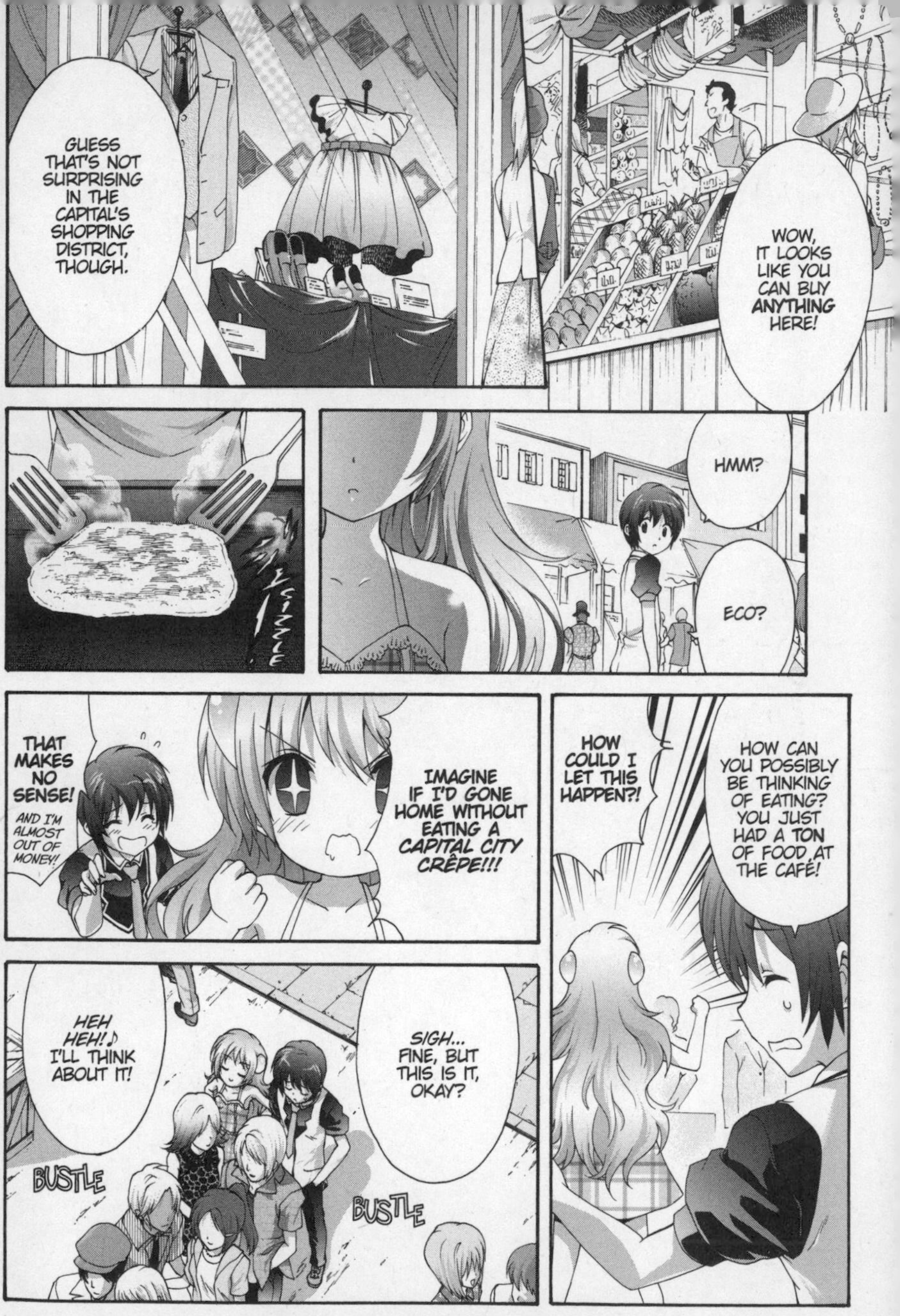
WOW, IT LOOKS LIKE YOU CAN BUY ANYTHING HERE!
GUESS THAT'S NOT SURPRISING IN THE CAPITAL'S SHOPPING DISTRICT, THOUGH.
HMM?
ECO?
SIZZLE
HOW CAN YOU POSSIBLY BE THINKING OF EATING? YOU JUST HAD A TON OF FOOD AT THE CAFÉ!
HOW COULD I LET THIS HAPPEN?!
IMAGINE IF I'D GONE HOME WITHOUT EATING A CAPITAL CITY CRÊPE!!!
THAT MAKES NO SENSE!
AND I'M ALMOST OUT OF MONEY!
SIGH... FINE, BUT THIS IS IT, OKAY?
HEH HEH!♪ I'LL THINK ABOUT IT!
BUSTLE
BUSTLE

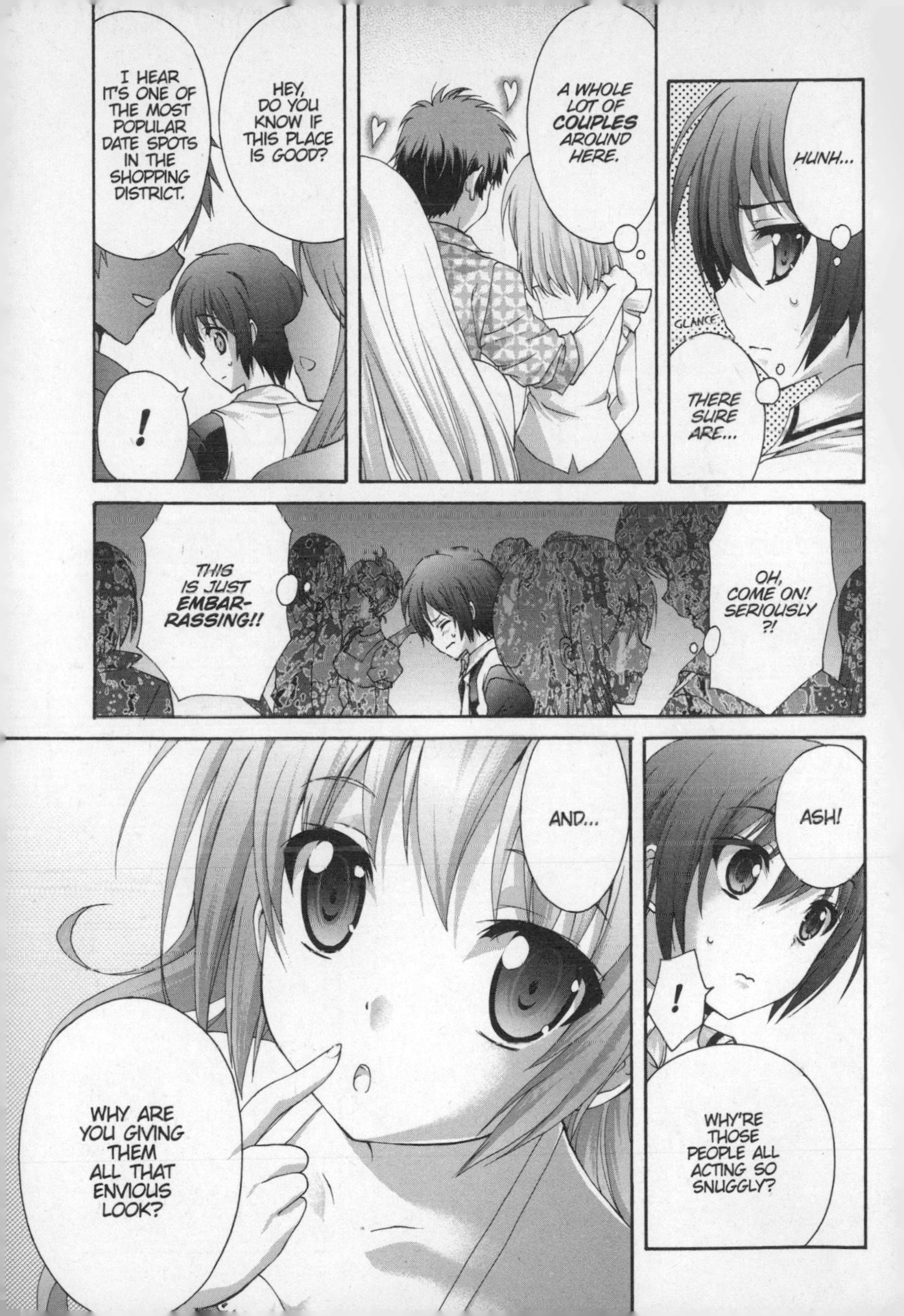
HUNH...
GLANCE
THERE SURE ARE...
A WHOLE LOT OF COUPLES AROUND HERE.
HEY, DO YOU KNOW IF THIS PLACE IS GOOD?
I HEAR IT'S ONE OF THE MOST POPULAR DATE SPOTS IN THE SHOPPING DISTRICT.
!
OH, COME ON! SERIOUSLY?!
THIS IS JUST EMBARRASSING!!
ASH!
!
WHY'RE THOSE PEOPLE ALL ACTING SO SNUGGLY?
AND...
WHY ARE YOU GIVING THEM ALL THAT ENVIOUS LOOK?

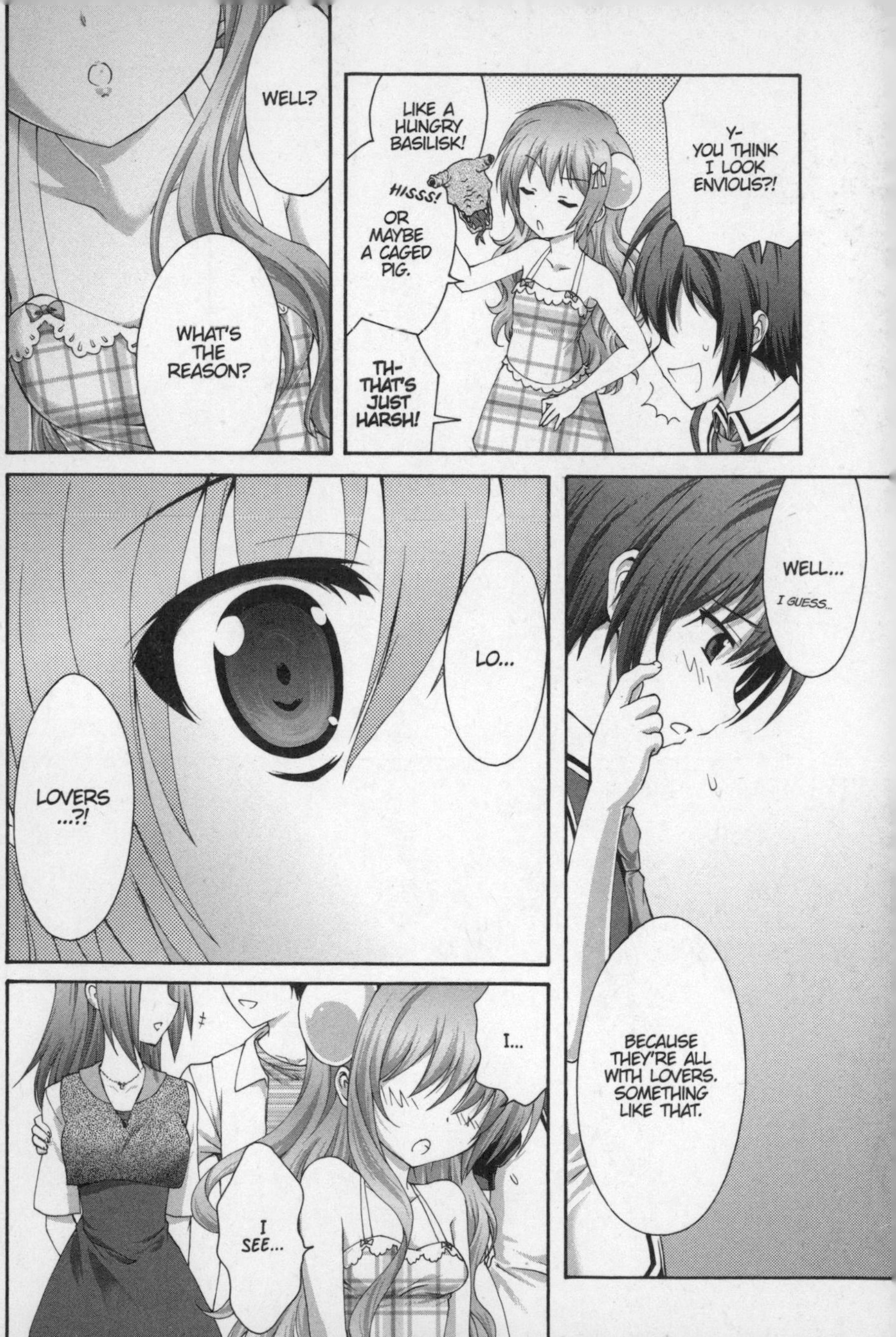
Y- YOU THINK I LOOK ENVIOUS?!
LIKE A HUNGRY BASILISK!
HISSS!
OR MAYBE A CAGED PIG.
TH- THAT'S JUST HARSH!
WELL?
WHAT'S THE REASON?
WELL...
I GUESS...
BECAUSE THEY'RE ALL WITH LOVERS. SOMETHING LIKE THAT.
LO...
LOVERS ...?!
I...
I SEE...

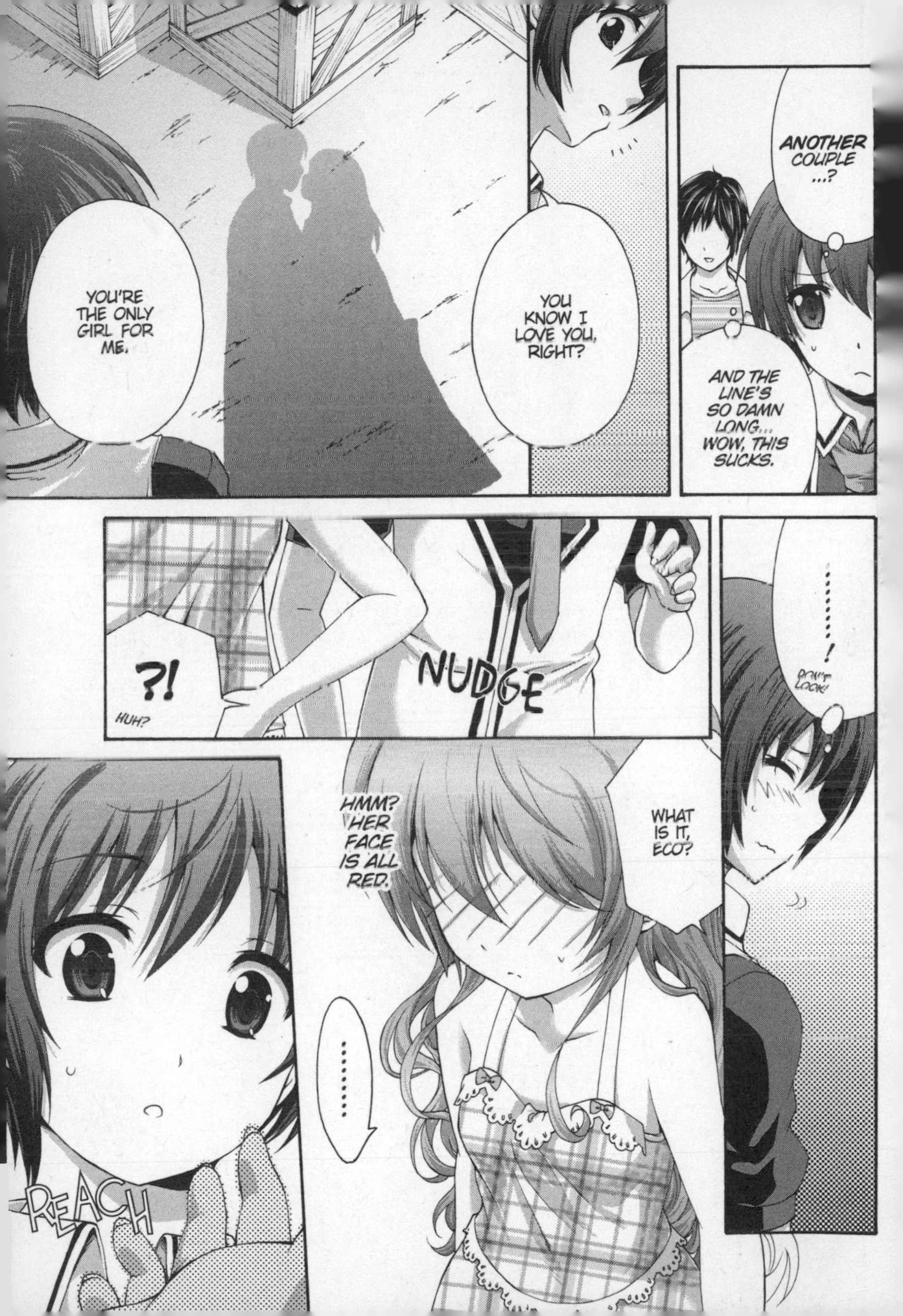

ANOTHER COUPLE ...?
AND THE LINE'S SO DAMN LONG... WOW, THIS SUCKS.
YOU KNOW I LOVE YOU, RIGHT?
YOU'RE THE ONLY GIRL FOR ME.
......!
DON'T LOOK!
WHAT IS IT, ECO?
NUDGE
?!
HUH?
HMM? HER FACE IS ALL RED.
......
REACH

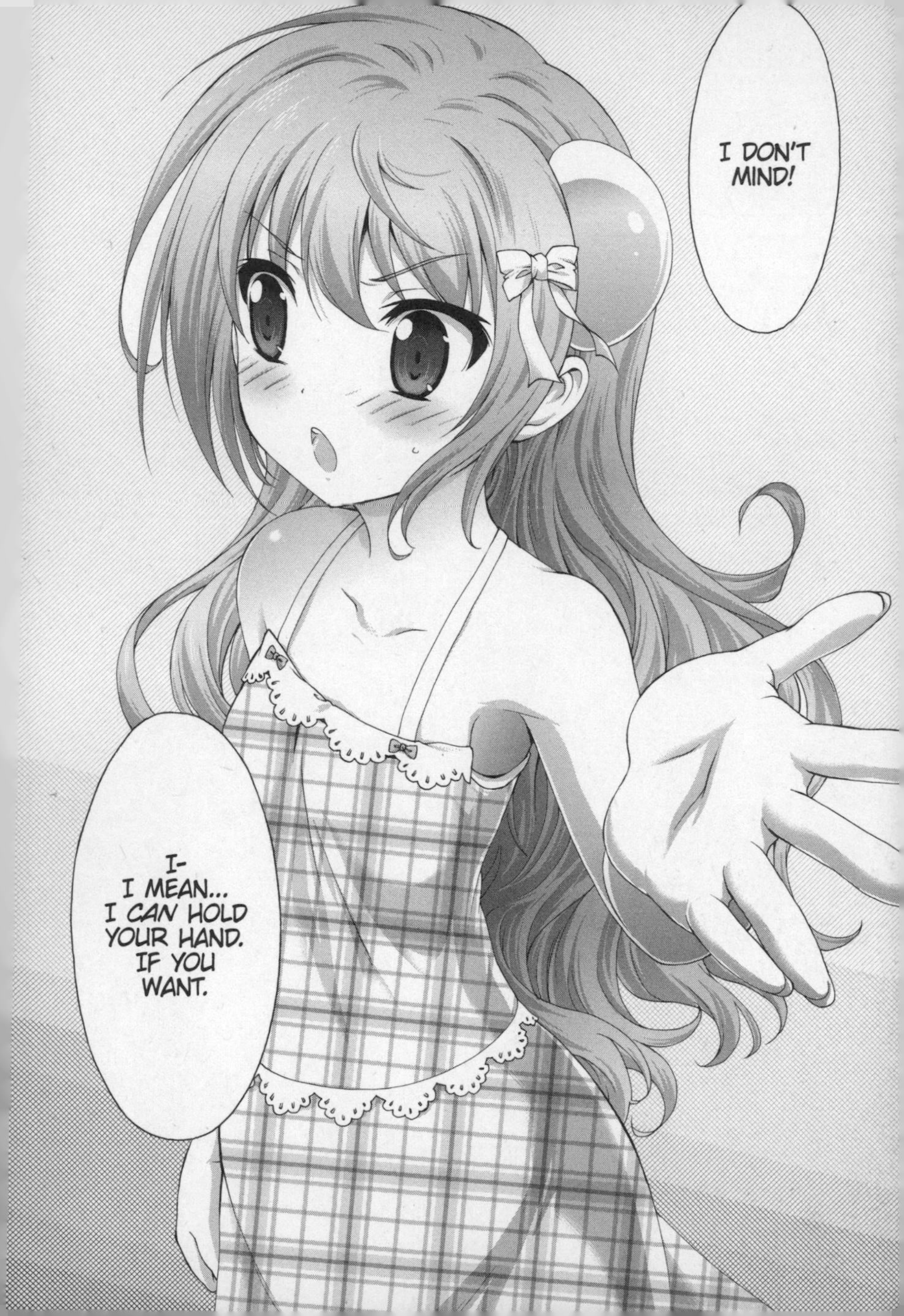
I DON'T MIND!
I- I MEAN... I CAN HOLD YOUR HAND. IF YOU WANT.

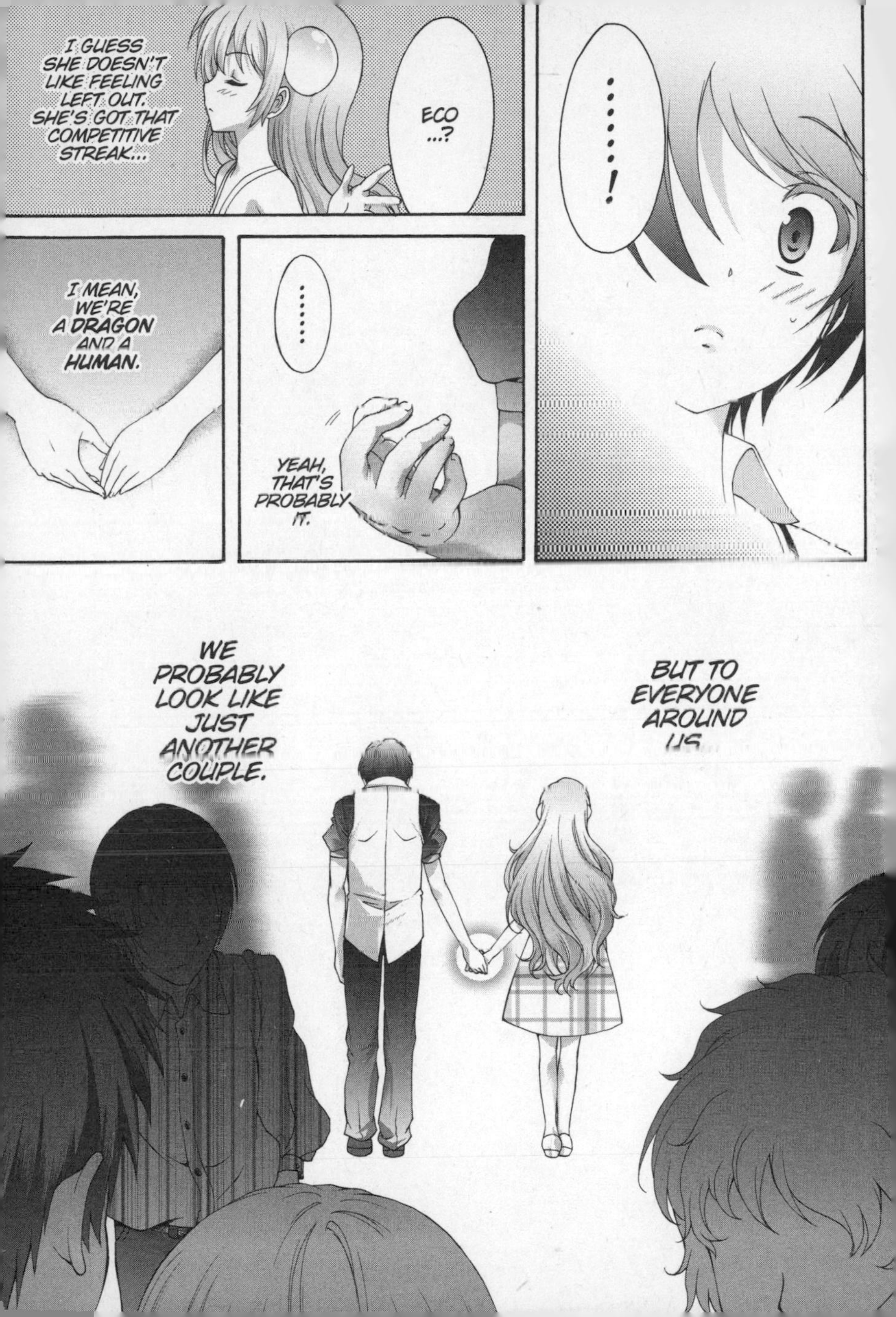
......!
ECO ...?
I GUESS SHE DOESN'T LIKE FEELING LEFT OUT. SHE'S GOT THAT COMPETITIVE STREAK...
......
YEAH, THAT'S PROBABLY IT.
I MEAN, WE'RE A DRAGON AND A HUMAN.
BUT TO EVERYONE AROUND US,
WE PROBABLY LOOK LIKE JUST ANOTHER COUPLE.

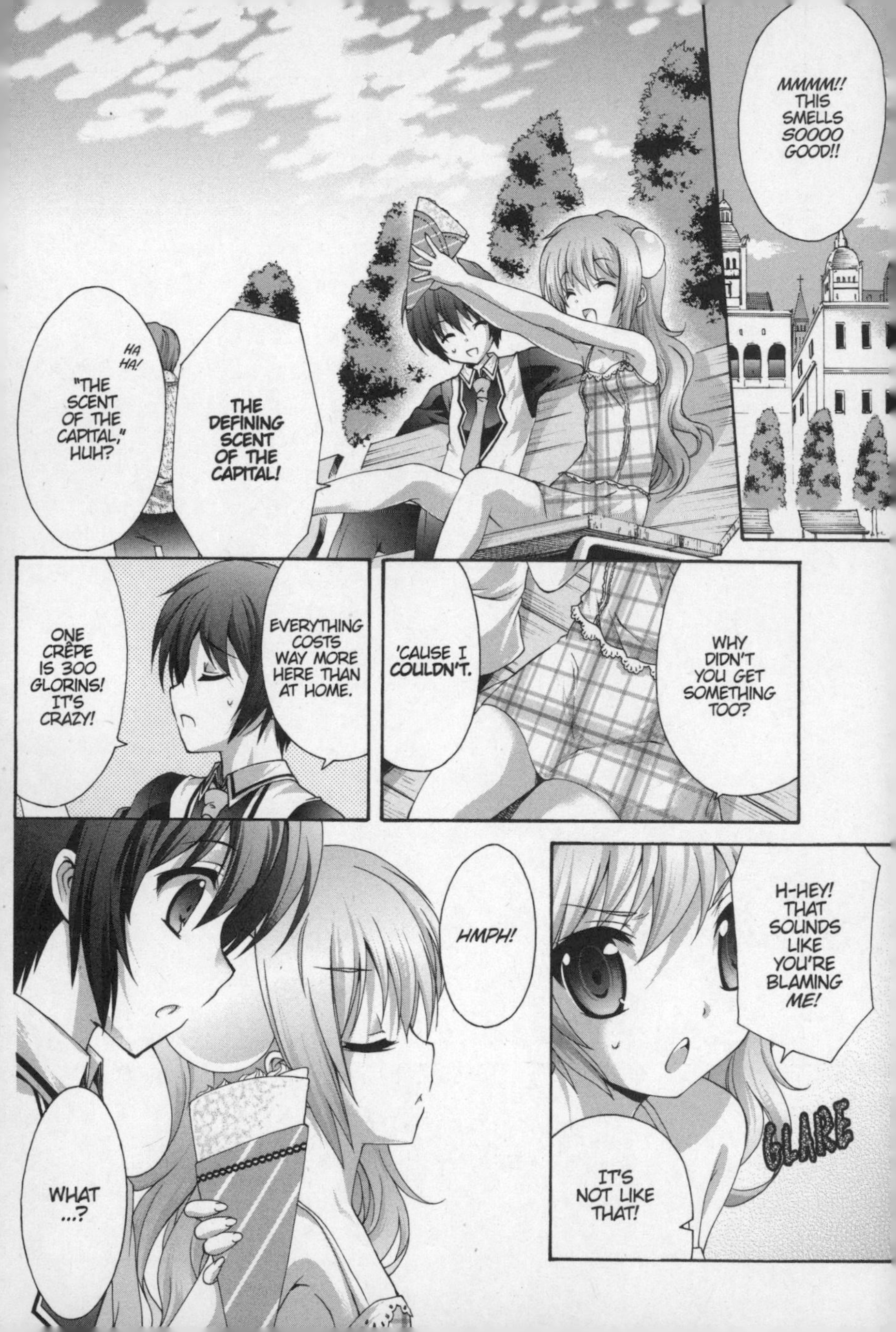
MMMM!! THIS SMELLS SOOOO GOOD!!
THE DEFINING SCENT OF THE CAPITAL!
HA HA!
"THE SCENT OF THE CAPITAL," HUH?
WHY DIDN'T YOU GET SOMETHING TOO?
'CAUSE I COULDN'T.
EVERYTHING COSTS WAY MORE HERE THAN AT HOME.
ONE CRÊPE IS 300 GLORINS! IT'S CRAZY!
H-HEY! THAT SOUNDS LIKE YOU'RE BLAMING ME!
GLARE
IT'S NOT LIKE THAT!
HMPH!
WHAT ...?

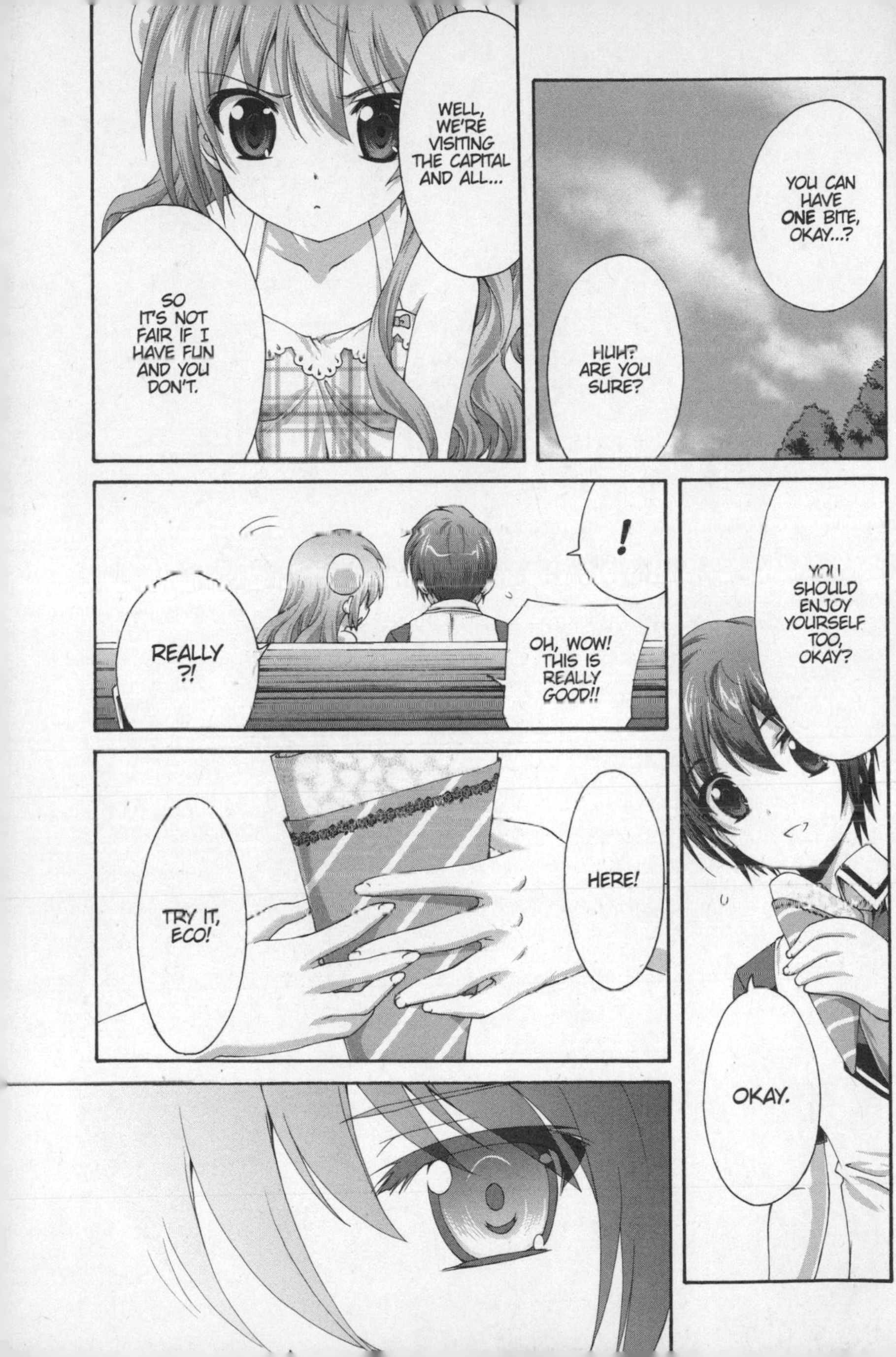
YOU CAN HAVE ONE BITE, OKAY...?
HUH? ARE YOU SURE?
WELL, WE'RE VISITING THE CAPITAL AND ALL...
SO IT'S NOT FAIR IF I HAVE FUN AND YOU DON'T.
YOU SHOULD ENJOY YOURSELF TOO, OKAY?
OKAY.
!
OH, WOW! THIS IS REALLY GOOD!!
REALLY ?!
HERE!
TRY IT, ECO!

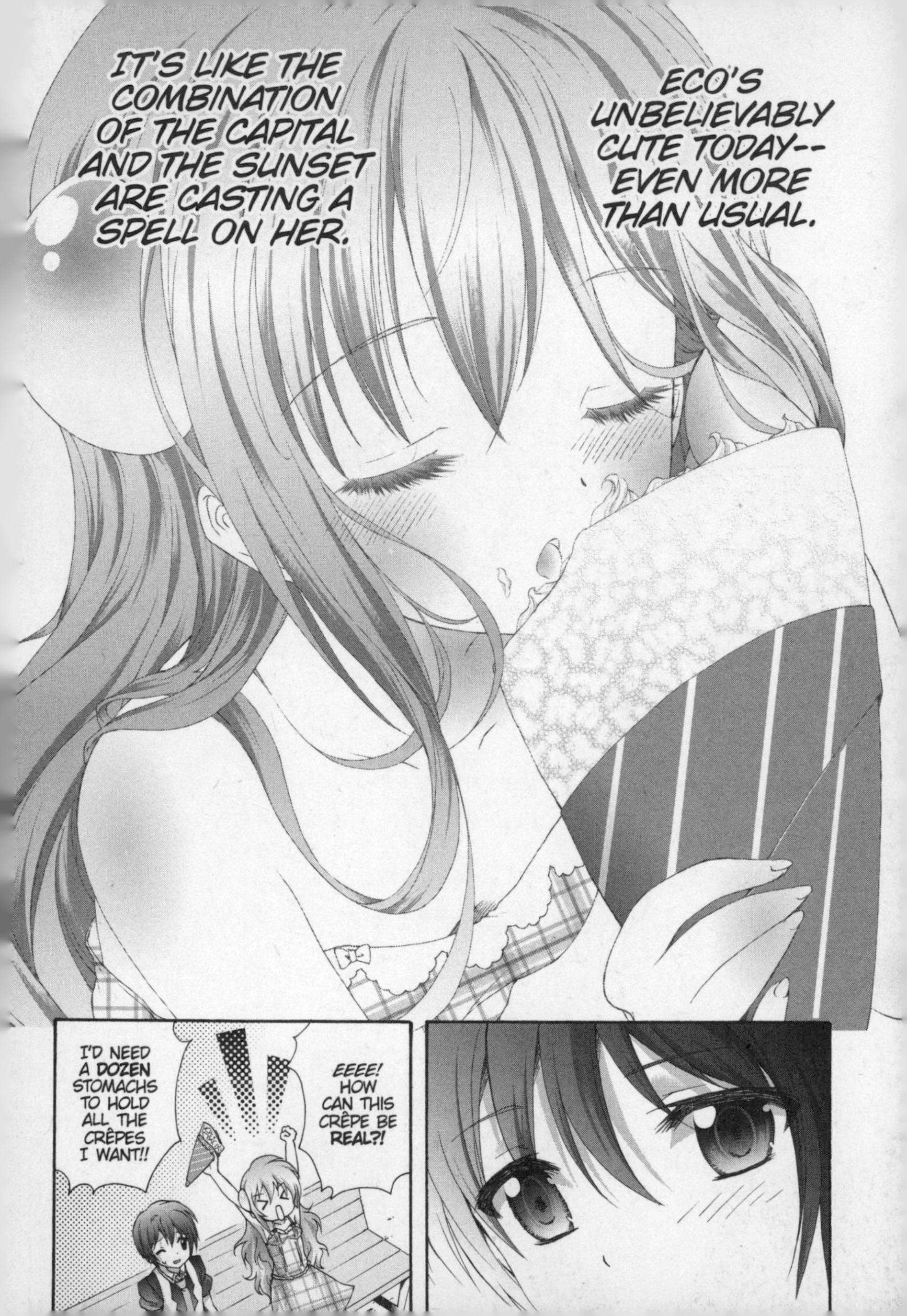
ECO'S UNBELIEVABLY CUTE TODAY-- EVEN MORE THAN USUAL.
IT'S LIKE THE COMBINATION OF THE CAPITAL AND THE SUNSET ARE CASTING A SPELL ON HER.
EEEE! HOW CAN THIS CRÊPE BE REAL?!
I'D NEED A DOZEN STOMACHS TO HOLD ALL THE CRÊPES I WANT!!

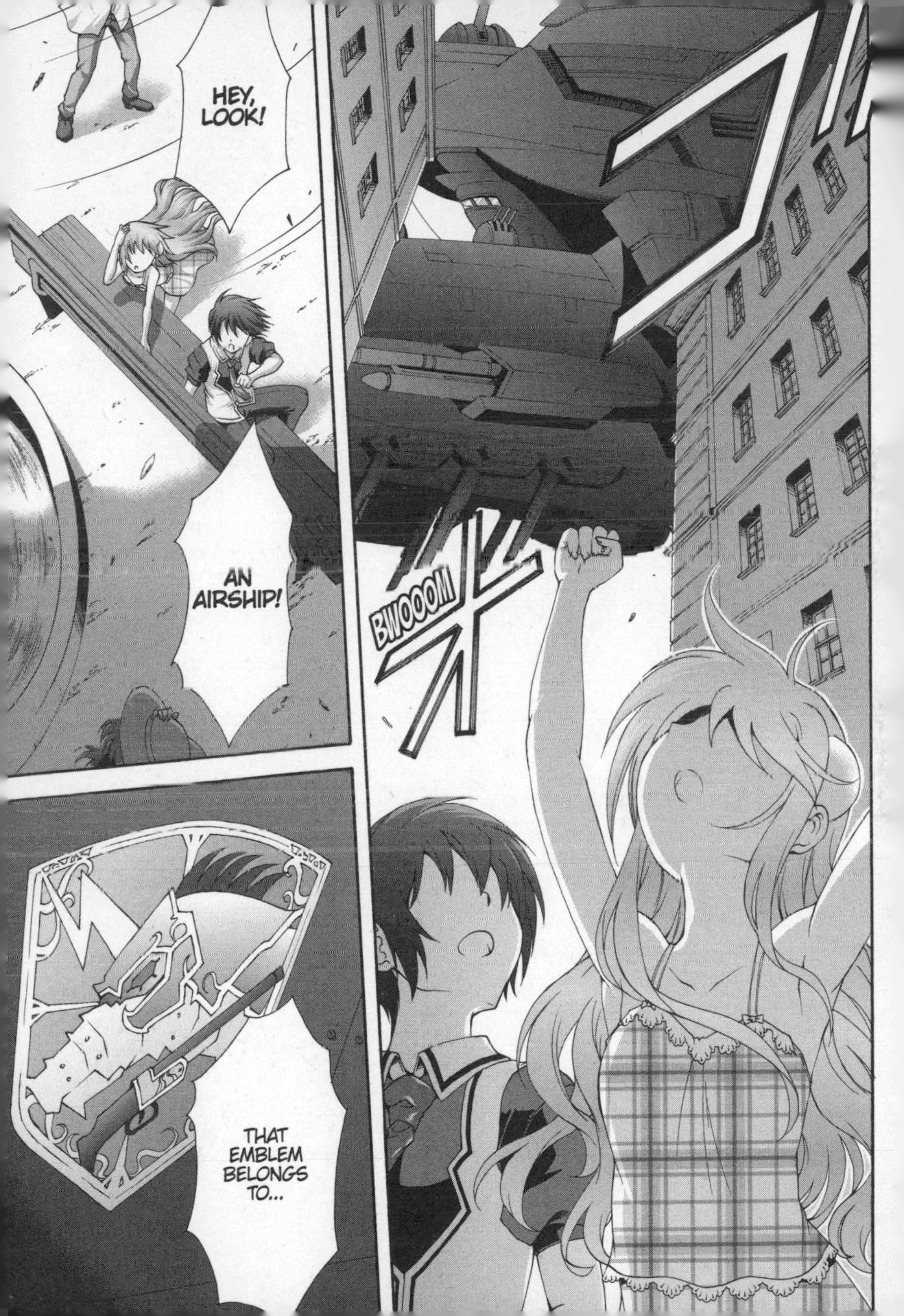
BWOOOM
HEY, LOOK!
AN AIRSHIP!
THAT EMBLEM BELONGS TO...

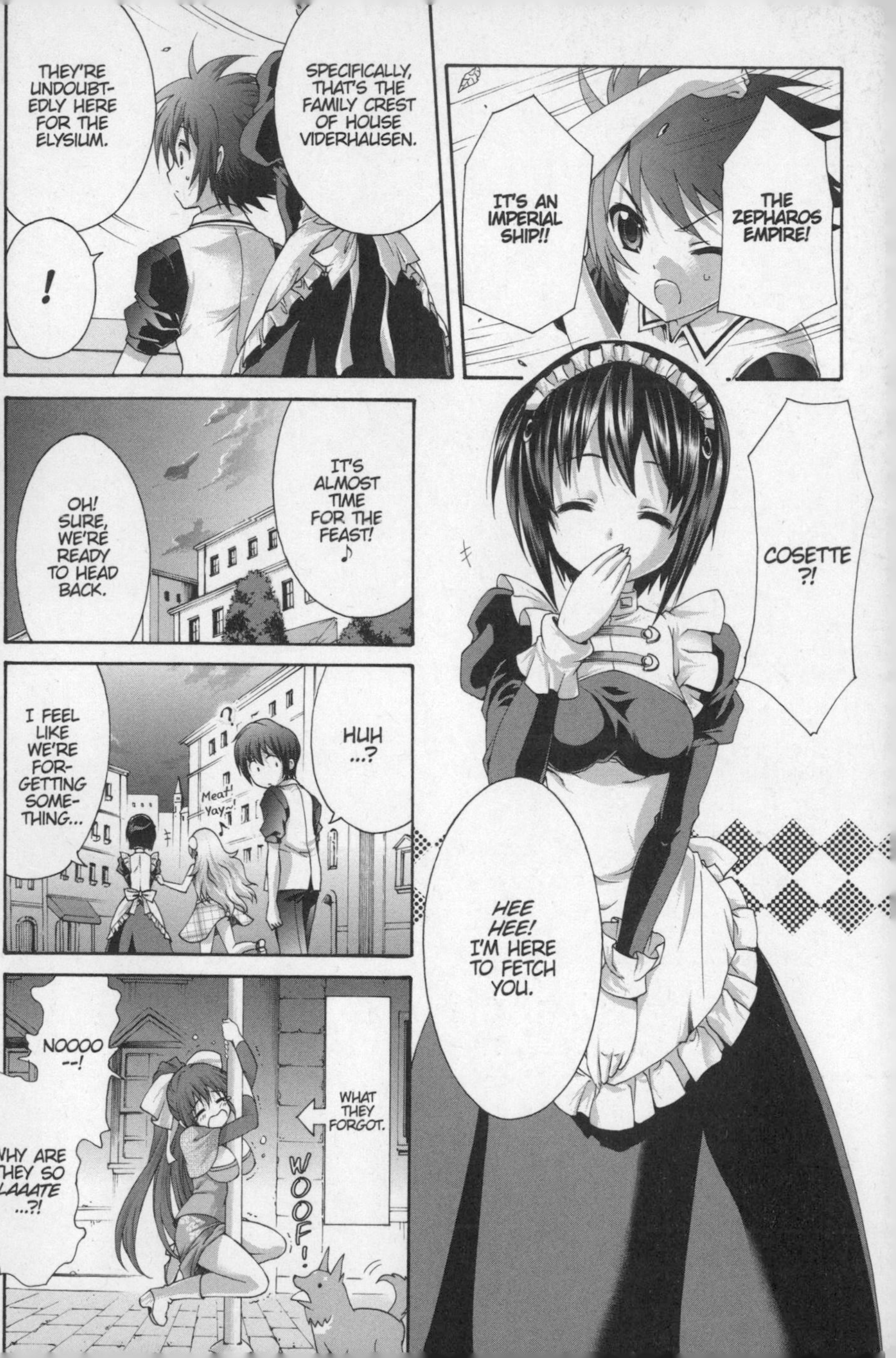
THE ZEPHAROS EMPIRE!
IT'S AN IMPERIAL SHIP!!
SPECIFICALLY, THAT'S THE FAMILY CREST OF HOUSE VIDERHAUSEN.
THEY'RE UNDOUBT-EDLY HERE FOR THE ELYSIUM.
!
COSETTE ?!
HEE HEE! I'M HERE TO FETCH YOU.
IT'S ALMOST TIME FOR THE FEAST! ♪
OH! SURE, WE'RE READY TO HEAD BACK.
HUH ...?
Meat! Yay~!
I FEEL LIKE WE'RE FOR-GETTING SOME-THING...
WHAT THEY FORGOT.
NOOOO --!
WOOF!
WHY ARE THEY SO LAAATE ...?!

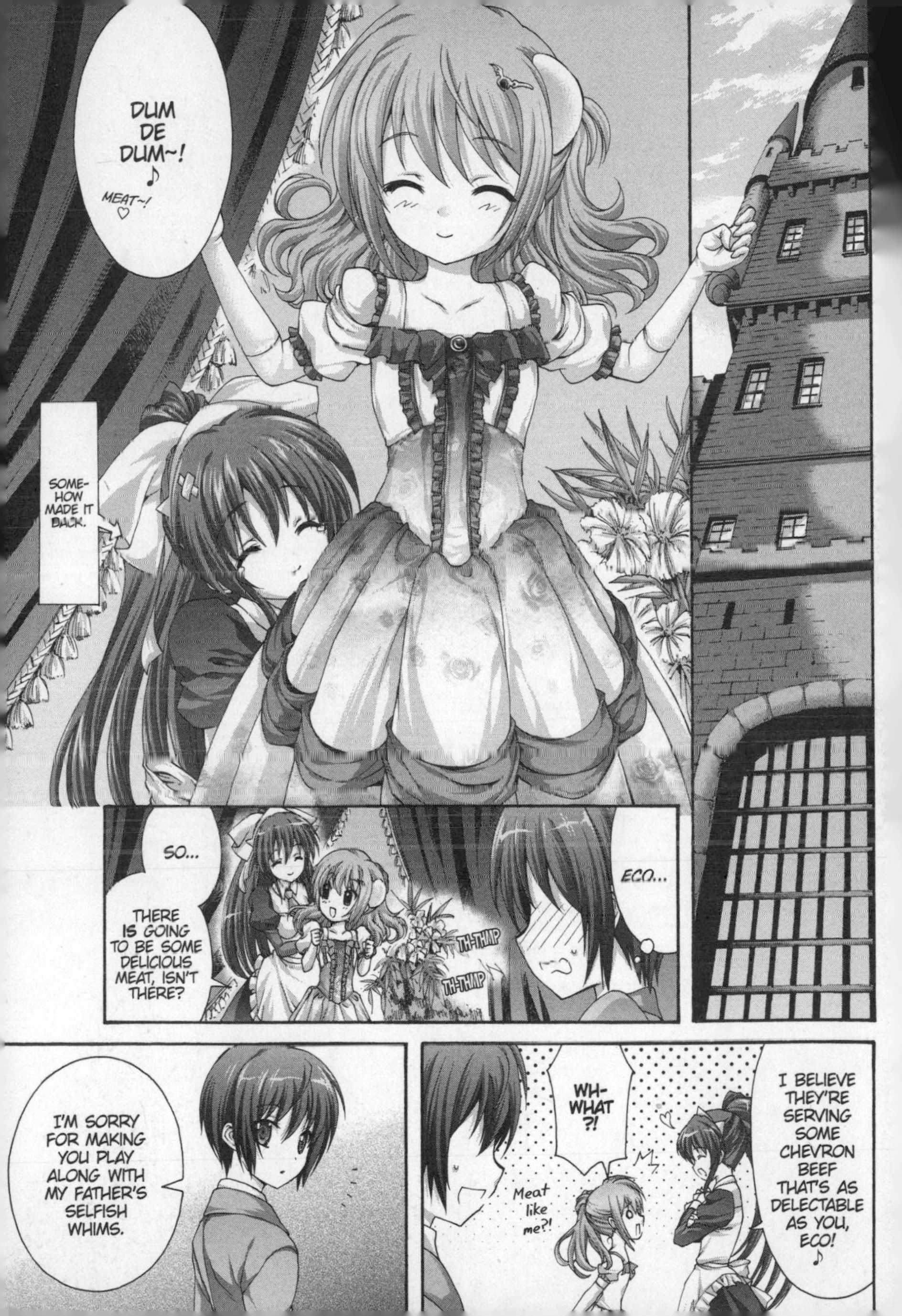
DUM DE DUM~! ♪
MEAT~! ♡
SOME-HOW MADE IT BACK.
ECO...
SO...
THERE IS GOING TO BE SOME DELICIOUS MEAT, ISN'T THERE?
TH-THMP
TH-THMP
I BELIEVE THEY'RE SERVING SOME CHEVRON BEEF THAT'S AS DELECTABLE AS YOU, ECO! ♪
WH-WHAT?!
Meat like me?!
I'M SORRY FOR MAKING YOU PLAY ALONG WITH MY FATHER'S SELFISH WHIMS.

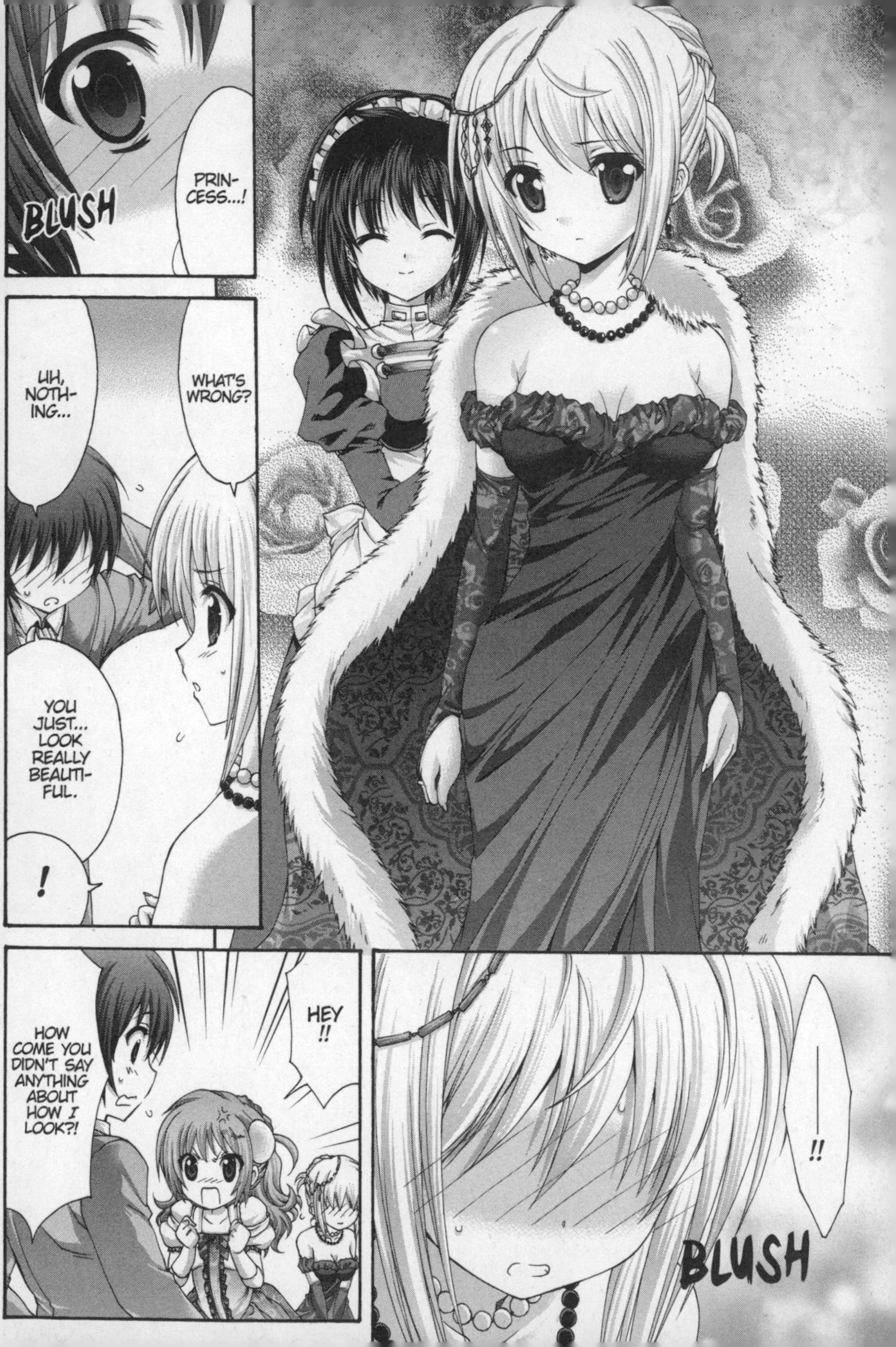
PRIN-CESS...!
BLUSH
WHAT'S WRONG?
UH, NOTH-ING...
YOU JUST... LOOK REALLY BEAUTI-FUL.
!
—!!
BLUSH
HEY!!
HOW COME YOU DIDN'T SAY ANYTHING ABOUT HOW I LOOK?!

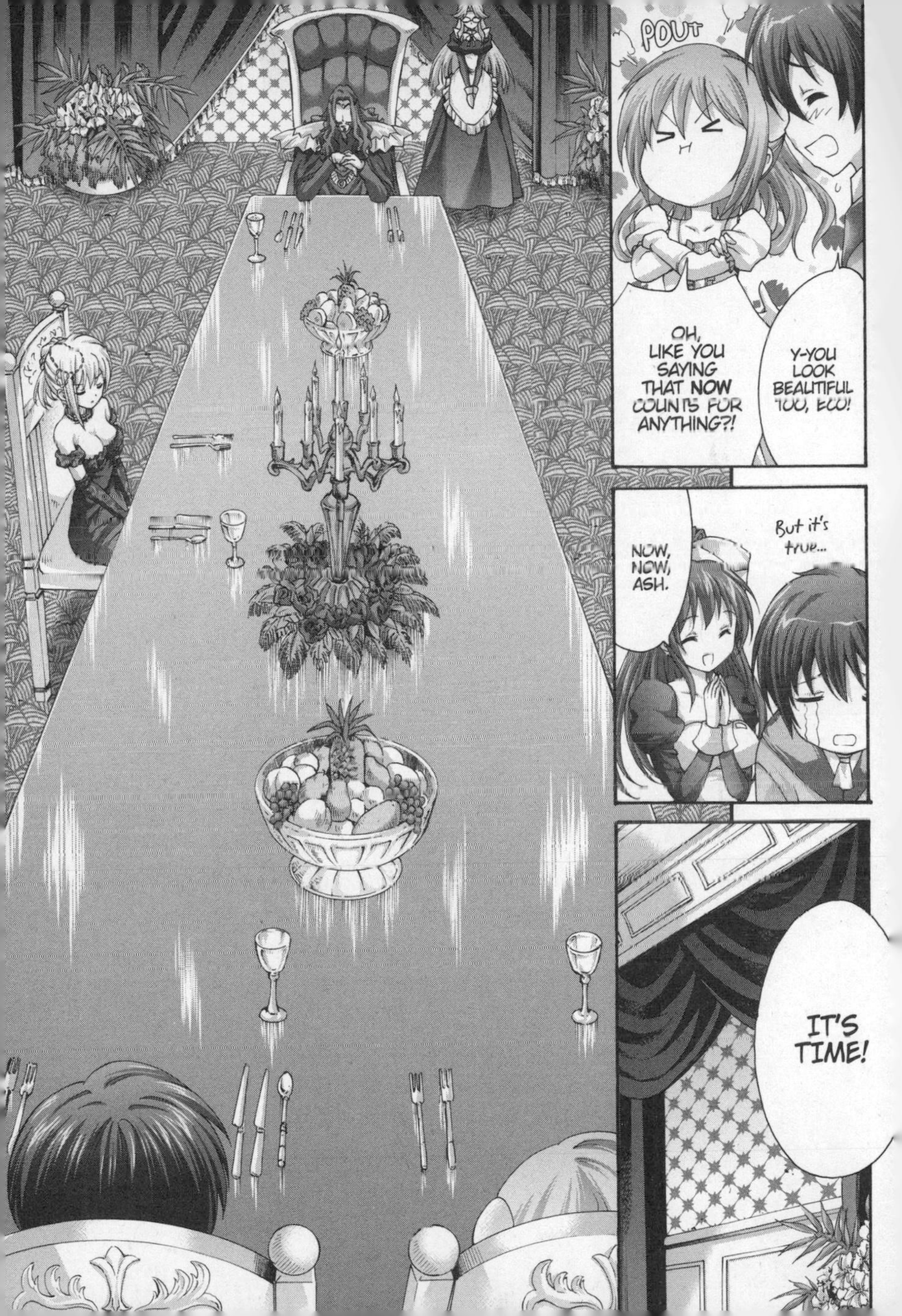
POUT
Y-YOU LOOK BEAUTIFUL TOO, ECO!
OH, LIKE YOU SAYING THAT NOW COUNTS FOR ANYTHING?!
NOW, NOW, ASH.
But it's true...
IT'S TIME!

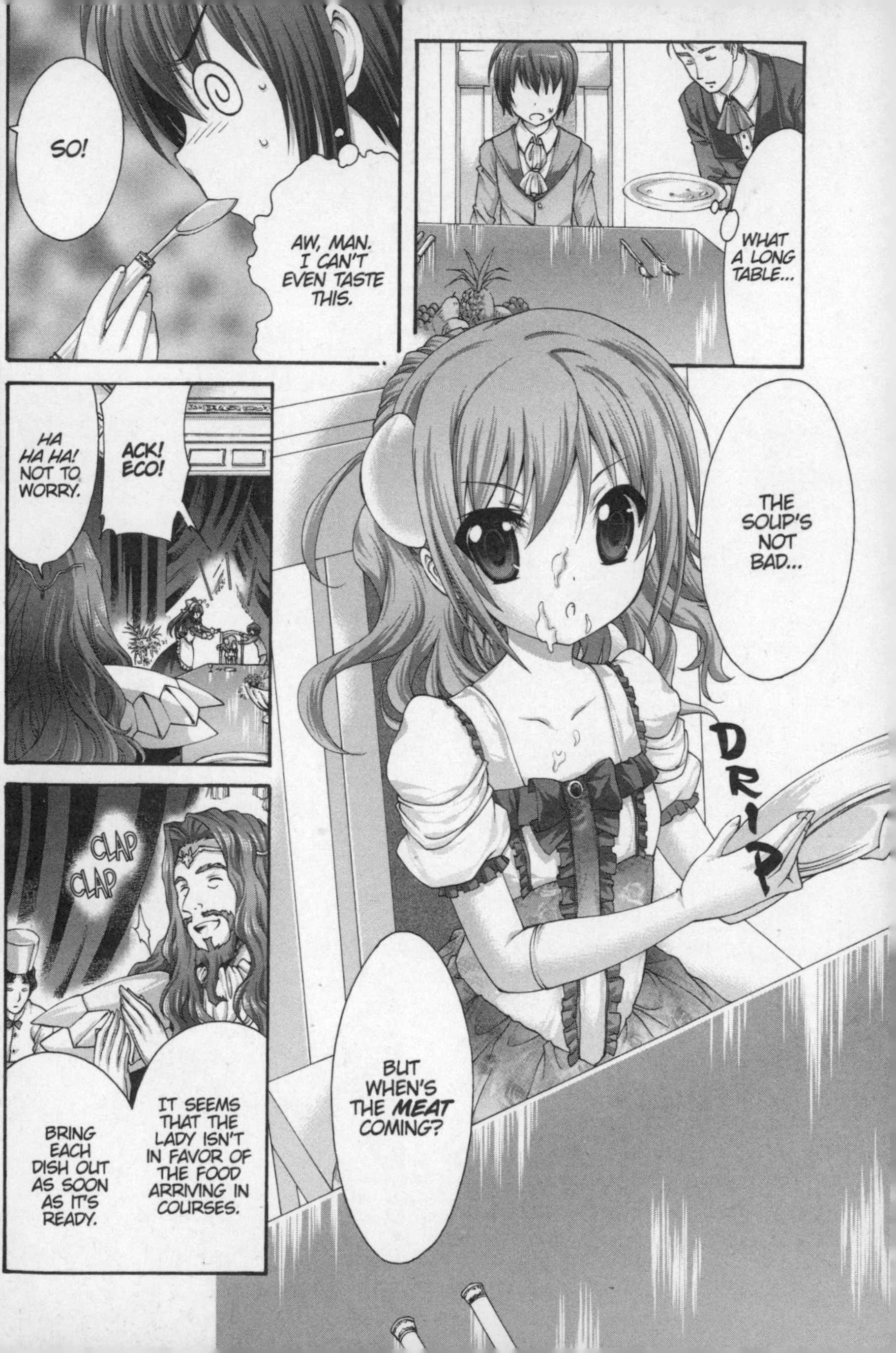
WHAT A LONG TABLE...
AW, MAN. I CAN'T EVEN TASTE THIS.
SO!
THE SOUP'S NOT BAD...
DRIP
BUT WHEN'S THE MEAT COMING?
ACK! ECO!
HA HA HA! NOT TO WORRY.
CLAP CLAP
IT SEEMS THAT THE LADY ISN'T IN FAVOR OF THE FOOD ARRIVING IN COURSES.
BRING EACH DISH OUT AS SOON AS IT'S READY.

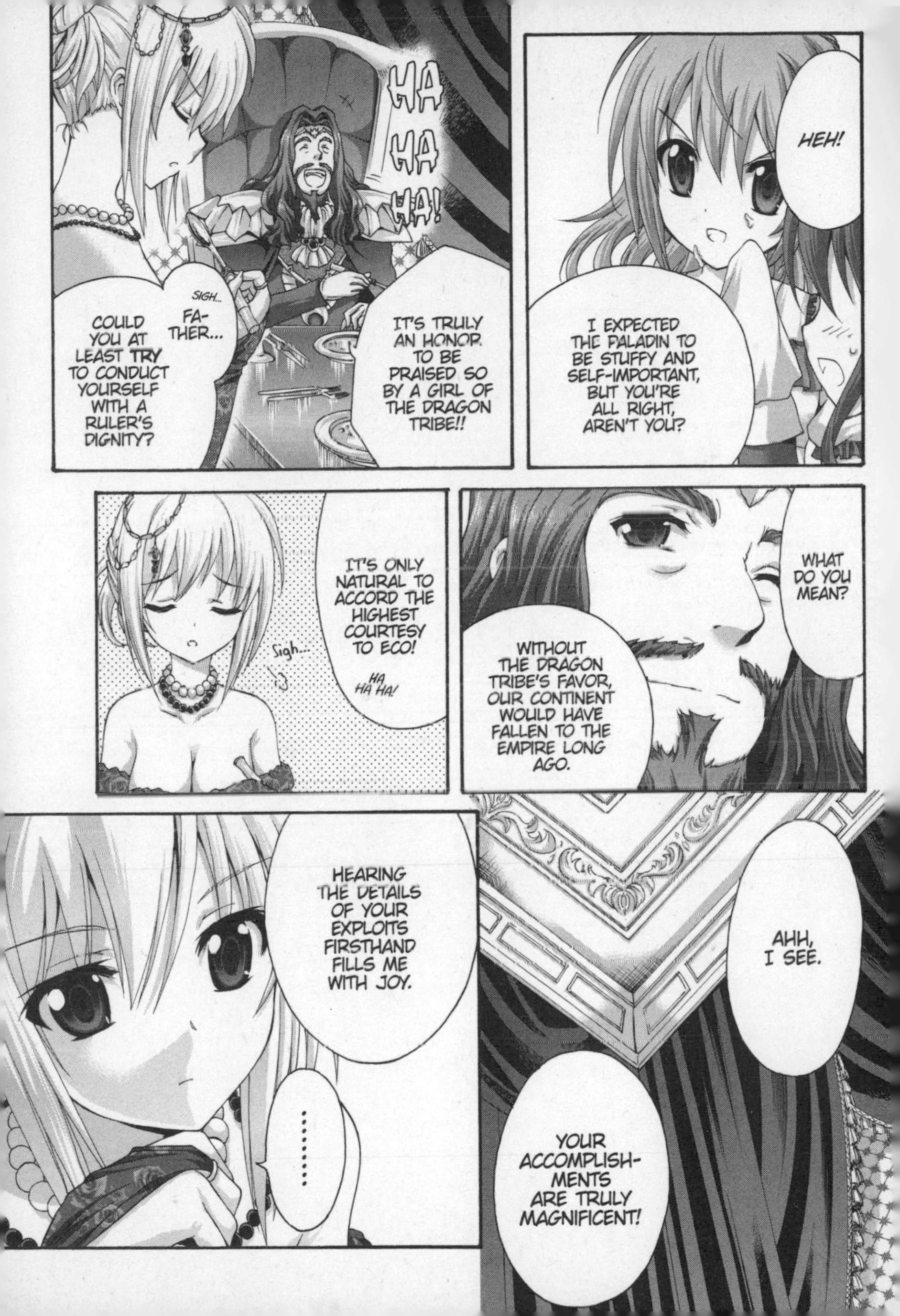
HEH!
I EXPECTED THE PALADIN TO BE STUFFY AND SELF-IMPORTANT, BUT YOU'RE ALL RIGHT, AREN'T YOU?
HA HA HA!
IT'S TRULY AN HONOR TO BE PRAISED SO BY A GIRL OF THE DRAGON TRIBE!!
SIGH...
FA-THER...
COULD YOU AT LEAST TRY TO CONDUCT YOURSELF WITH A RULER'S DIGNITY?
WHAT DO YOU MEAN?
WITHOUT THE DRAGON TRIBE'S FAVOR, OUR CONTINENT WOULD HAVE FALLEN TO THE EMPIRE LONG AGO.
IT'S ONLY NATURAL TO ACCORD THE HIGHEST COURTESY TO ECO!
HA HA HA!
Sigh...
AHH, I SEE.
YOUR ACCOMPLISH-MENTS ARE TRULY MAGNIFICENT!
HEARING THE DETAILS OF YOUR EXPLOITS FIRSTHAND FILLS ME WITH JOY.
......

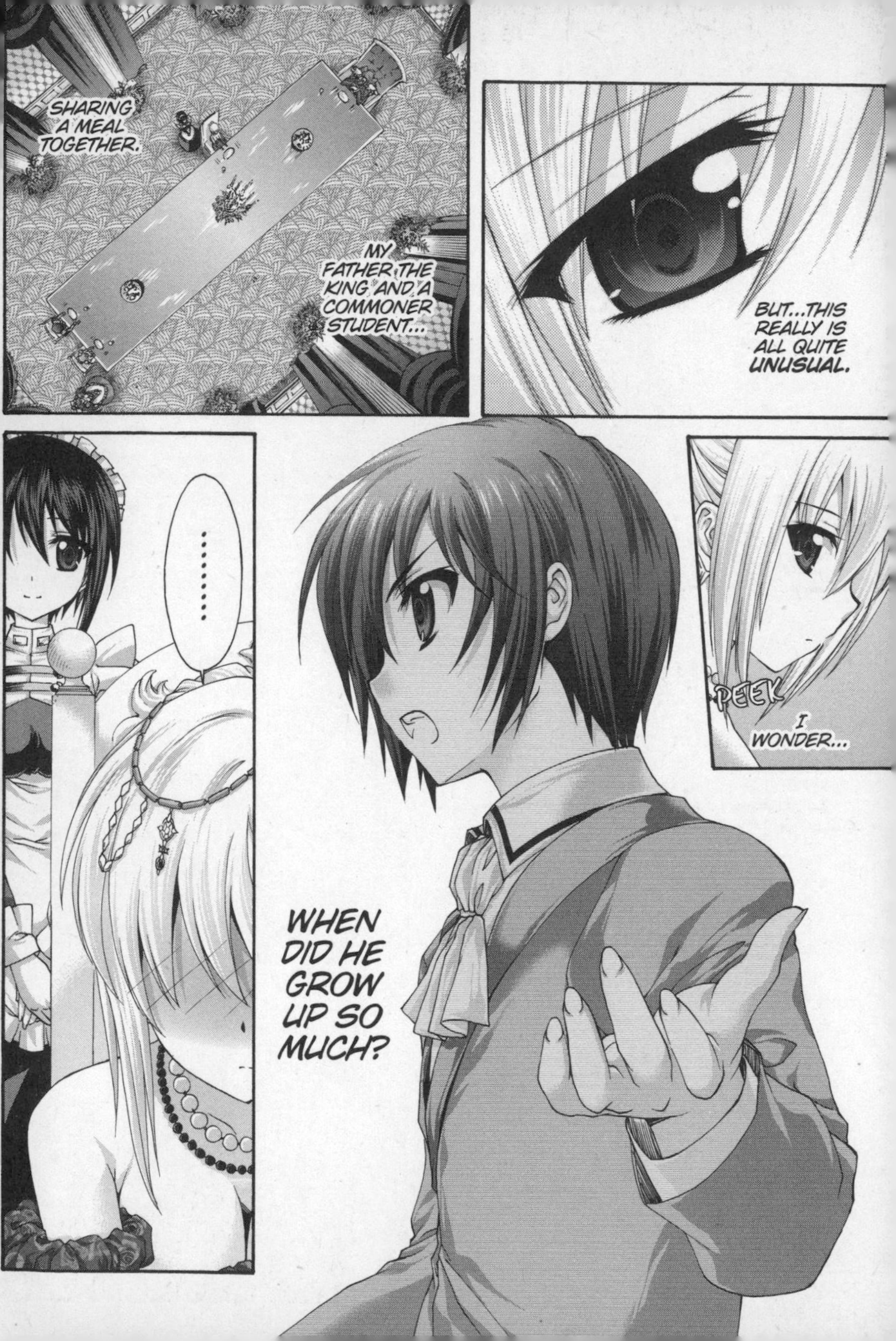
BUT...THIS REALLY IS ALL QUITE UNUSUAL.
MY FATHER THE KING AND A COMMONER STUDENT...
SHARING A MEAL TOGETHER.
PEEK
I WONDER...
WHEN DID HE GROW UP SO MUCH?
......

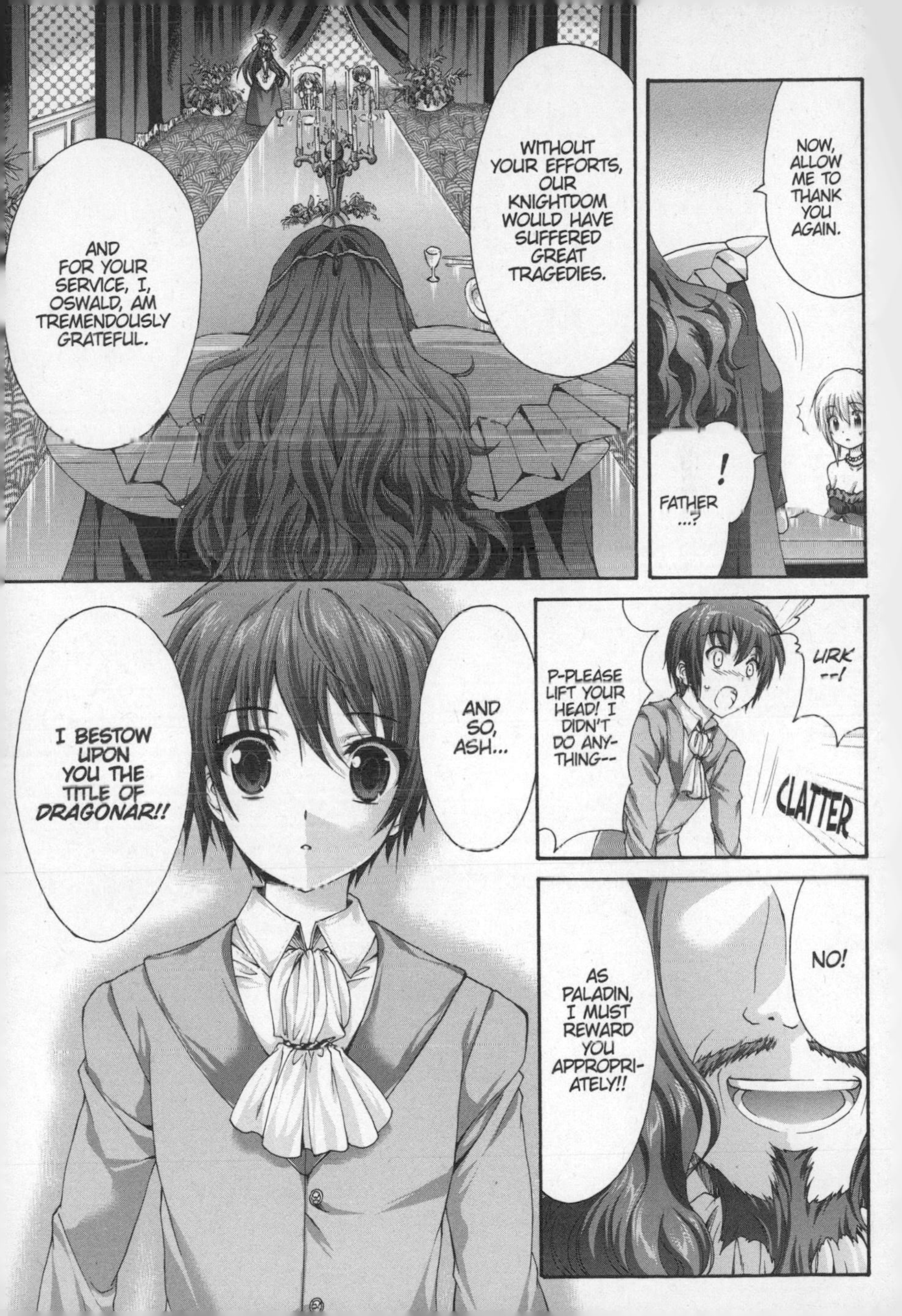
NOW, ALLOW ME TO THANK YOU AGAIN.
!
FATHER ...?
WITHOUT YOUR EFFORTS, OUR KNIGHTDOM WOULD HAVE SUFFERED GREAT TRAGEDIES.
AND FOR YOUR SERVICE, I, OSWALD, AM TREMENDOUSLY GRATEFUL.
URK--!
P-PLEASE LIFT YOUR HEAD! I DIDN'T DO ANY-THING--
CLATTER
NO!
AS PALADIN, I MUST REWARD YOU APPROPRI-ATELY!!
AND SO, ASH...
I BESTOW UPON YOU THE TITLE OF *DRAGONAR*!!

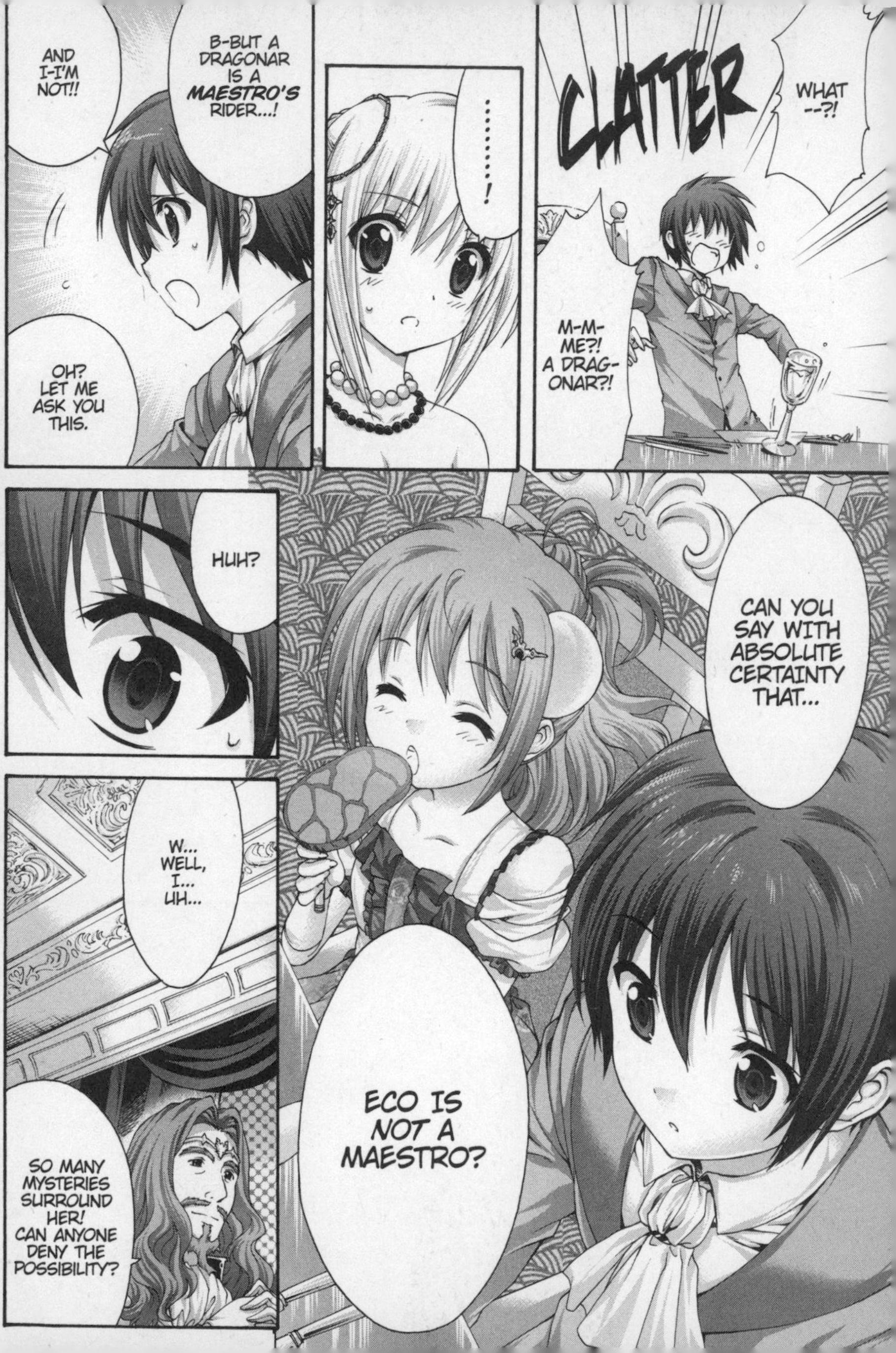
CLATTER
WHAT --?!
M-M-ME?! A DRAG-ONAR?!
......!
B-BUT A DRAGONAR IS A *MAESTRO'S* RIDER...!
AND I-I'M NOT!!
OH? LET ME ASK YOU THIS.
CAN YOU SAY WITH ABSOLUTE CERTAINTY THAT...
ECO IS *NOT* A MAESTRO?
HUH?
W... WELL, I... UH...
SO MANY MYSTERIES SURROUND HER! CAN ANYONE DENY THE POSSIBILITY?

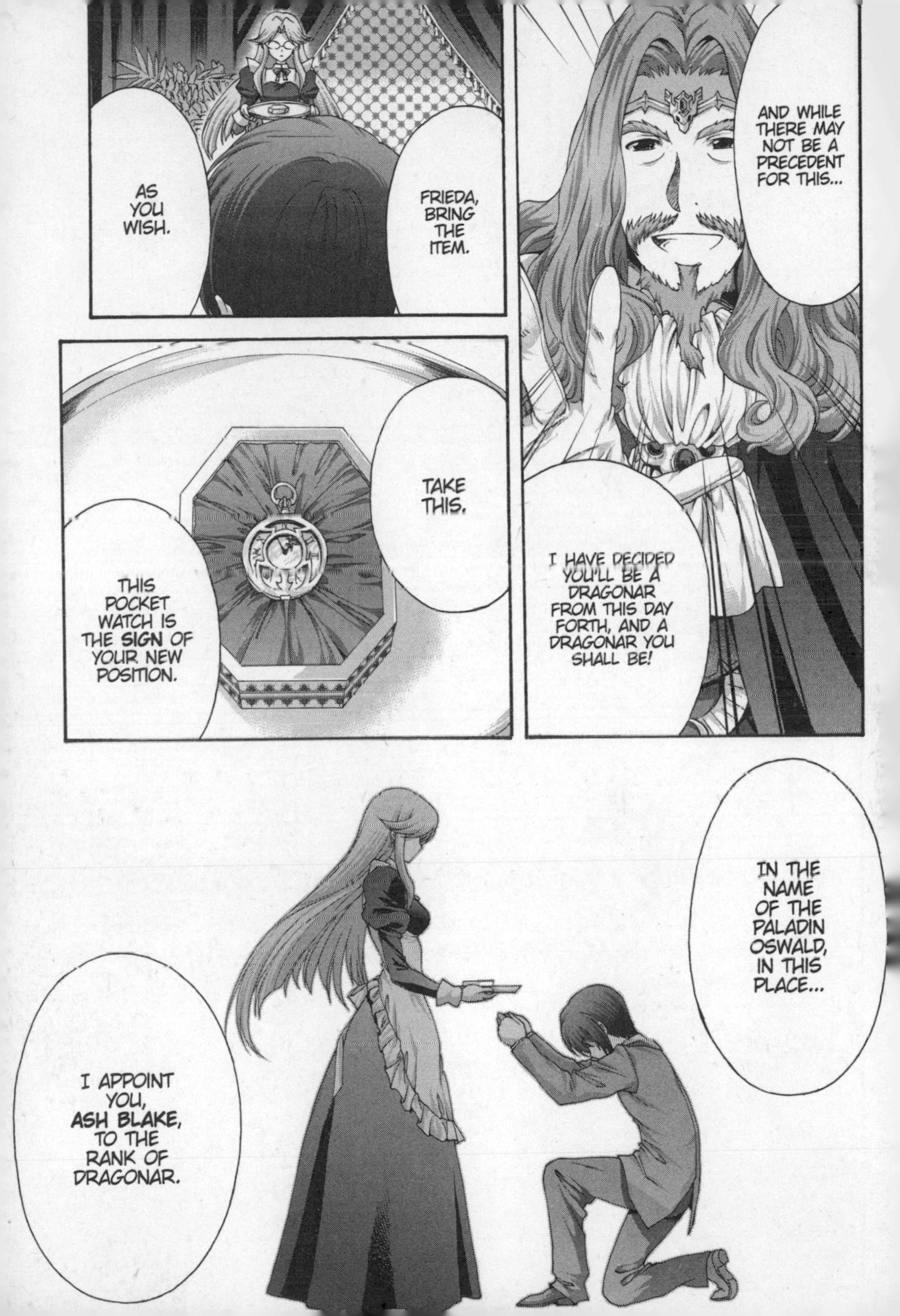
AND WHILE THERE MAY NOT BE A PRECEDENT FOR THIS...
I HAVE DECIDED YOU'LL BE A DRAGONAR FROM THIS DAY FORTH, AND A DRAGONAR YOU SHALL BE!
FRIEDA, BRING THE ITEM.
AS YOU WISH.
TAKE THIS.
THIS POCKET WATCH IS THE **SIGN** OF YOUR NEW POSITION.
IN THE NAME OF THE PALADIN OSWALD, IN THIS PLACE...
I APPOINT YOU, **ASH BLAKE**, TO THE RANK OF DRAGONAR.

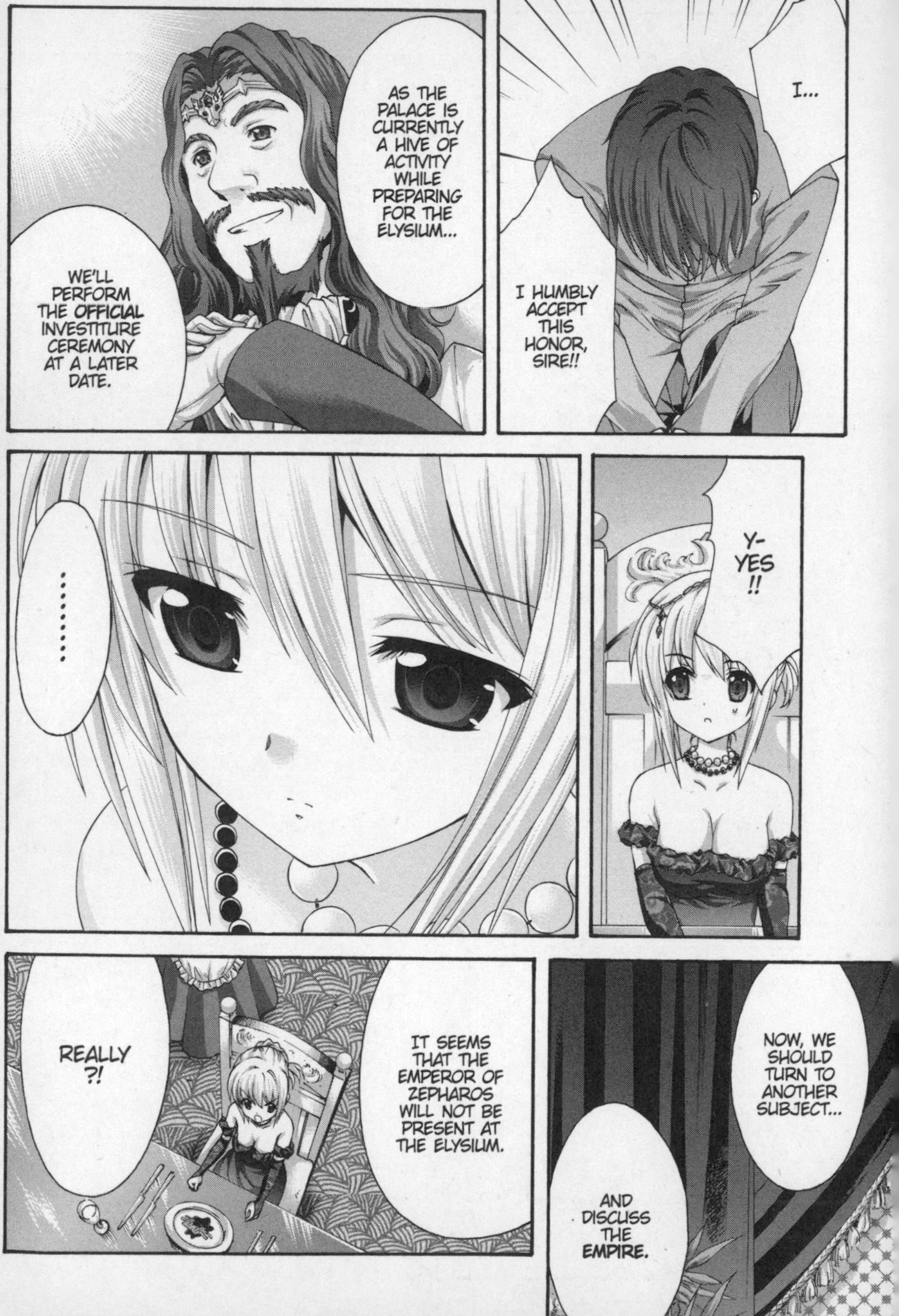

I...
I HUMBLY ACCEPT THIS HONOR, SIRE!!
AS THE PALACE IS CURRENTLY A HIVE OF ACTIVITY WHILE PREPARING FOR THE ELYSIUM...
WE'LL PERFORM THE OFFICIAL INVESTITURE CEREMONY AT A LATER DATE.
Y-YES!!
......
NOW, WE SHOULD TURN TO ANOTHER SUBJECT...
AND DISCUSS THE EMPIRE.
IT SEEMS THAT THE EMPEROR OF ZEPHAROS WILL NOT BE PRESENT AT THE ELYSIUM.
REALLY?!

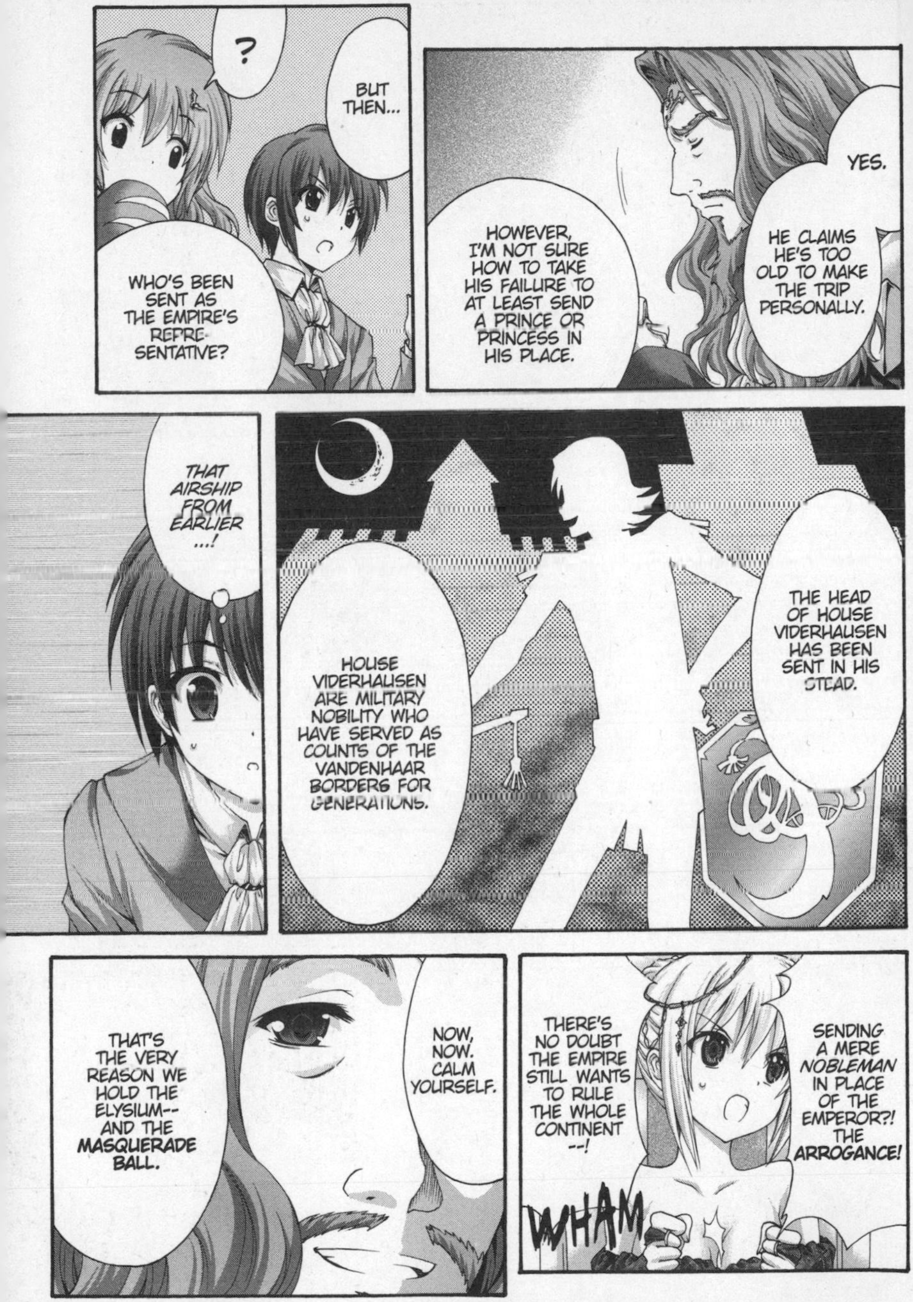
YES.
HE CLAIMS HE'S TOO OLD TO MAKE THE TRIP PERSONALLY.
HOWEVER, I'M NOT SURE HOW TO TAKE HIS FAILURE TO AT LEAST SEND A PRINCE OR PRINCESS IN HIS PLACE.
BUT THEN...
?
WHO'S BEEN SENT AS THE EMPIRE'S REPRE-SENTATIVE?
THE HEAD OF HOUSE VIDERHAUSEN HAS BEEN SENT IN HIS STEAD.
HOUSE VIDERHAUSEN ARE MILITARY NOBILITY WHO HAVE SERVED AS COUNTS OF THE VANDENHAAR BORDERS FOR GENERATIONS.
THAT AIRSHIP FROM EARLIER ...!
SENDING A MERE NOBLEMAN IN PLACE OF THE EMPEROR?! THE ARROGANCE!
THERE'S NO DOUBT THE EMPIRE STILL WANTS TO RULE THE WHOLE CONTINENT --!
WHAM
NOW, NOW. CALM YOURSELF.
THAT'S THE VERY REASON WE HOLD THE ELYSIUM-- AND THE MASQUERADE BALL.

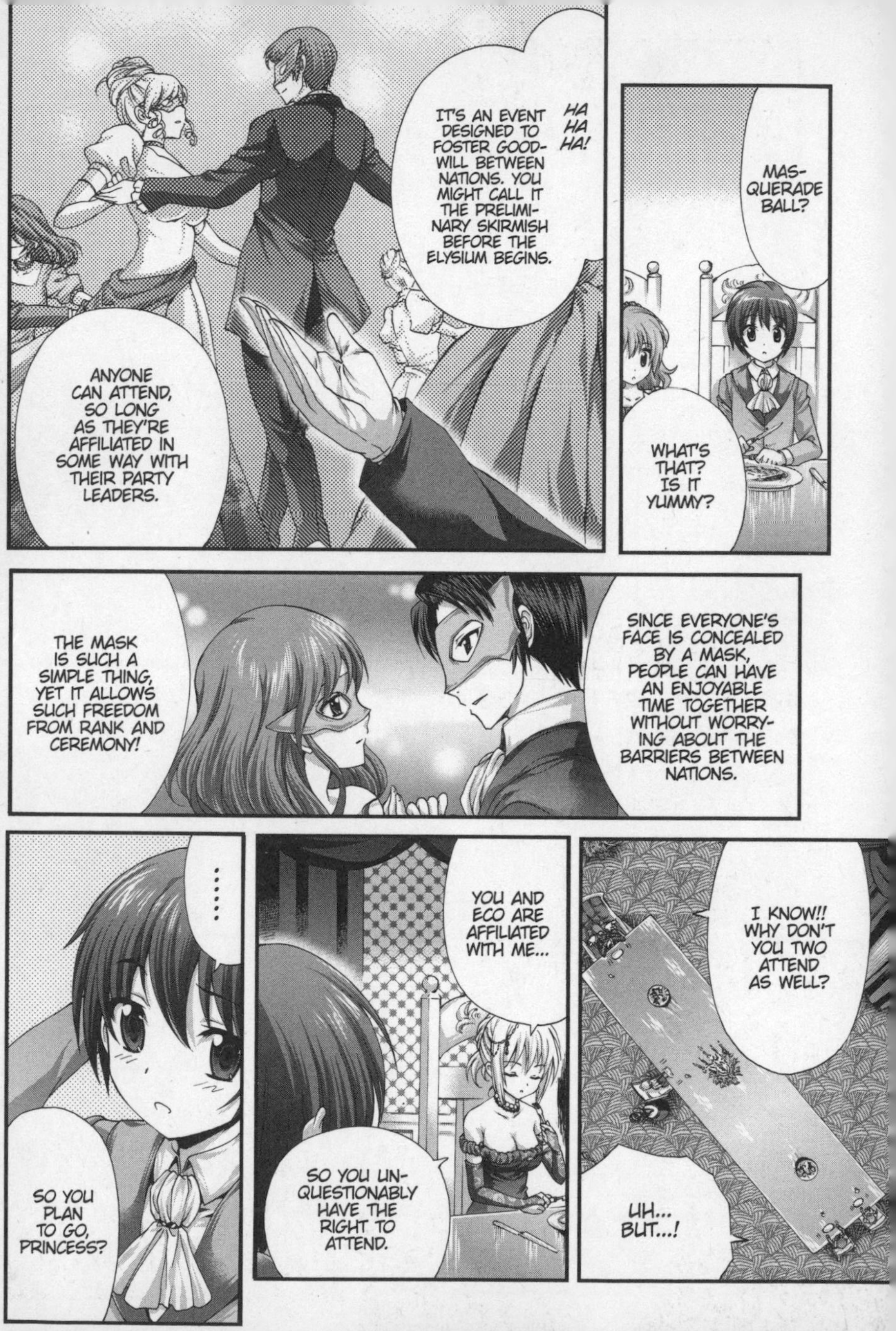
MAS-QUERADE BALL?
WHAT'S THAT? IS IT YUMMY?
HA HA HA!
IT'S AN EVENT DESIGNED TO FOSTER GOOD-WILL BETWEEN NATIONS. YOU MIGHT CALL IT THE PRELIMI-NARY SKIRMISH BEFORE THE ELYSIUM BEGINS.
ANYONE CAN ATTEND, SO LONG AS THEY'RE AFFILIATED IN SOME WAY WITH THEIR PARTY LEADERS.
SINCE EVERYONE'S FACE IS CONCEALED BY A MASK, PEOPLE CAN HAVE AN ENJOYABLE TIME TOGETHER WITHOUT WORRY-ING ABOUT THE BARRIERS BETWEEN NATIONS.
THE MASK IS SUCH A SIMPLE THING, YET IT ALLOWS SUCH FREEDOM FROM RANK AND CEREMONY!
I KNOW!! WHY DON'T YOU TWO ATTEND AS WELL?
UH... BUT...!
YOU AND ECO ARE AFFILIATED WITH ME...
SO YOU UN-QUESTIONABLY HAVE THE RIGHT TO ATTEND.
......
SO YOU PLAN TO GO, PRINCESS?

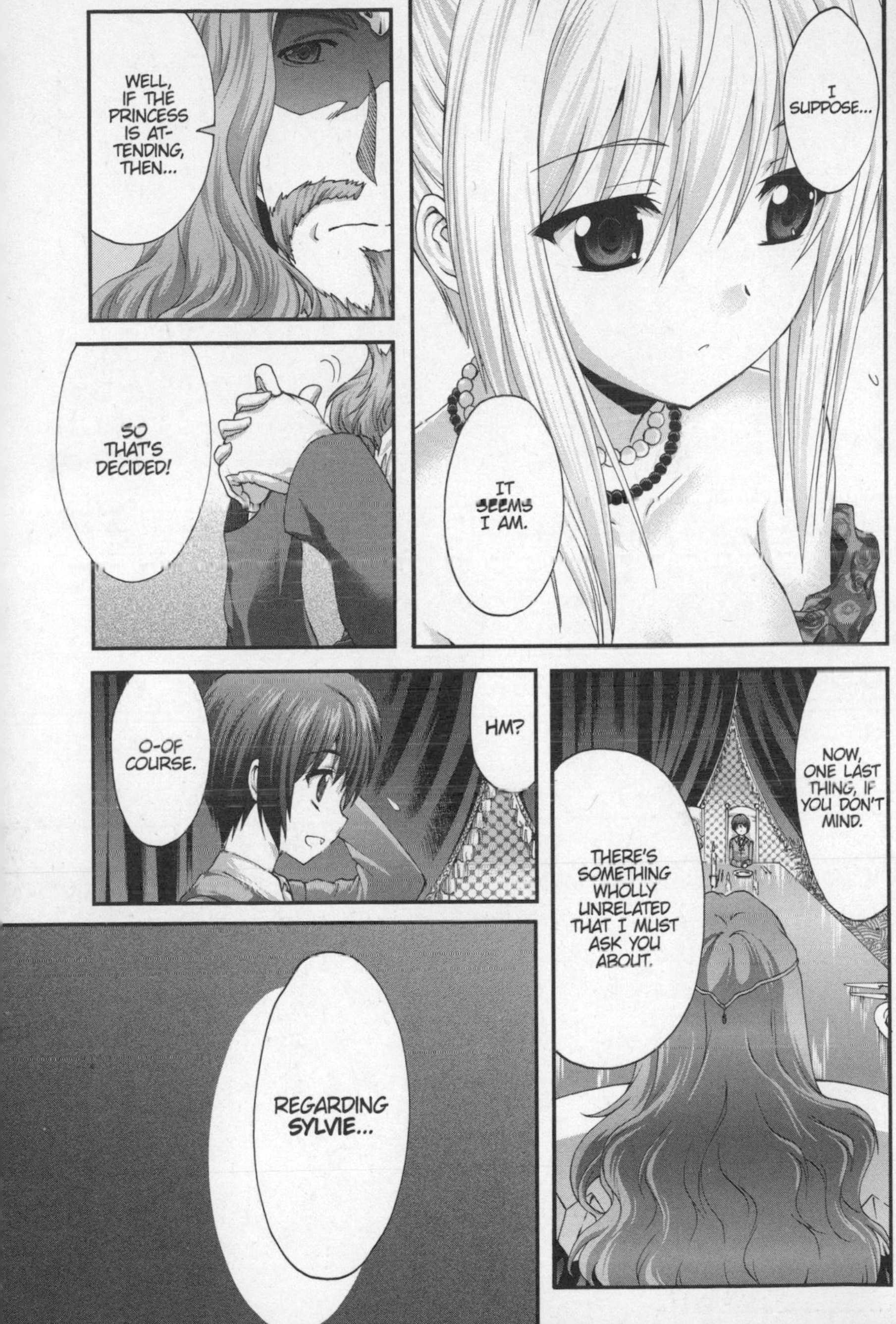
I SUPPOSE...
IT SEEMS I AM.
WELL, IF THE PRINCESS IS AT-TENDING, THEN...
SO THAT'S DECIDED!
NOW, ONE LAST THING, IF YOU DON'T MIND.
THERE'S SOMETHING WHOLLY UNRELATED THAT I MUST ASK YOU ABOUT.
HM?
O-OF COURSE.
REGARDING SYLVIE...

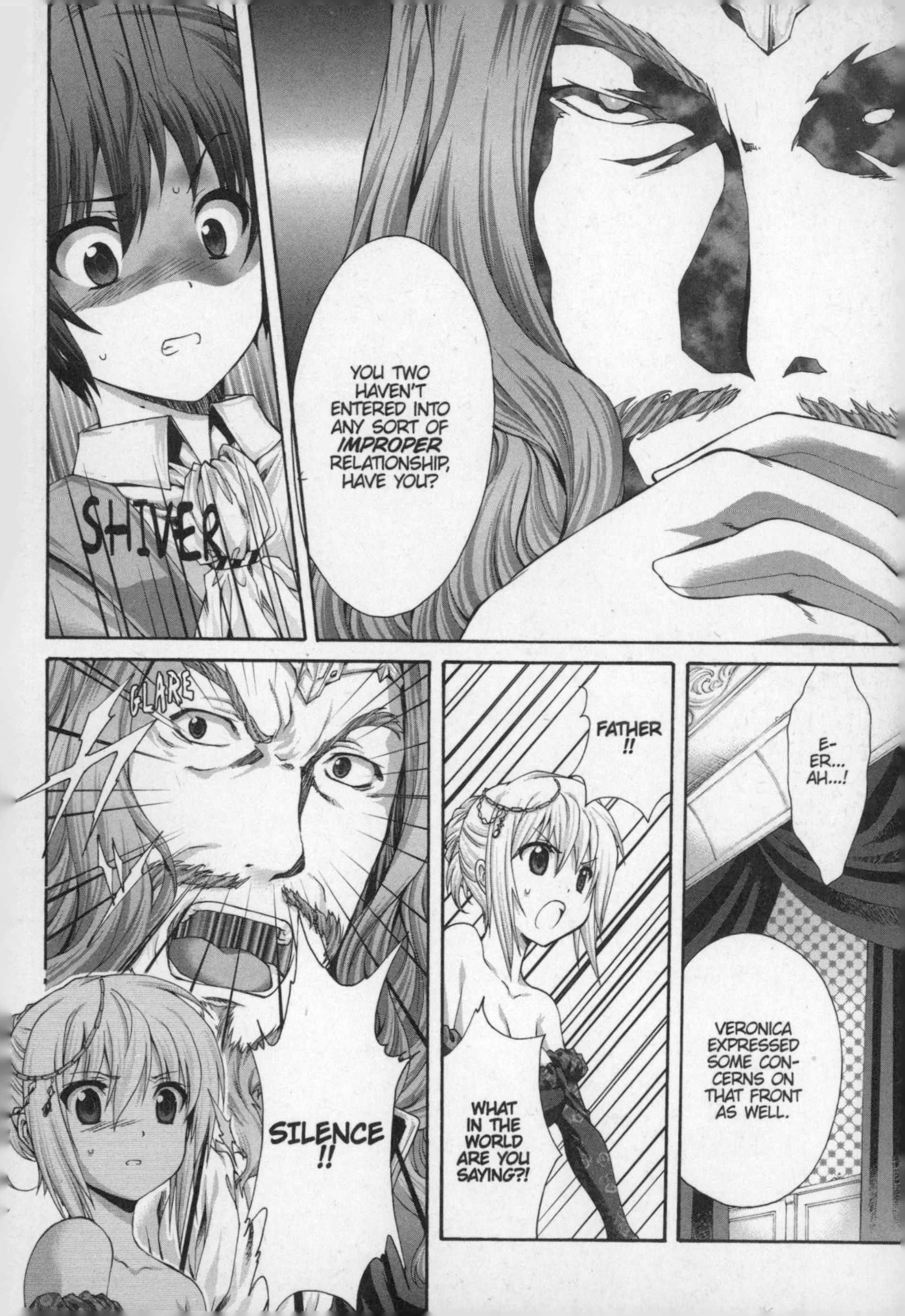
YOU TWO HAVEN'T ENTERED INTO ANY SORT OF *IMPROPER* RELATIONSHIP, HAVE YOU?
SHIVER
E- ER... AH...!
VERONICA EXPRESSED SOME CONCERNS ON THAT FRONT AS WELL.
FATHER !!
WHAT IN THE WORLD ARE YOU SAYING?!
GLARE
SILENCE !!

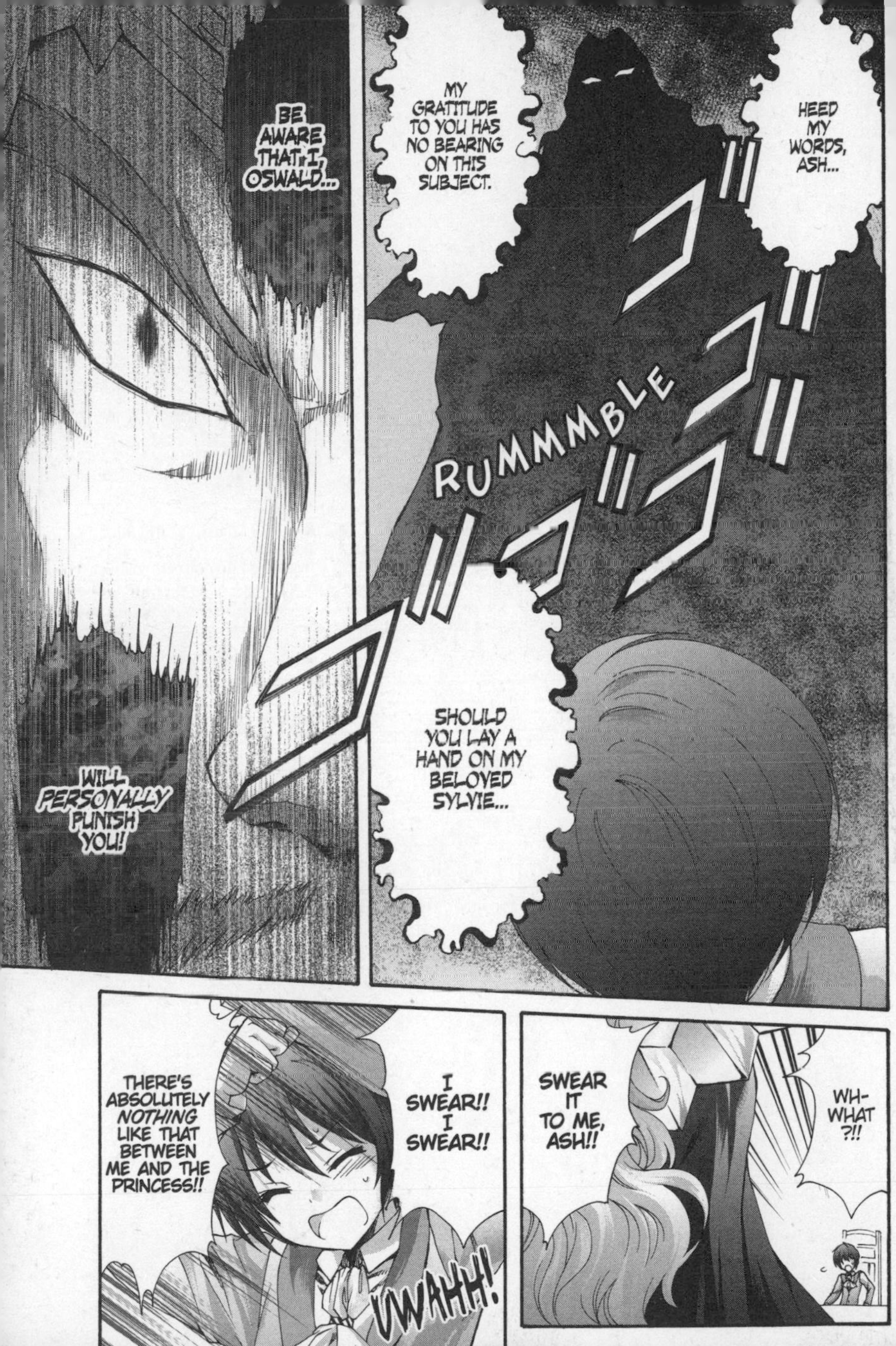
HEED MY WORDS, ASH...
MY GRATITUDE TO YOU HAS NO BEARING ON THIS SUBJECT.
RUMMMBLE
SHOULD YOU LAY A HAND ON MY BELOVED SYLVIE...
BE AWARE THAT I, OSWALD...
WILL PERSONALLY PUNISH YOU!
WH-WHAT?!!
SWEAR IT TO ME, ASH!!
I SWEAR!! I SWEAR!!
THERE'S ABSOLUTELY NOTHING LIKE THAT BETWEEN ME AND THE PRINCESS!!
UWAHH!

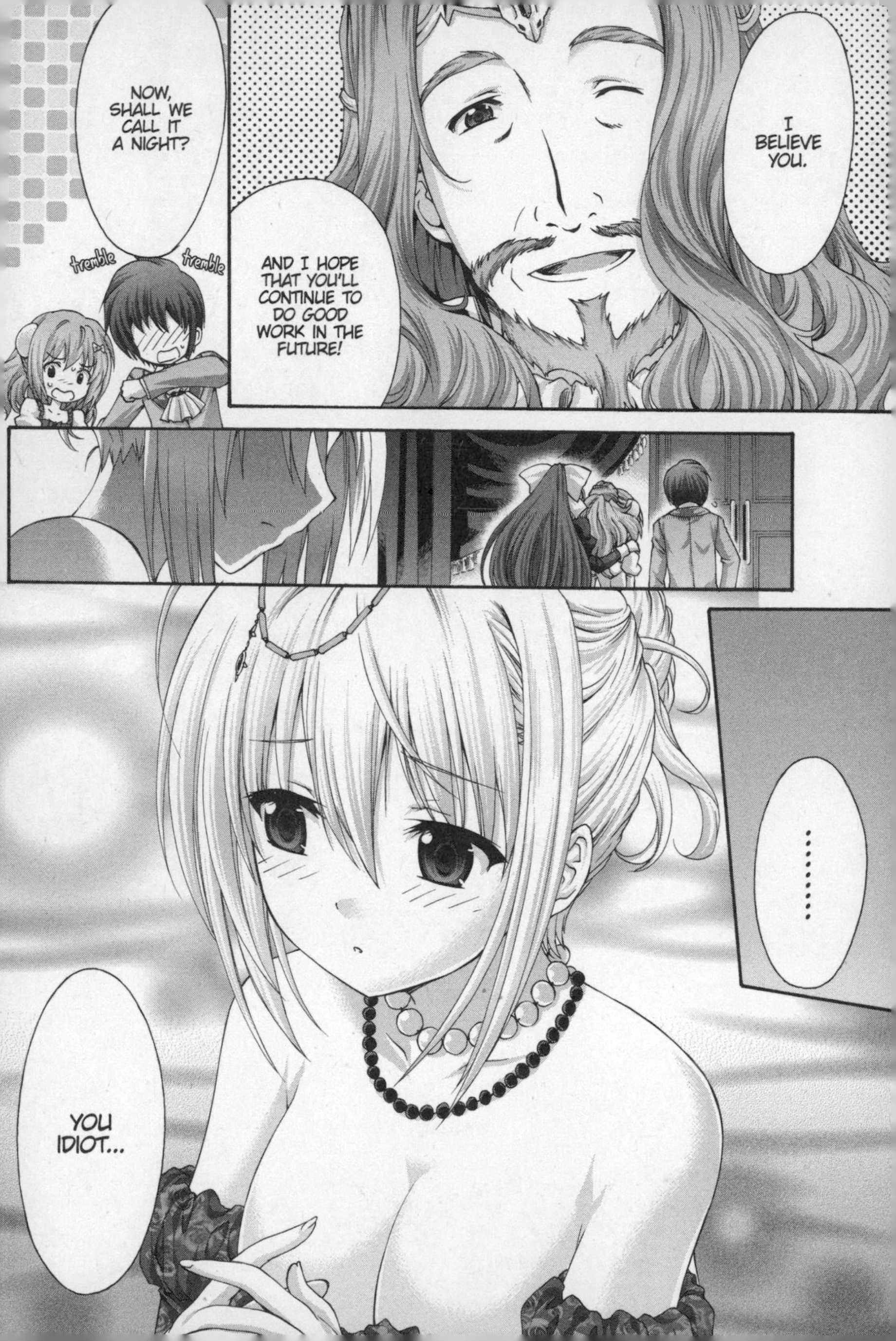
I BELIEVE YOU.
AND I HOPE THAT YOU'LL CONTINUE TO DO GOOD WORK IN THE FUTURE!
NOW, SHALL WE CALL IT A NIGHT?
tremble
tremble
......
YOU IDIOT...

DRAGONAR
ACADEMY

星刻の竜騎士

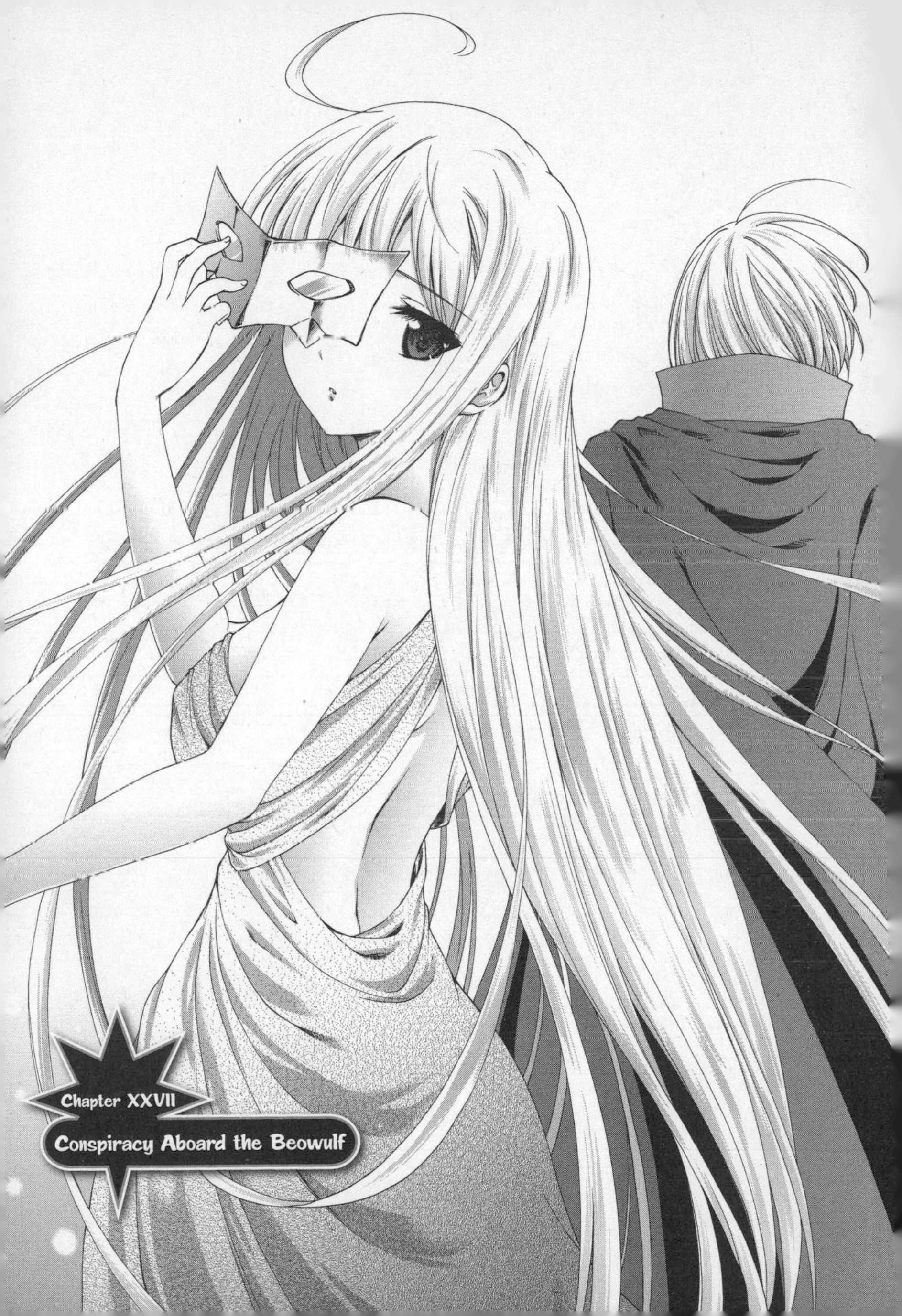
Chapter XXVII
Conspiracy Aboard the Beowulf

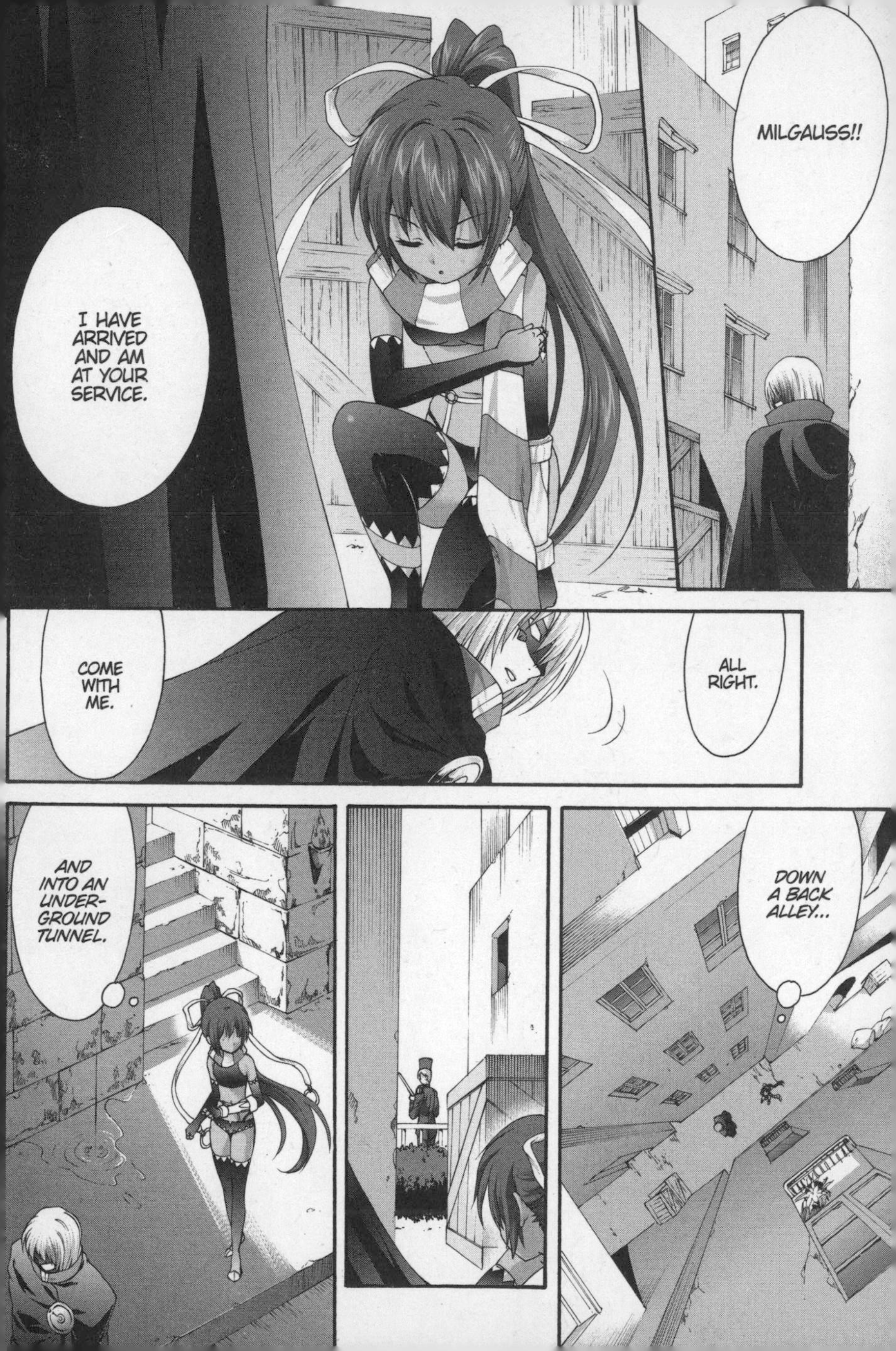
MILGAUSS!!
I HAVE ARRIVED AND AM AT YOUR SERVICE.
ALL RIGHT.
COME WITH ME.
DOWN A BACK ALLEY...
AND INTO AN UNDER-GROUND TUNNEL.

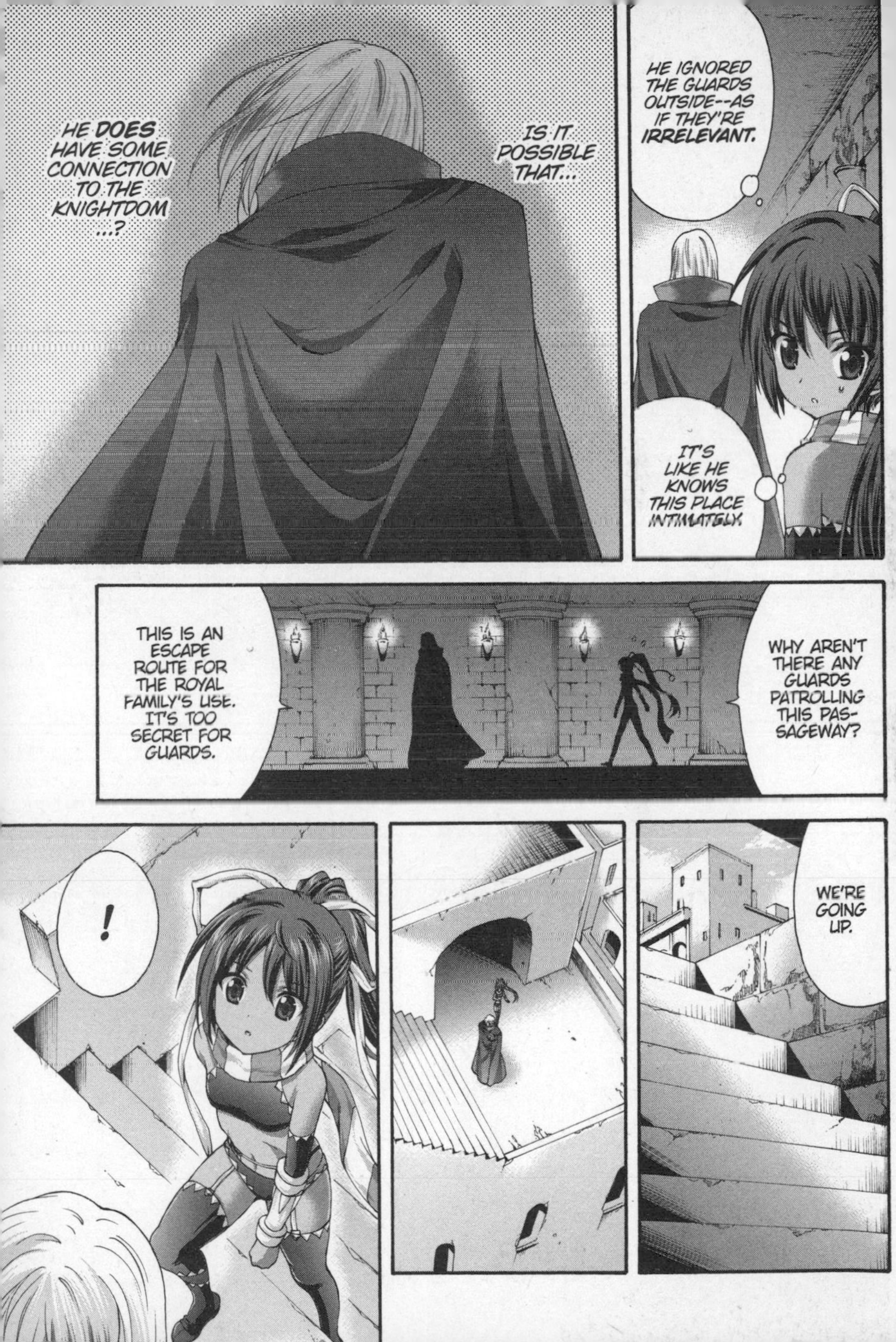
HE IGNORED THE GUARDS OUTSIDE--AS IF THEY'RE IRRELEVANT.
IT'S LIKE HE KNOWS THIS PLACE INTIMATELY.
IS IT POSSIBLE THAT...
HE DOES HAVE SOME CONNECTION TO THE KNIGHTDOM ...?
WHY AREN'T THERE ANY GUARDS PATROLLING THIS PAS-SAGEWAY?
THIS IS AN ESCAPE ROUTE FOR THE ROYAL FAMILY'S USE. IT'S TOO SECRET FOR GUARDS.
WE'RE GOING UP.
!

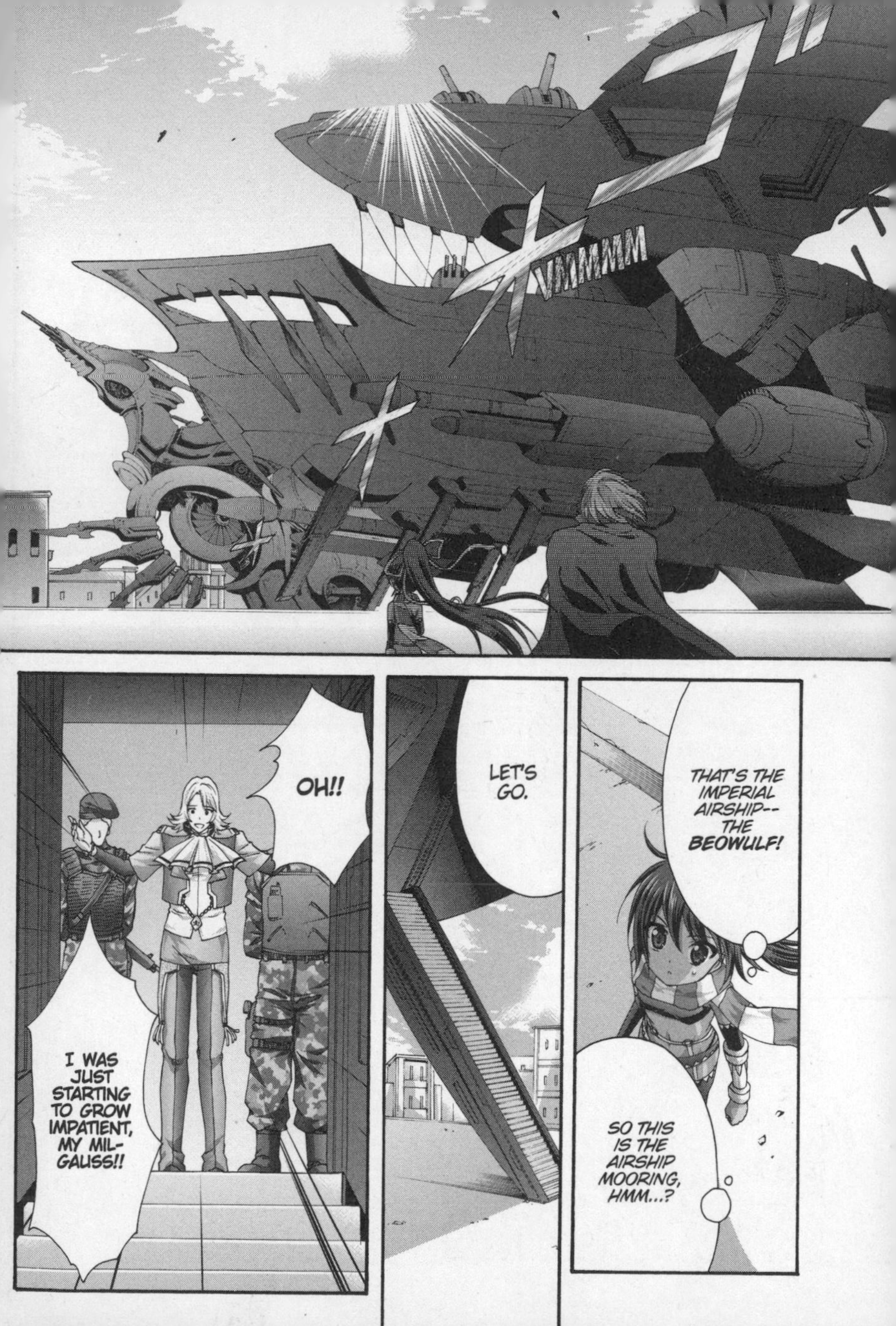
VMMMMM
THAT'S THE IMPERIAL AIRSHIP-- THE BEOWULF!
SO THIS IS THE AIRSHIP MOORING, HMM...?
LET'S GO.
OH!!
I WAS JUST STARTING TO GROW IMPATIENT, MY MIL-GAUSS!!

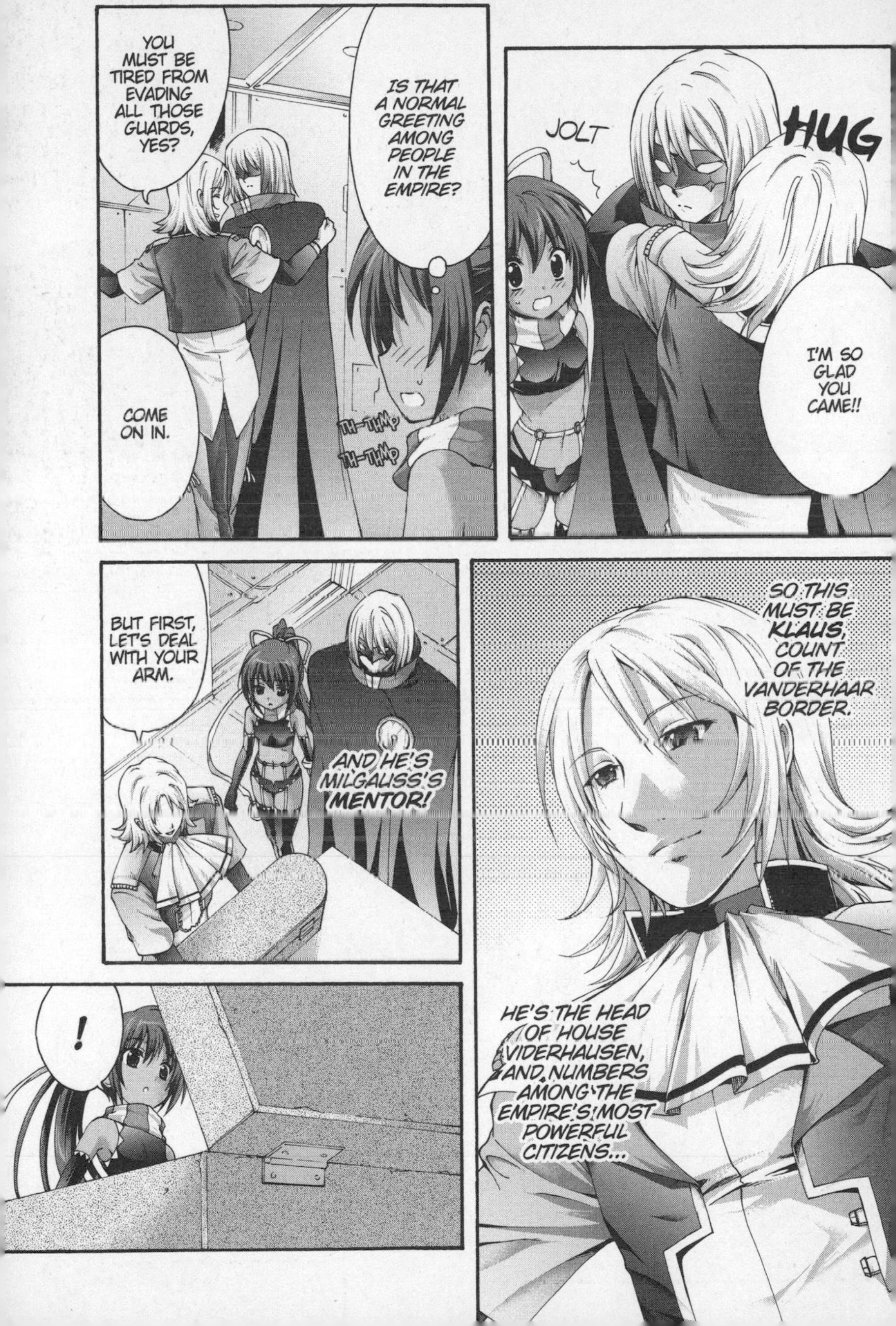
HUG
I'M SO GLAD YOU CAME!!
JOLT
IS THAT A NORMAL GREETING AMONG PEOPLE IN THE EMPIRE?
YOU MUST BE TIRED FROM EVADING ALL THOSE GUARDS, YES?
COME ON IN.
TH-THMP
TH-THMP
SO THIS MUST BE KLAUS, COUNT OF THE VANDERHAAR BORDER.
HE'S THE HEAD OF HOUSE VIDERHAUSEN, AND NUMBERS AMONG THE EMPIRE'S MOST POWERFUL CITIZENS...
BUT FIRST, LET'S DEAL WITH YOUR ARM.
AND HE'S MILGAUSS'S MENTOR!
!

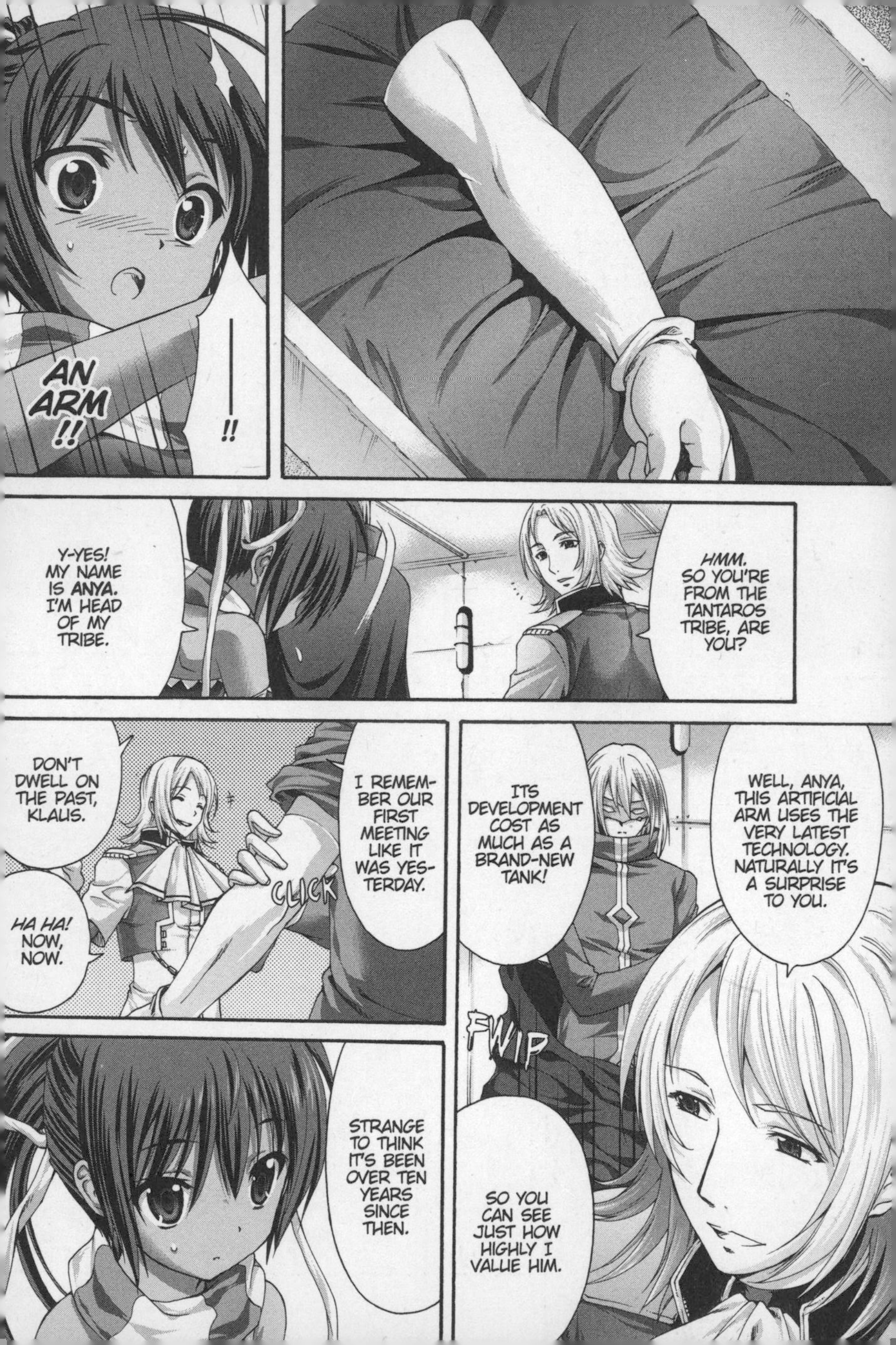
——!!
AN ARM!!
HMM. SO YOU'RE FROM THE TANTAROS TRIBE, ARE YOU?
Y-YES! MY NAME IS ANYA. I'M HEAD OF MY TRIBE.
WELL, ANYA, THIS ARTIFICIAL ARM USES THE VERY LATEST TECHNOLOGY. NATURALLY IT'S A SURPRISE TO YOU.
ITS DEVELOPMENT COST AS MUCH AS A BRAND-NEW TANK!
FWIP
SO YOU CAN SEE JUST HOW HIGHLY I VALUE HIM.
I REMEMBER OUR FIRST MEETING LIKE IT WAS YESTERDAY.
CLICK
DON'T DWELL ON THE PAST, KLAUS.
HA HA! NOW, NOW.
STRANGE TO THINK IT'S BEEN OVER TEN YEARS SINCE THEN.

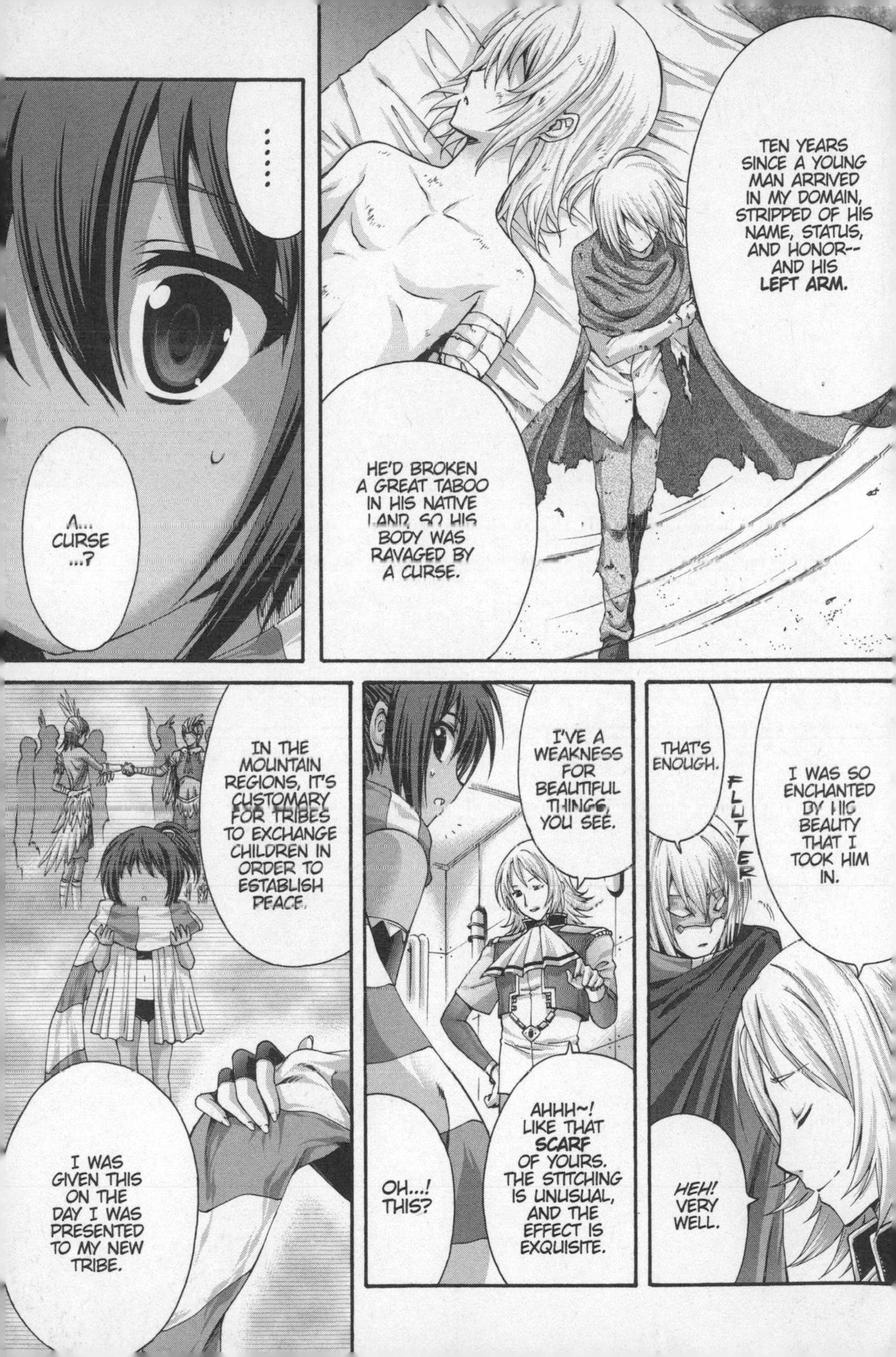
TEN YEARS SINCE A YOUNG MAN ARRIVED IN MY DOMAIN, STRIPPED OF HIS NAME, STATUS, AND HONOR-- AND HIS LEFT ARM.
HE'D BROKEN A GREAT TABOO IN HIS NATIVE LAND, SO HIS BODY WAS RAVAGED BY A CURSE.
......
A... CURSE ...?
I WAS SO ENCHANTED BY HIS BEAUTY THAT I TOOK HIM IN.
THAT'S ENOUGH.
FLUTTER
HEH! VERY WELL.
I'VE A WEAKNESS FOR BEAUTIFUL THINGS, YOU SEE.
AHHH~! LIKE THAT SCARF OF YOURS. THE STITCHING IS UNUSUAL, AND THE EFFECT IS EXQUISITE.
OH...! THIS?
IN THE MOUNTAIN REGIONS, IT'S CUSTOMARY FOR TRIBES TO EXCHANGE CHILDREN IN ORDER TO ESTABLISH PEACE.
I WAS GIVEN THIS ON THE DAY I WAS PRESENTED TO MY NEW TRIBE.

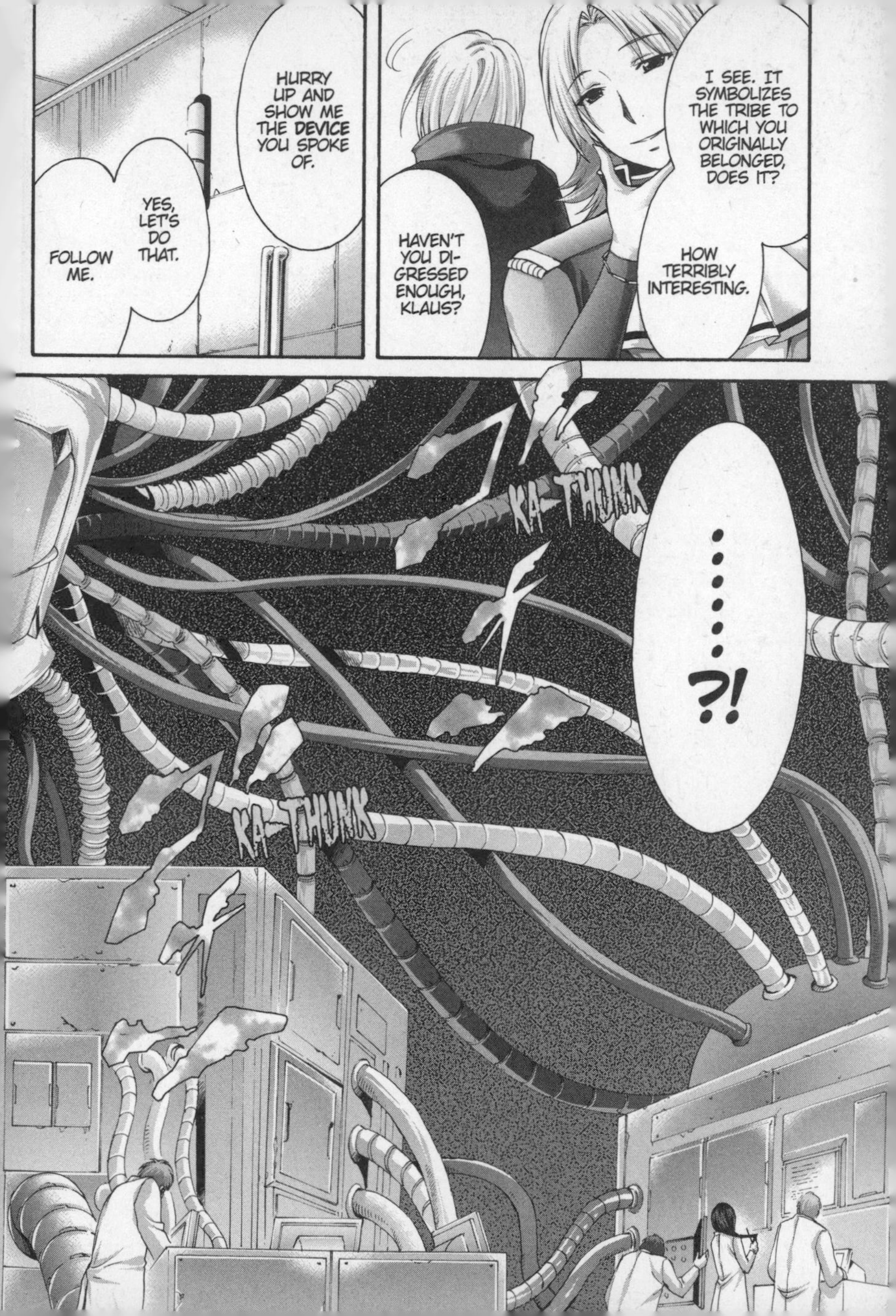
I SEE. IT SYMBOLIZES THE TRIBE TO WHICH YOU ORIGINALLY BELONGED, DOES IT?
HOW TERRIBLY INTERESTING.
HAVEN'T YOU DIGRESSED ENOUGH, KLAUS?
HURRY UP AND SHOW ME THE DEVICE YOU SPOKE OF.
YES, LET'S DO THAT.
FOLLOW ME.
......?!
KA-THUNK
KA-THUNK

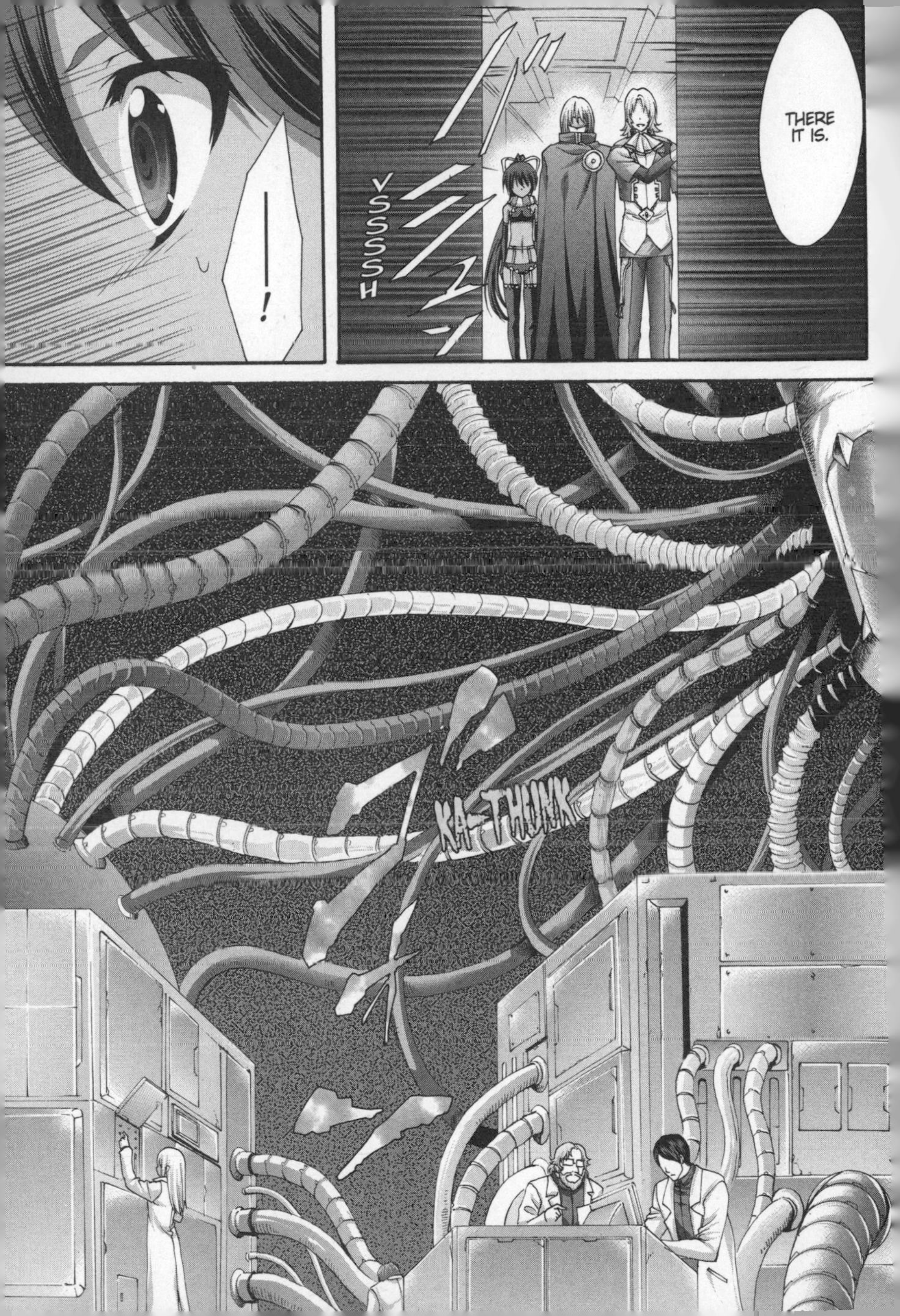
THERE IT IS.
VSSSSH
—!
KA-THUNK

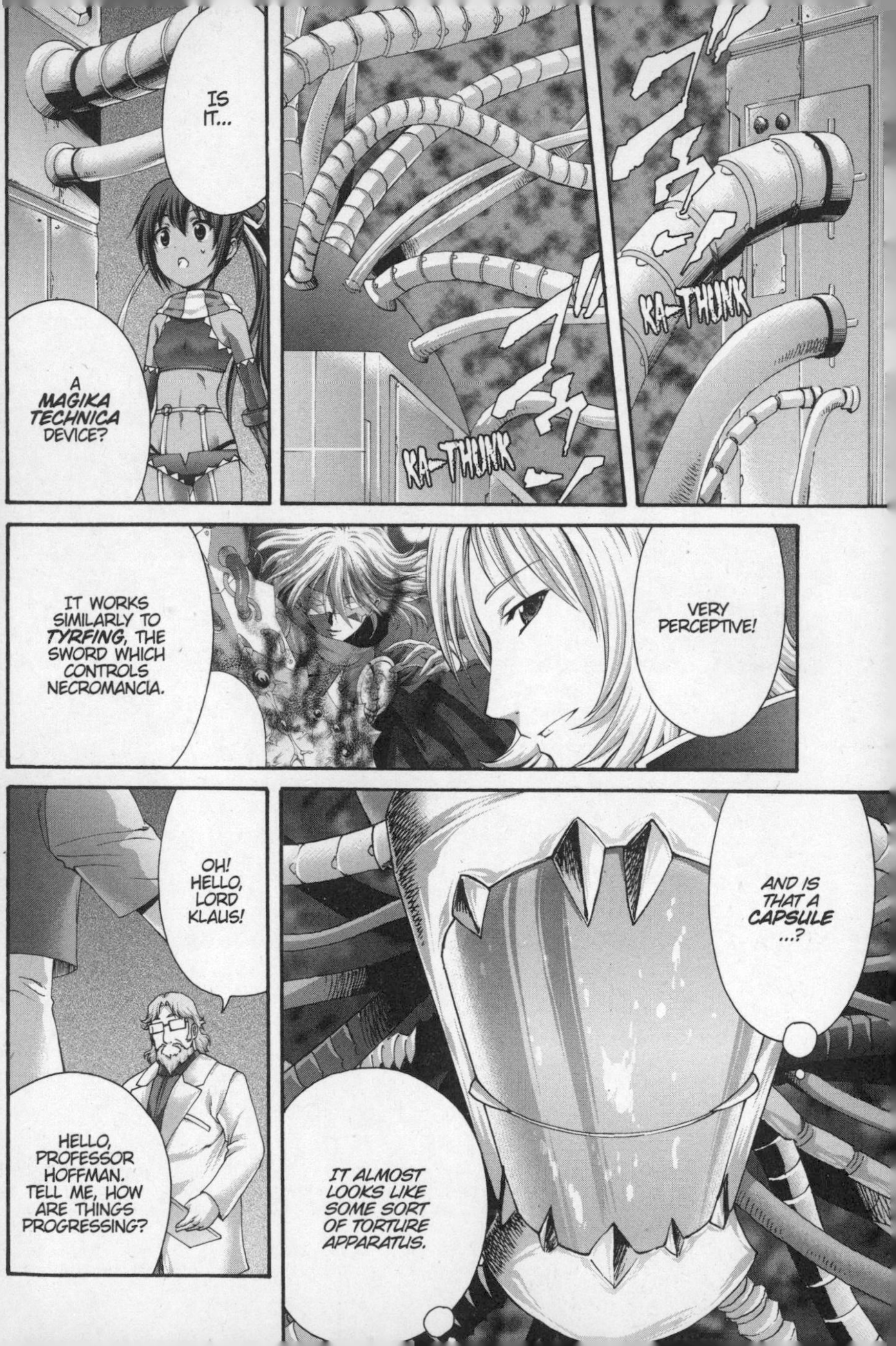
KA-THUNK
KA-THUNK
IS IT...
A *MAGIKA TECHNICA* DEVICE?
VERY PERCEPTIVE!
IT WORKS SIMILARLY TO *TYRFING*, THE SWORD WHICH CONTROLS NECROMANCIA.
AND IS THAT A **CAPSULE** ...?
IT ALMOST LOOKS LIKE SOME SORT OF TORTURE APPARATUS.
OH! HELLO, LORD KLAUS!
HELLO, PROFESSOR HOFFMAN. TELL ME, HOW ARE THINGS PROGRESSING?

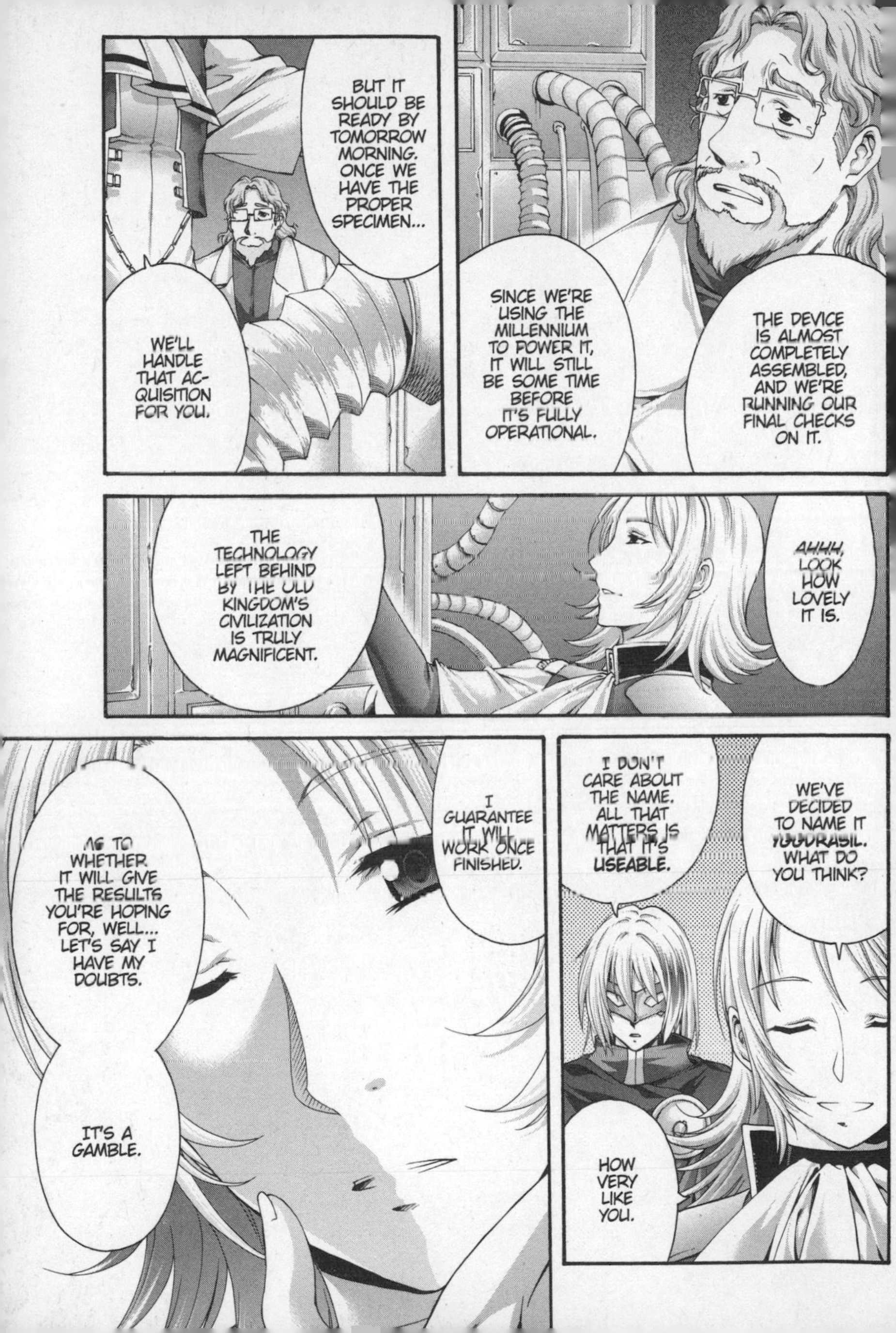
THE DEVICE IS ALMOST COMPLETELY ASSEMBLED, AND WE'RE RUNNING OUR FINAL CHECKS ON IT.
SINCE WE'RE USING THE MILLENNIUM TO POWER IT, IT WILL STILL BE SOME TIME BEFORE IT'S FULLY OPERATIONAL.
BUT IT SHOULD BE READY BY TOMORROW MORNING. ONCE WE HAVE THE PROPER SPECIMEN...
WE'LL HANDLE THAT AC-QUISITION FOR YOU.
AHHH, LOOK HOW LOVELY IT IS.
THE TECHNOLOGY LEFT BEHIND BY THE OLD KINGDOM'S CIVILIZATION IS TRULY MAGNIFICENT.
WE'VE DECIDED TO NAME IT YGGDRASIL. WHAT DO YOU THINK?
I DON'T CARE ABOUT THE NAME. ALL THAT MATTERS IS THAT IT'S USEABLE.
HOW VERY LIKE YOU.
I GUARANTEE IT WILL WORK ONCE FINISHED.
AS TO WHETHER IT WILL GIVE THE RESULTS YOU'RE HOPING FOR, WELL... LET'S SAY I HAVE MY DOUBTS.
IT'S A GAMBLE.

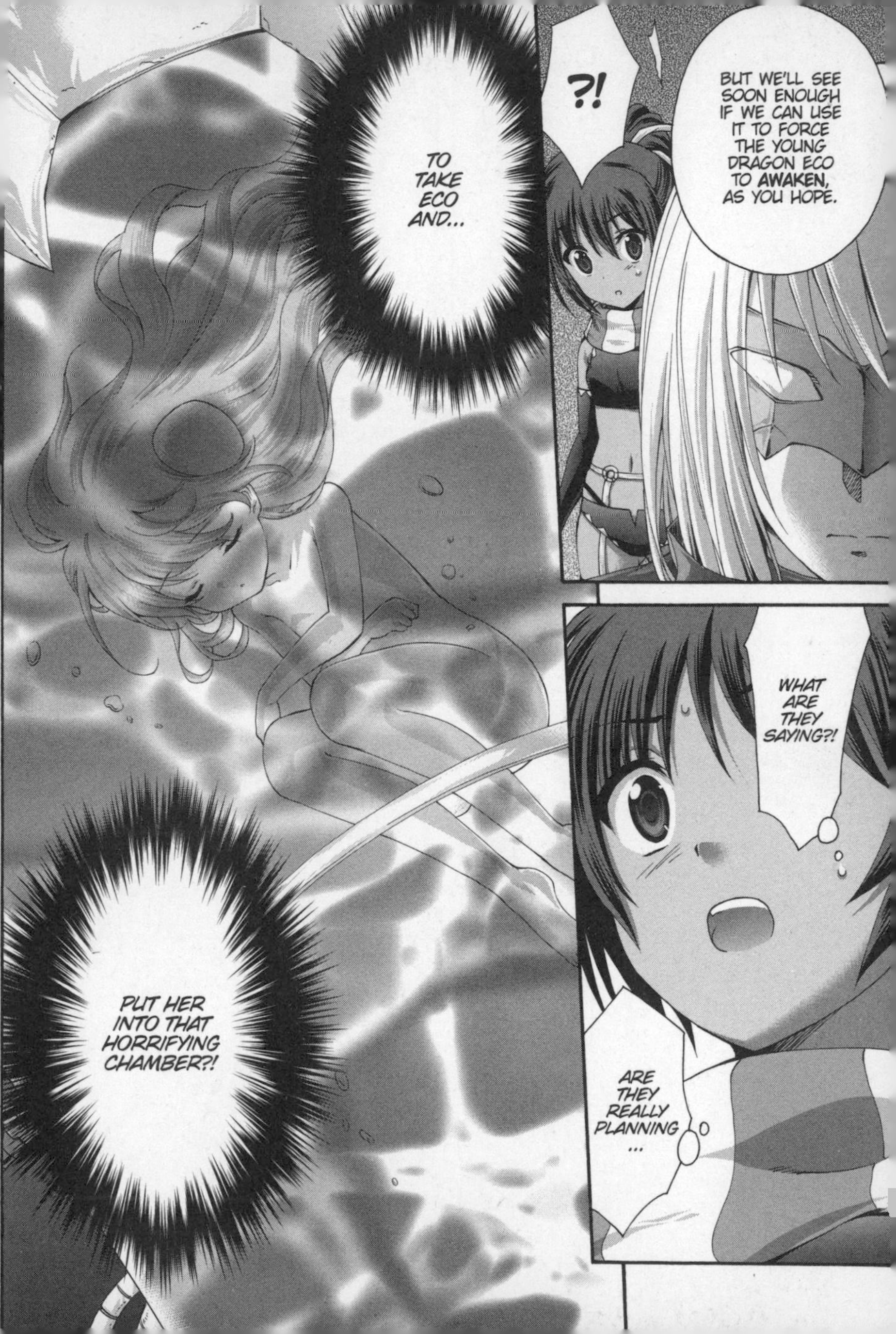
BUT WE'LL SEE SOON ENOUGH IF WE CAN USE IT TO FORCE THE YOUNG DRAGON ECO TO AWAKEN, AS YOU HOPE.
?!
WHAT ARE THEY SAYING?!
ARE THEY REALLY PLANNING ...
TO TAKE ECO AND...
PUT HER INTO THAT HORRIFYING CHAMBER?!

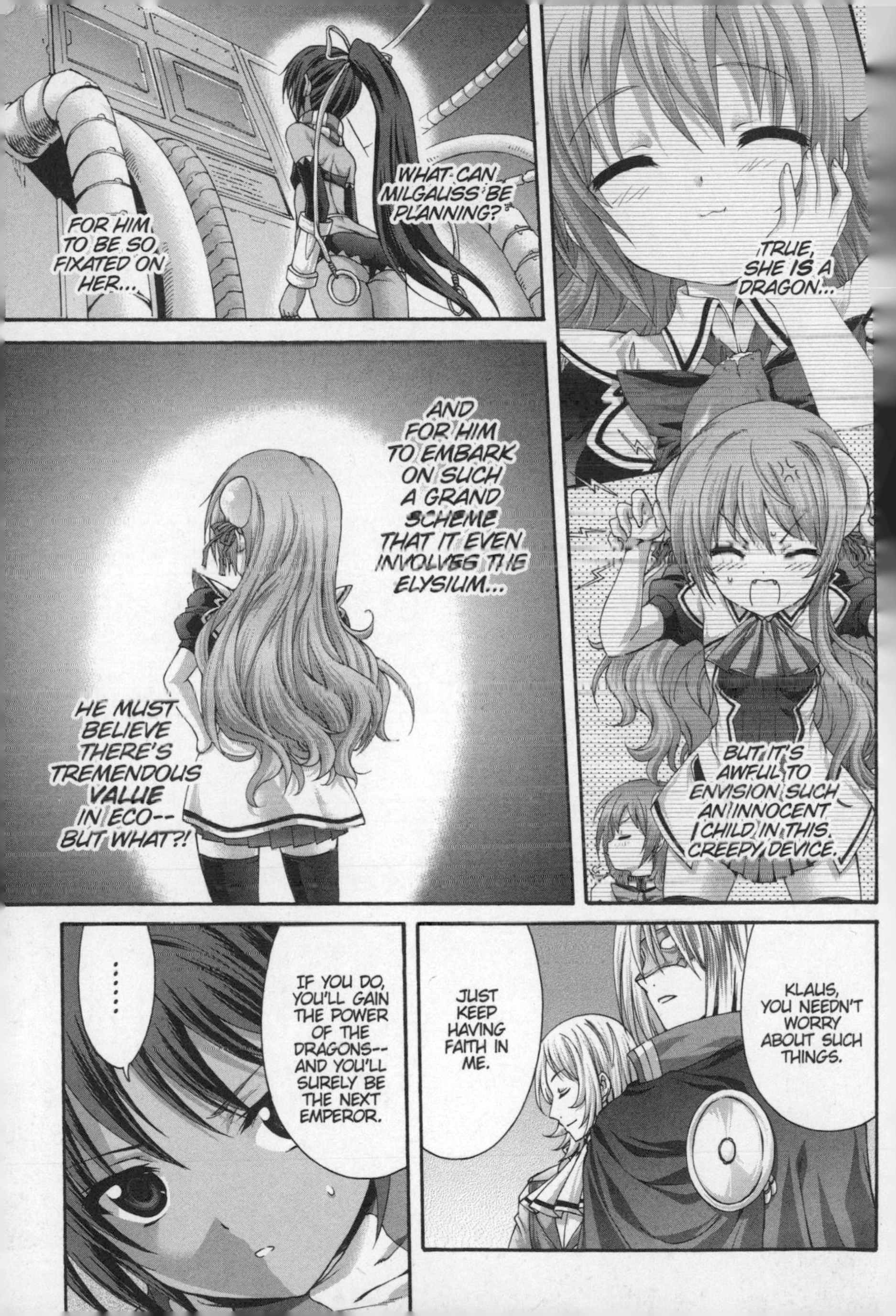
TRUE, SHE IS A DRAGON...
WHAT CAN MILGAUSS BE PLANNING?
FOR HIM TO BE SO FIXATED ON HER...
BUT IT'S AWFUL TO ENVISION SUCH AN INNOCENT CHILD IN THIS CREEPY DEVICE.
AND FOR HIM TO EMBARK ON SUCH A GRAND SCHEME THAT IT EVEN INVOLVES THE ELYSIUM...
HE MUST BELIEVE THERE'S TREMENDOUS VALUE IN ECO-- BUT WHAT?!
KLAUS, YOU NEEDN'T WORRY ABOUT SUCH THINGS.
JUST KEEP HAVING FAITH IN ME.
IF YOU DO, YOU'LL GAIN THE POWER OF THE DRAGONS-- AND YOU'LL SURELY BE THE NEXT EMPEROR.
......

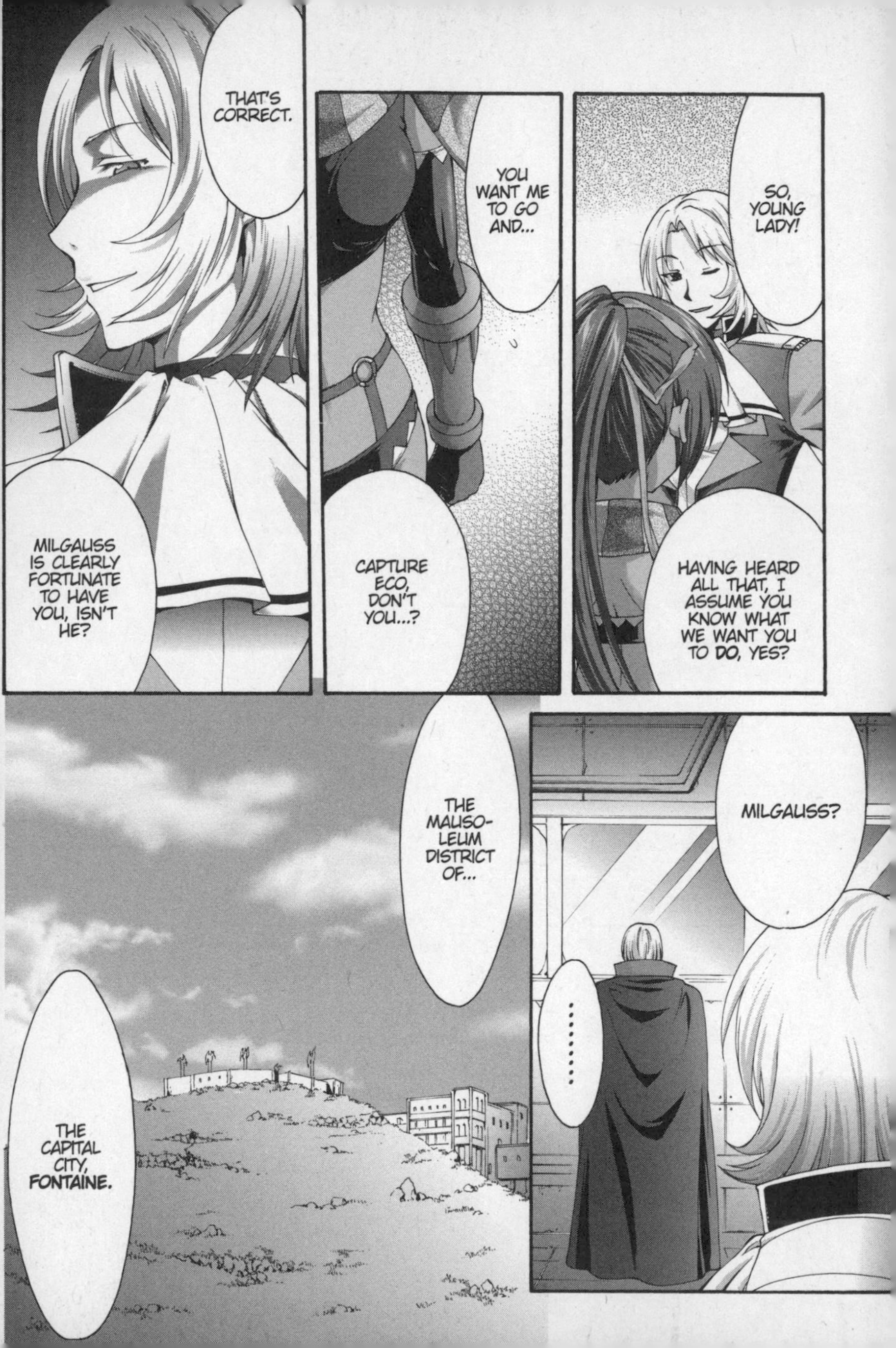
SO, YOUNG LADY!
HAVING HEARD ALL THAT, I ASSUME YOU KNOW WHAT WE WANT YOU TO DO, YES?
YOU WANT ME TO GO AND...
CAPTURE ECO, DON'T YOU...?
THAT'S CORRECT.
MILGAUSS IS CLEARLY FORTUNATE TO HAVE YOU, ISN'T HE?
MILGAUSS?
......
THE MAUSO-LEUM DISTRICT OF...
THE CAPITAL CITY, FONTAINE.

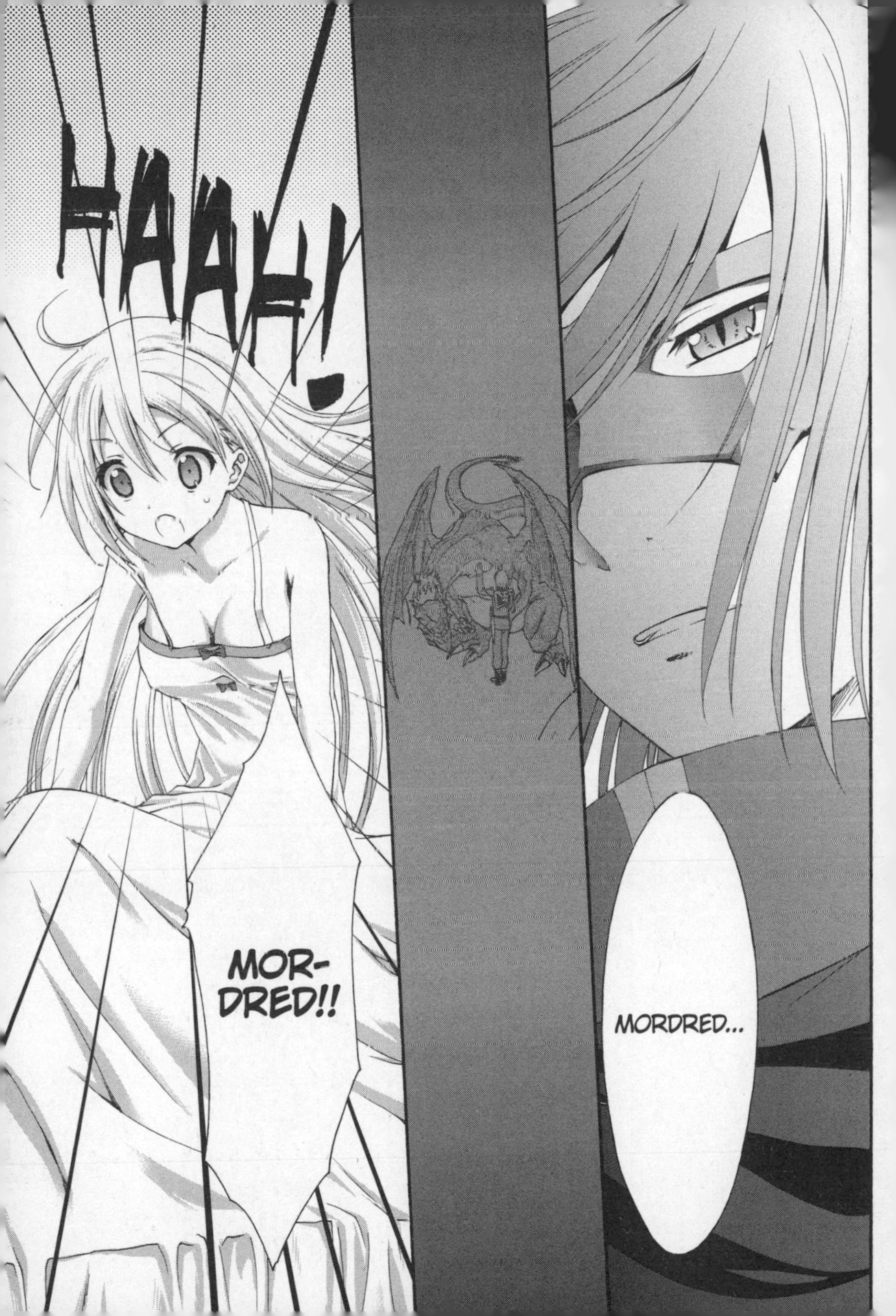
MORDRED...
HAAAH!
MOR-DRED!!

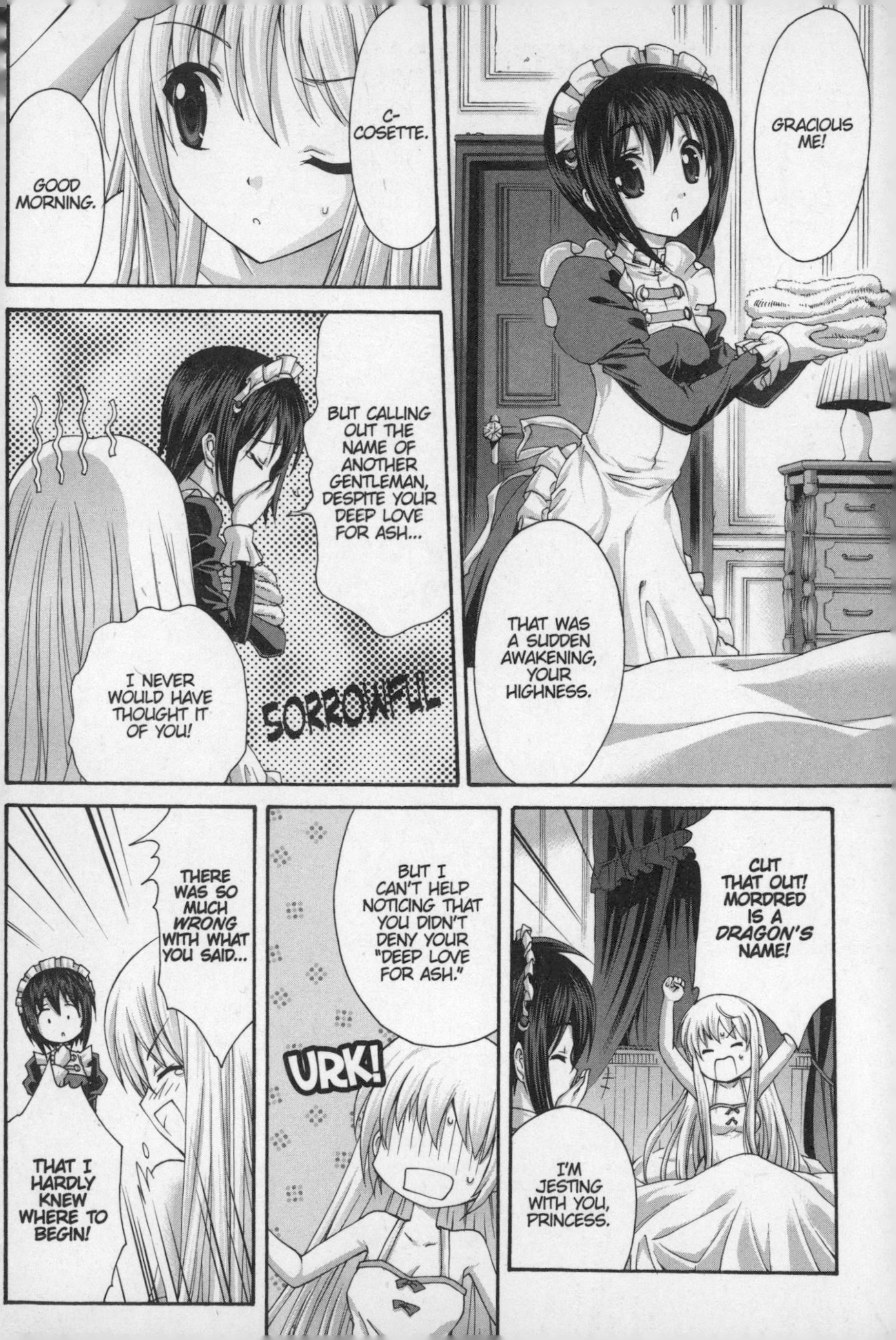
GRACIOUS ME!
THAT WAS A SUDDEN AWAKENING, YOUR HIGHNESS.
C- COSETTE.
GOOD MORNING.
BUT CALLING OUT THE NAME OF ANOTHER GENTLEMAN, DESPITE YOUR DEEP LOVE FOR ASH...
SORROWFUL
I NEVER WOULD HAVE THOUGHT IT OF YOU!
CUT THAT OUT! MORDRED IS A DRAGON'S NAME!
I'M JESTING WITH YOU, PRINCESS.
BUT I CAN'T HELP NOTICING THAT YOU DIDN'T DENY YOUR "DEEP LOVE FOR ASH."
URK!
THERE WAS SO MUCH *WRONG* WITH WHAT YOU SAID...
THAT I HARDLY KNEW WHERE TO BEGIN!

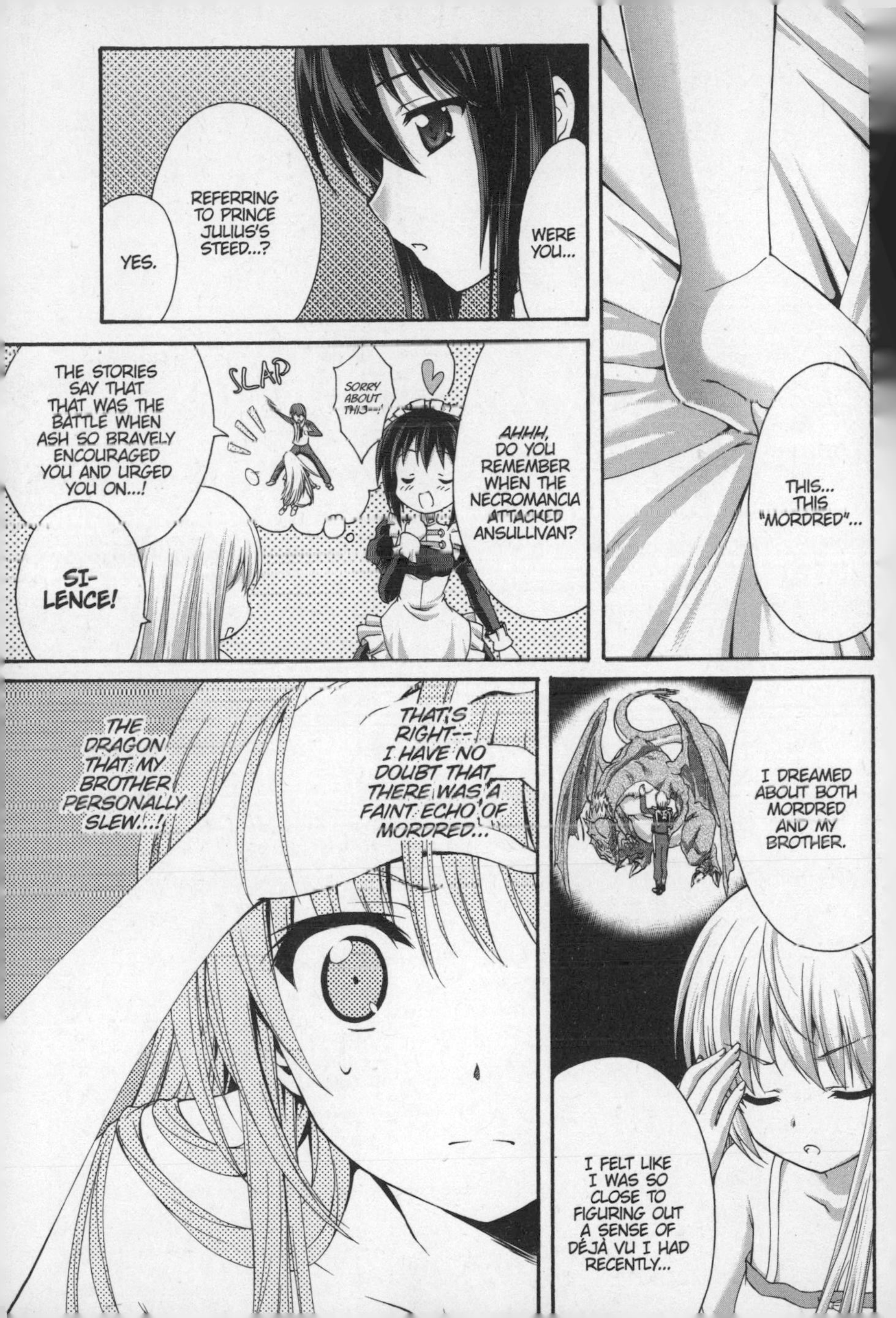
THIS... THIS "MORDRED"...
WERE YOU...
REFERRING TO PRINCE JULIUS'S STEED...?
YES.
AHHH, DO YOU REMEMBER WHEN THE NECROMANCIA ATTACKED ANSULLIVAN?
SORRY ABOUT THIS--!
SLAP
THE STORIES SAY THAT THAT WAS THE BATTLE WHEN ASH SO BRAVELY ENCOURAGED YOU AND URGED YOU ON...!
SI-LENCE!
I DREAMED ABOUT BOTH MORDRED AND MY BROTHER.
I FELT LIKE I WAS SO CLOSE TO FIGURING OUT A SENSE OF DÉJÀ VU I HAD RECENTLY...
THAT'S RIGHT-- I HAVE NO DOUBT THAT THERE WAS A FAINT ECHO OF MORDRED...
THE DRAGON THAT MY BROTHER PERSONALLY SLEW...!

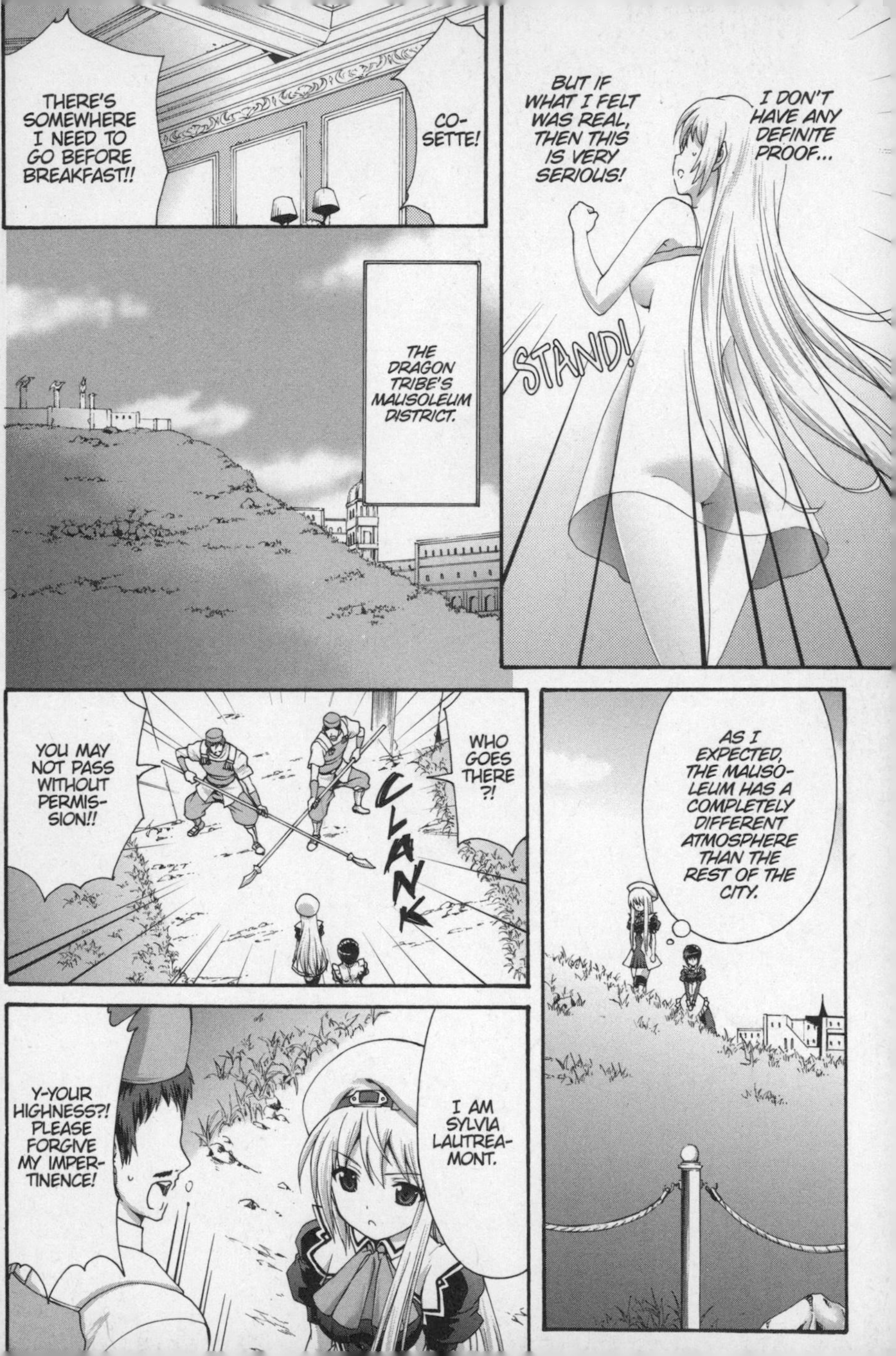
I DON'T HAVE ANY DEFINITE PROOF...
BUT IF WHAT I FELT WAS REAL, THEN THIS IS VERY SERIOUS!
STAND!
CO-SETTE!
THERE'S SOMEWHERE I NEED TO GO BEFORE BREAKFAST!!
THE DRAGON TRIBE'S MAUSOLEUM DISTRICT.
AS I EXPECTED, THE MAUSO-LEUM HAS A COMPLETELY DIFFERENT ATMOSPHERE THAN THE REST OF THE CITY.
WHO GOES THERE?!
CLANK
YOU MAY NOT PASS WITHOUT PERMIS-SION!!
I AM SYLVIA LAUTREA-MONT.
Y-YOUR HIGHNESS?! PLEASE FORGIVE MY IMPER-TINENCE!

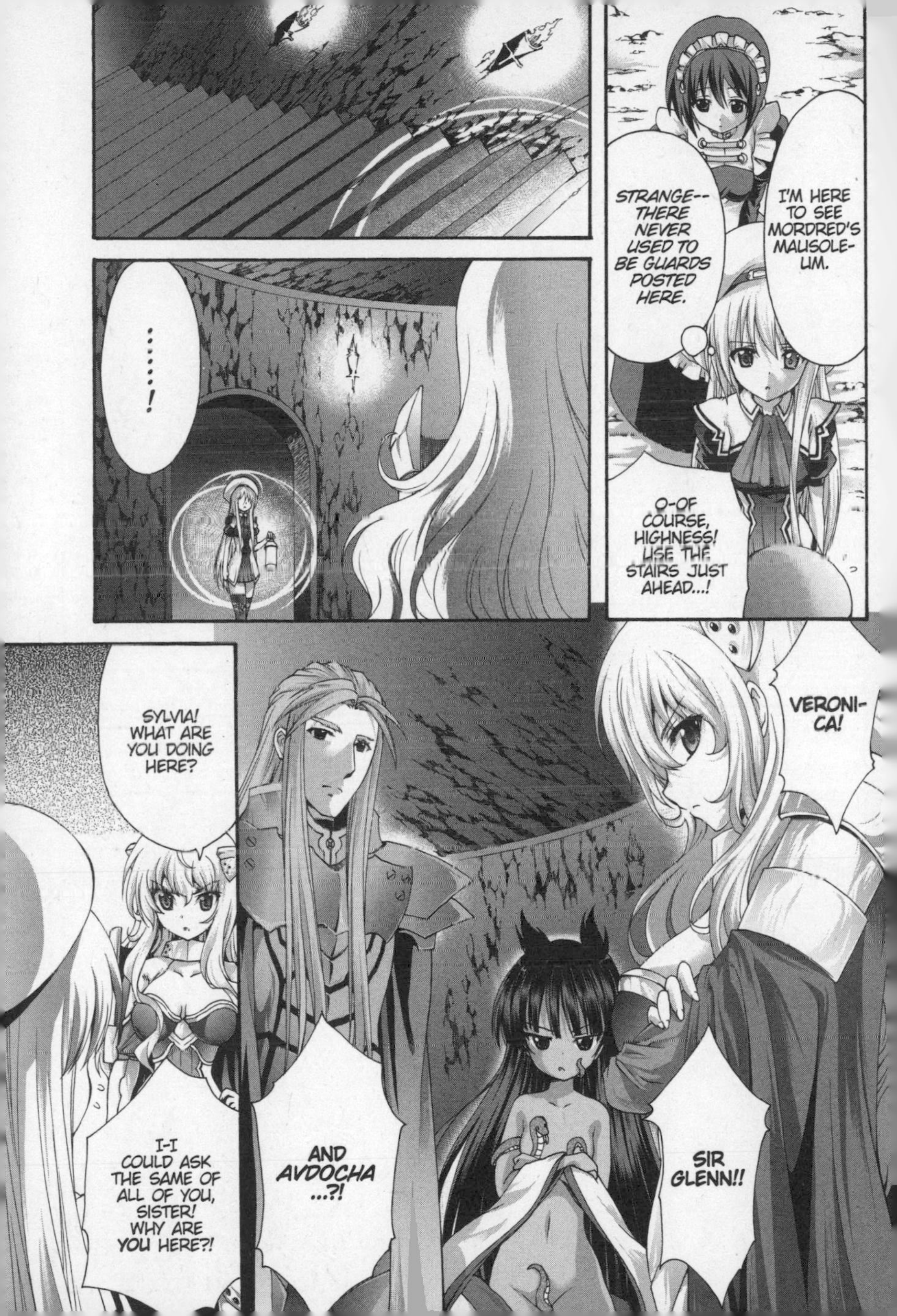
I'M HERE TO SEE MORDRED'S MAUSOLE-UM.
STRANGE-- THERE NEVER USED TO BE GUARDS POSTED HERE.
O-OF COURSE, HIGHNESS! USE THE STAIRS JUST AHEAD...!
......!
VERONI-CA!
SYLVIA! WHAT ARE YOU DOING HERE?
SIR GLENN!!
AND AVDOCHA ...?!
I-I COULD ASK THE SAME OF ALL OF YOU, SISTER! WHY ARE YOU HERE?!

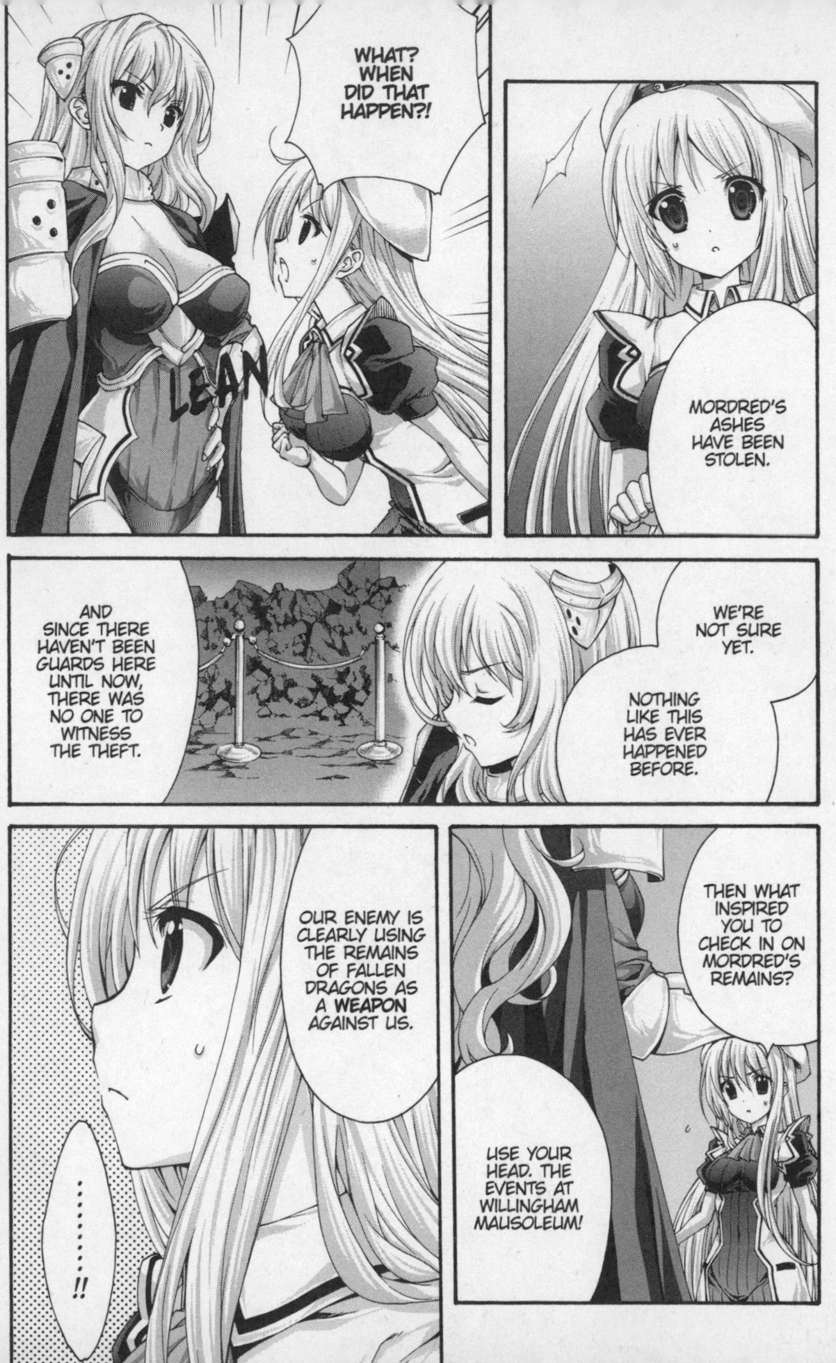
MORDRED'S ASHES HAVE BEEN STOLEN.
WHAT? WHEN DID THAT HAPPEN?!
LEAN
WE'RE NOT SURE YET.
NOTHING LIKE THIS HAS EVER HAPPENED BEFORE.
AND SINCE THERE HAVEN'T BEEN GUARDS HERE UNTIL NOW, THERE WAS NO ONE TO WITNESS THE THEFT.
THEN WHAT INSPIRED YOU TO CHECK IN ON MORDRED'S REMAINS?
USE YOUR HEAD. THE EVENTS AT WILLINGHAM MAUSOLEUM!
OUR ENEMY IS CLEARLY USING THE REMAINS OF FALLEN DRAGONS AS A WEAPON AGAINST US.
.........!!

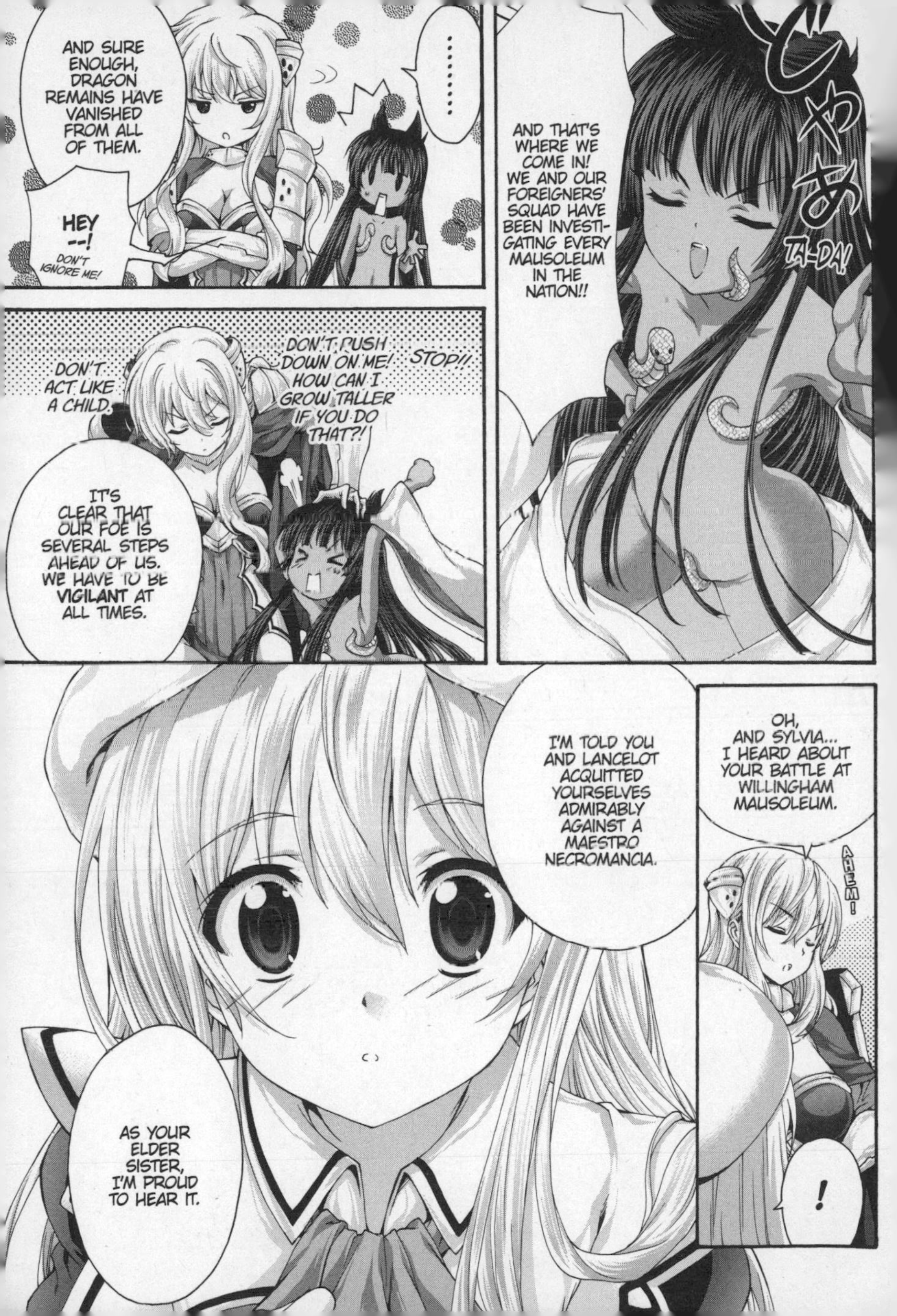
じゃあ
TA-DA!
AND THAT'S WHERE WE COME IN! WE AND OUR FOREIGNERS' SQUAD HAVE BEEN INVESTI-GATING EVERY MAUSOLEUM IN THE NATION!!
......
AND SURE ENOUGH, DRAGON REMAINS HAVE VANISHED FROM ALL OF THEM.
HEY--!
DON'T IGNORE ME!
STOP!!
DON'T PUSH DOWN ON ME! HOW CAN I GROW TALLER IF YOU DO THAT?!
DON'T ACT LIKE A CHILD.
IT'S CLEAR THAT OUR FOE IS SEVERAL STEPS AHEAD OF US. WE HAVE TO BE VIGILANT AT ALL TIMES.
OH, AND SYLVIA... I HEARD ABOUT YOUR BATTLE AT WILLINGHAM MAUSOLEUM.
AHEM!
!
I'M TOLD YOU AND LANCELOT ACQUITTED YOURSELVES ADMIRABLY AGAINST A MAESTRO NECROMANCIA.
AS YOUR ELDER SISTER, I'M PROUD TO HEAR IT.

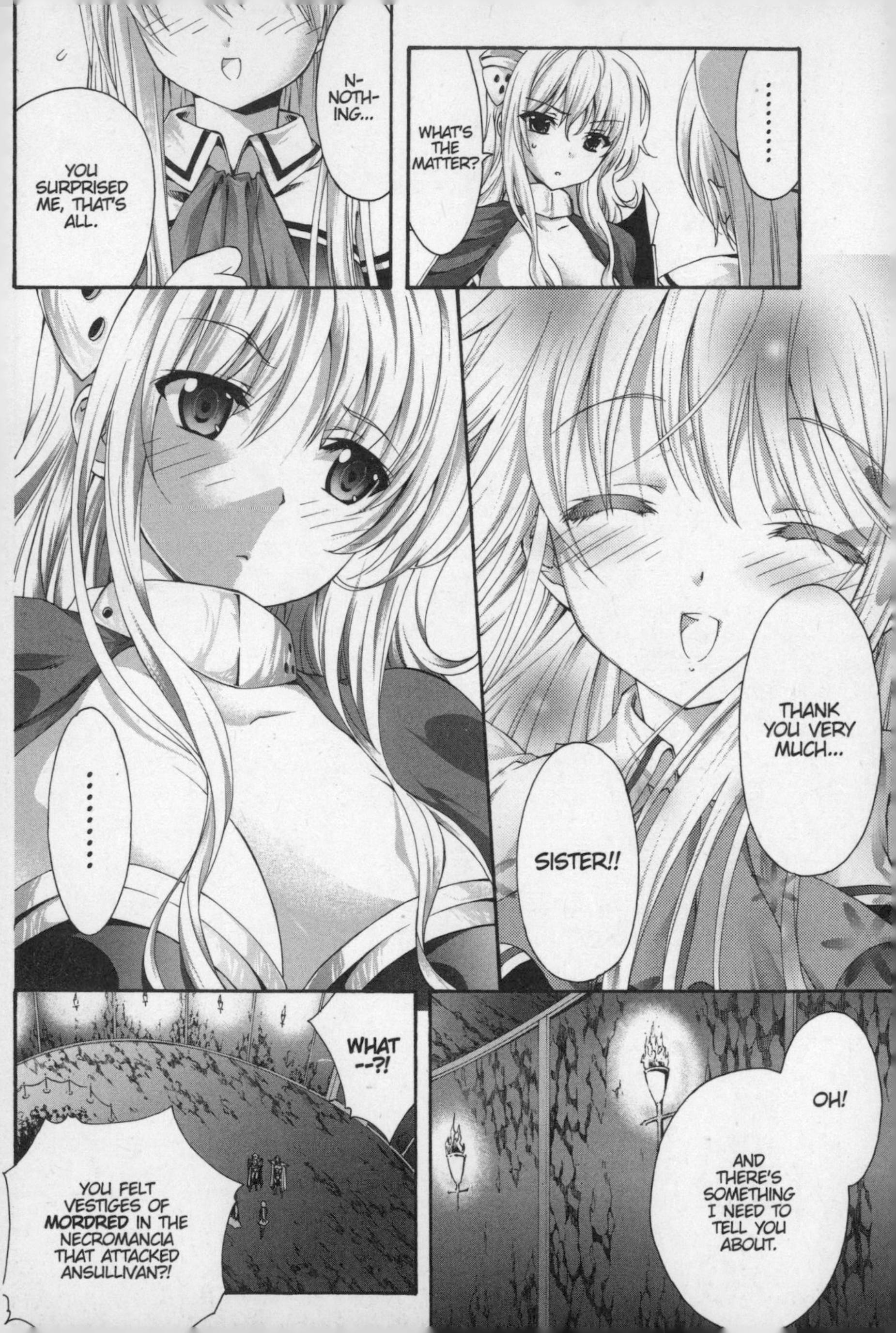
......
WHAT'S THE MATTER?
N-NOTHING...
YOU SURPRISED ME, THAT'S ALL.
THANK YOU VERY MUCH...
SISTER!!
....
OH!
AND THERE'S SOMETHING I NEED TO TELL YOU ABOUT.
WHAT--?!
YOU FELT VESTIGES OF MORDRED IN THE NECROMANCIA THAT ATTACKED ANSULLIVAN?!

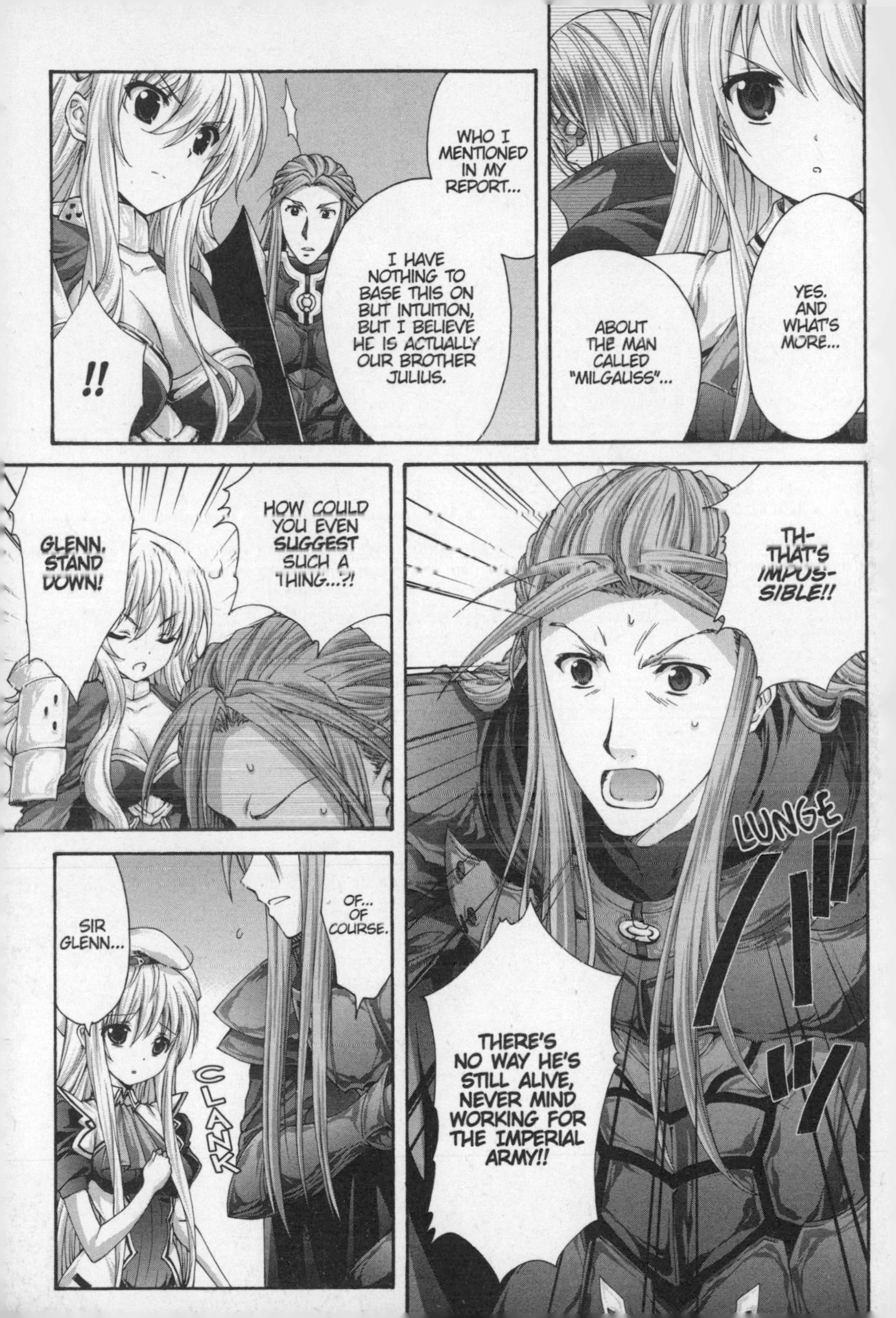
YES. AND WHAT'S MORE...
ABOUT THE MAN CALLED "MILGAUSS"...
WHO I MENTIONED IN MY REPORT...
I HAVE NOTHING TO BASE THIS ON BUT INTUITION, BUT I BELIEVE HE IS ACTUALLY OUR BROTHER JULIUS.
!!
TH-THAT'S IMPOSSIBLE!!
LUNGE
THERE'S NO WAY HE'S STILL ALIVE, NEVER MIND WORKING FOR THE IMPERIAL ARMY!!
HOW COULD YOU EVEN SUGGEST SUCH A THING...?!
GLENN, STAND DOWN!
OF... OF COURSE.
SIR GLENN...
CLANK

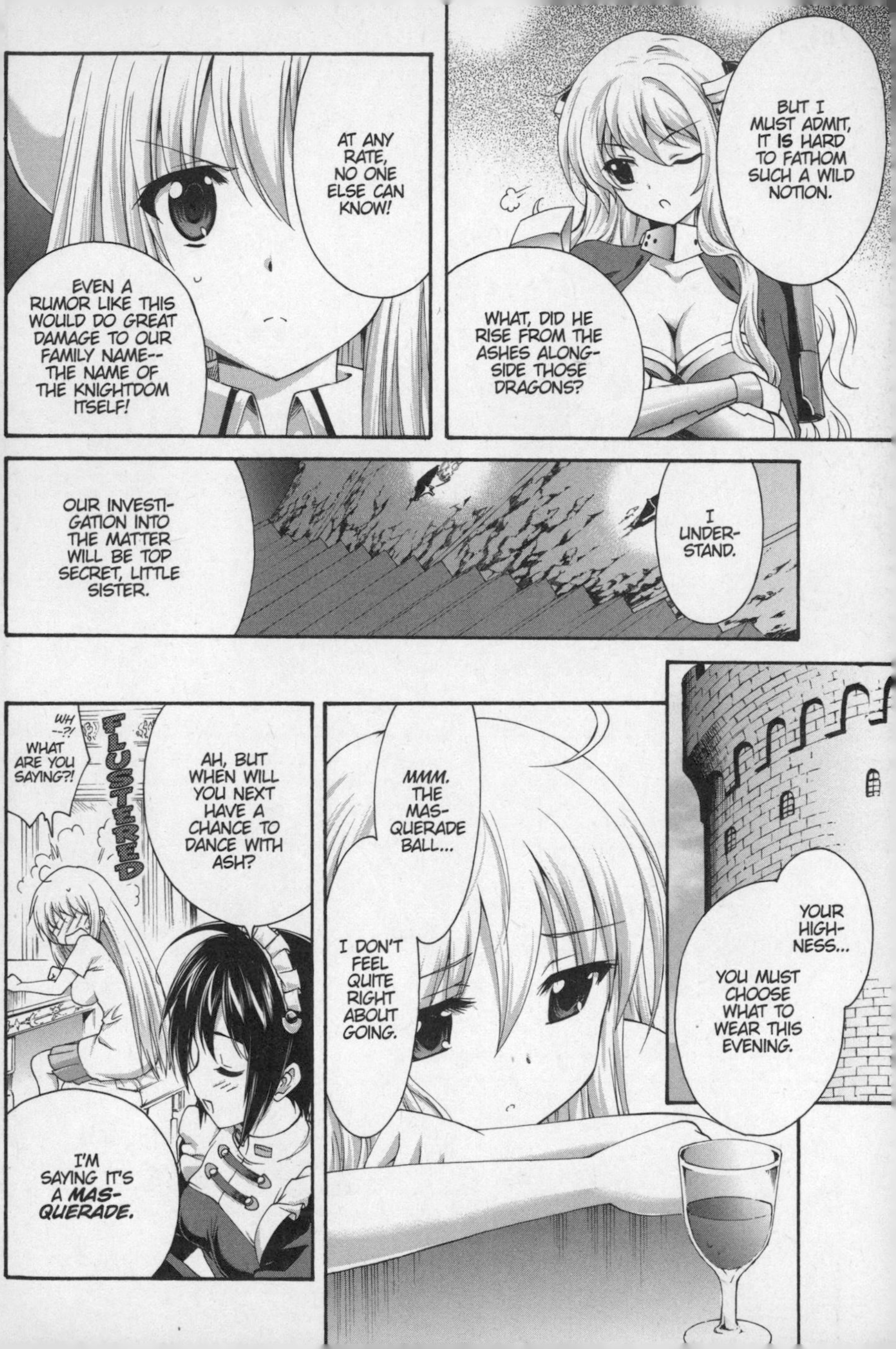
BUT I MUST ADMIT, IT IS HARD TO FATHOM SUCH A WILD NOTION.
WHAT, DID HE RISE FROM THE ASHES ALONG-SIDE THOSE DRAGONS?
AT ANY RATE, NO ONE ELSE CAN KNOW!
EVEN A RUMOR LIKE THIS WOULD DO GREAT DAMAGE TO OUR FAMILY NAME-- THE NAME OF THE KNIGHTDOM ITSELF!
OUR INVESTI-GATION INTO THE MATTER WILL BE TOP SECRET, LITTLE SISTER.
I UNDER-STAND.
YOUR HIGH-NESS...
YOU MUST CHOOSE WHAT TO WEAR THIS EVENING.
MMM. THE MAS-QUERADE BALL...
I DON'T FEEL QUITE RIGHT ABOUT GOING.
AH, BUT WHEN WILL YOU NEXT HAVE A CHANCE TO DANCE WITH ASH?
FLUSTERED
WH--?! WHAT ARE YOU SAYING?!
I'M SAYING IT'S A ***MAS-QUERADE.***

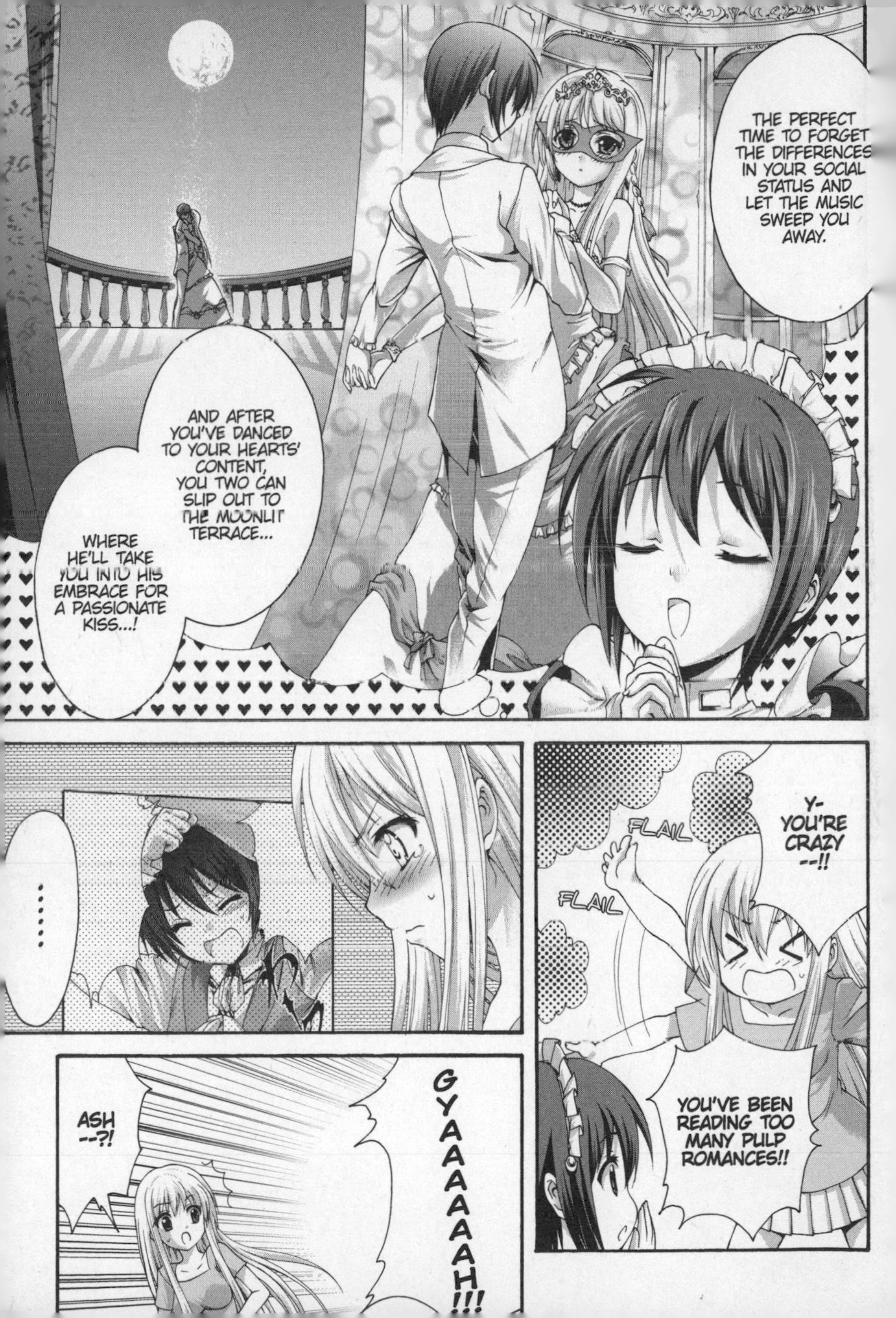
THE PERFECT TIME TO FORGET THE DIFFERENCES IN YOUR SOCIAL STATUS AND LET THE MUSIC SWEEP YOU AWAY.
AND AFTER YOU'VE DANCED TO YOUR HEARTS' CONTENT, YOU TWO CAN SLIP OUT TO THE MOONLIT TERRACE...
WHERE HE'LL TAKE YOU INTO HIS EMBRACE FOR A PASSIONATE KISS...!
Y-YOU'RE CRAZY--!!
FLAIL
FLAIL
YOU'VE BEEN READING TOO MANY PULP ROMANCES!!
......
GYAAAAAAH!!!
ASH--?!

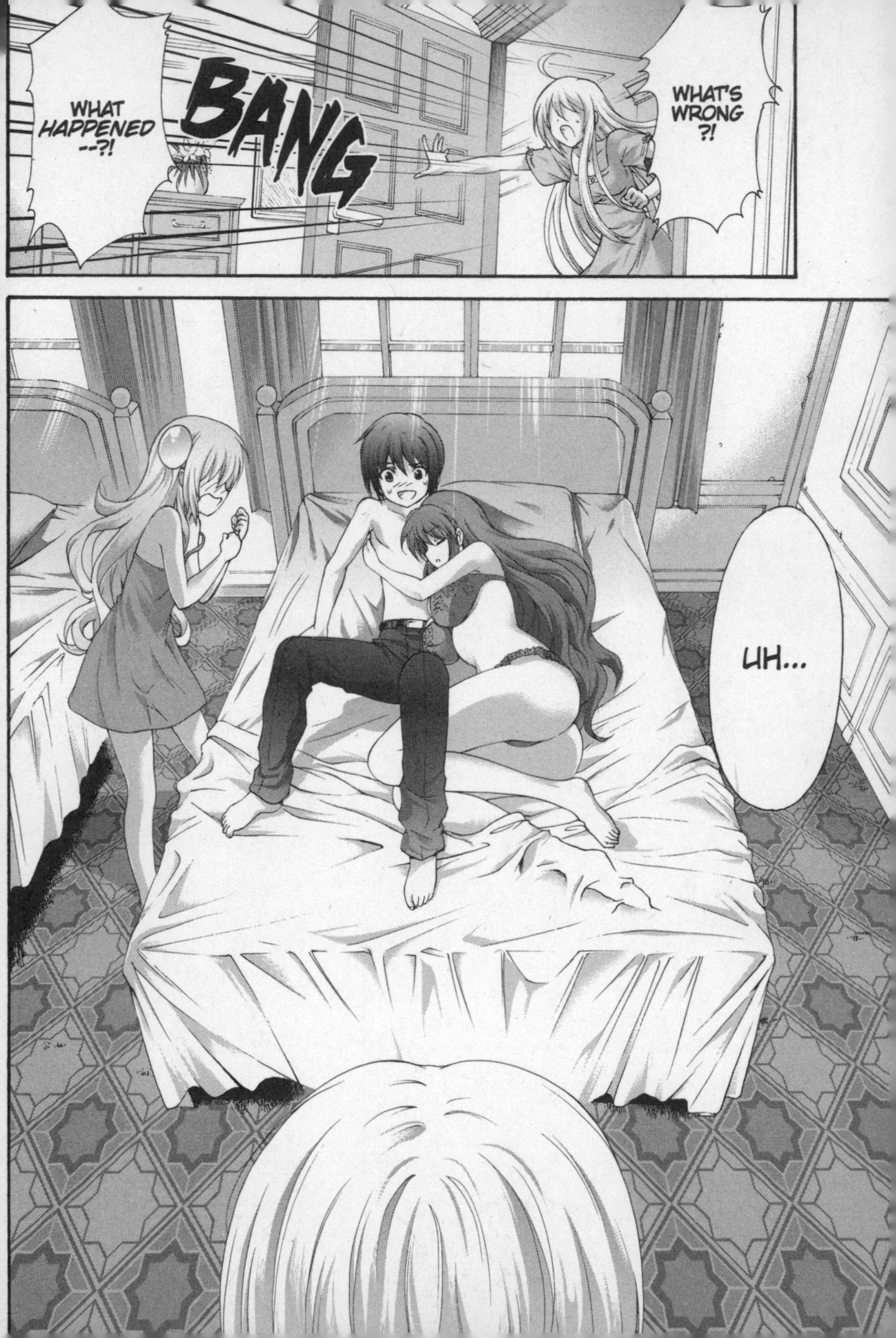
WHAT'S WRONG ?!
BANG
WHAT HAPPENED --?!
UH...

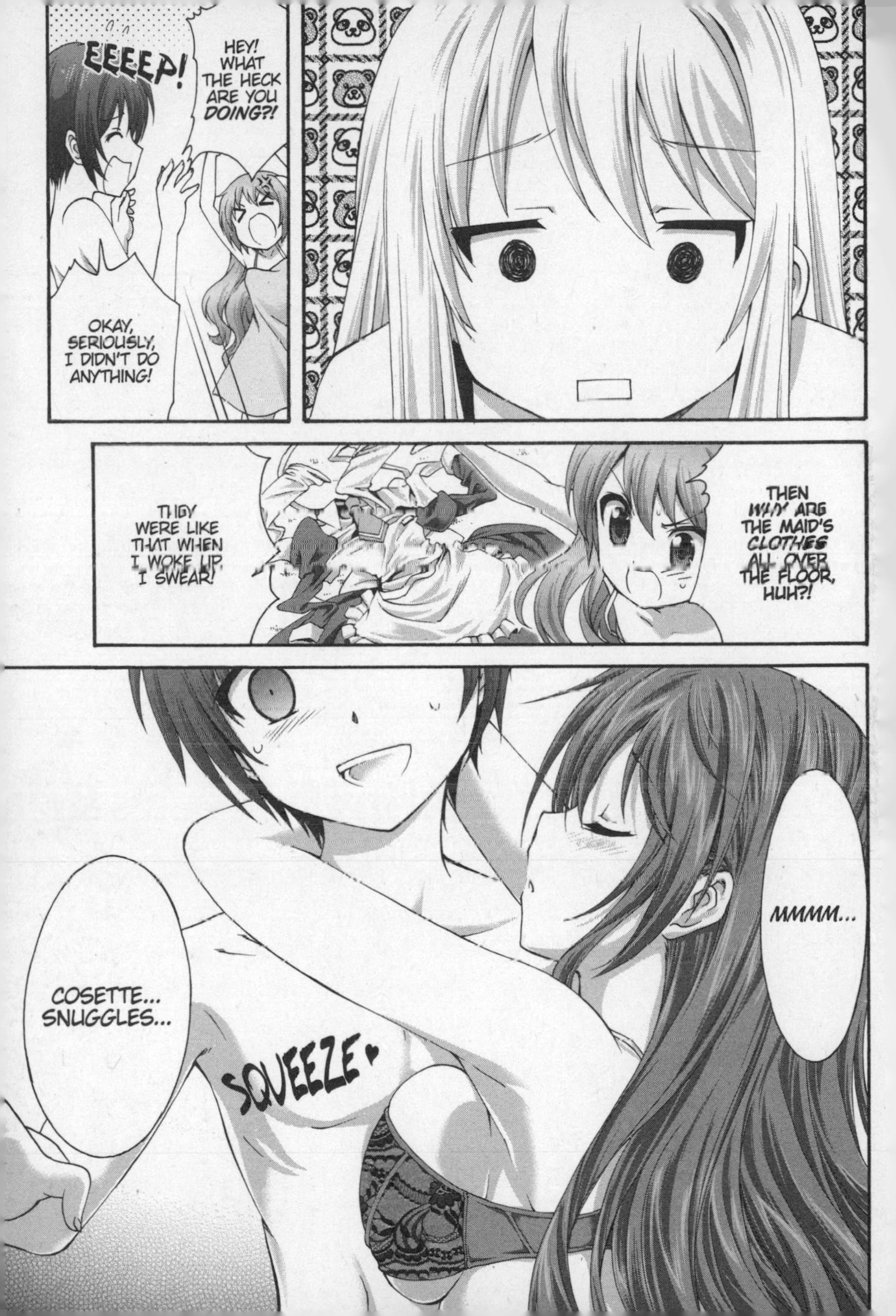
HEY! WHAT THE HECK ARE YOU DOING?!
EEEEP!
OKAY, SERIOUSLY, I DIDN'T DO ANYTHING!
THEN WHY ARE THE MAID'S CLOTHES ALL OVER THE FLOOR, HUH?!
THEY WERE LIKE THAT WHEN I WOKE UP, I SWEAR!
MMMM...
COSETTE... SNUGGLES...
SQUEEZE♥

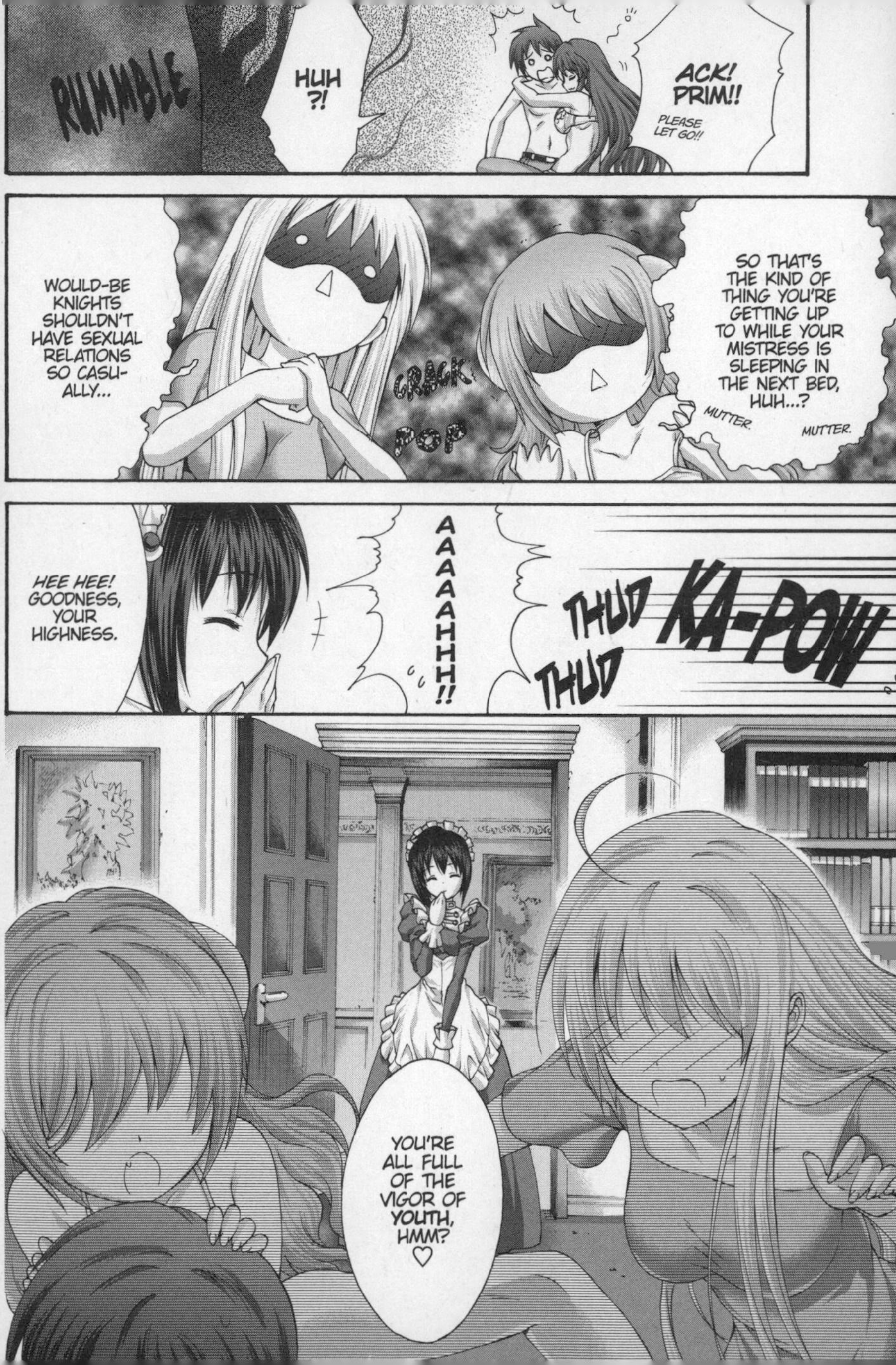
ACK! PRIM!!
PLEASE LET GO!!
HUH ?!
RUMMBLE
SO THAT'S THE KIND OF THING YOU'RE GETTING UP TO WHILE YOUR MISTRESS IS SLEEPING IN THE NEXT BED, HUH...?
MUTTER.
MUTTER.
CRACK
POP
WOULD-BE KNIGHTS SHOULDN'T HAVE SEXUAL RELATIONS SO CASU-ALLY...
KA-POW
THUD
THUD
AAAAAAHHHH!!
HEE HEE! GOODNESS, YOUR HIGHNESS.
YOU'RE ALL FULL OF THE VIGOR OF YOUTH, HMM? ♡

DRAGONAR
ACADEMY

星刻の竜騎士

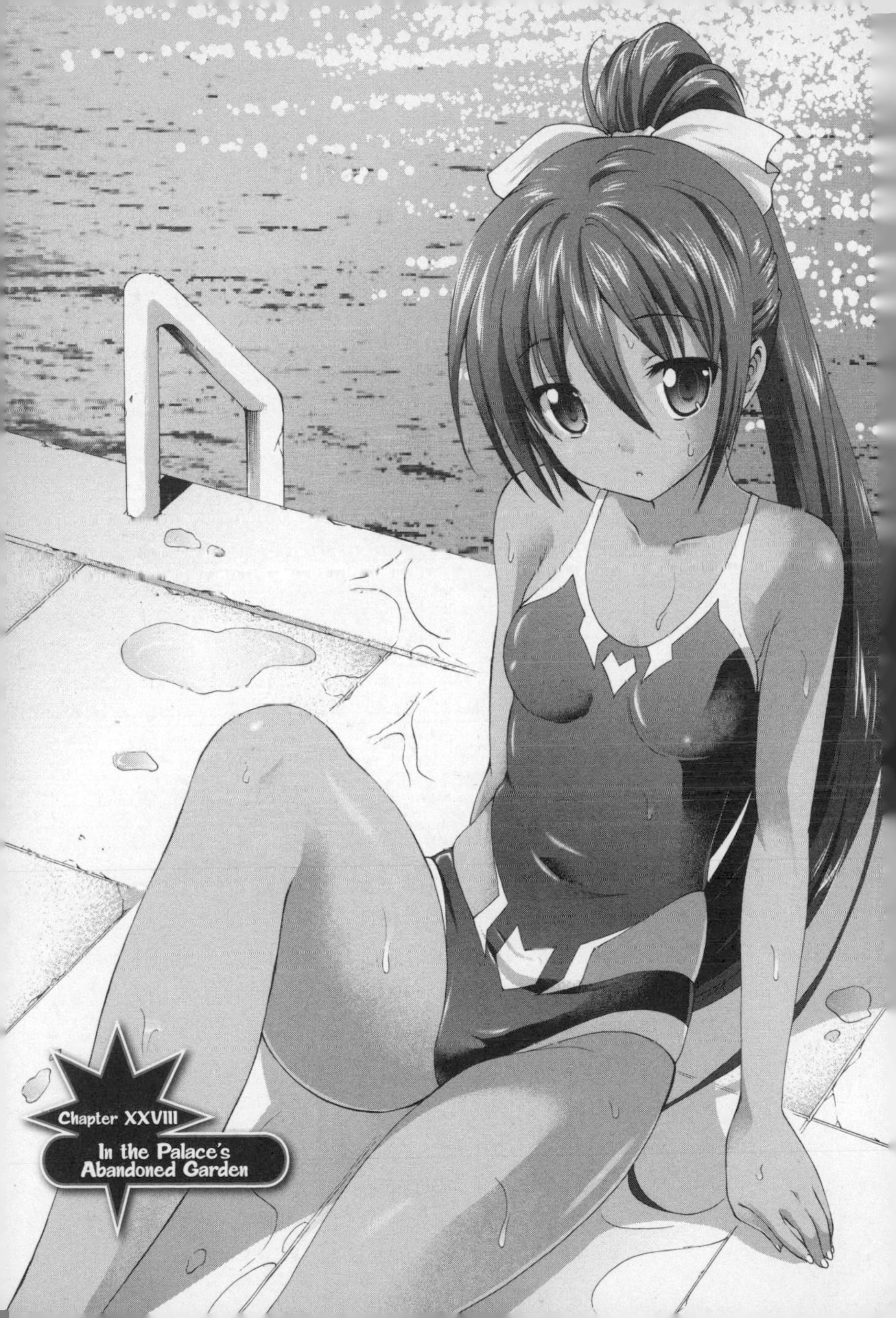
Chapter XXVIII
In the Palace's Abandoned Garden

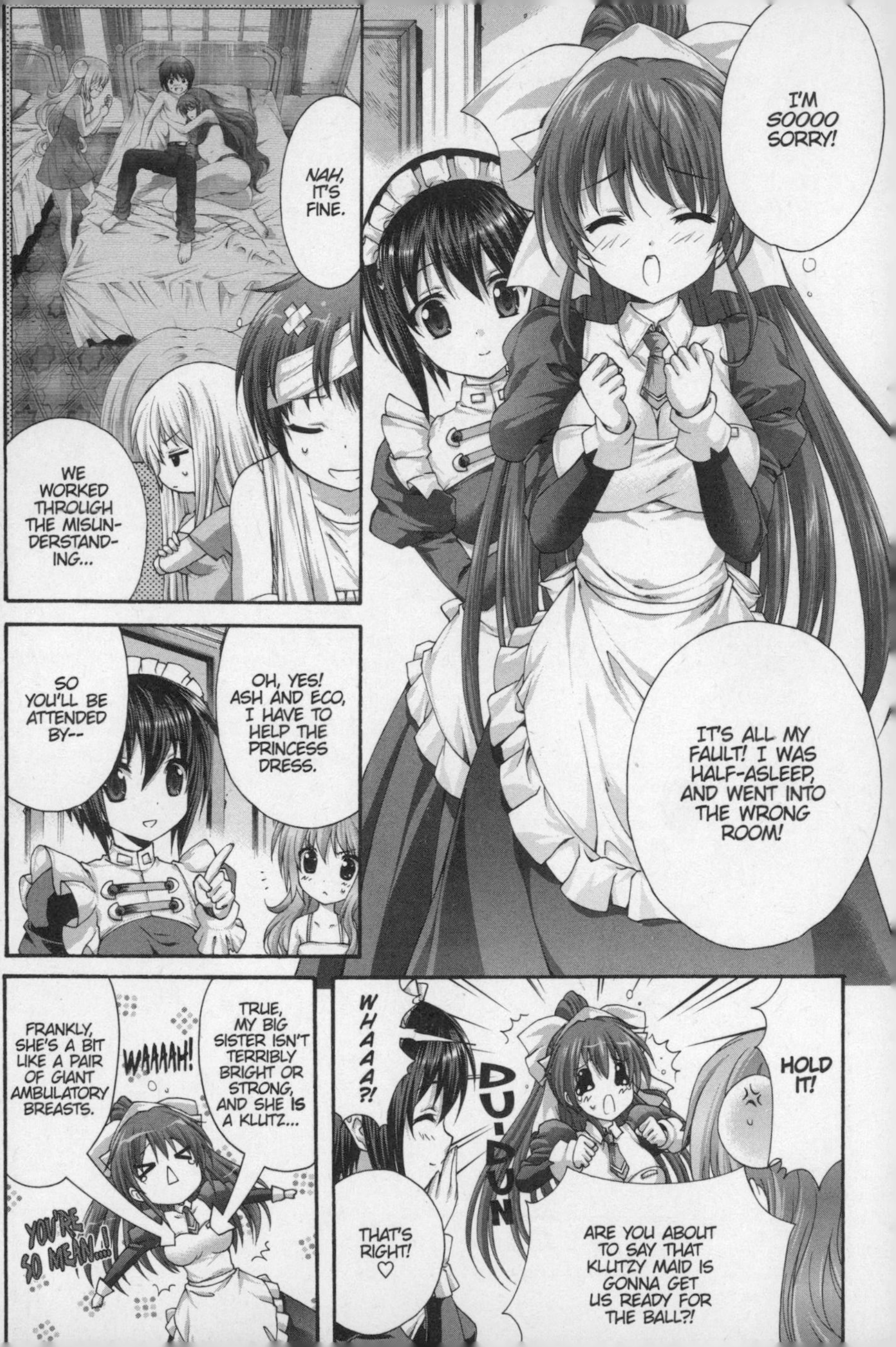
I'M SOOOO SORRY!
IT'S ALL MY FAULT! I WAS HALF-ASLEEP, AND WENT INTO THE WRONG ROOM!
NAH, IT'S FINE.
WE WORKED THROUGH THE MISUNDERSTANDING...
OH, YES! ASH AND ECO, I HAVE TO HELP THE PRINCESS DRESS.
SO YOU'LL BE ATTENDED BY--
HOLD IT!
WHAAAA?!
DU-DUN
ARE YOU ABOUT TO SAY THAT KLUTZY MAID IS GONNA GET US READY FOR THE BALL?!
THAT'S RIGHT! ♡
TRUE, MY BIG SISTER ISN'T TERRIBLY BRIGHT OR STRONG, AND SHE IS A KLUTZ...
FRANKLY, SHE'S A BIT LIKE A PAIR OF GIANT AMBULATORY BREASTS.
WAAAAH!
YOU'RE SO MEAN...!

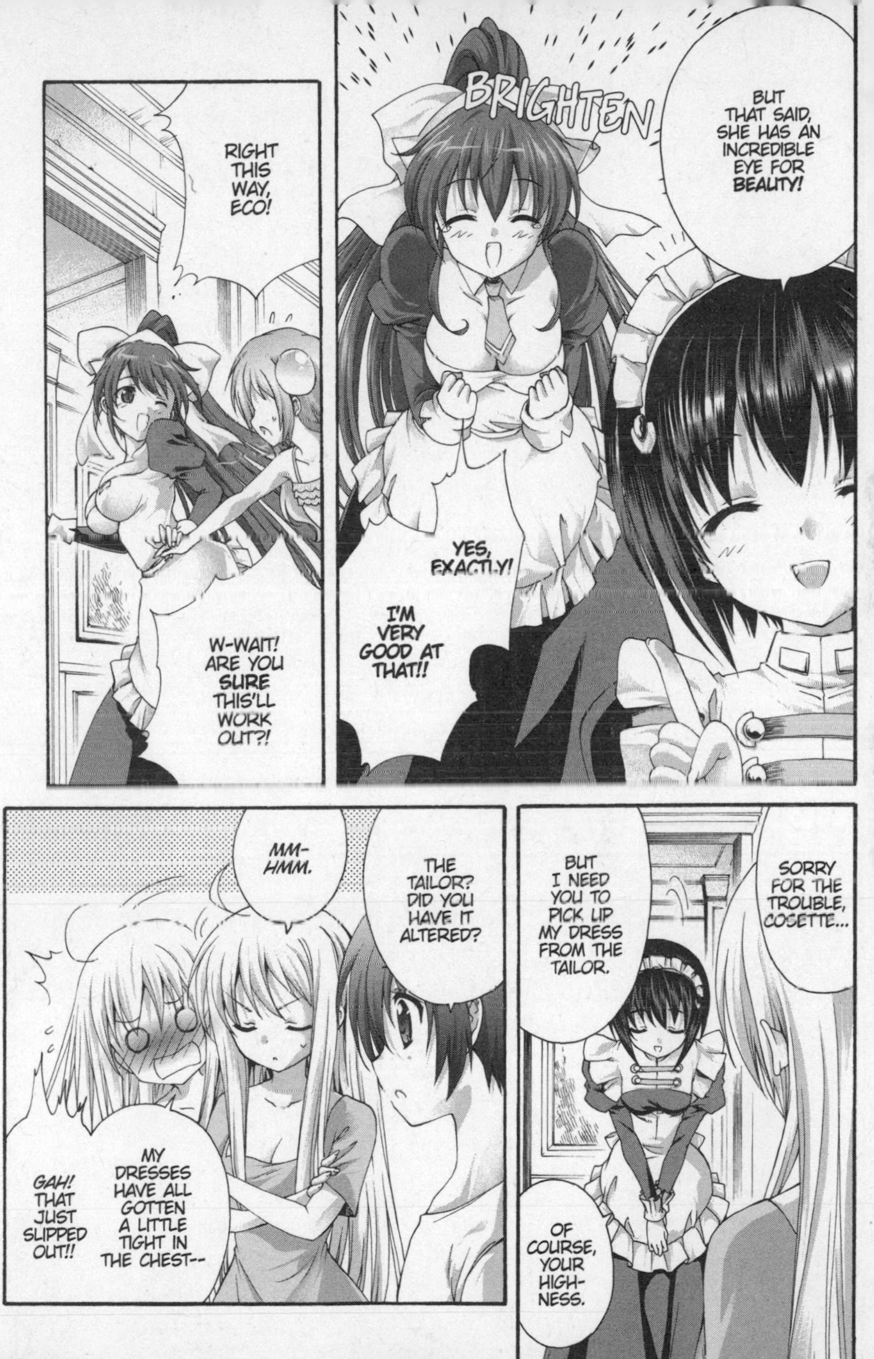
BUT THAT SAID, SHE HAS AN INCREDIBLE EYE FOR BEAUTY!
BRIGHTEN
YES, EXACTLY!
I'M VERY GOOD AT THAT!!
RIGHT THIS WAY, ECO!
W-WAIT! ARE YOU SURE THIS'LL WORK OUT?!
SORRY FOR THE TROUBLE, COSETTE...
BUT I NEED YOU TO PICK UP MY DRESS FROM THE TAILOR.
OF COURSE, YOUR HIGHNESS.
THE TAILOR? DID YOU HAVE IT ALTERED?
MM-HMM.
MY DRESSES HAVE ALL GOTTEN A LITTLE TIGHT IN THE CHEST--
GAH! THAT JUST SLIPPED OUT!!

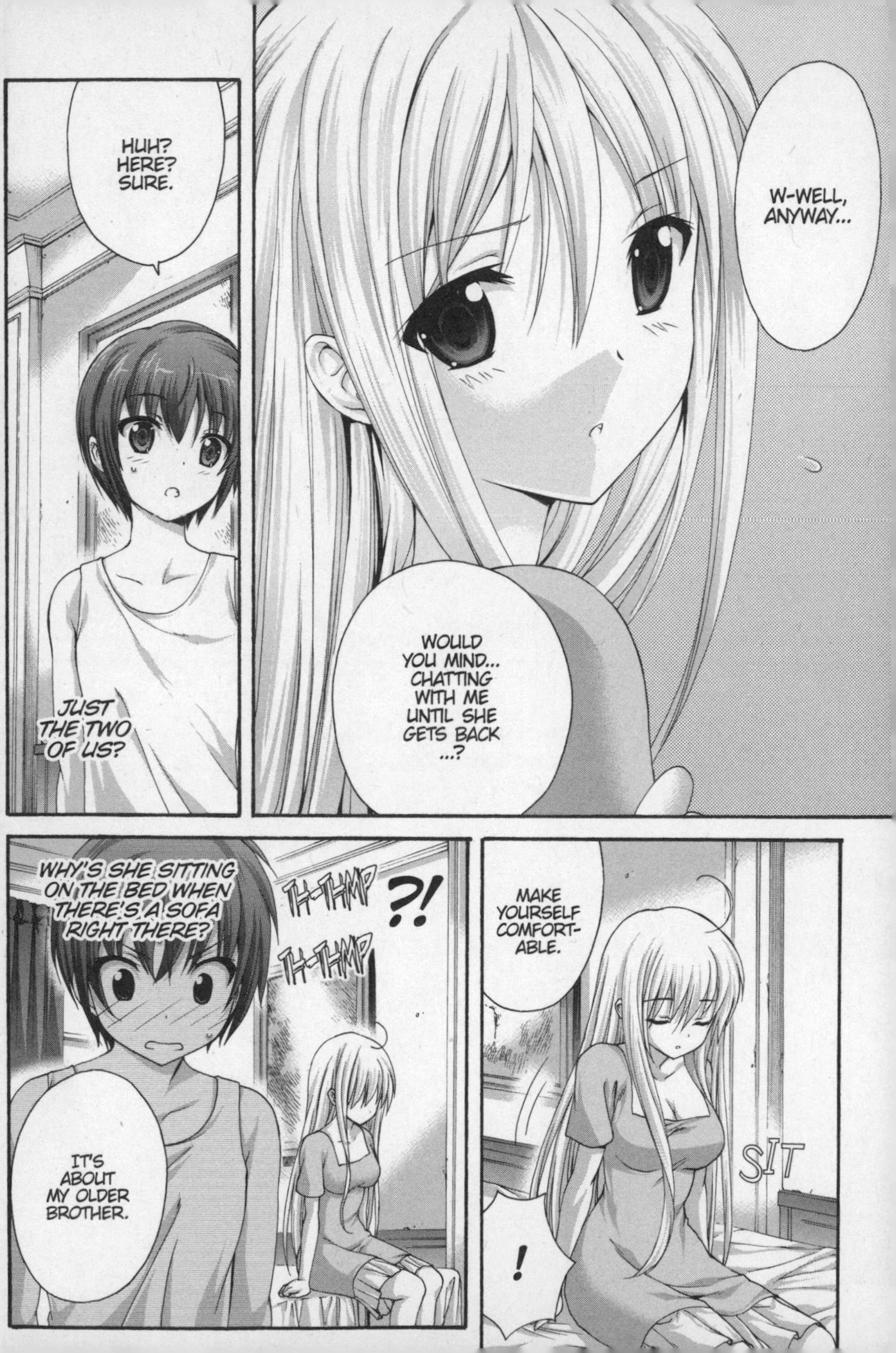
W-WELL, ANYWAY...
WOULD YOU MIND... CHATTING WITH ME UNTIL SHE GETS BACK ...?
HUH? HERE? SURE.
JUST THE TWO OF US?
MAKE YOURSELF COMFORT-ABLE.
SIT
!
TH-THMP
?!
TH-THMP
WHY'S SHE SITTING ON THE BED WHEN THERE'S A SOFA RIGHT THERE?
IT'S ABOUT MY OLDER BROTHER.

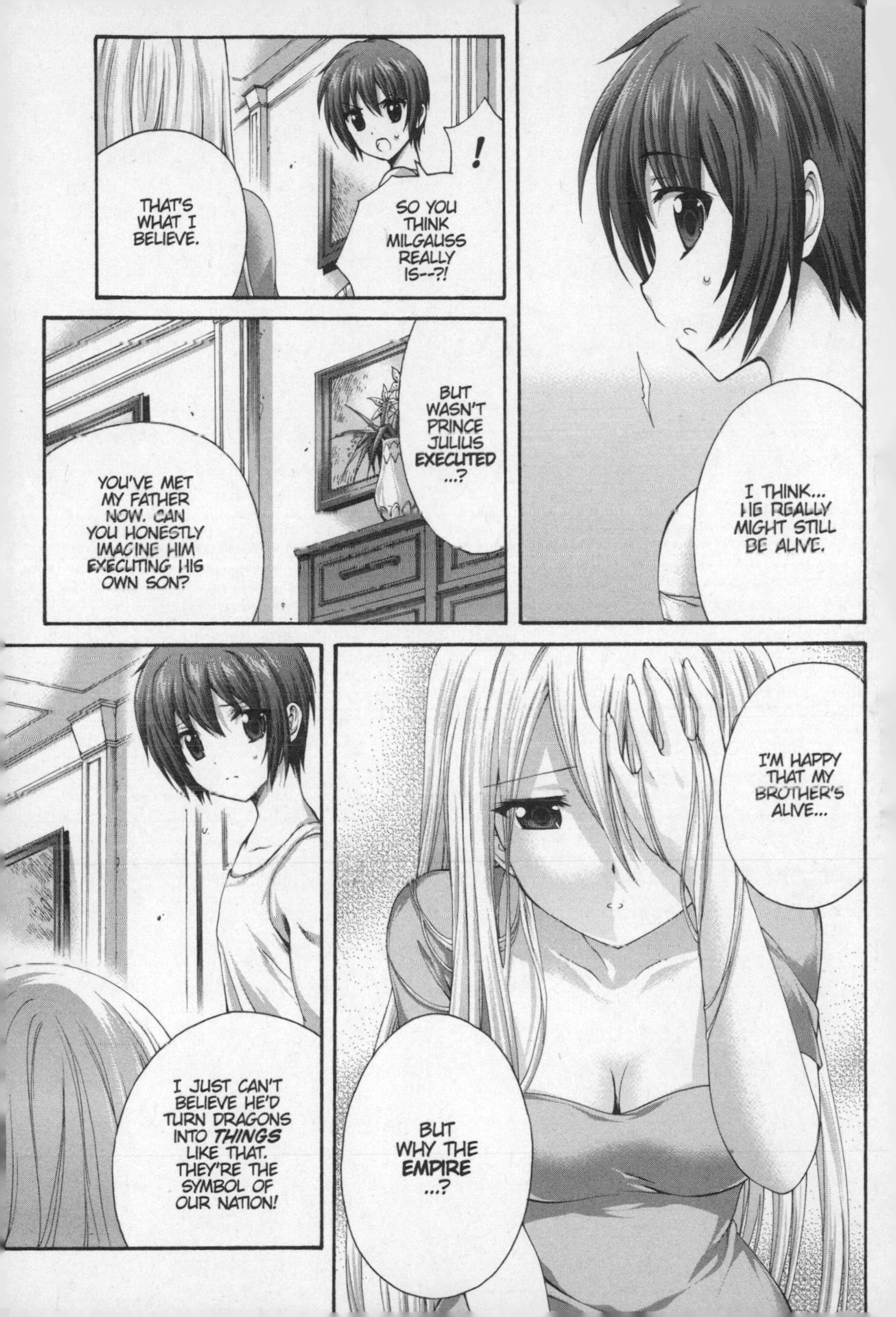
I THINK... HE REALLY MIGHT STILL BE ALIVE.
!
SO YOU THINK MILGAUSS REALLY IS--?!
THAT'S WHAT I BELIEVE.
BUT WASN'T PRINCE JULIUS EXECUTED ...?
YOU'VE MET MY FATHER NOW. CAN YOU HONESTLY IMAGINE HIM EXECUTING HIS OWN SON?
I'M HAPPY THAT MY BROTHER'S ALIVE...
BUT WHY THE EMPIRE ...?
I JUST CAN'T BELIEVE HE'D TURN DRAGONS INTO THINGS LIKE THAT. THEY'RE THE SYMBOL OF OUR NATION!

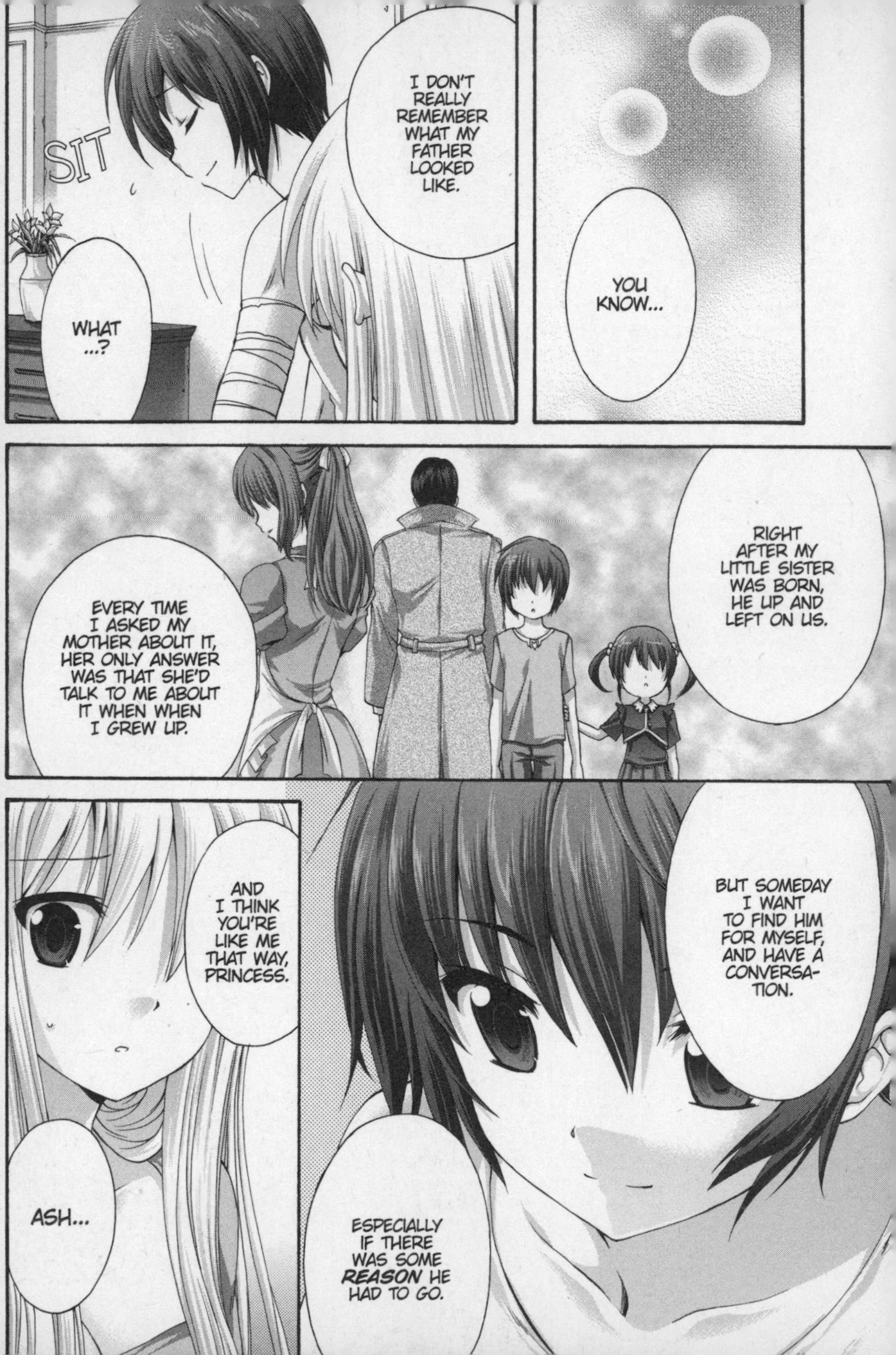
YOU KNOW...
I DON'T REALLY REMEMBER WHAT MY FATHER LOOKED LIKE.
SIT
WHAT ...?
RIGHT AFTER MY LITTLE SISTER WAS BORN, HE UP AND LEFT ON US.
EVERY TIME I ASKED MY MOTHER ABOUT IT, HER ONLY ANSWER WAS THAT SHE'D TALK TO ME ABOUT IT WHEN WHEN I GREW UP.
BUT SOMEDAY I WANT TO FIND HIM FOR MYSELF, AND HAVE A CONVERSA-TION.
ESPECIALLY IF THERE WAS SOME **REASON** HE HAD TO GO.
AND I THINK YOU'RE LIKE ME THAT WAY, PRINCESS.
ASH...

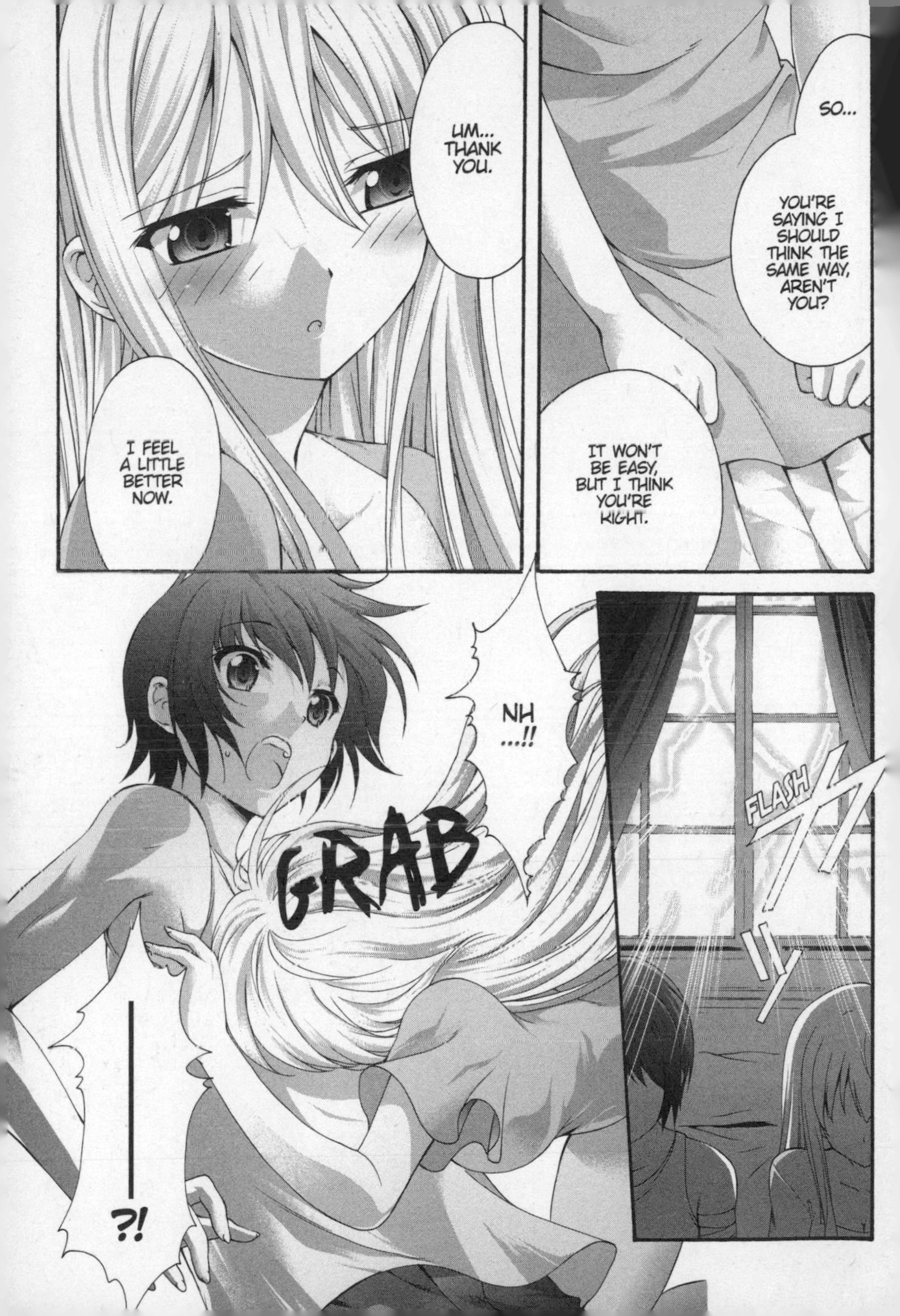
SO...
YOU'RE SAYING I SHOULD THINK THE SAME WAY, AREN'T YOU?
IT WON'T BE EASY, BUT I THINK YOU'RE RIGHT.
UM... THANK YOU.
I FEEL A LITTLE BETTER NOW.
FLASH
NH ...!!
GRAB
?!

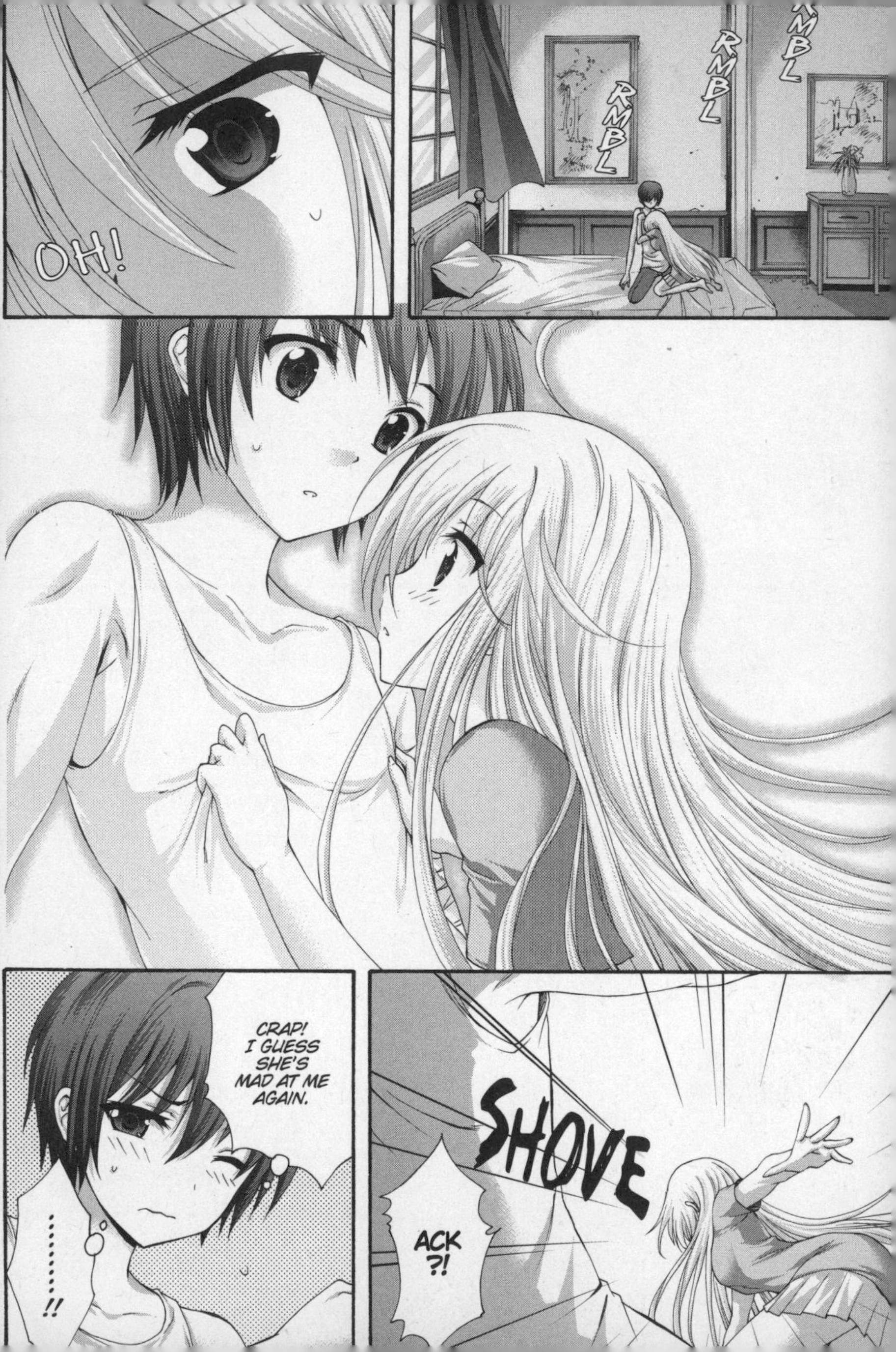
RMBL
RMBL
OH!
SHOVE
ACK?!
CRAP! I GUESS SHE'S MAD AT ME AGAIN.
......!!

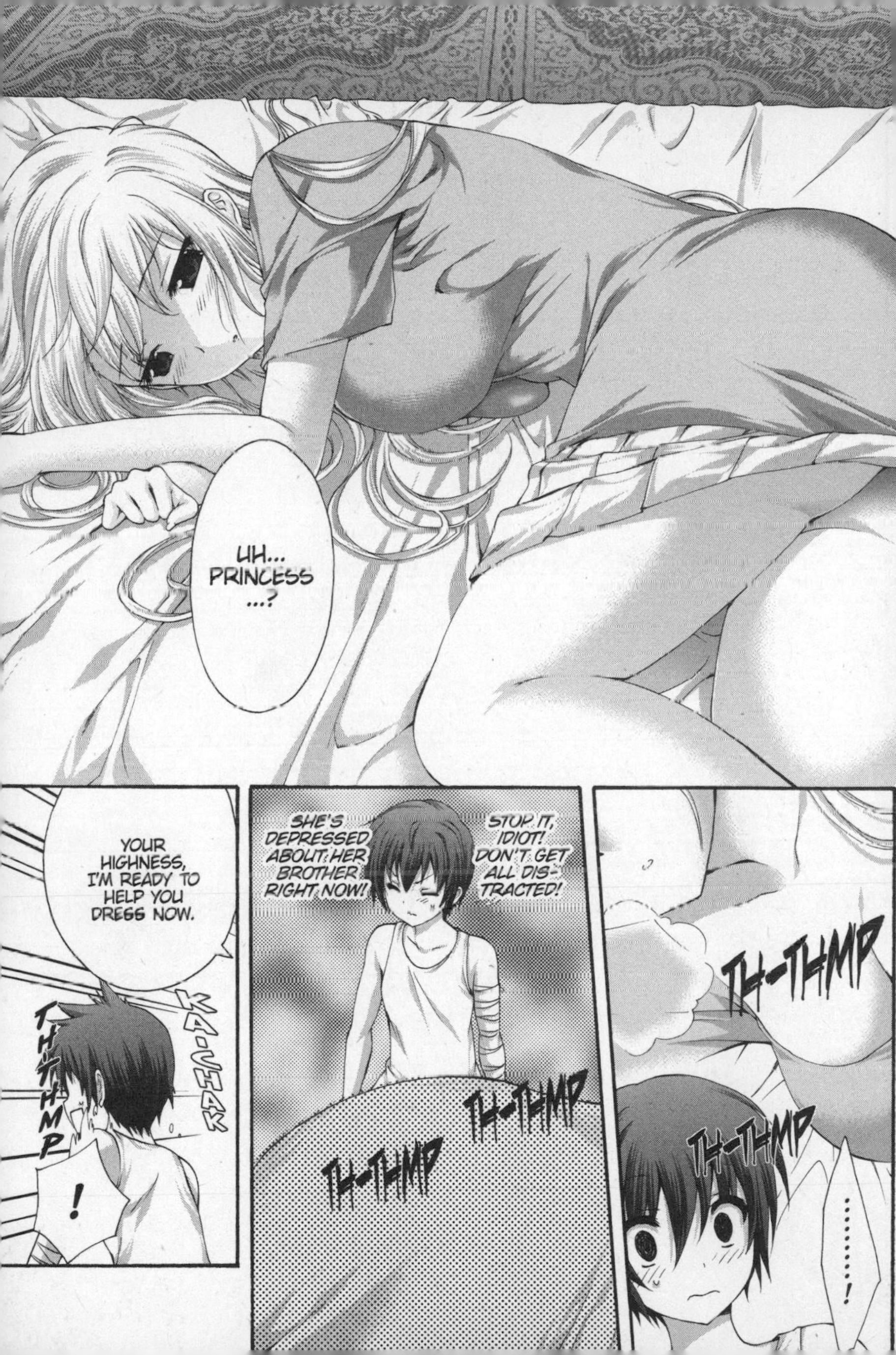
UH... PRINCESS ...?
TH-THMP
TH-THMP
......!
STOP IT, IDIOT! DON'T GET ALL DIS-TRACTED!
SHE'S DEPRESSED ABOUT HER BROTHER RIGHT NOW!
TH-THMP
TH-THMP
YOUR HIGHNESS, I'M READY TO HELP YOU DRESS NOW.
KA-CHAK
TH-THMP
!

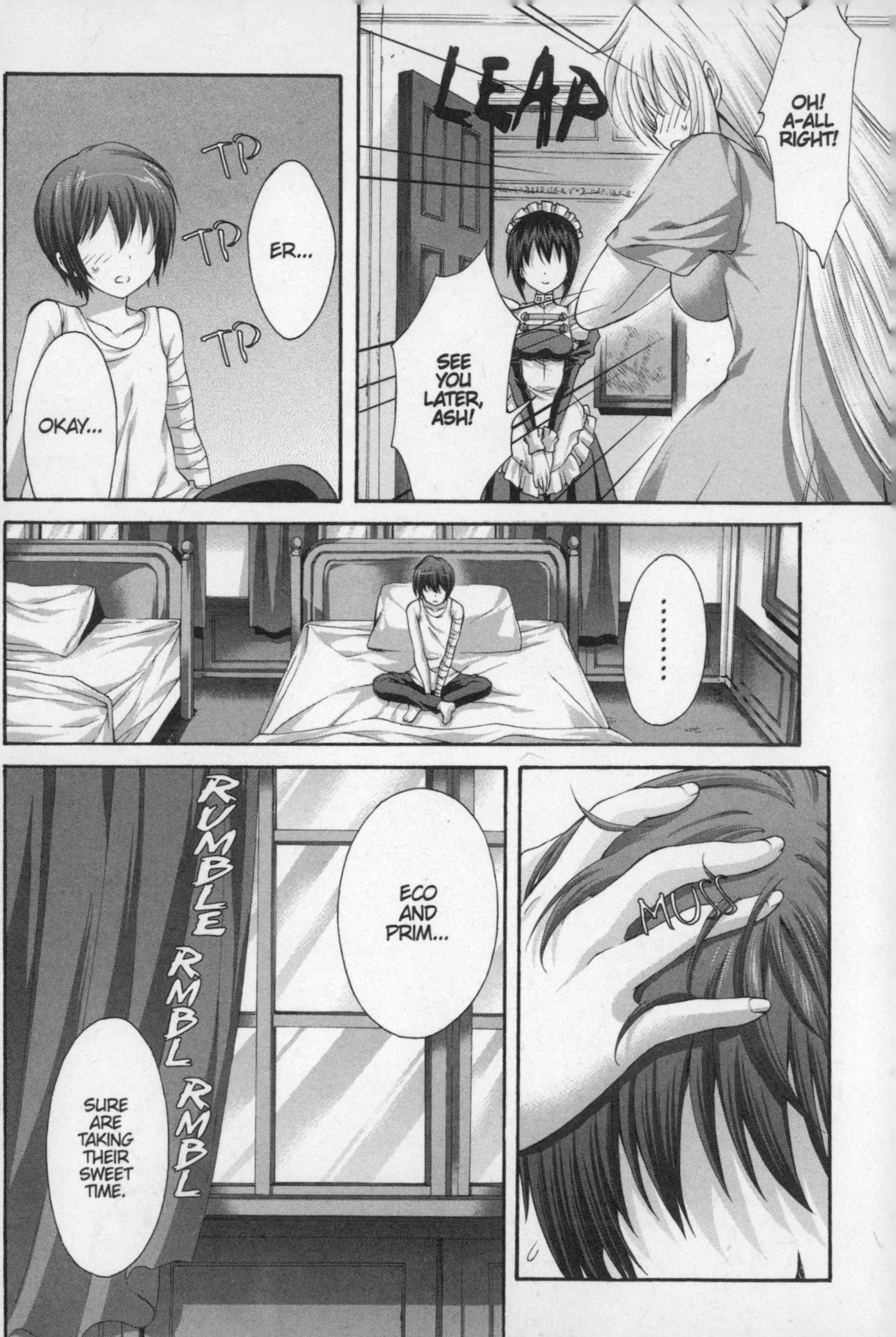
LEAP
OH! A-ALL RIGHT!
SEE YOU LATER, ASH!
TP
TP
TP
ER...
OKAY...
....
MUSS
ECO AND PRIM...
SURE ARE TAKING THEIR SWEET TIME.
RUMBLE RMBL RMBL

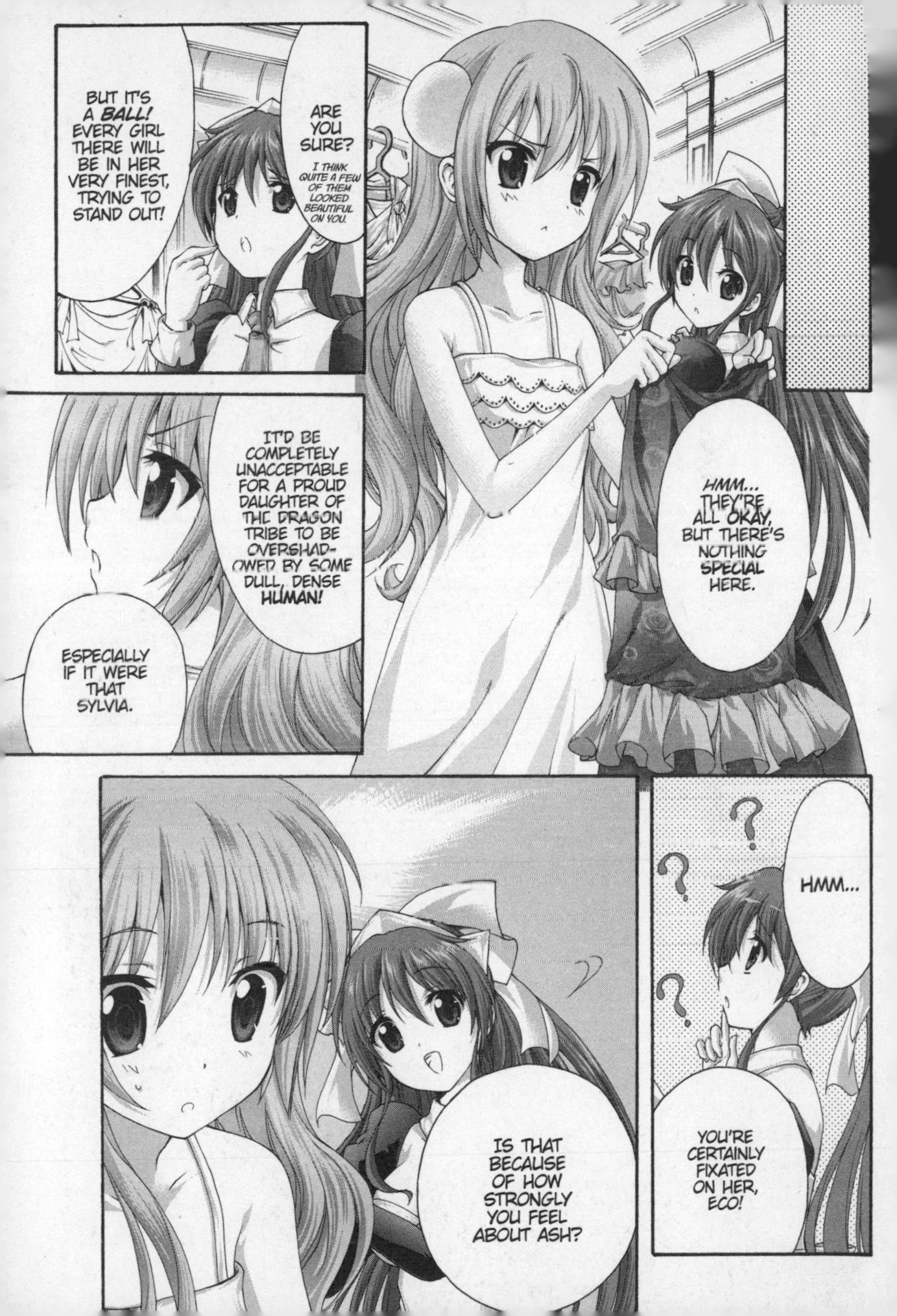
HMM... THEY'RE ALL OKAY, BUT THERE'S NOTHING SPECIAL HERE.
ARE YOU SURE?
I THINK QUITE A FEW OF THEM LOOKED BEAUTIFUL ON YOU.
BUT IT'S A BALL! EVERY GIRL THERE WILL BE IN HER VERY FINEST, TRYING TO STAND OUT!
IT'D BE COMPLETELY UNACCEPTABLE FOR A PROUD DAUGHTER OF THE DRAGON TRIBE TO BE OVERSHADOWED BY SOME DULL, DENSE HUMAN!
ESPECIALLY IF IT WERE THAT SYLVIA.
HMM...
YOU'RE CERTAINLY FIXATED ON HER, ECO!
IS THAT BECAUSE OF HOW STRONGLY YOU FEEL ABOUT ASH?

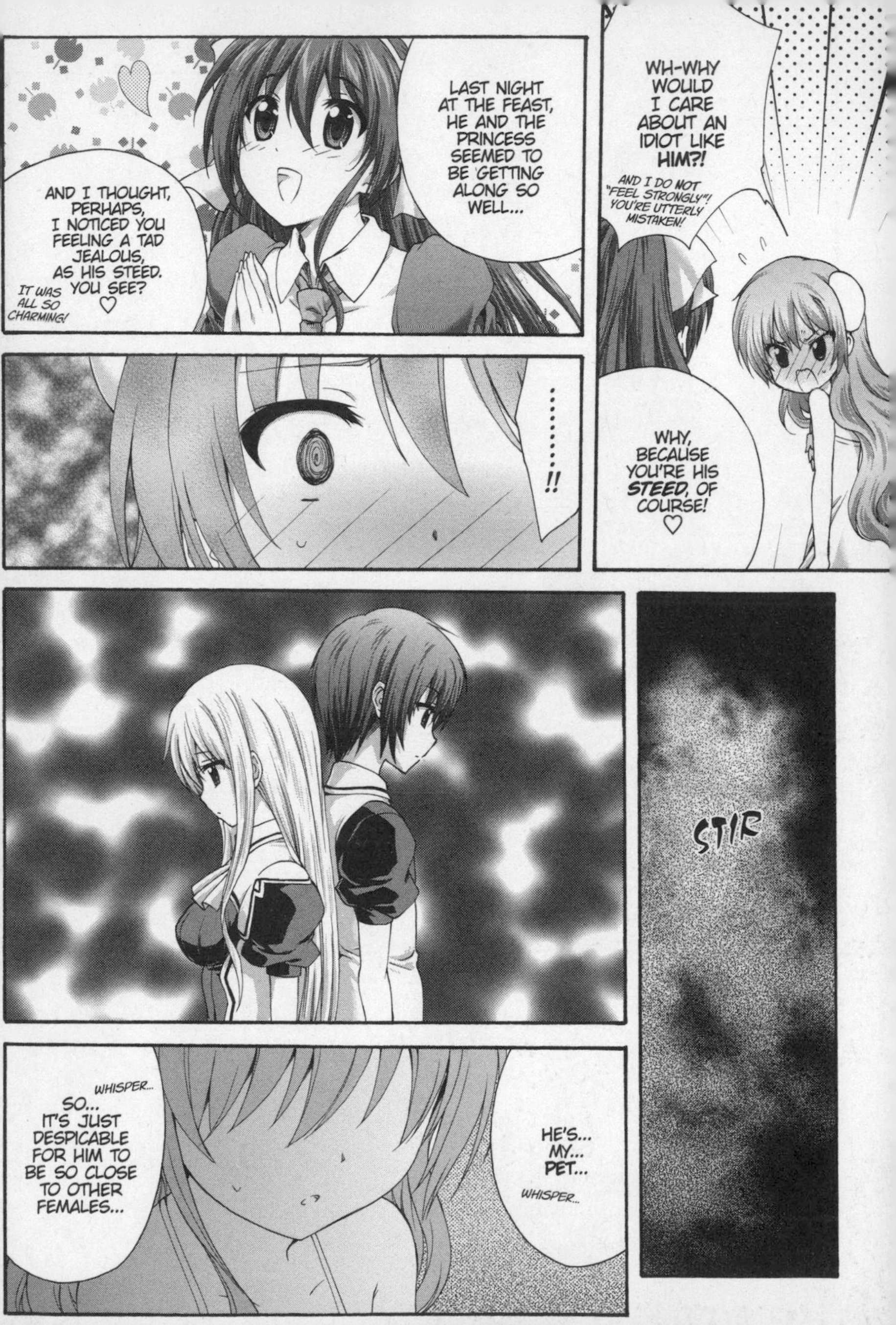
WH-WHY WOULD I CARE ABOUT AN IDIOT LIKE HIM?!
AND I DO NOT "FEEL STRONGLY"! YOU'RE UTTERLY MISTAKEN!
WHY, BECAUSE YOU'RE HIS STEED, OF COURSE! ♡
LAST NIGHT AT THE FEAST, HE AND THE PRINCESS SEEMED TO BE GETTING ALONG SO WELL...
AND I THOUGHT, PERHAPS, I NOTICED YOU FEELING A TAD JEALOUS, AS HIS STEED. YOU SEE? ♡
IT WAS ALL SO CHARMING!
......!!
STIR
HE'S... MY... PET...
WHISPER...
WHISPER...
SO... IT'S JUST DESPICABLE FOR HIM TO BE SO CLOSE TO OTHER FEMALES...

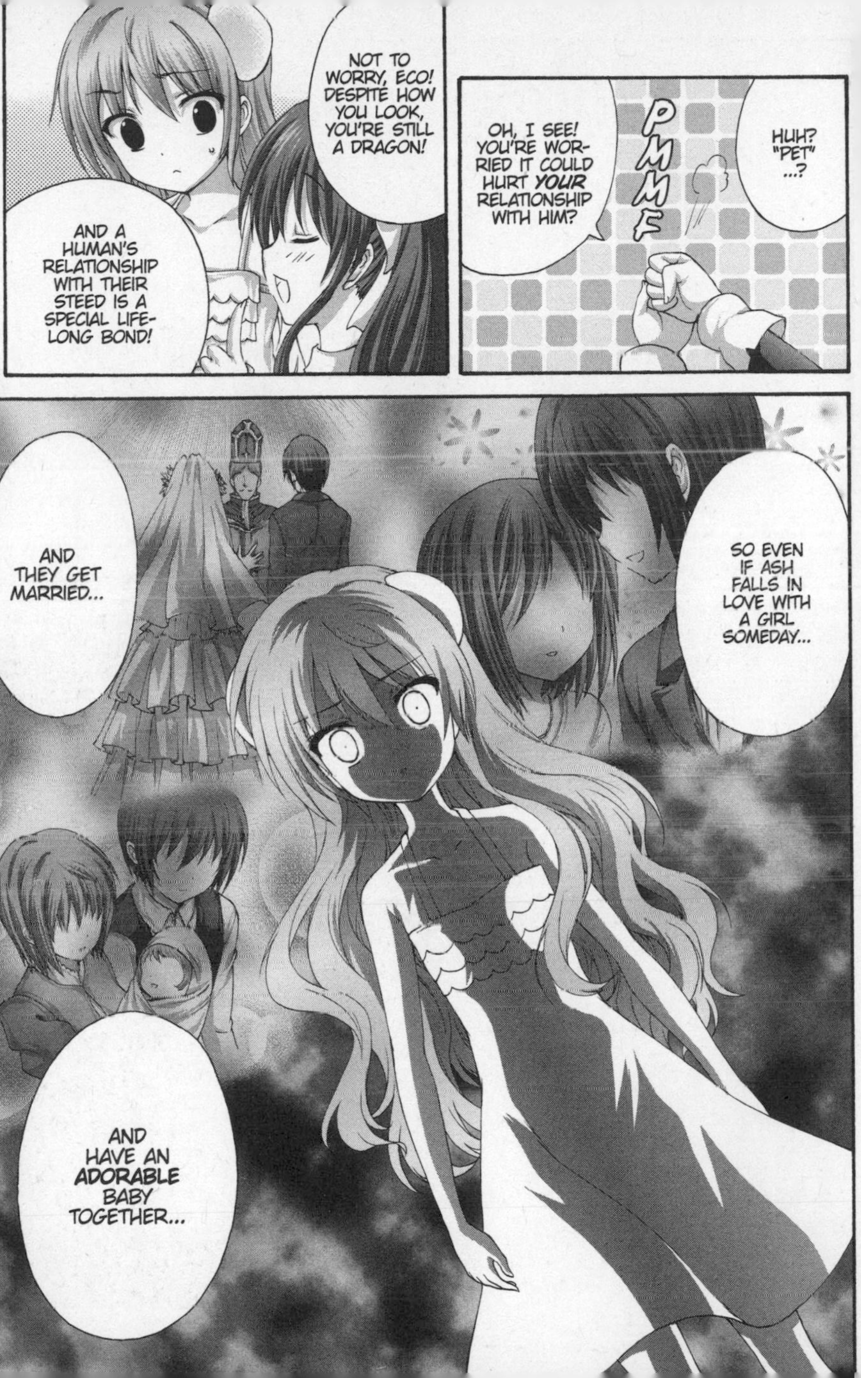
HUH? "PET" ...?
PMMF
OH, I SEE! YOU'RE WORRIED IT COULD HURT YOUR RELATIONSHIP WITH HIM?
NOT TO WORRY, ECO! DESPITE HOW YOU LOOK, YOU'RE STILL A DRAGON!
AND A HUMAN'S RELATIONSHIP WITH THEIR STEED IS A SPECIAL LIFE-LONG BOND!
SO EVEN IF ASH FALLS IN LOVE WITH A GIRL SOMEDAY...
AND THEY GET MARRIED...
AND HAVE AN ADORABLE BABY TOGETHER...

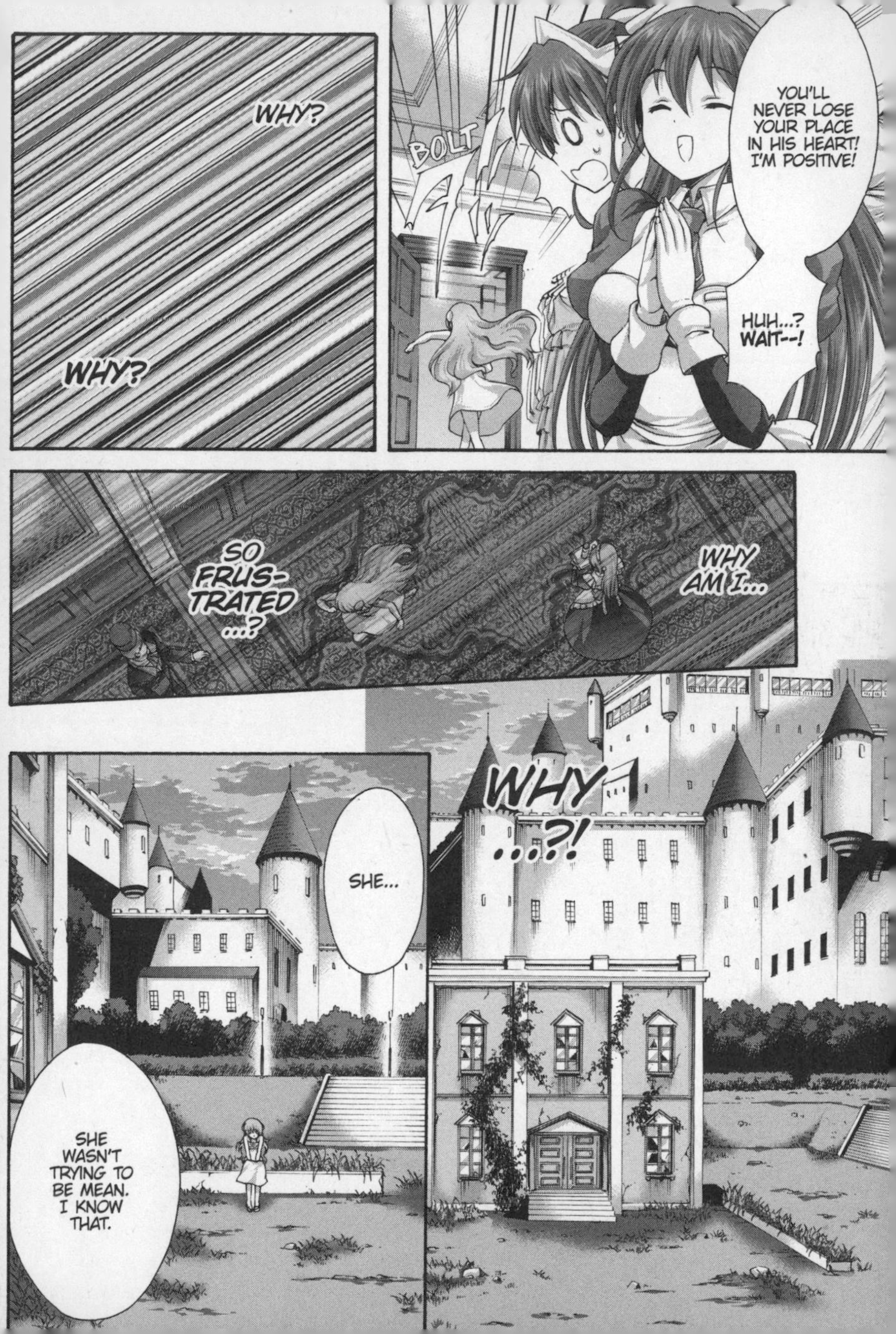

YOU'LL NEVER LOSE YOUR PLACE IN HIS HEART! I'M POSITIVE!
BOLT
HUH...? WAIT--!
WHY?
WHY?
WHY AM I...
SO FRUS-TRATED ...?
WHY ...?!
SHE...
SHE WASN'T TRYING TO BE MEAN. I KNOW THAT.

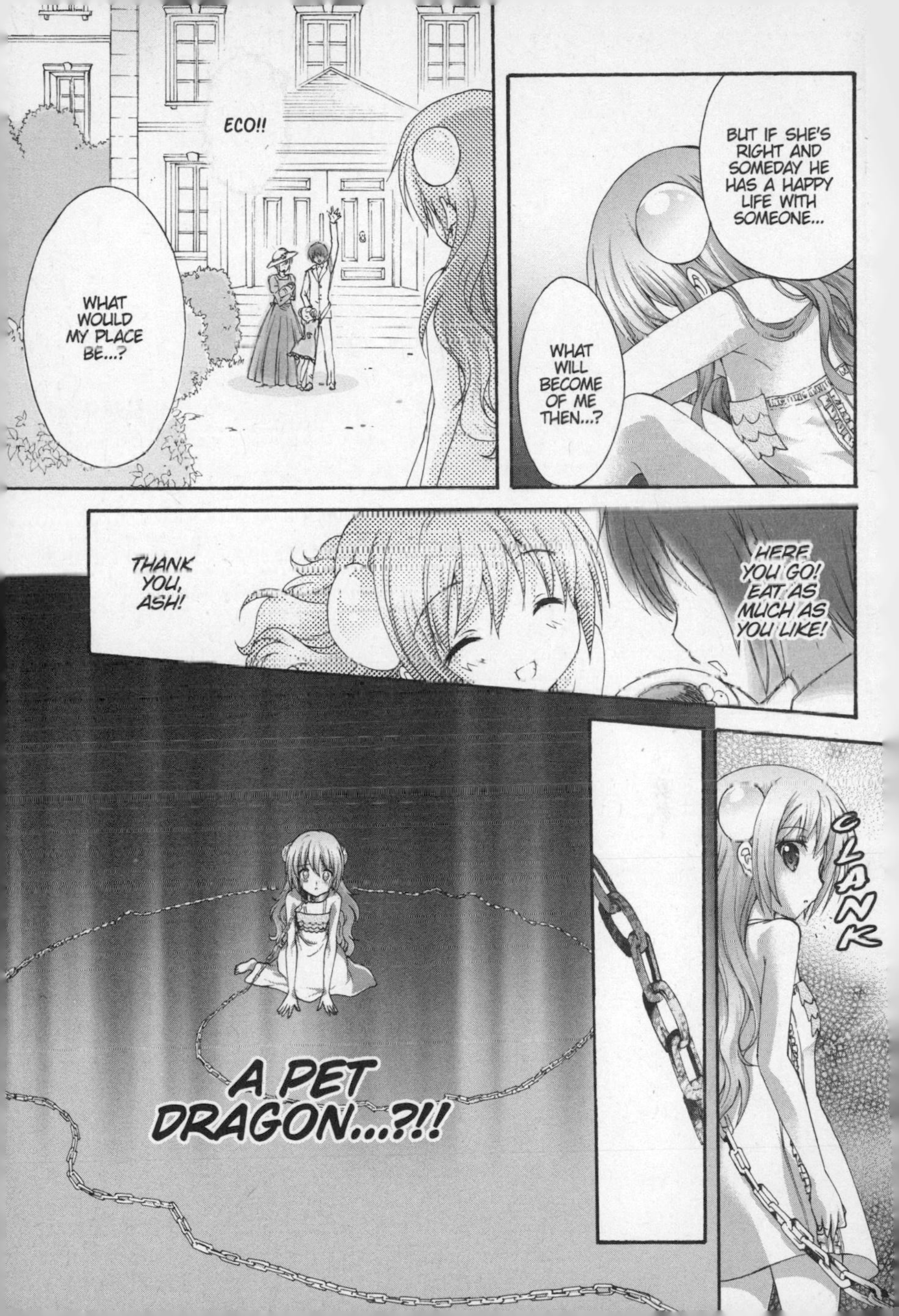
BUT IF SHE'S RIGHT AND SOMEDAY HE HAS A HAPPY LIFE WITH SOMEONE...
WHAT WILL BECOME OF ME THEN...?
ECO!!
WHAT WOULD MY PLACE BE...?
HERE YOU GO! EAT AS MUCH AS YOU LIKE!
THANK YOU, ASH!
CLANK
A PET DRAGON...?!!

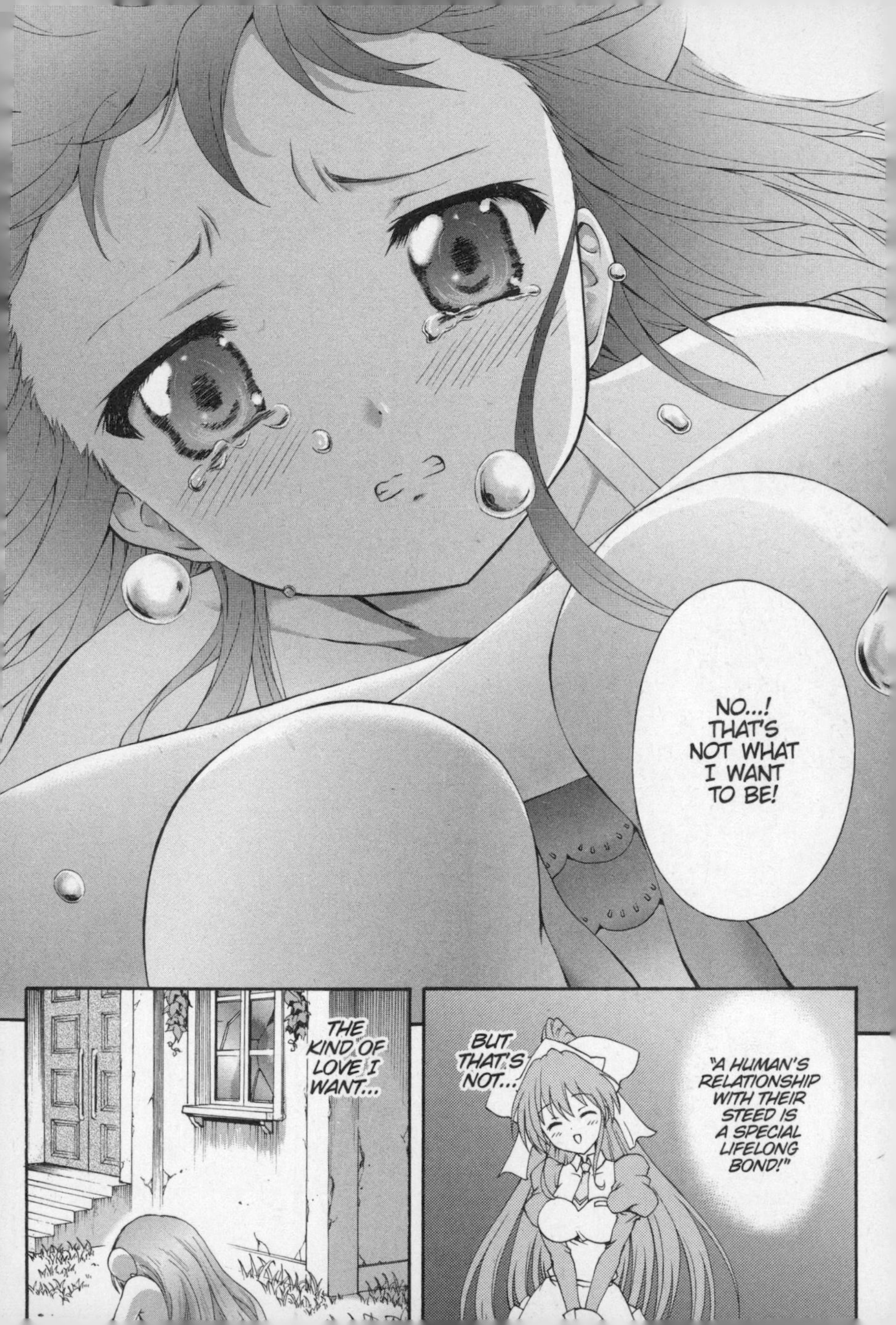
NO...! THAT'S NOT WHAT I WANT TO BE!
"A HUMAN'S RELATIONSHIP WITH THEIR STEED IS A SPECIAL LIFELONG BOND!"
BUT THAT'S NOT...
THE KIND OF LOVE I WANT...

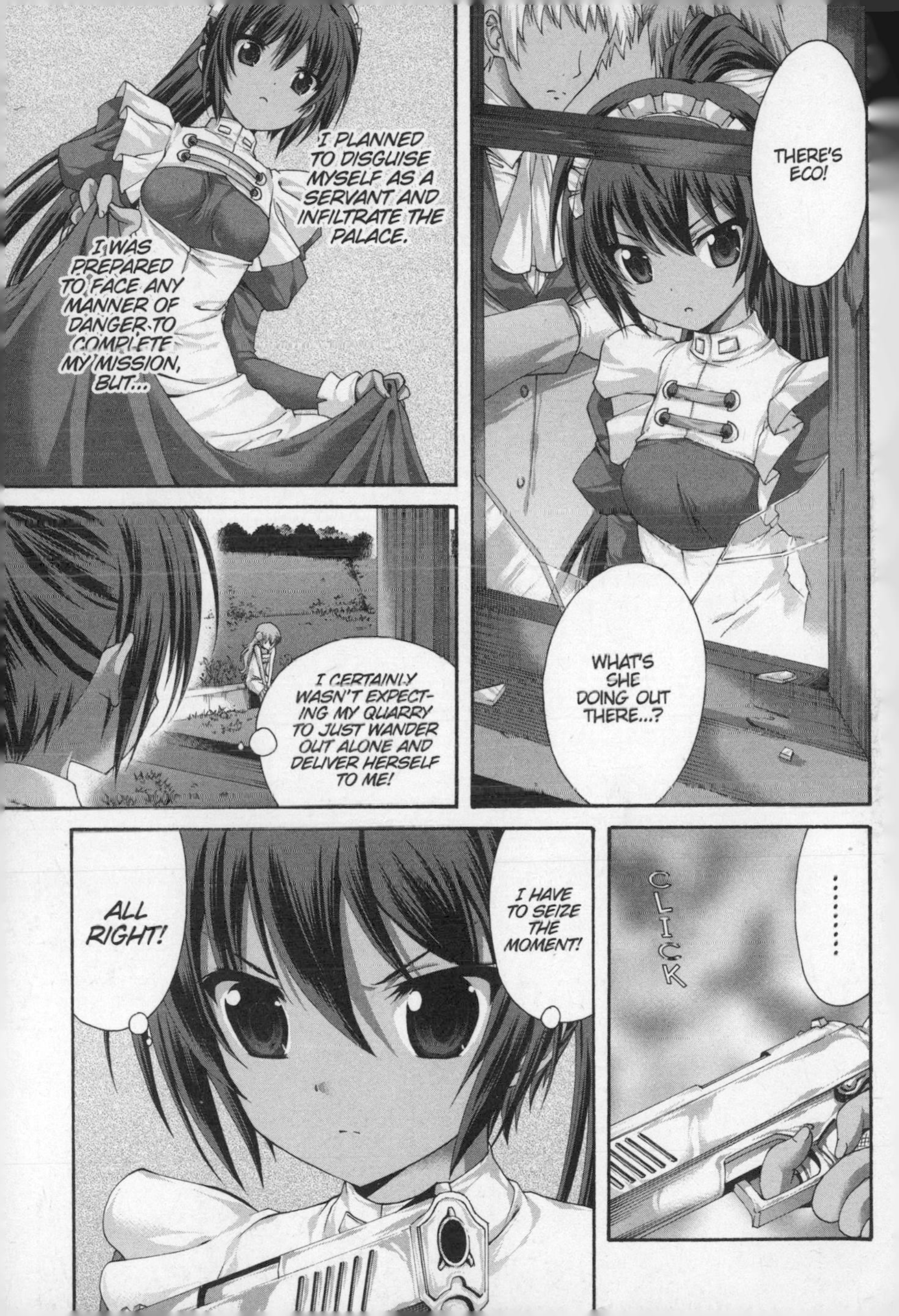
THERE'S ECO!
WHAT'S SHE DOING OUT THERE...?
I PLANNED TO DISGUISE MYSELF AS A SERVANT AND INFILTRATE THE PALACE.
I WAS PREPARED TO FACE ANY MANNER OF DANGER TO COMPLETE MY MISSION, BUT...
I CERTAINLY WASN'T EXPECTING MY QUARRY TO JUST WANDER OUT ALONE AND DELIVER HERSELF TO ME!
......
CLICK
I HAVE TO SEIZE THE MOMENT!
ALL RIGHT!

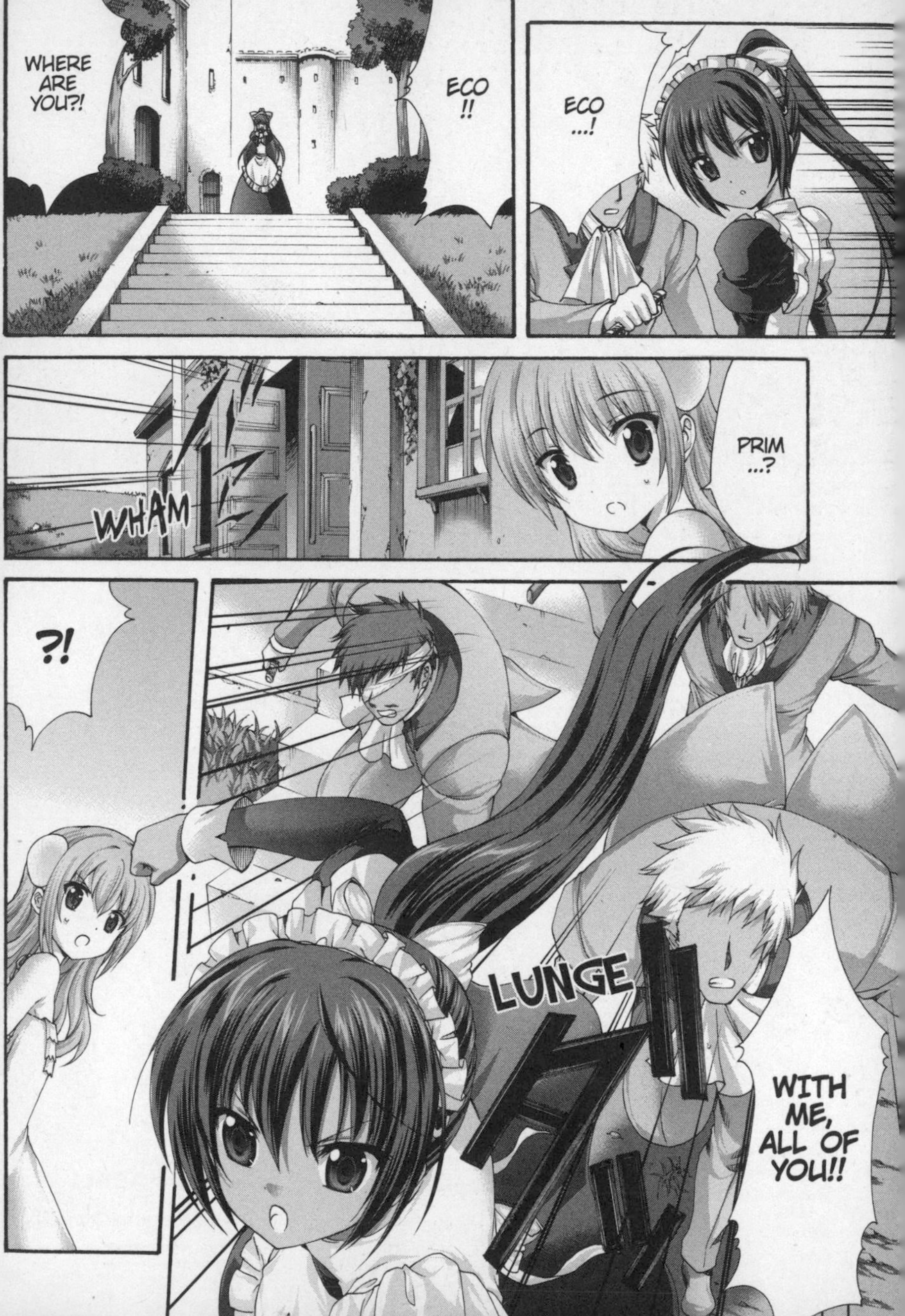
ECO ...!
ECO !!
WHERE ARE YOU?!
PRIM ...?
WHAM
LUNGE
WITH ME, ALL OF YOU!!
?!

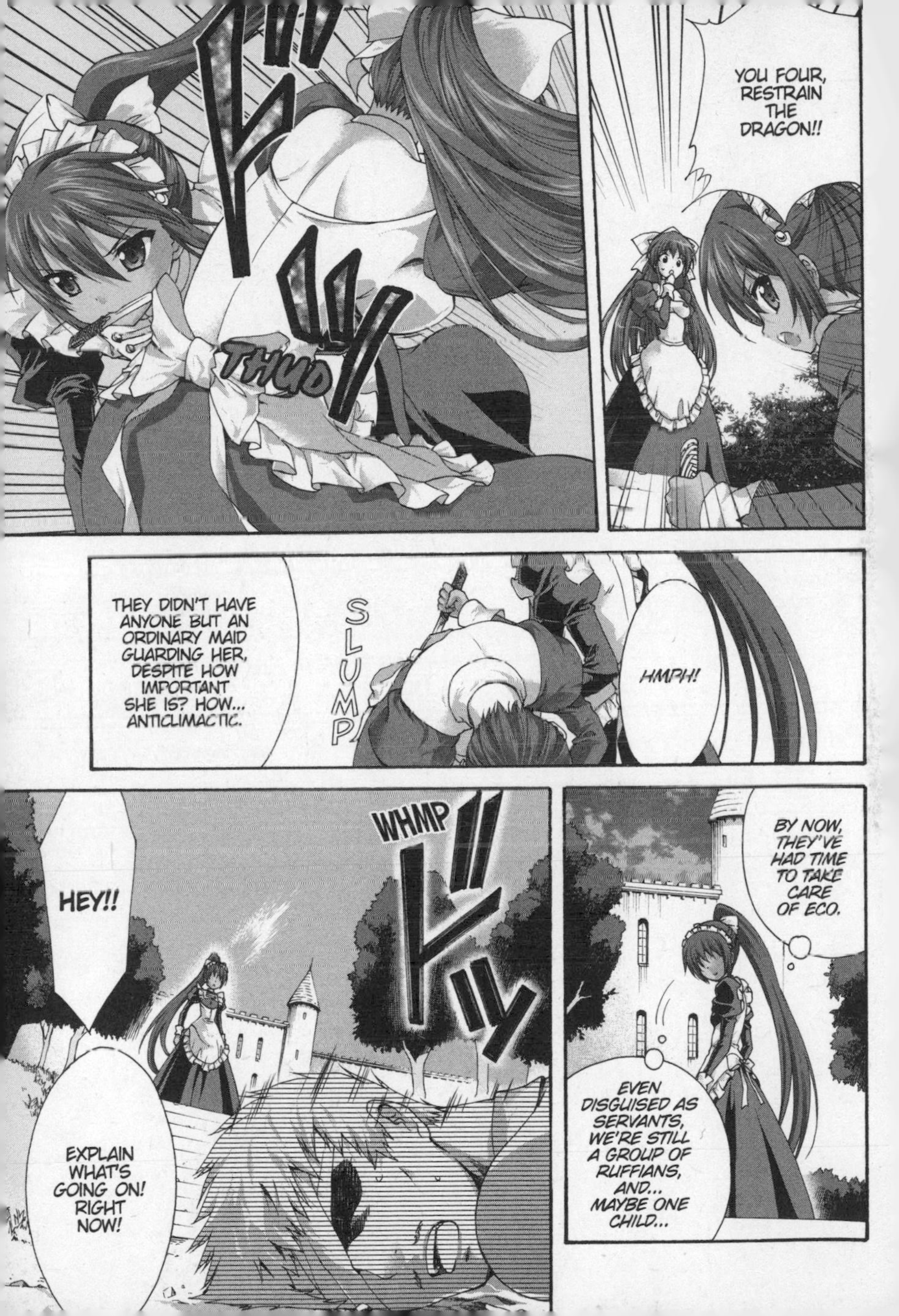
YOU FOUR, RESTRAIN THE DRAGON!!
THUD
HMPH!
SLUMP
THEY DIDN'T HAVE ANYONE BUT AN ORDINARY MAID GUARDING HER, DESPITE HOW IMPORTANT SHE IS? HOW... ANTICLIMACTIC.
BY NOW, THEY'VE HAD TIME TO TAKE CARE OF ECO.
EVEN DISGUISED AS SERVANTS, WE'RE STILL A GROUP OF RUFFIANS, AND... MAYBE ONE CHILD...
WHMP
HEY!!
EXPLAIN WHAT'S GOING ON! RIGHT NOW!

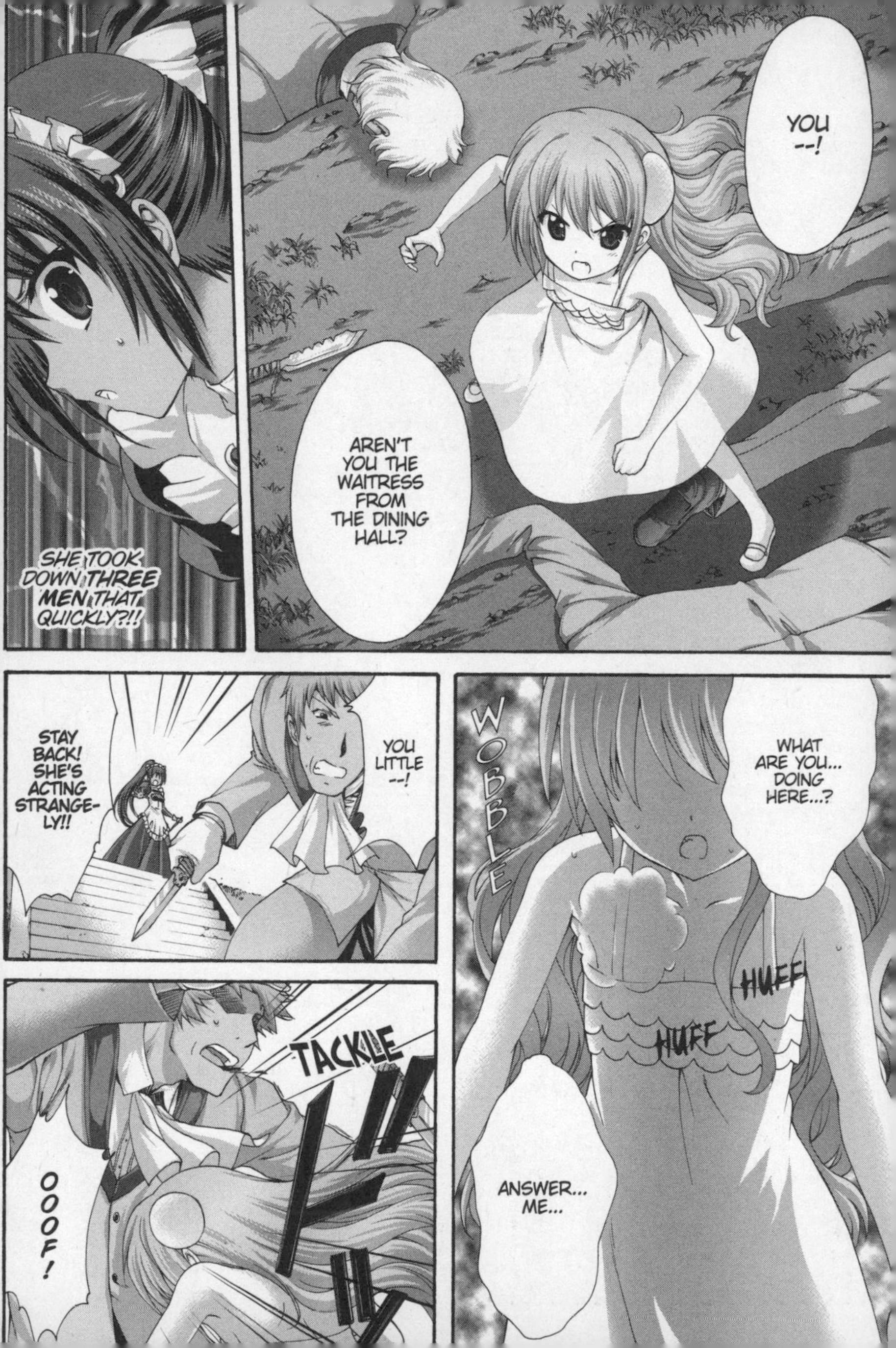
YOU --!
AREN'T YOU THE WAITRESS FROM THE DINING HALL?
SHE TOOK DOWN THREE MEN THAT QUICKLY?!!
WOBBLE
WHAT ARE YOU... DOING HERE...?
HUFF
HUFF
ANSWER... ME...
YOU LITTLE --!
STAY BACK! SHE'S ACTING STRANGE-LY!!
TACKLE
OOOF!

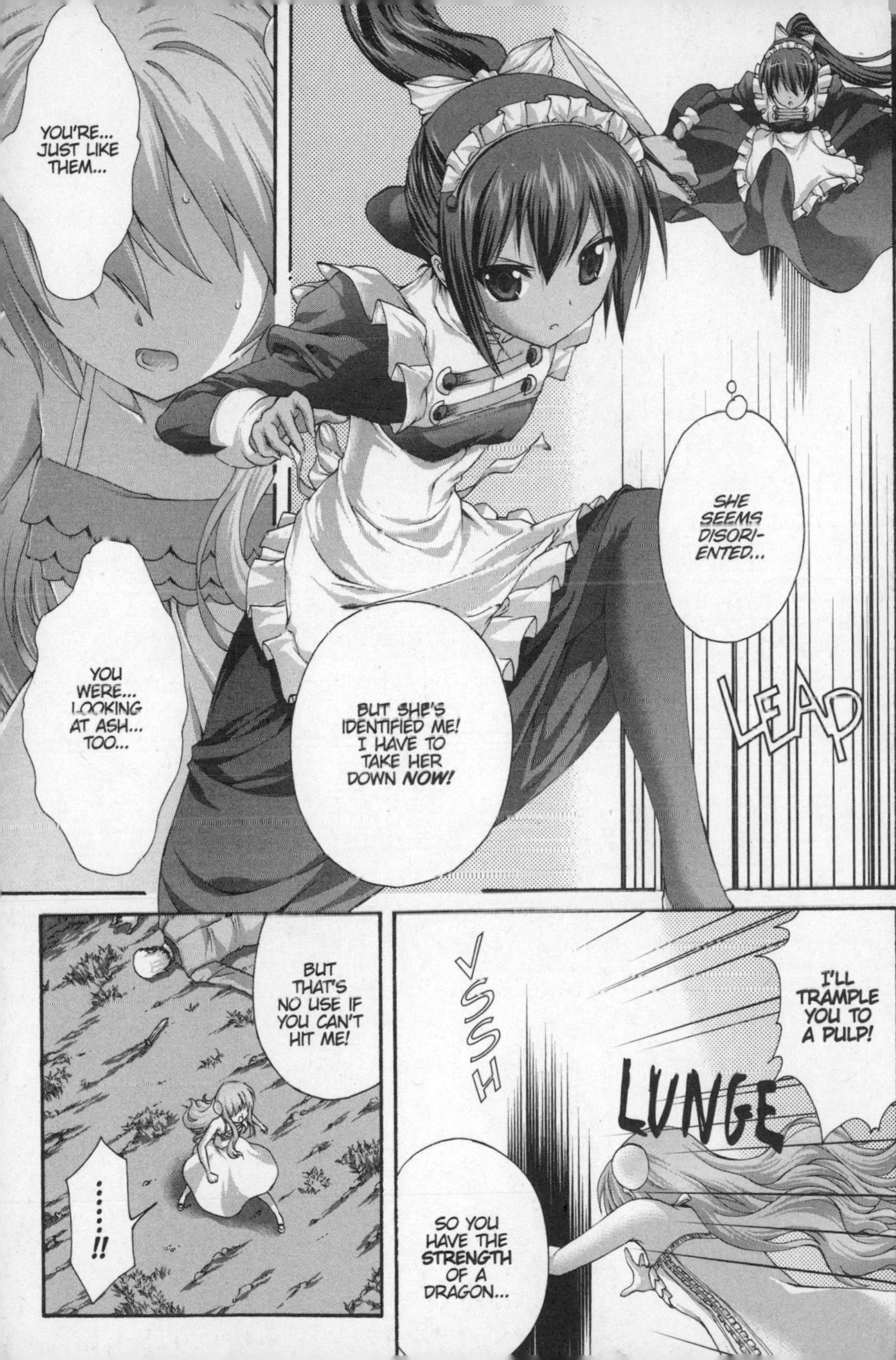
SHE SEEMS DISORI-ENTED...
LEAP
BUT SHE'S IDENTIFIED ME! I HAVE TO TAKE HER DOWN *NOW!*
YOU'RE... JUST LIKE THEM...
YOU WERE... LOOKING AT ASH... TOO...
I'LL TRAMPLE YOU TO A PULP!
VSSH
LUNGE
SO YOU HAVE THE STRENGTH OF A DRAGON...
BUT THAT'S NO USE IF YOU CAN'T HIT ME!
......!!

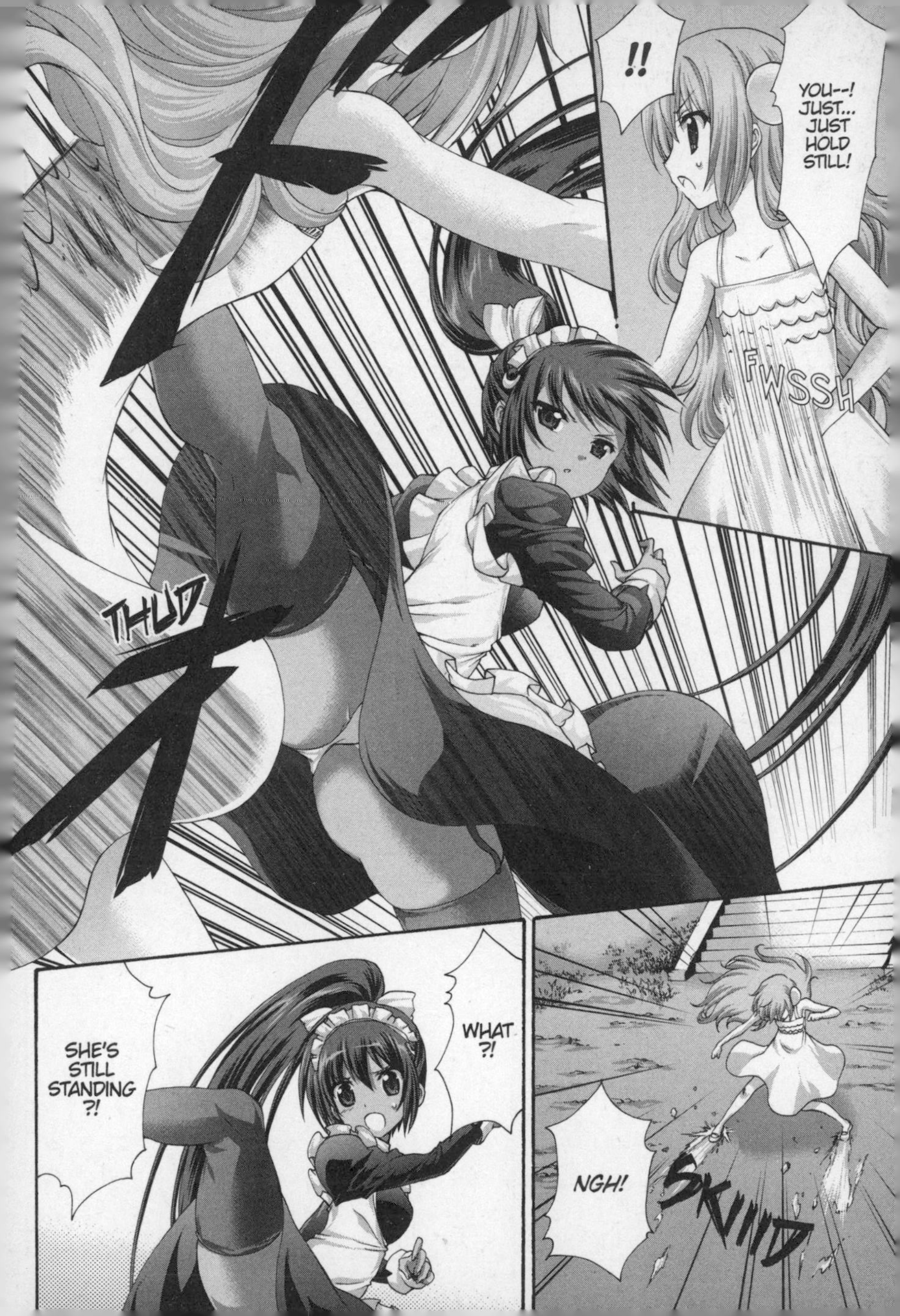
YOU--! JUST... JUST HOLD STILL!
!!
FWSSH
THUD
NGH!
SKIIID
WHAT?!
SHE'S STILL STANDING?!

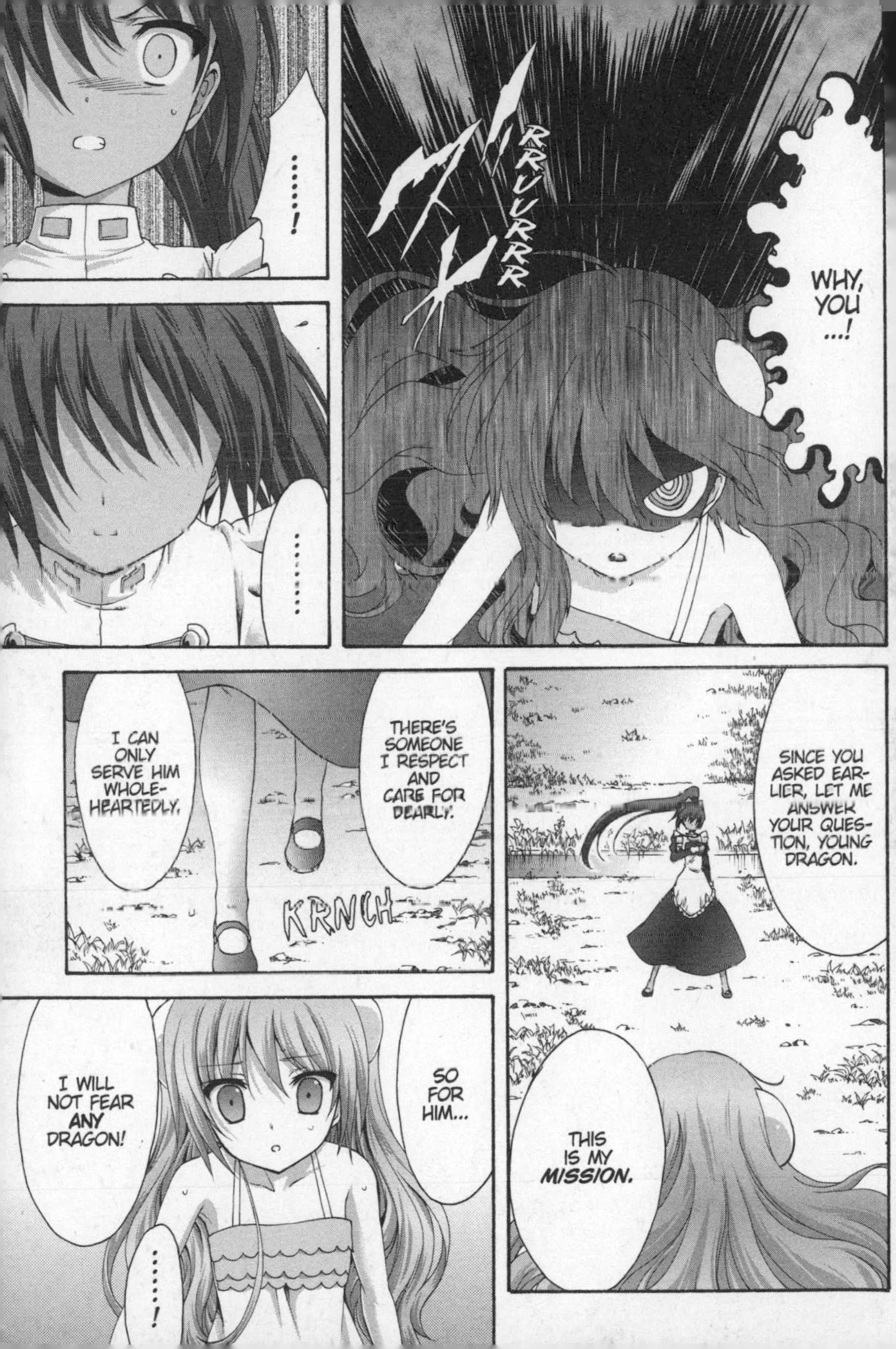
RRUURRRR
WHY, YOU ...!
......!
......
SINCE YOU ASKED EARLIER, LET ME ANSWER YOUR QUESTION, YOUNG DRAGON.
THIS IS MY MISSION.
THERE'S SOMEONE I RESPECT AND CARE FOR DEARLY.
I CAN ONLY SERVE HIM WHOLEHEARTEDLY.
KRNCH
SO FOR HIM...
I WILL NOT FEAR ANY DRAGON!
......!

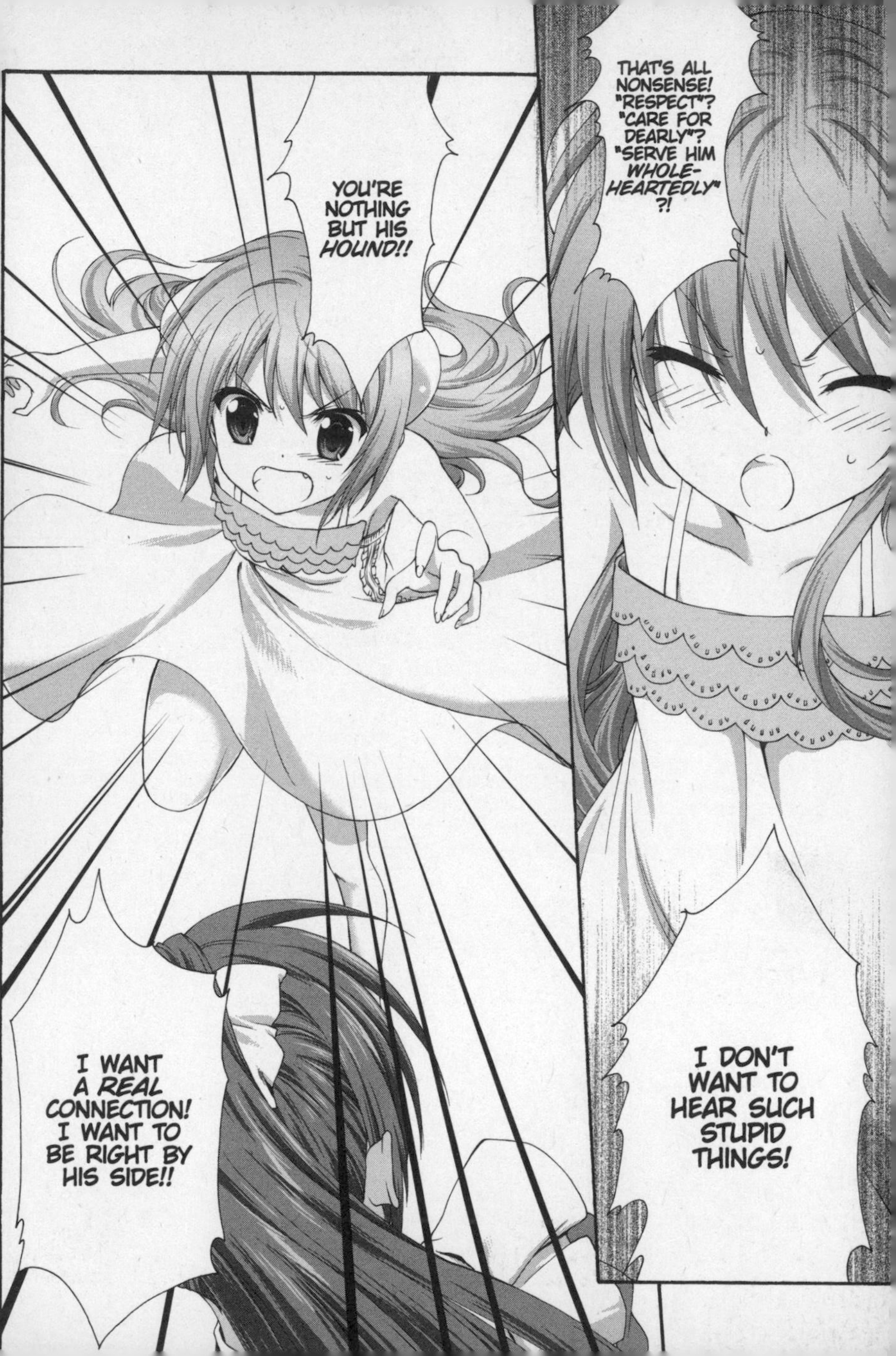
THAT'S ALL NONSENSE! "RESPECT"? "CARE FOR DEARLY"? "SERVE HIM *WHOLE-HEARTEDLY*"?!
I DON'T WANT TO HEAR SUCH STUPID THINGS!
YOU'RE NOTHING BUT HIS *HOUND!!*
I WANT A *REAL* CONNECTION! I WANT TO BE RIGHT BY HIS SIDE!!

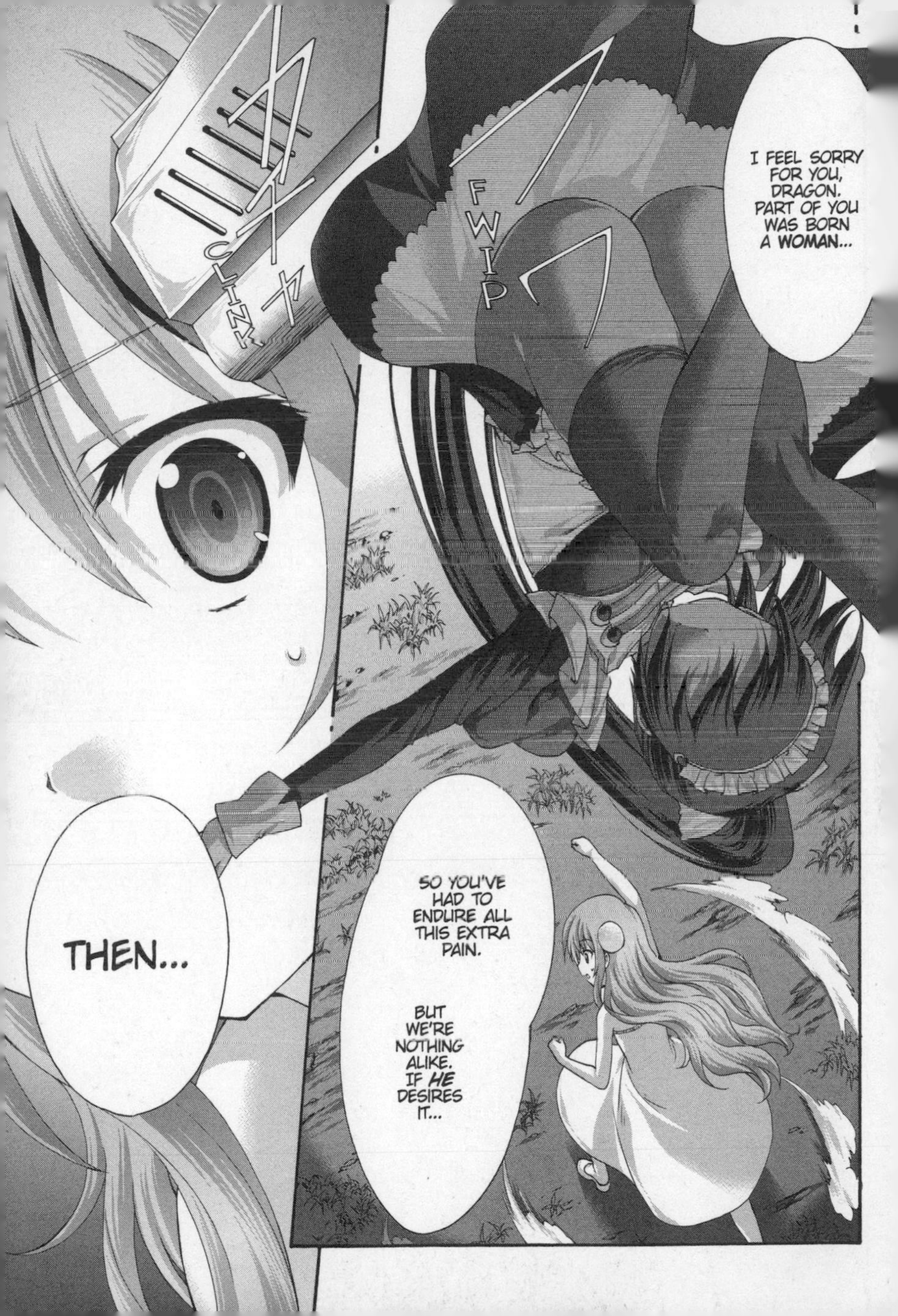
FWIP
I FEEL SORRY FOR YOU, DRAGON. PART OF YOU WAS BORN A **WOMAN**...
SO YOU'VE HAD TO ENDURE ALL THIS EXTRA PAIN.
BUT WE'RE NOTHING ALIKE. IF ***HE*** DESIRES IT...
CLINK
THEN...

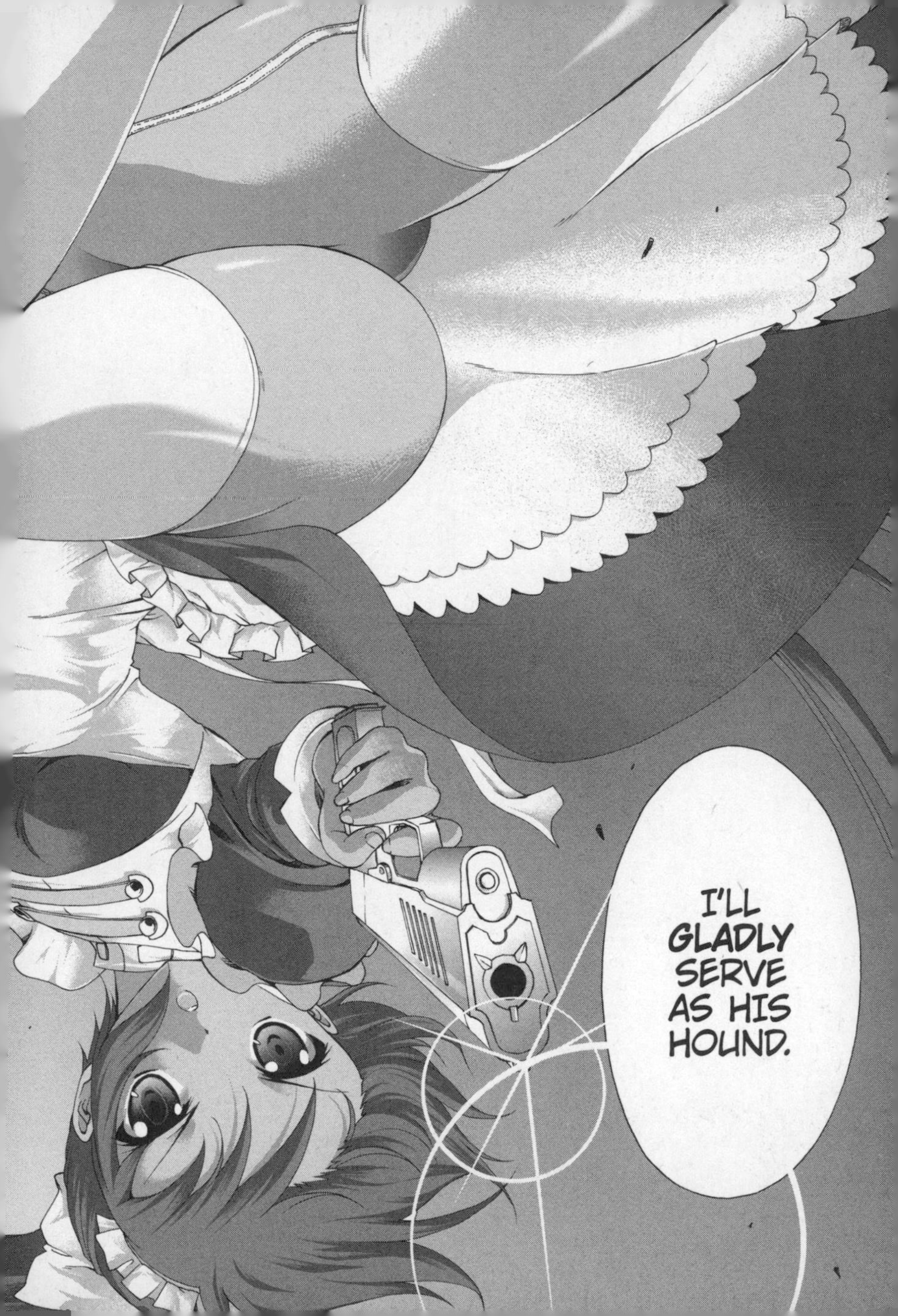
I'LL GLADLY SERVE AS HIS HOUND.

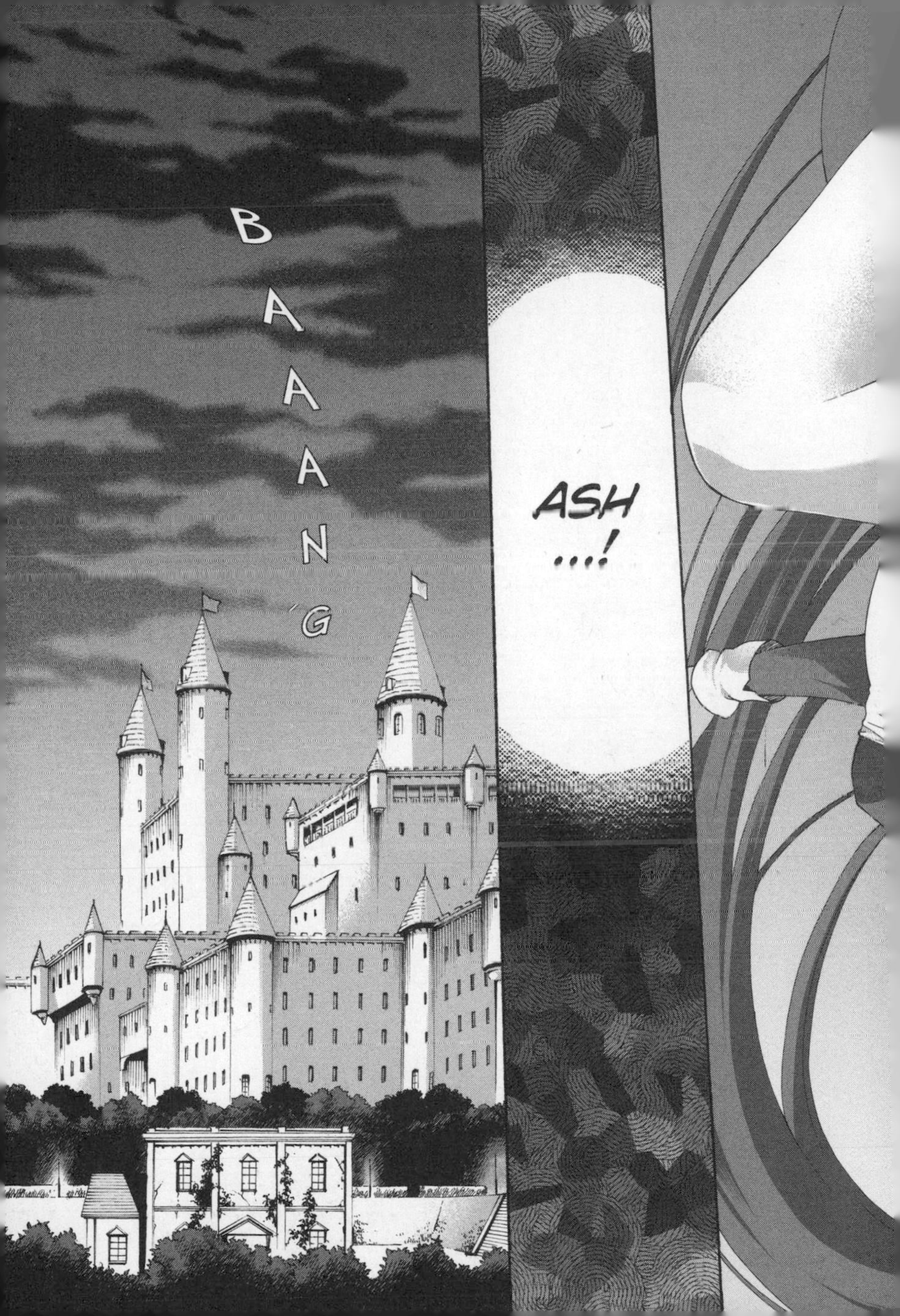
ASH ...!
BAAAANG

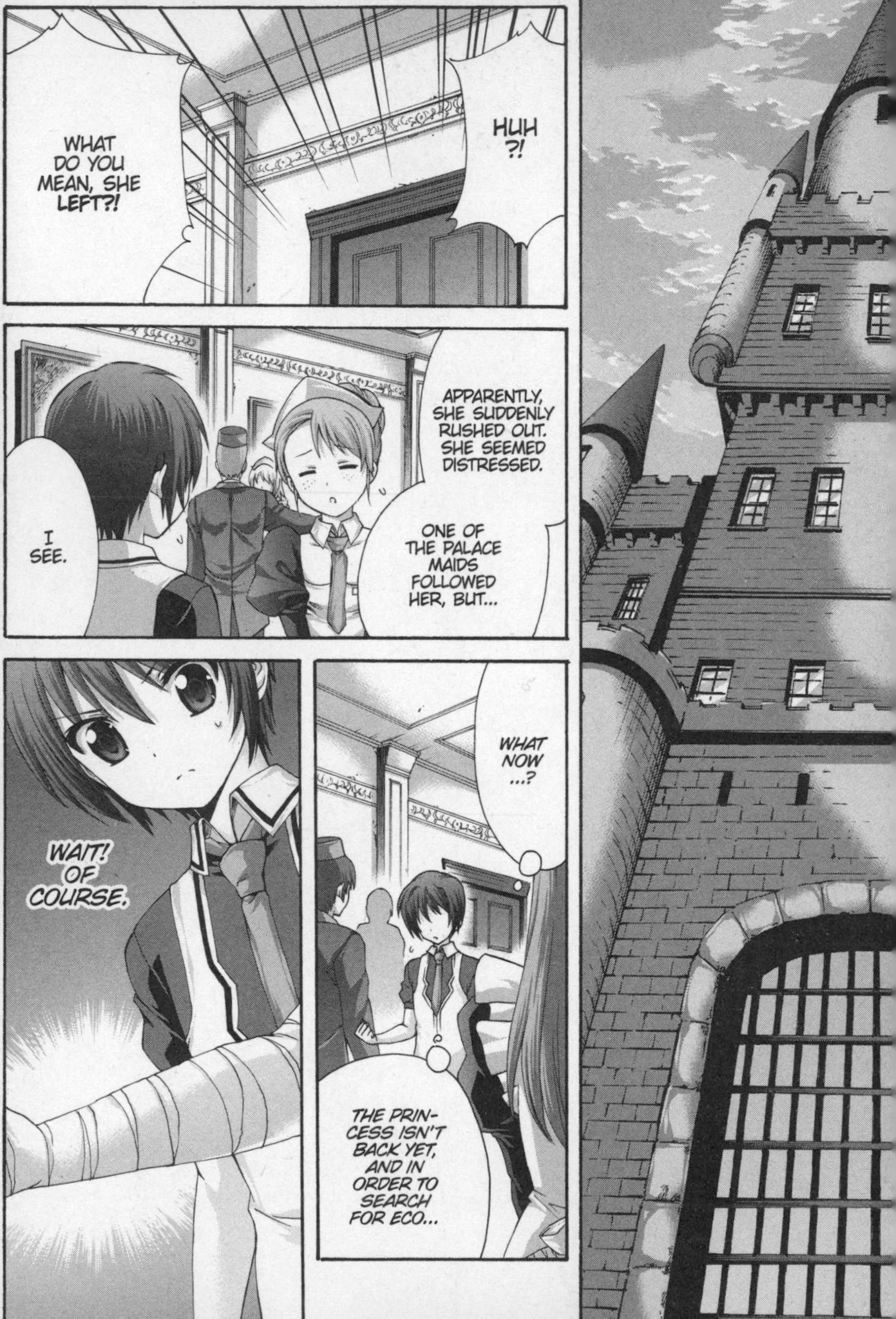
HUH ?!
WHAT DO YOU MEAN, SHE LEFT?!
APPARENTLY, SHE SUDDENLY RUSHED OUT. SHE SEEMED DISTRESSED.
ONE OF THE PALACE MAIDS FOLLOWED HER, BUT...
I SEE.
WHAT NOW ...?
THE PRIN-CESS ISN'T BACK YET, AND IN ORDER TO SEARCH FOR ECO...
WAIT! OF COURSE.

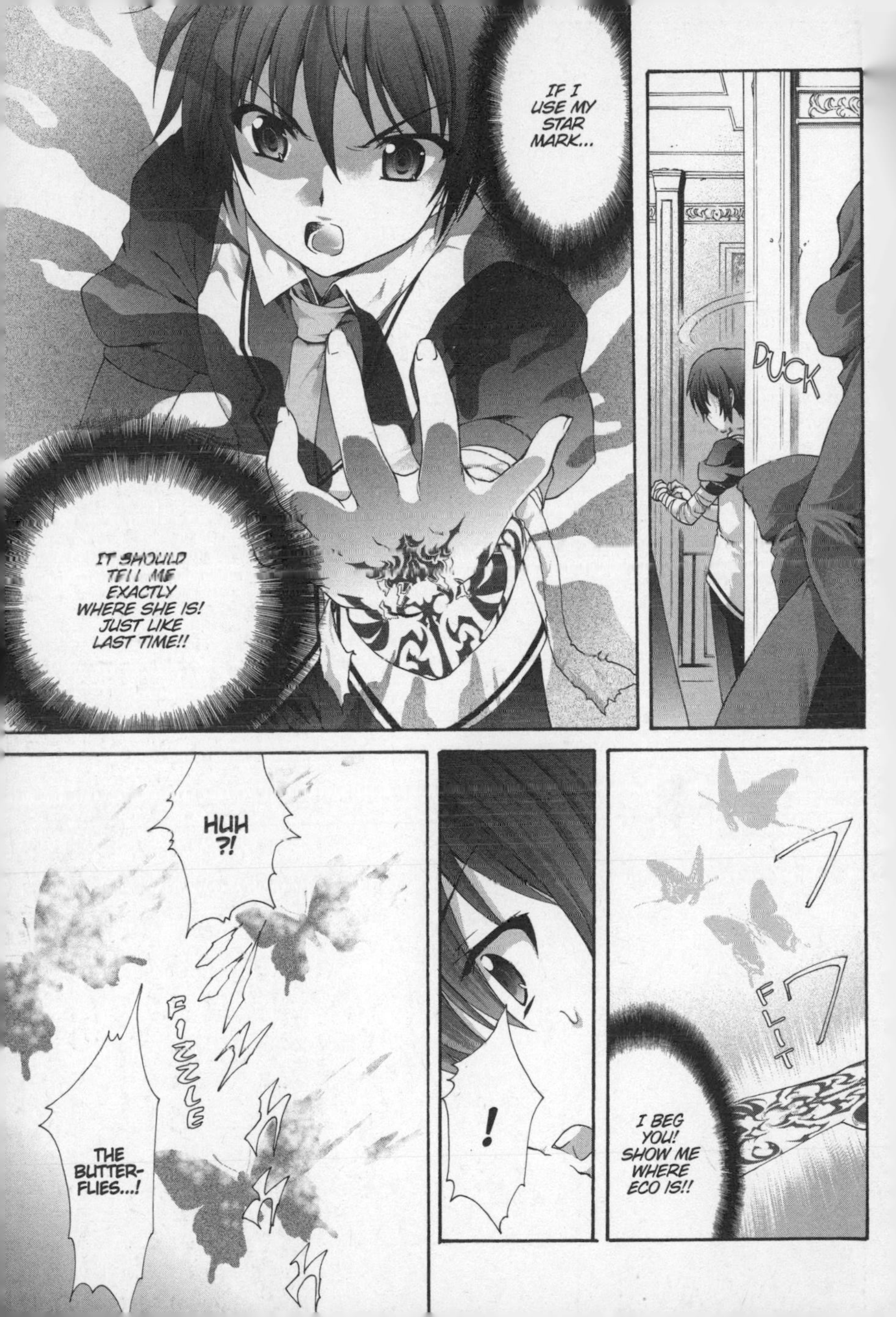
DUCK
IF I USE MY STAR MARK...
IT SHOULD TELL ME EXACTLY WHERE SHE IS! JUST LIKE LAST TIME!!
FLIT
I BEG YOU! SHOW ME WHERE ECO IS!!
!
HUH ?!
FIZZLE
THE BUTTER-FLIES...!

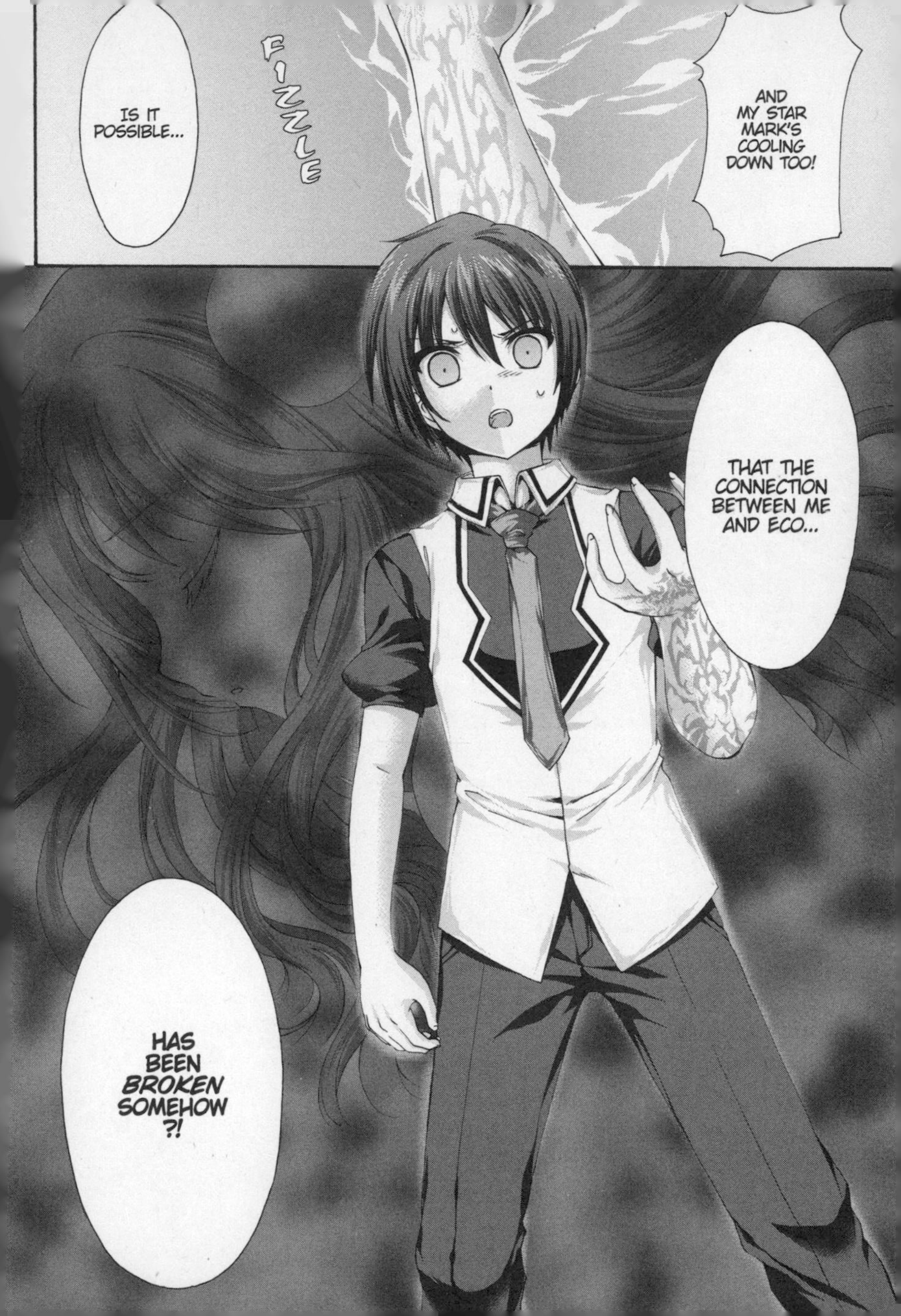
AND MY STAR MARK'S COOLING DOWN TOO!
FIZZLE
IS IT POSSIBLE...
THAT THE CONNECTION BETWEEN ME AND ECO...
HAS BEEN *BROKEN* SOMEHOW?!

DRAGONAR
ACADEMY

星刻の竜騎士

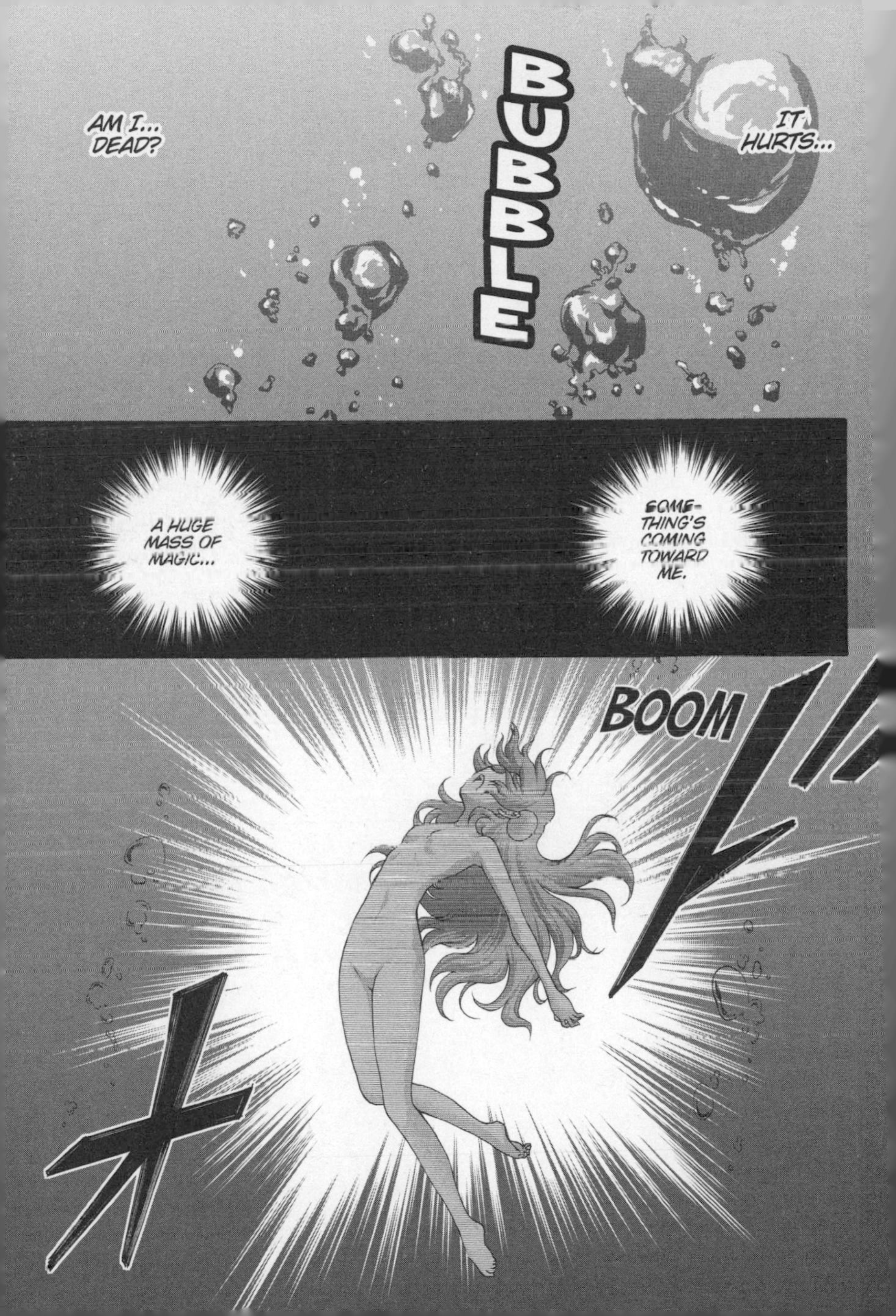
IT HURTS...
BUBBLE
AM I... DEAD?
SOME-THING'S COMING TOWARD ME.
A HUGE MASS OF MAGIC...
BOOM

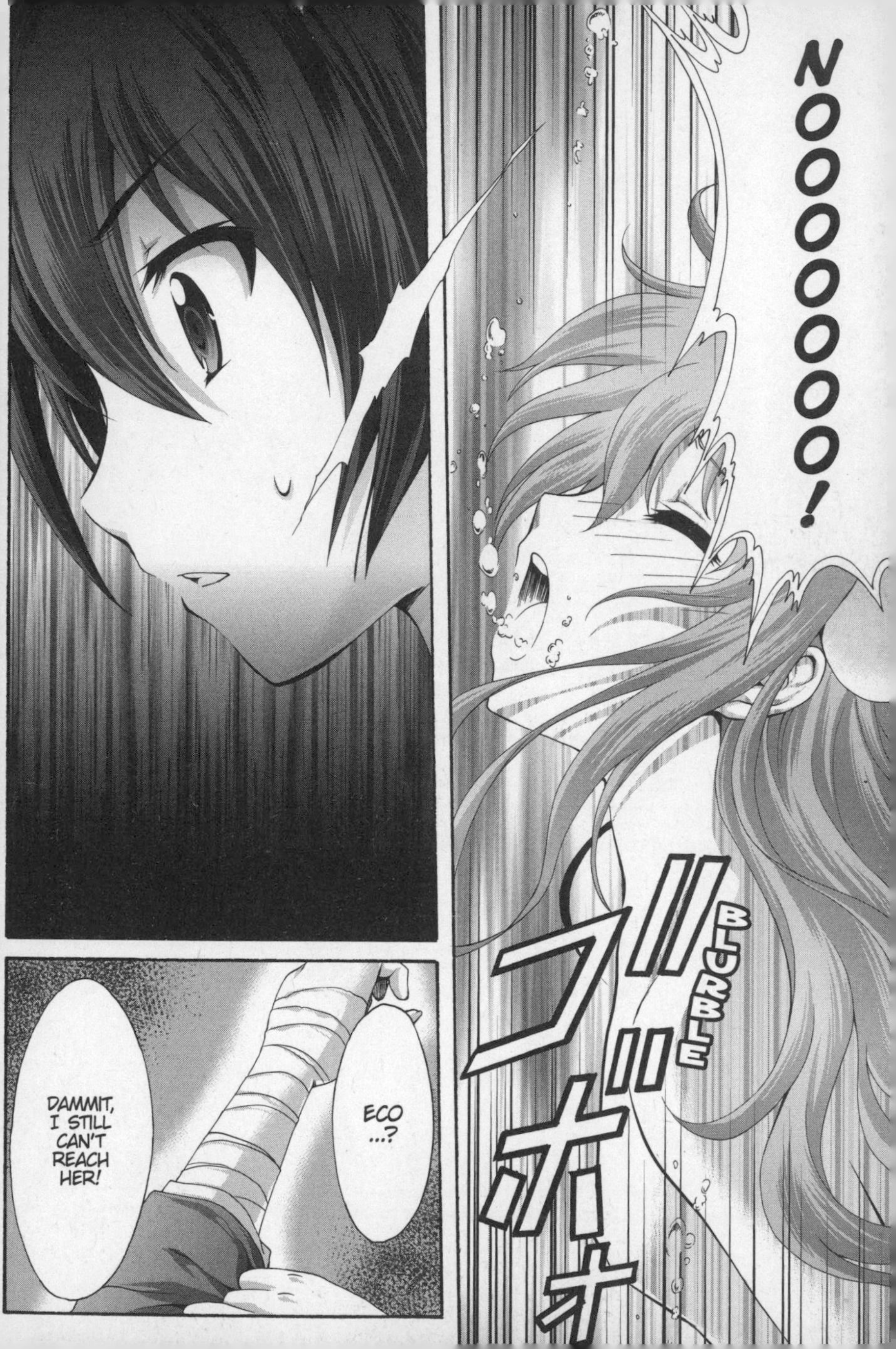
NOOOOOOO!
BLURBLE
ECO ...?
DAMMIT, I STILL CAN'T REACH HER!

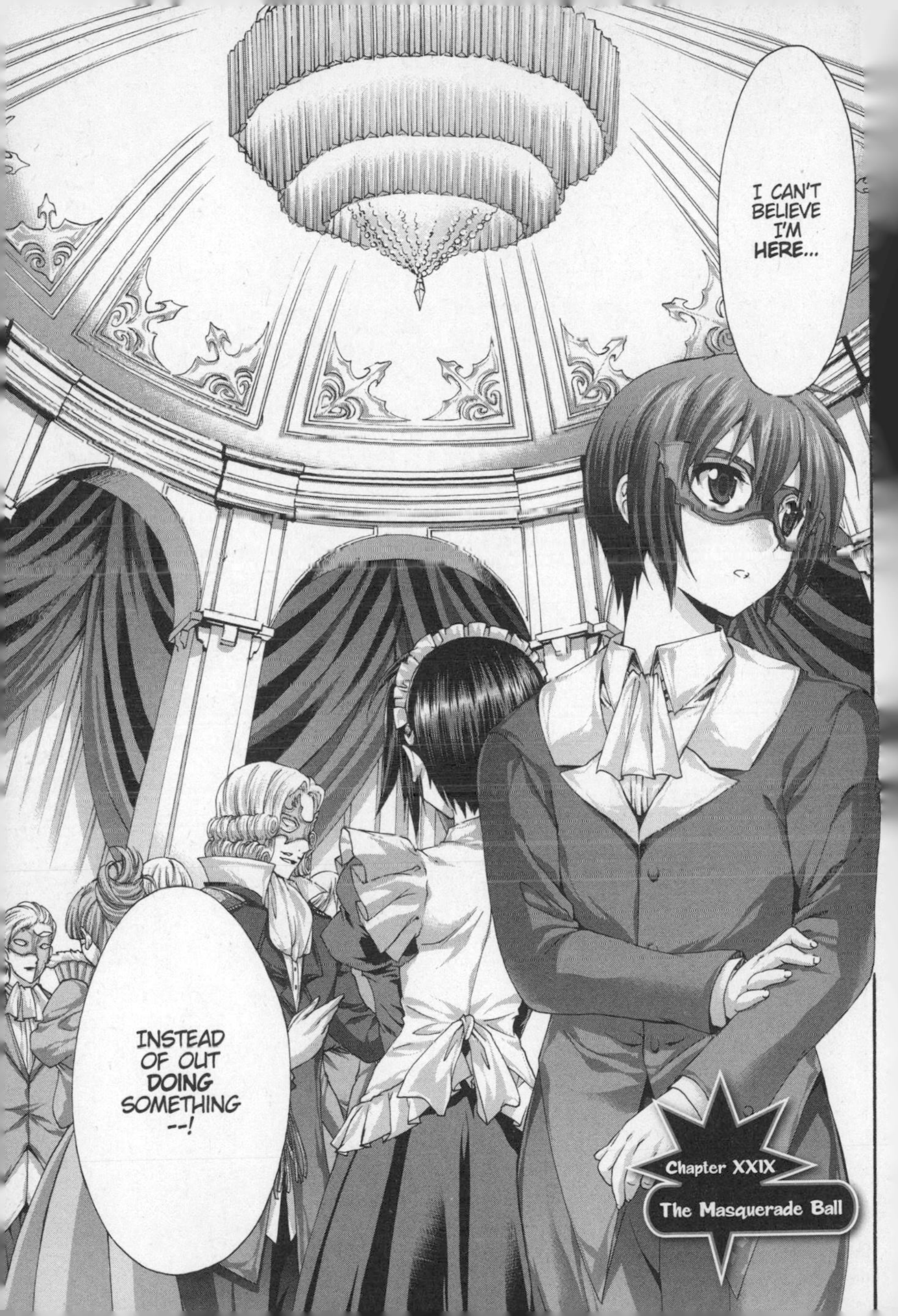
I CAN'T BELIEVE I'M HERE...
INSTEAD OF OUT DOING SOMETHING --!
Chapter XXIX
The Masquerade Ball

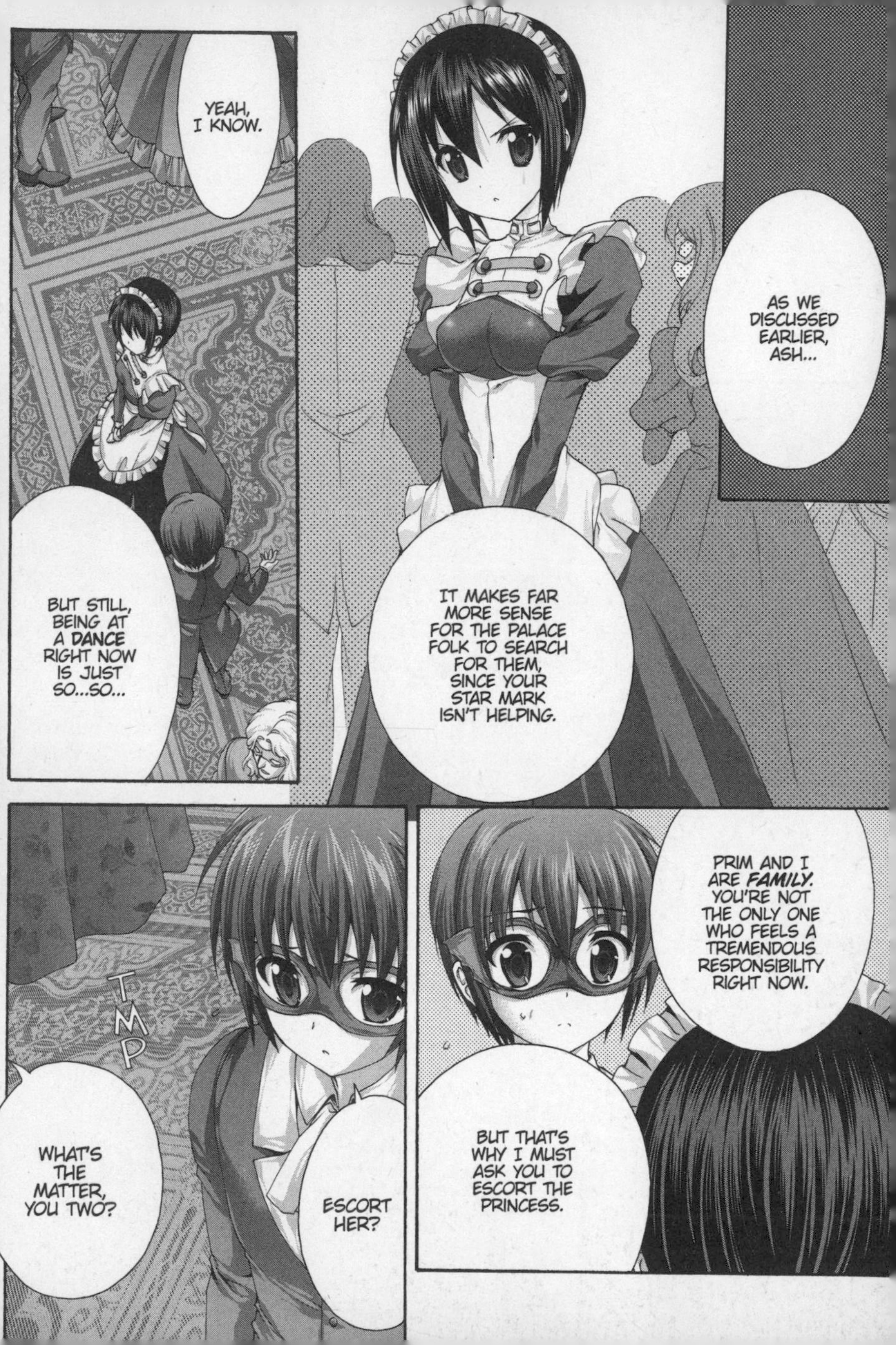
AS WE DISCUSSED EARLIER, ASH...
IT MAKES FAR MORE SENSE FOR THE PALACE FOLK TO SEARCH FOR THEM, SINCE YOUR STAR MARK ISN'T HELPING.
YEAH, I KNOW.
BUT STILL, BEING AT A DANCE RIGHT NOW IS JUST SO...SO...
PRIM AND I ARE FAMILY. YOU'RE NOT THE ONLY ONE WHO FEELS A TREMENDOUS RESPONSIBILITY RIGHT NOW.
BUT THAT'S WHY I MUST ASK YOU TO ESCORT THE PRINCESS.
ESCORT HER?
TMP
WHAT'S THE MATTER, YOU TWO?

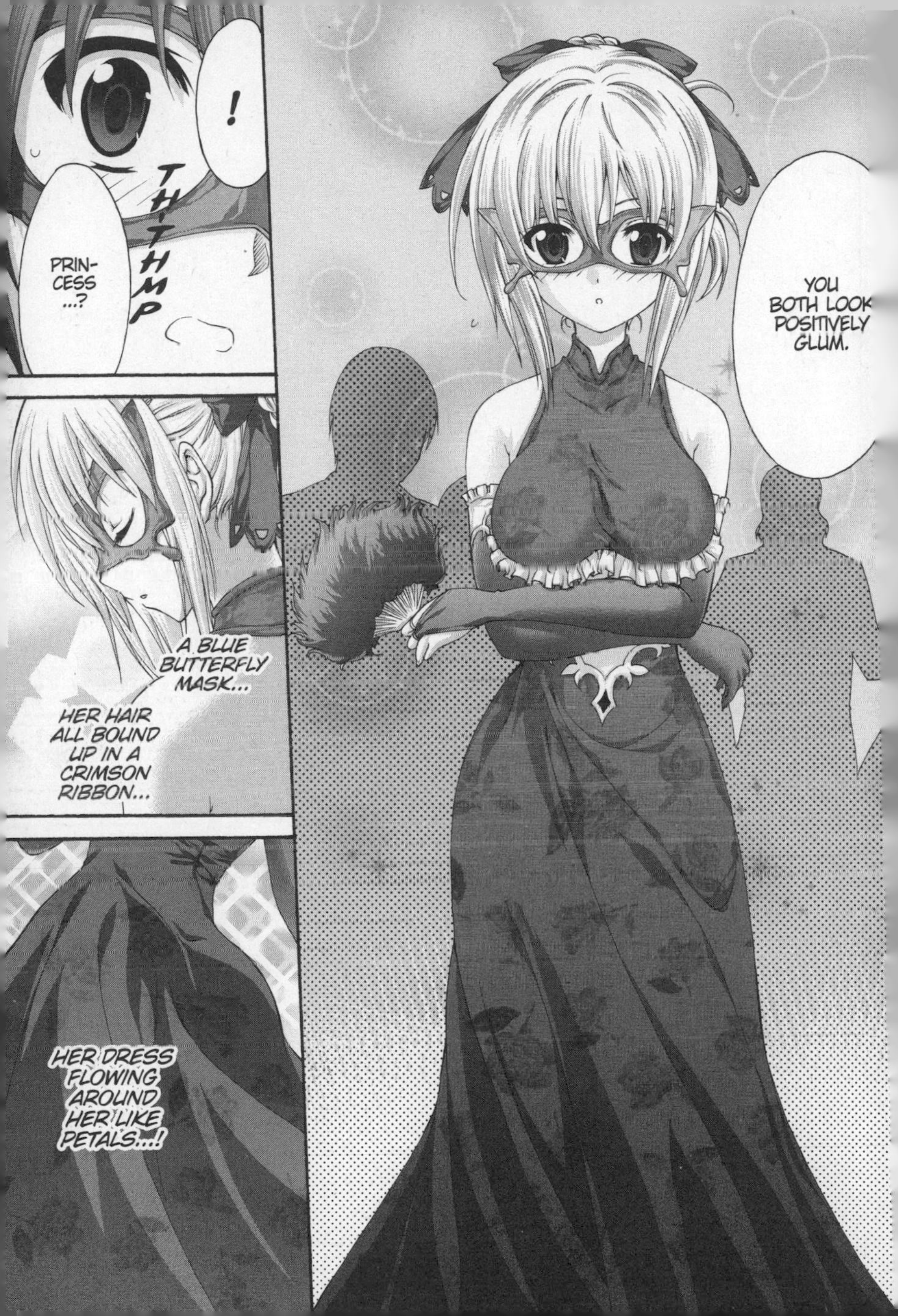

YOU BOTH LOOK POSITIVELY GLUM.
!
THTHMP
PRIN-CESS ...?
A BLUE BUTTERFLY MASK...
HER HAIR ALL BOUND UP IN A CRIMSON RIBBON...
HER DRESS FLOWING AROUND HER LIKE PETALS...!

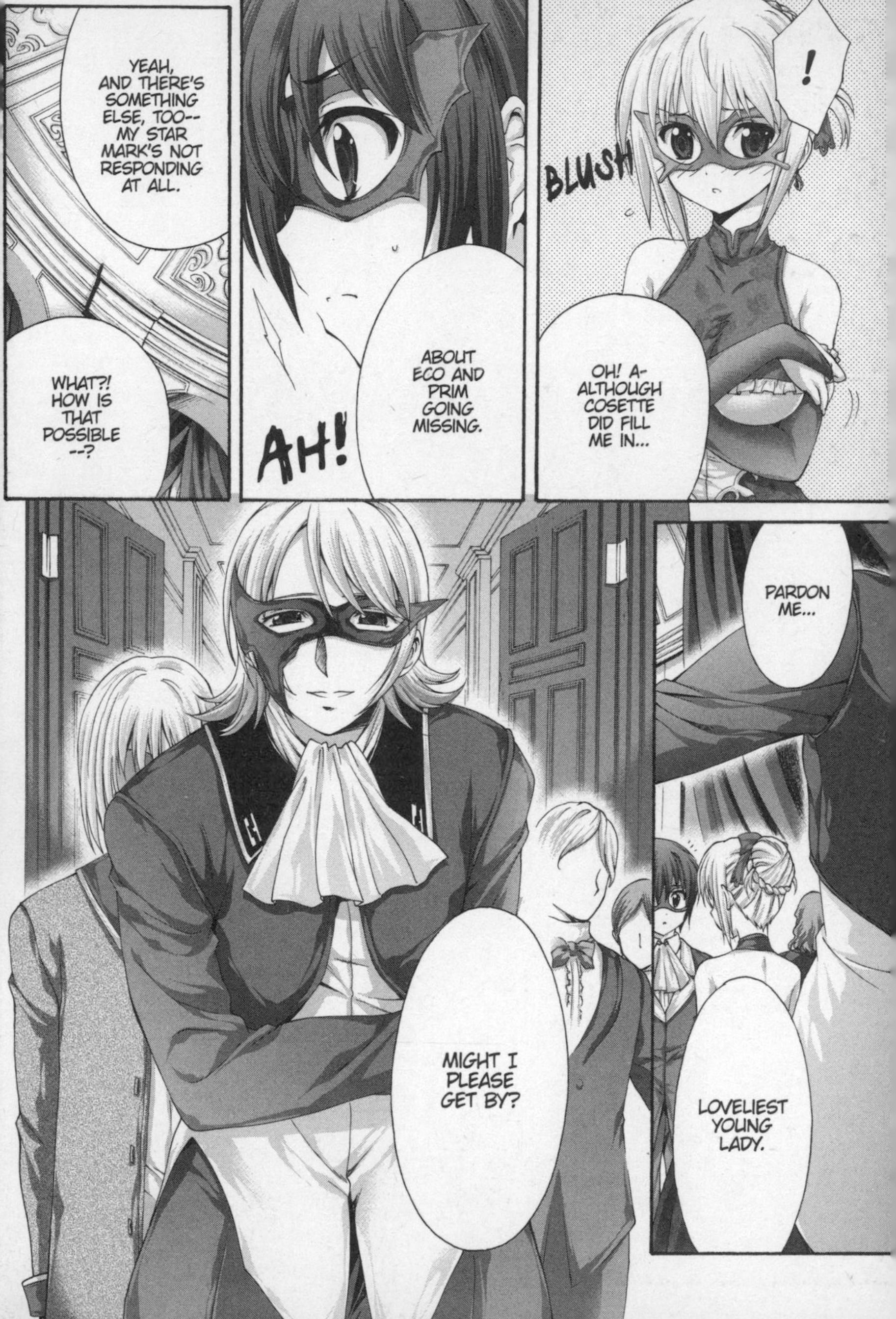
!
BLUSH
OH! A-ALTHOUGH COSETTE DID FILL ME IN...
ABOUT ECO AND PRIM GOING MISSING.
AH!
YEAH, AND THERE'S SOMETHING ELSE, TOO-- MY STAR MARK'S NOT RESPONDING AT ALL.
WHAT?! HOW IS THAT POSSIBLE --?
PARDON ME...
LOVELIEST YOUNG LADY.
MIGHT I PLEASE GET BY?

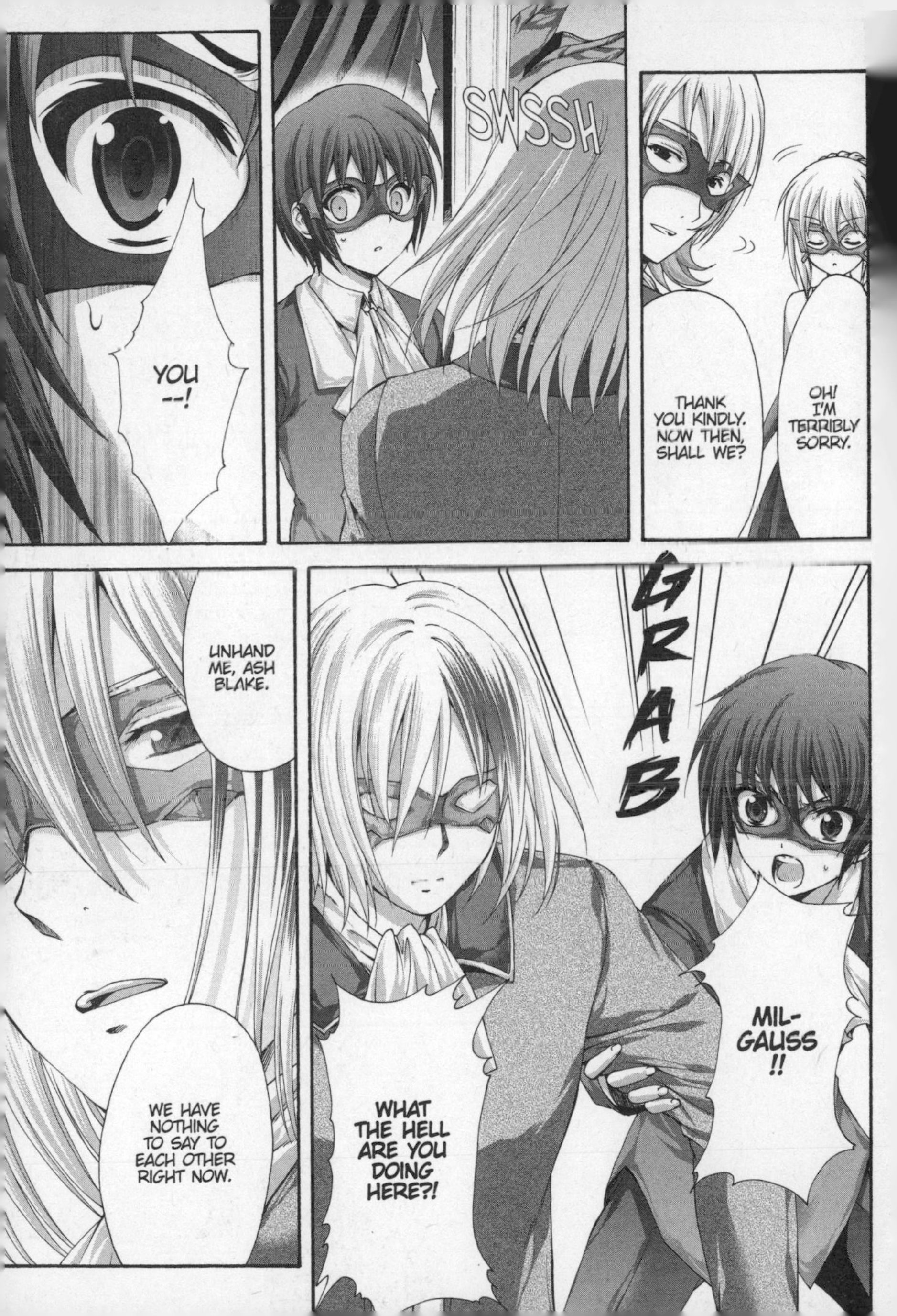
OH! I'M TERRIBLY SORRY.
THANK YOU KINDLY. NOW THEN, SHALL WE?
SWSSH
YOU --!
GRAB
MIL-GAUSS !!
WHAT THE HELL ARE YOU DOING HERE?!
UNHAND ME, ASH BLAKE.
WE HAVE NOTHING TO SAY TO EACH OTHER RIGHT NOW.

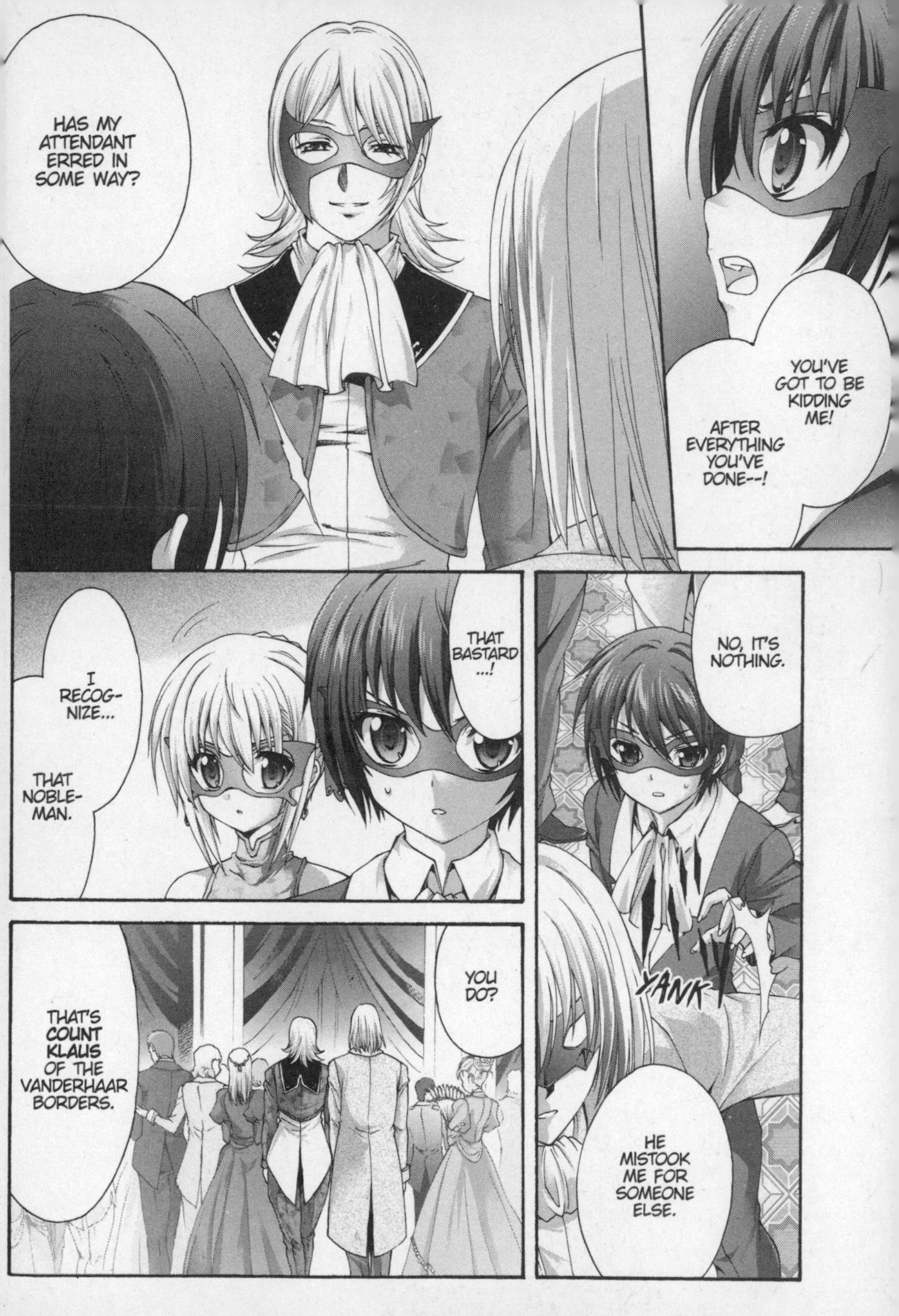
YOU'VE GOT TO BE KIDDING ME!
AFTER EVERYTHING YOU'VE DONE--!
HAS MY ATTENDANT ERRED IN SOME WAY?
NO, IT'S NOTHING.
YANK
HE MISTOOK ME FOR SOMEONE ELSE.
THAT BASTARD ...!
I RECOG-NIZE...
THAT NOBLE-MAN.
YOU DO?
THAT'S COUNT KLAUS OF THE VANDERHAAR BORDERS.

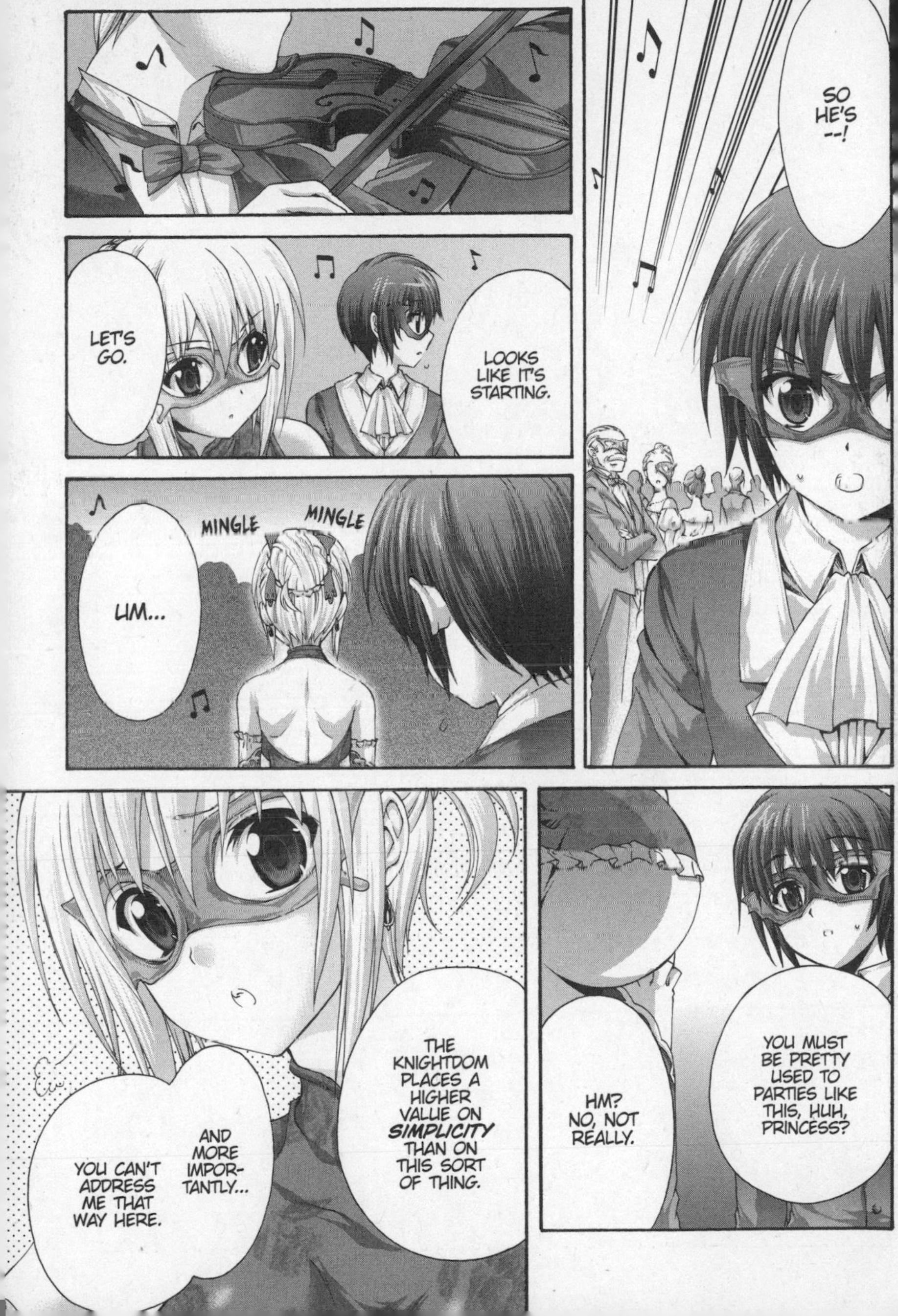
SO HE'S --!
LOOKS LIKE IT'S STARTING.
LET'S GO.
MINGLE
MINGLE
UM...
YOU MUST BE PRETTY USED TO PARTIES LIKE THIS, HUH, PRINCESS?
HM? NO, NOT REALLY.
THE KNIGHTDOM PLACES A HIGHER VALUE ON SIMPLICITY THAN ON THIS SORT OF THING.
AND MORE IMPORTANTLY...
YOU CAN'T ADDRESS ME THAT WAY HERE.

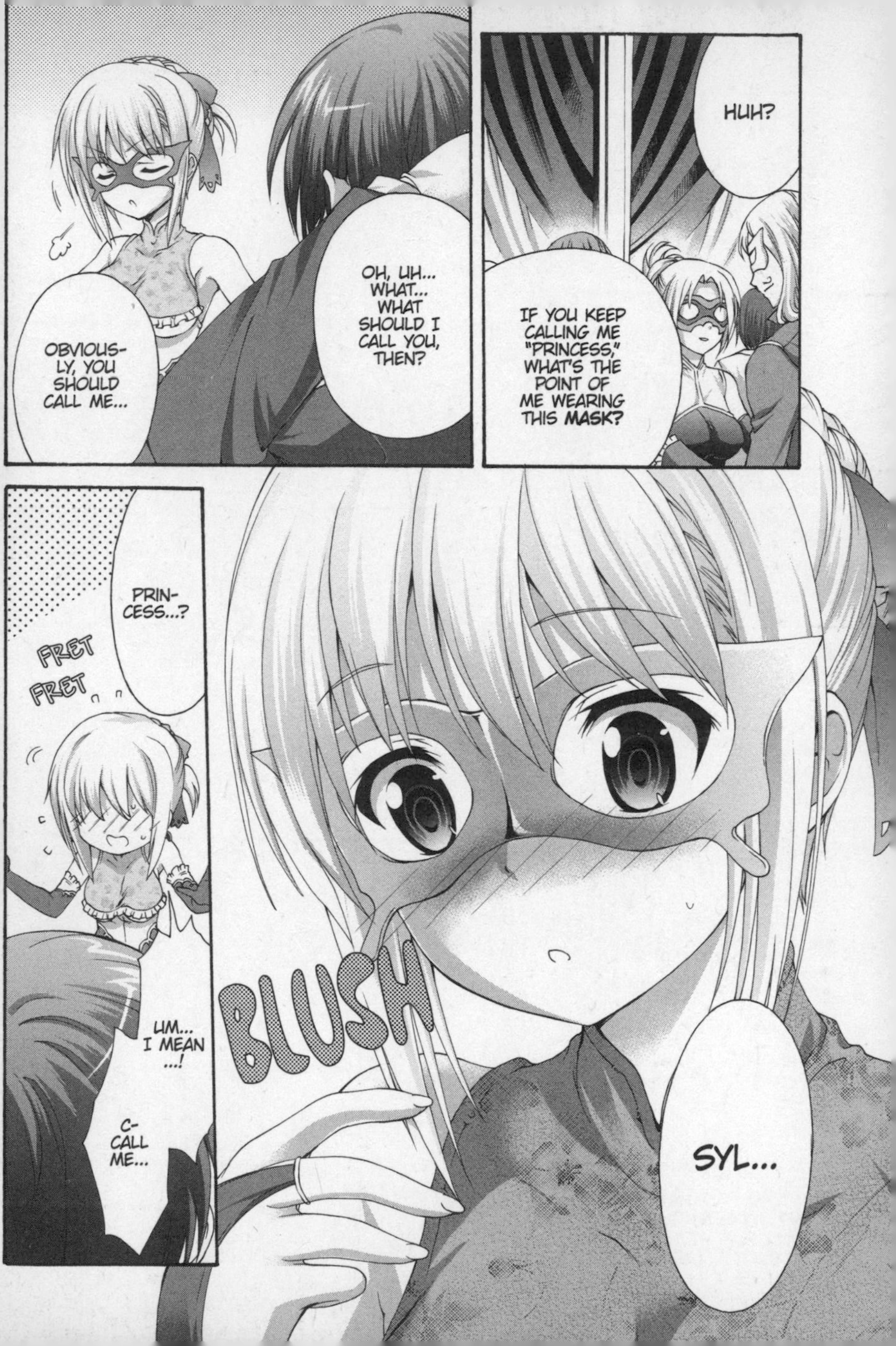
HUH?
IF YOU KEEP CALLING ME "PRINCESS," WHAT'S THE POINT OF ME WEARING THIS MASK?
OH, UH... WHAT... WHAT SHOULD I CALL YOU, THEN?
OBVIOUS-LY, YOU SHOULD CALL ME...
BLUSH
SYL...
PRIN-CESS...?
FRET FRET
UM... I MEAN ...!
C-CALL ME...

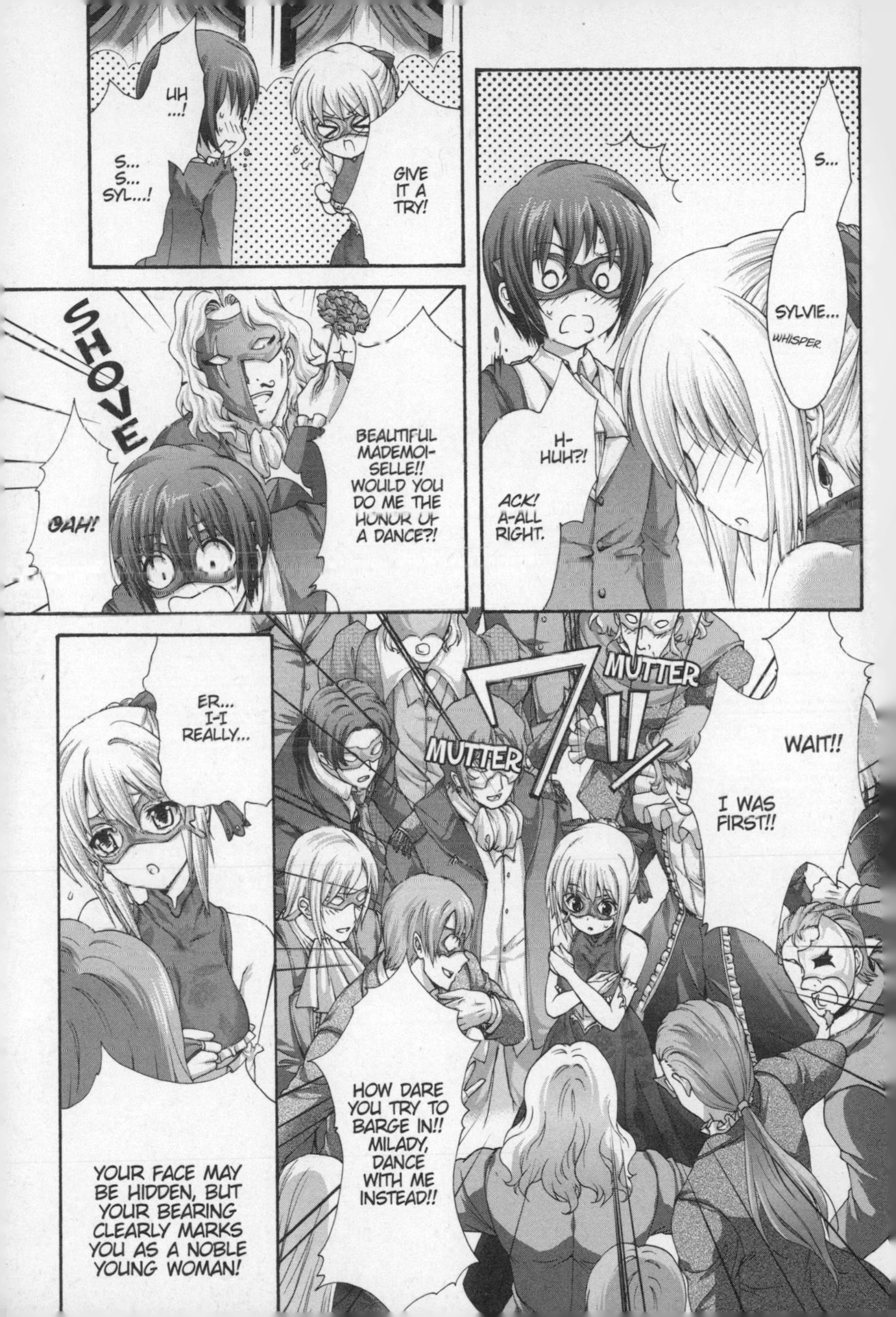
S...
SYLVIE...
WHISPER
H-HUH?!
ACK! A-ALL RIGHT.
UH ...!
S... S... SYL...!
GIVE IT A TRY!
SHOVE
BEAUTIFUL MADEMOISELLE!! WOULD YOU DO ME THE HONOR OF A DANCE?!
OAH!
WAIT!!
I WAS FIRST!!
MUTTER
MUTTER
HOW DARE YOU TRY TO BARGE IN!! MILADY, DANCE WITH ME INSTEAD!!
ER... I-I REALLY...
YOUR FACE MAY BE HIDDEN, BUT YOUR BEARING CLEARLY MARKS YOU AS A NOBLE YOUNG WOMAN!

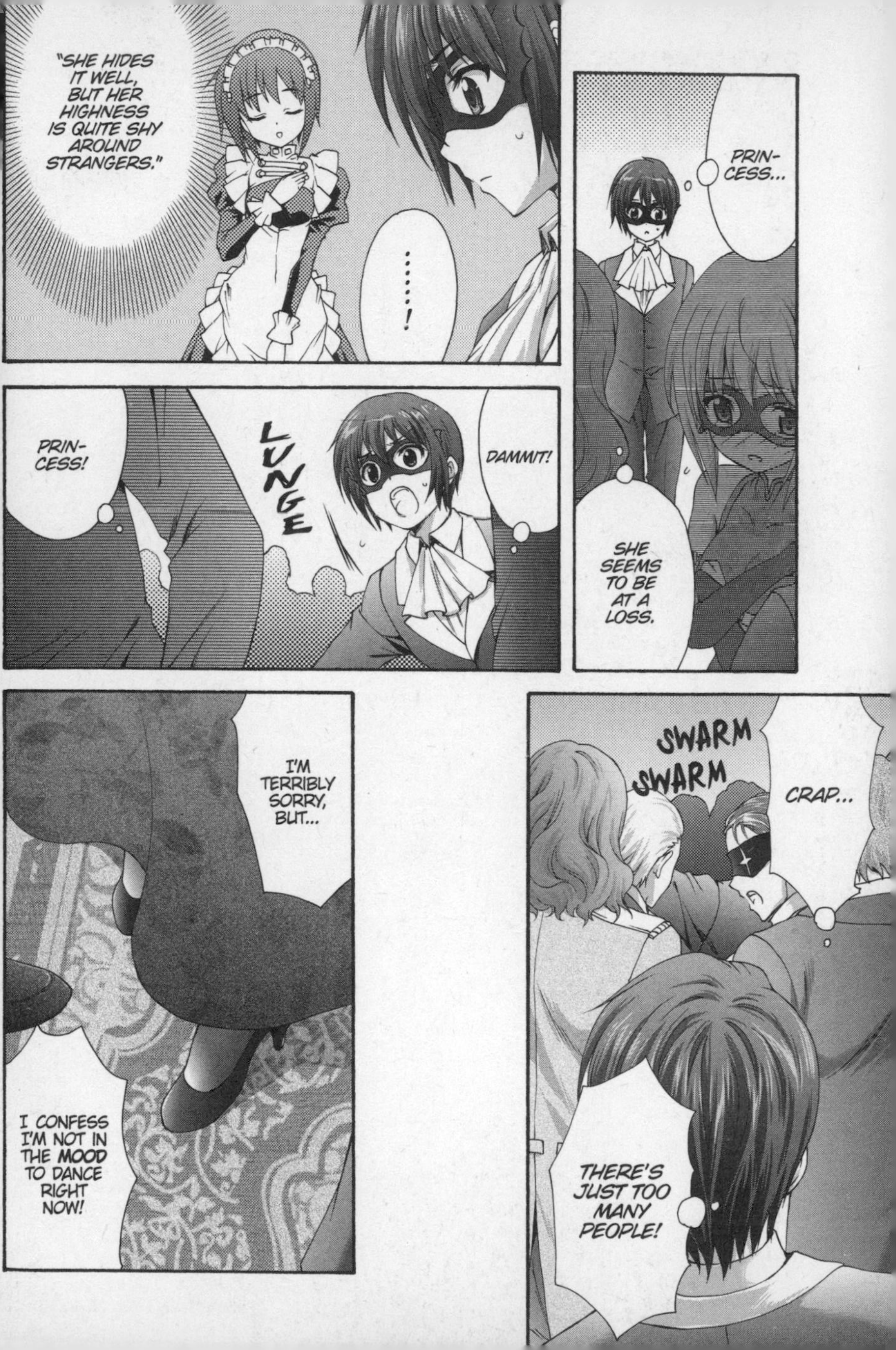
PRIN-CESS...
SHE SEEMS TO BE AT A LOSS.
.....!
"SHE HIDES IT WELL, BUT HER HIGHNESS IS QUITE SHY AROUND STRANGERS."
DAMMIT!
LUNGE
PRIN-CESS!
CRAP...
SWARM SWARM
THERE'S JUST TOO MANY PEOPLE!
I'M TERRIBLY SORRY, BUT...
I CONFESS I'M NOT IN THE MOOD TO DANCE RIGHT NOW!

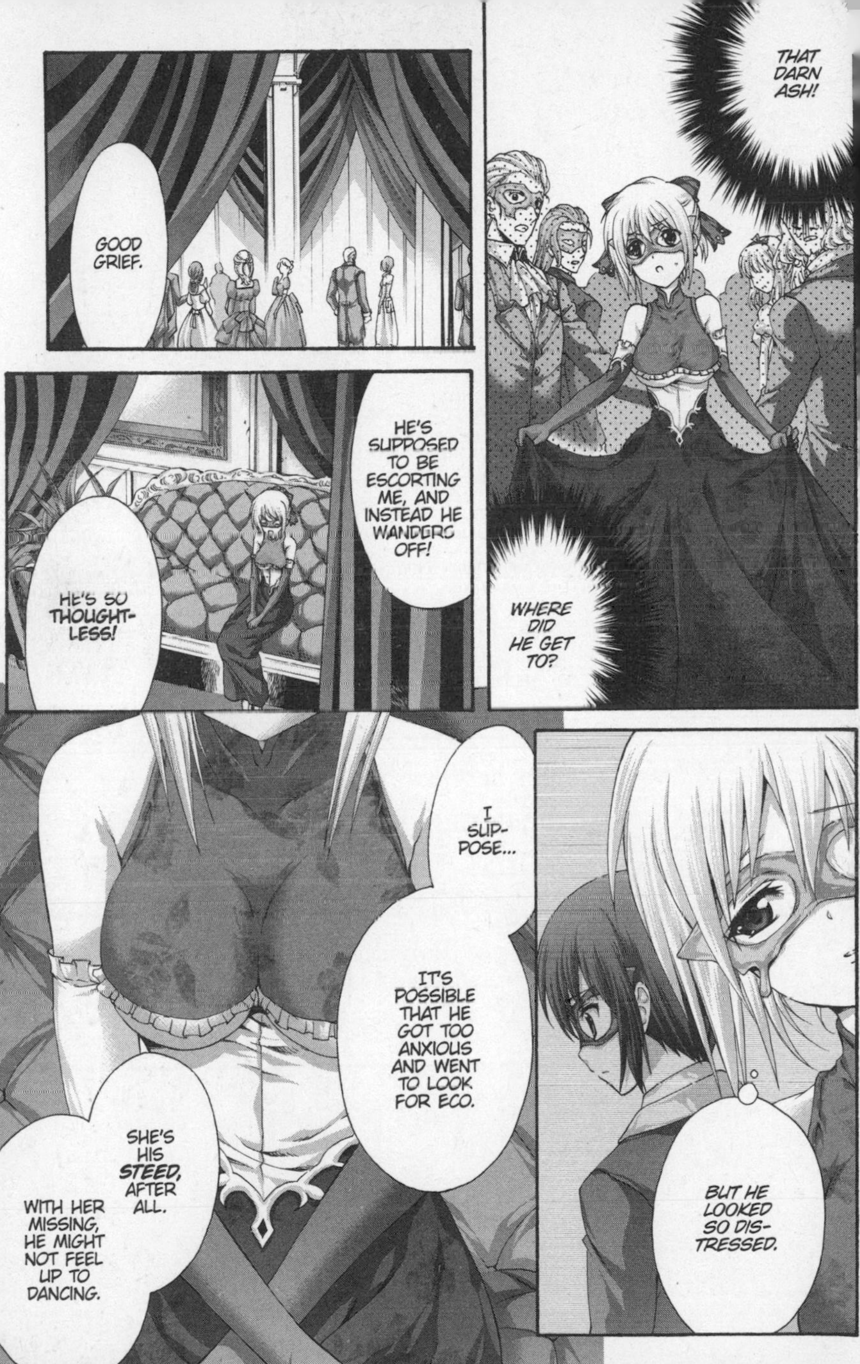
THAT DARN ASH!
WHERE DID HE GET TO?
GOOD GRIEF.
HE'S SUPPOSED TO BE ESCORTING ME, AND INSTEAD HE WANDERS OFF!
HE'S SO THOUGHTLESS!
BUT HE LOOKED SO DISTRESSED.
I SUPPOSE...
IT'S POSSIBLE THAT HE GOT TOO ANXIOUS AND WENT TO LOOK FOR ECO.
SHE'S HIS STEED, AFTER ALL.
WITH HER MISSING, HE MIGHT NOT FEEL UP TO DANCING.

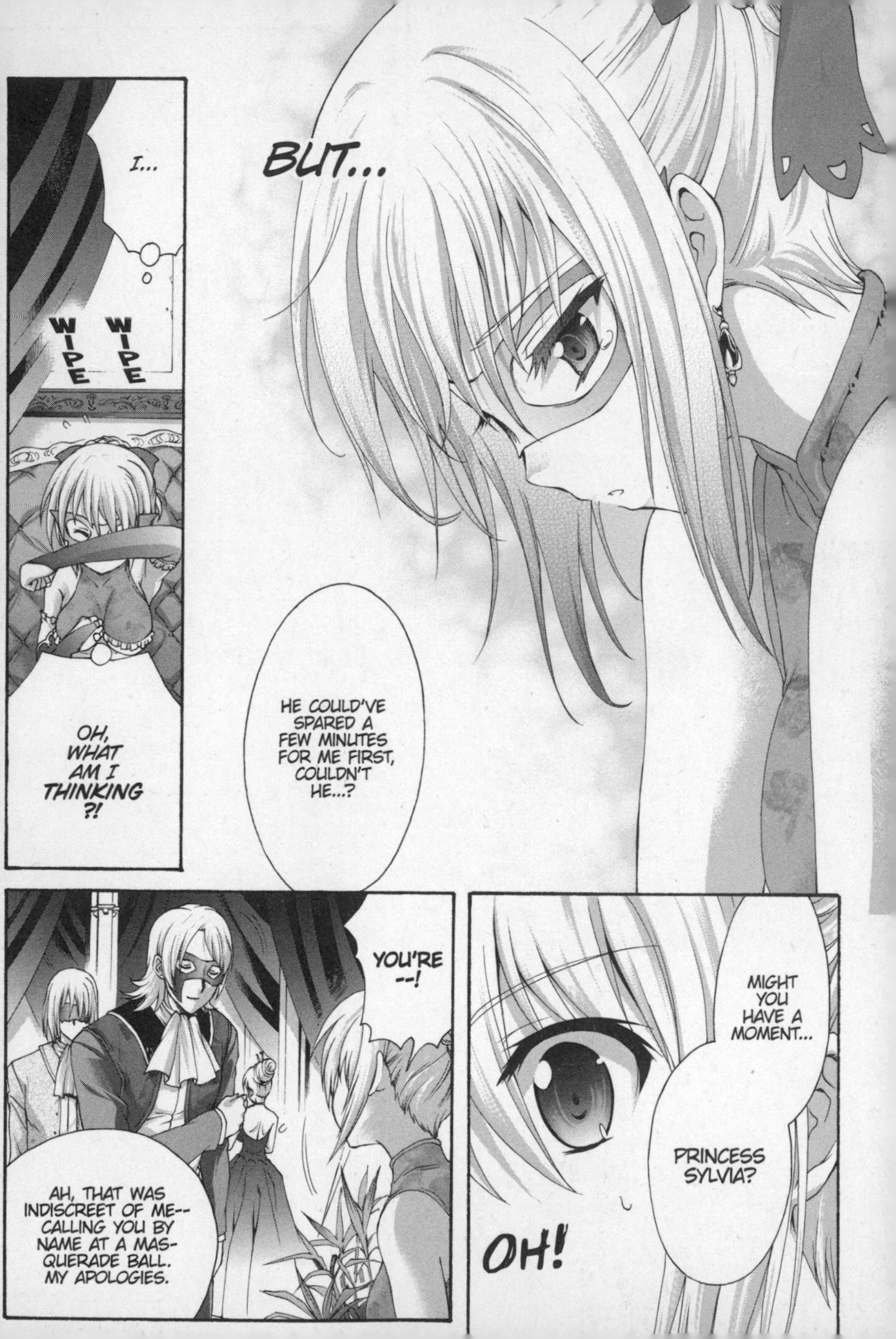
BUT...
HE COULD'VE SPARED A FEW MINUTES FOR ME FIRST, COULDN'T HE...?
I...
WIPE WIPE
OH, WHAT AM I THINKING ?!
MIGHT YOU HAVE A MOMENT...
PRINCESS SYLVIA?
OH!
YOU'RE --!
AH, THAT WAS INDISCREET OF ME-- CALLING YOU BY NAME AT A MASQUERADE BALL. MY APOLOGIES.

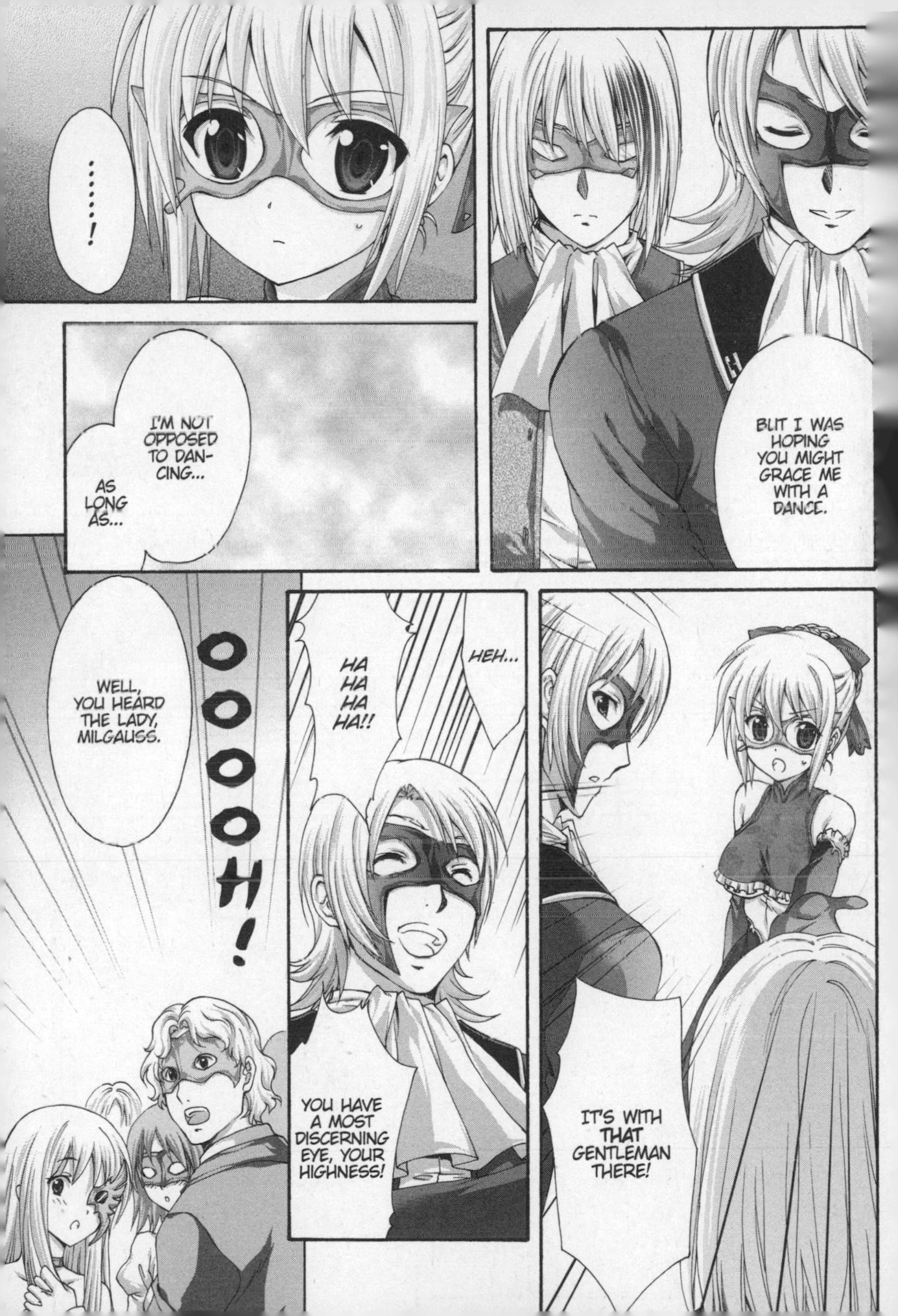
BUT I WAS HOPING YOU MIGHT GRACE ME WITH A DANCE.
......!
I'M NOT OPPOSED TO DANCING...
AS LONG AS...
IT'S WITH THAT GENTLEMAN THERE!
HEH...
HA HA HA HA!!
YOU HAVE A MOST DISCERNING EYE, YOUR HIGHNESS!
WELL, YOU HEARD THE LADY, MILGAUSS.
OOOOOH!

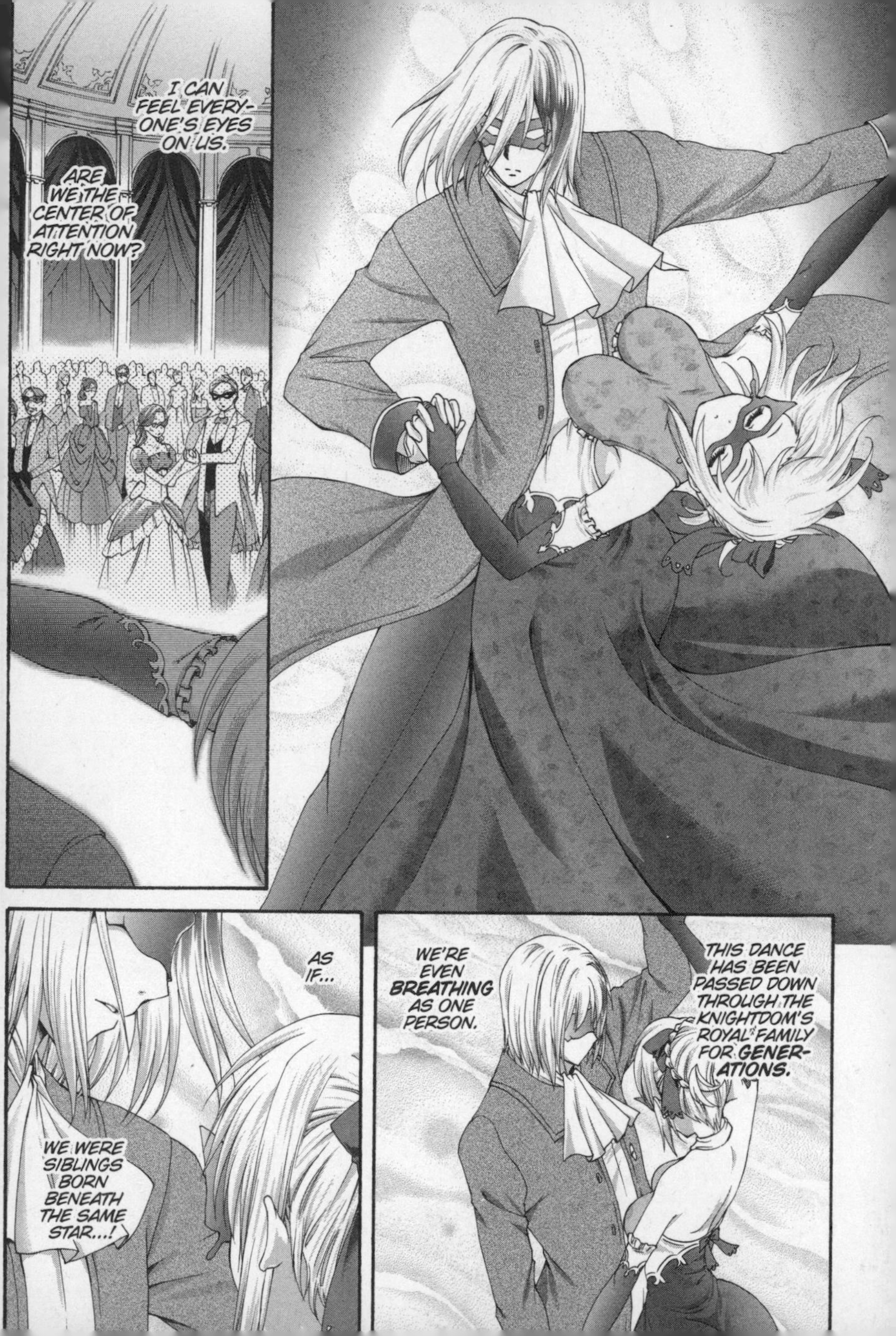
I CAN FEEL EVERY-ONE'S EYES ON US.
ARE WE THE CENTER OF ATTENTION RIGHT NOW?
THIS DANCE HAS BEEN PASSED DOWN THROUGH THE KNIGHTDOM'S ROYAL FAMILY FOR **GENER-ATIONS.**
WE'RE EVEN **BREATHING** AS ONE PERSON.
AS IF...
WE WERE SIBLINGS BORN BENEATH THE SAME STAR...!

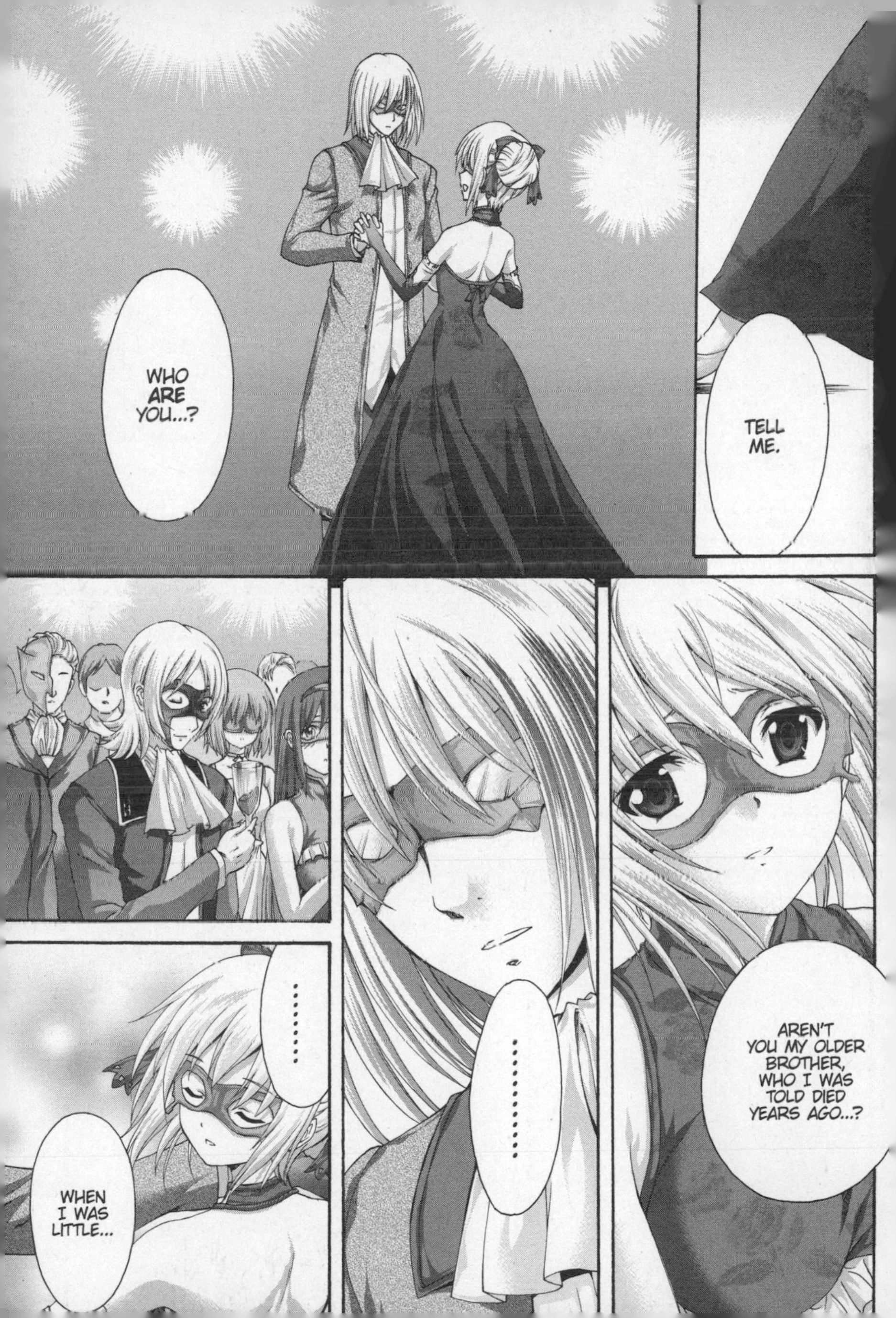
TELL ME.
WHO ARE YOU...?
AREN'T YOU MY OLDER BROTHER, WHO I WAS TOLD DIED YEARS AGO...?
......
......
WHEN I WAS LITTLE...

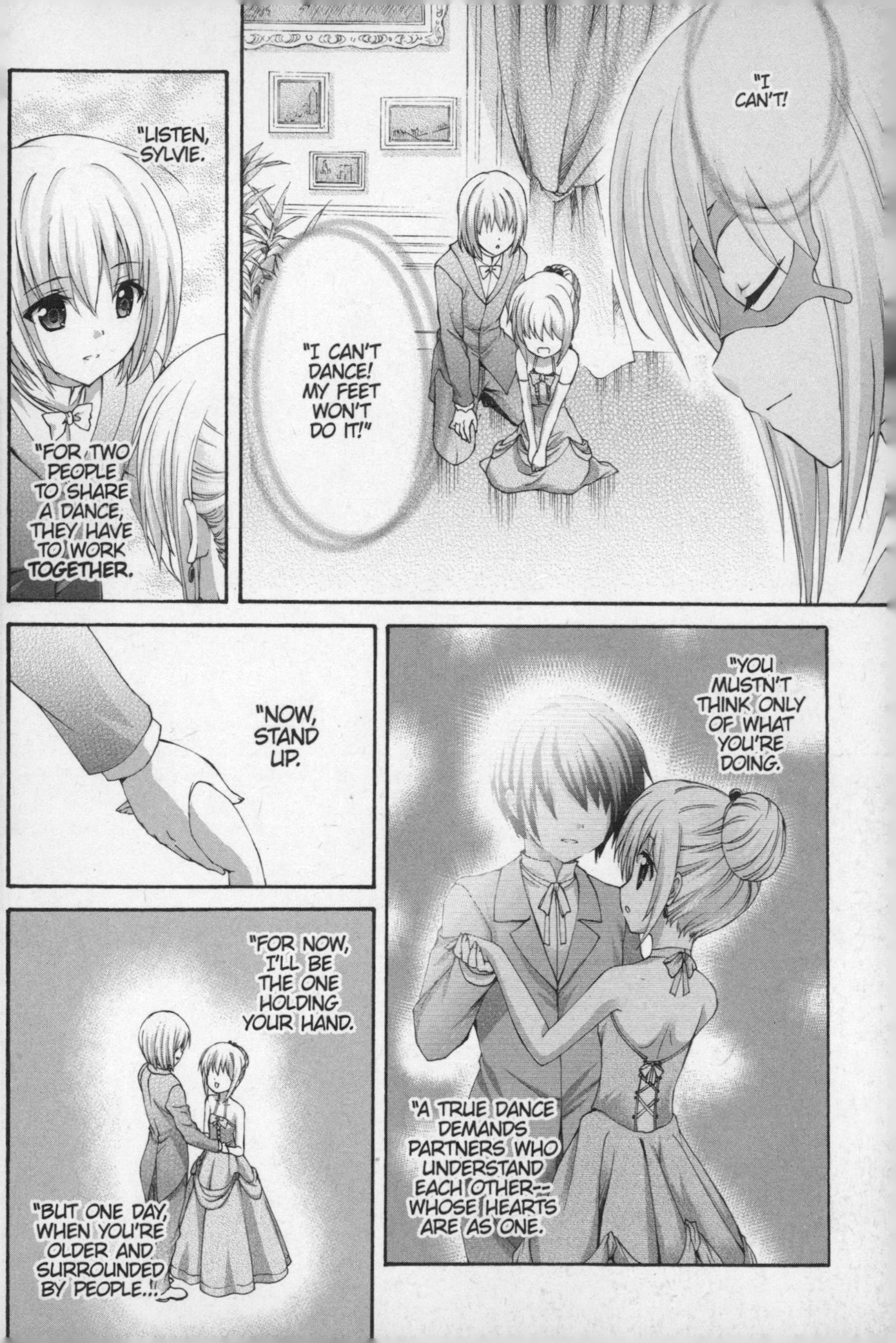
"I CAN'T!
"I CAN'T DANCE! MY FEET WON'T DO IT!"
"LISTEN, SYLVIE.
"FOR TWO PEOPLE TO SHARE A DANCE, THEY HAVE TO WORK TOGETHER.
"YOU MUSTN'T THINK ONLY OF WHAT YOU'RE DOING.
"A TRUE DANCE DEMANDS PARTNERS WHO UNDERSTAND EACH OTHER-- WHOSE HEARTS ARE AS ONE.
"NOW, STAND UP.
"FOR NOW, I'LL BE THE ONE HOLDING YOUR HAND.
"BUT ONE DAY, WHEN YOU'RE OLDER AND SURROUNDED BY PEOPLE...

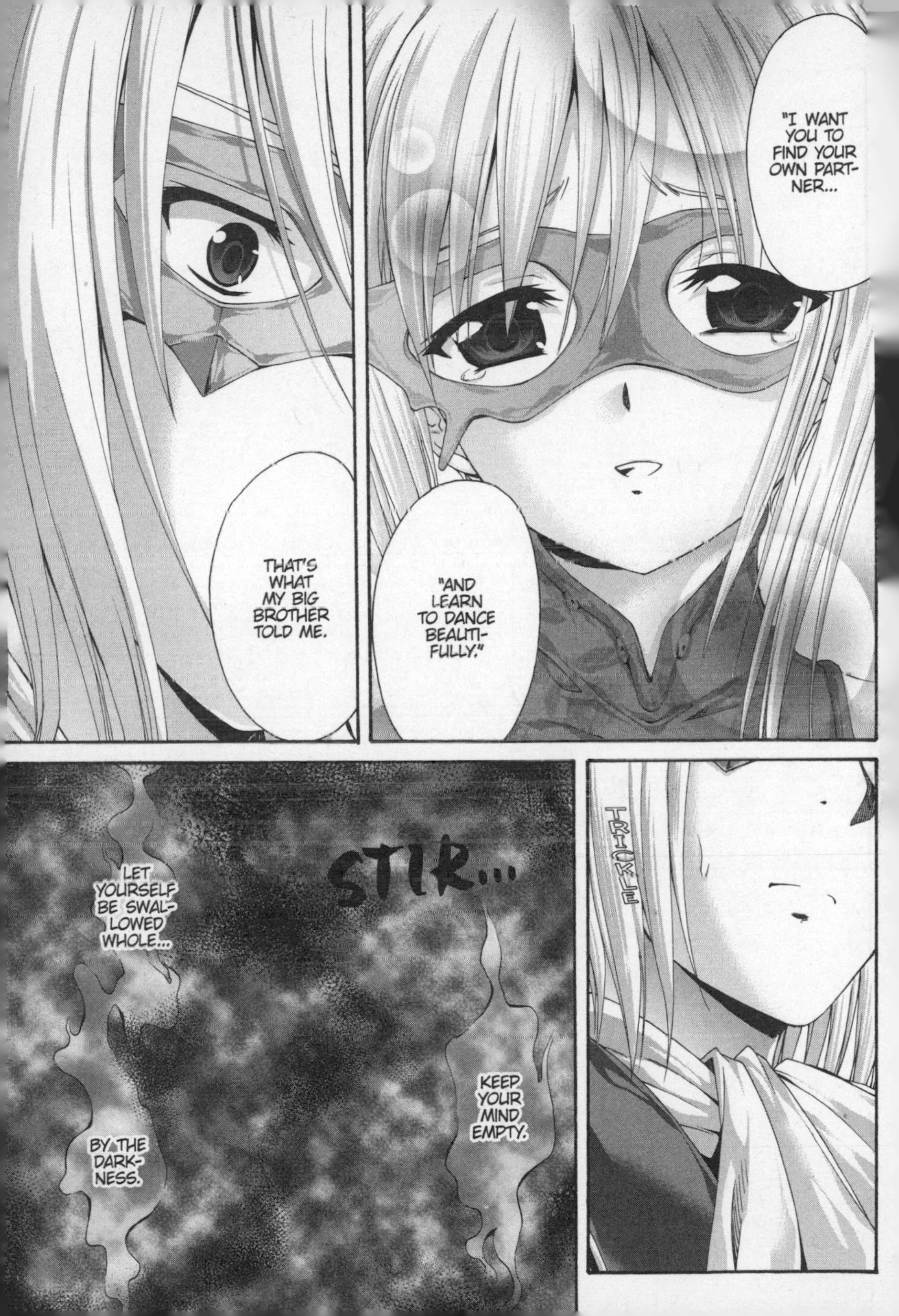
"I WANT YOU TO FIND YOUR OWN PARTNER...
"AND LEARN TO DANCE BEAUTIFULLY."
THAT'S WHAT MY BIG BROTHER TOLD ME.
TRICKLE
STIR...
LET YOURSELF BE SWALLOWED WHOLE...
KEEP YOUR MIND EMPTY.
BY THE DARKNESS.

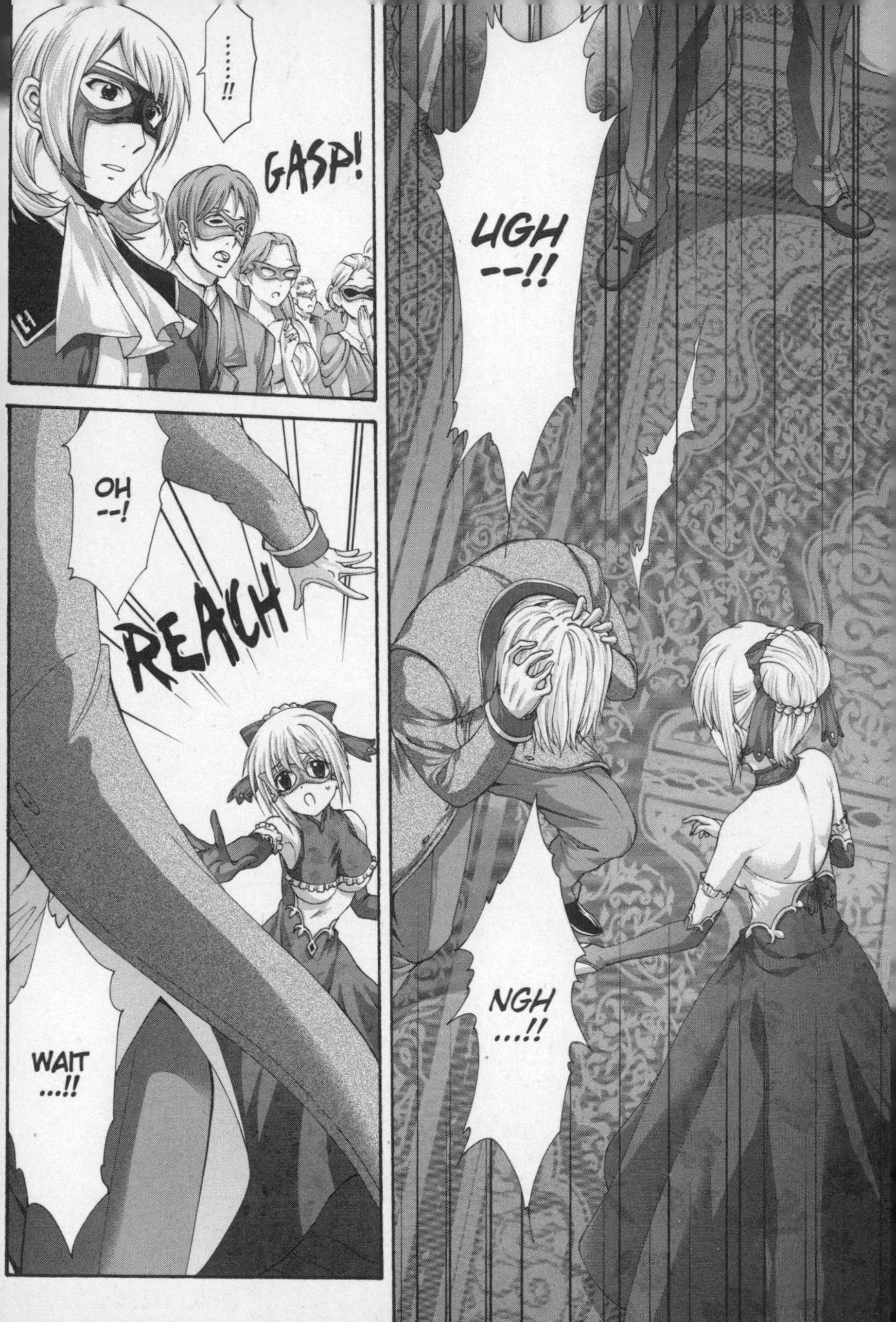
UGH --!!
NGH ...!!
......!!
GASP!
OH --!
REACH
WAIT ...!!

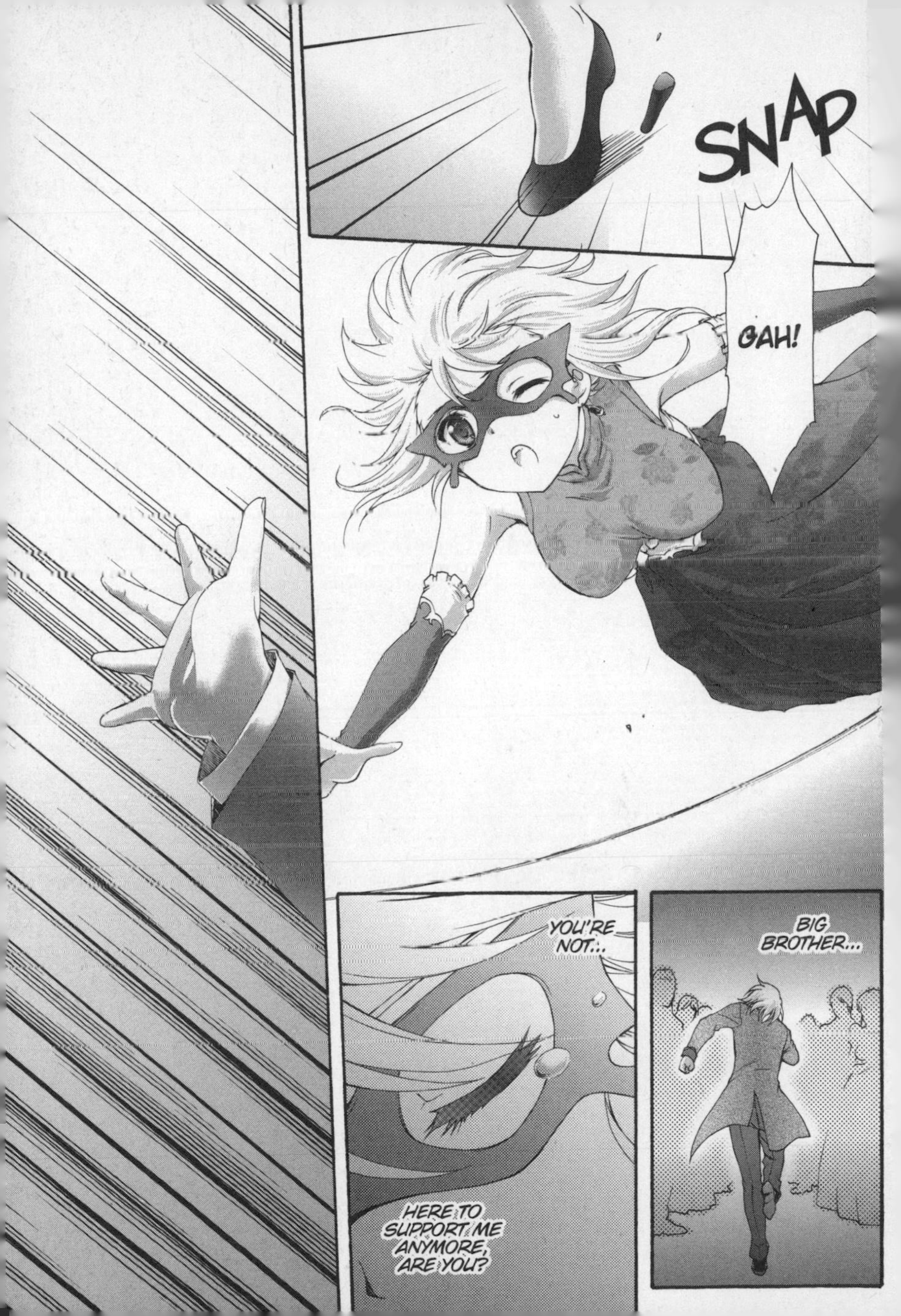
SNAP
GAH!
BIG BROTHER...
YOU'RE NOT...
HERE TO SUPPORT ME ANYMORE, ARE YOU?

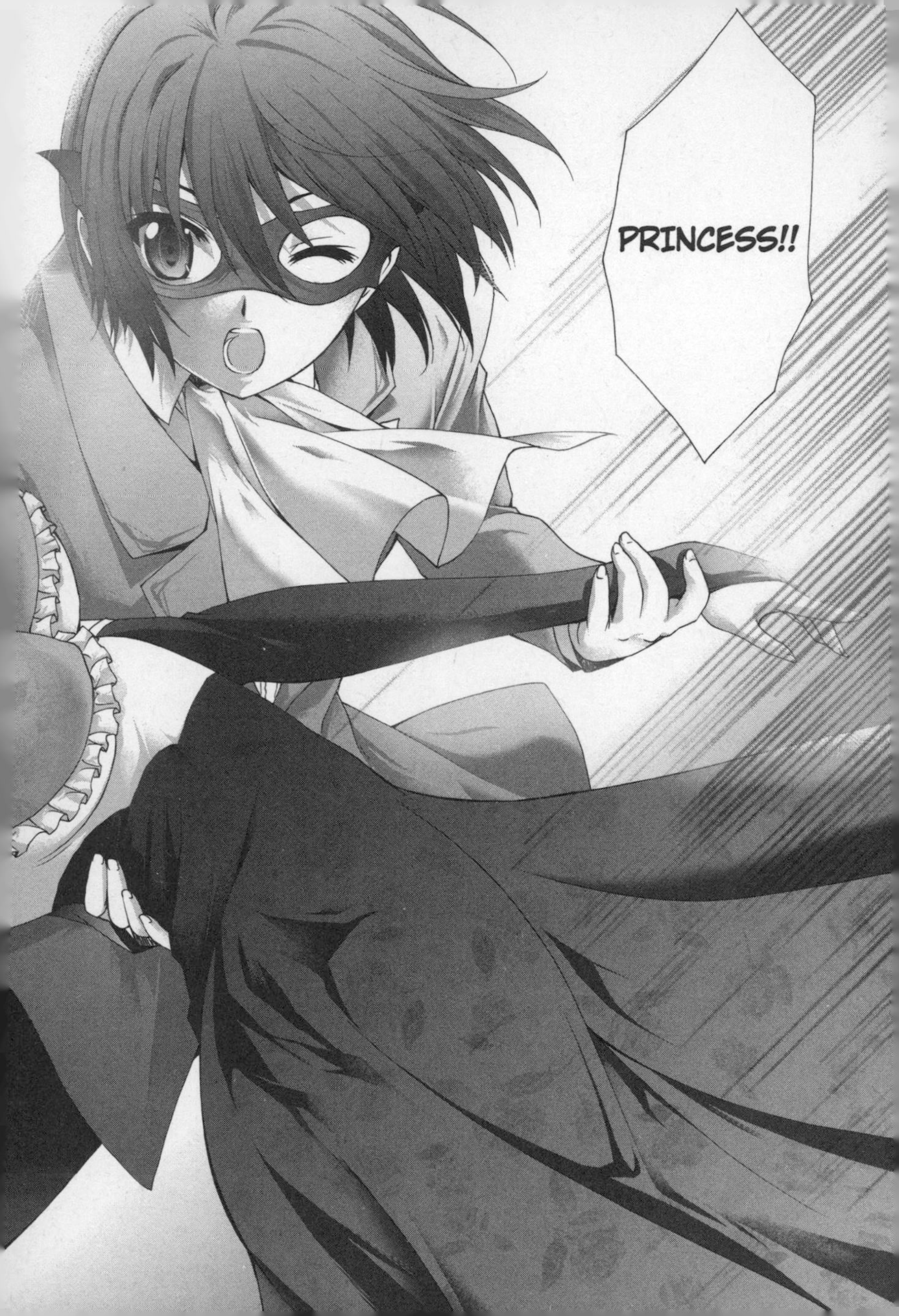
PRINCESS!!

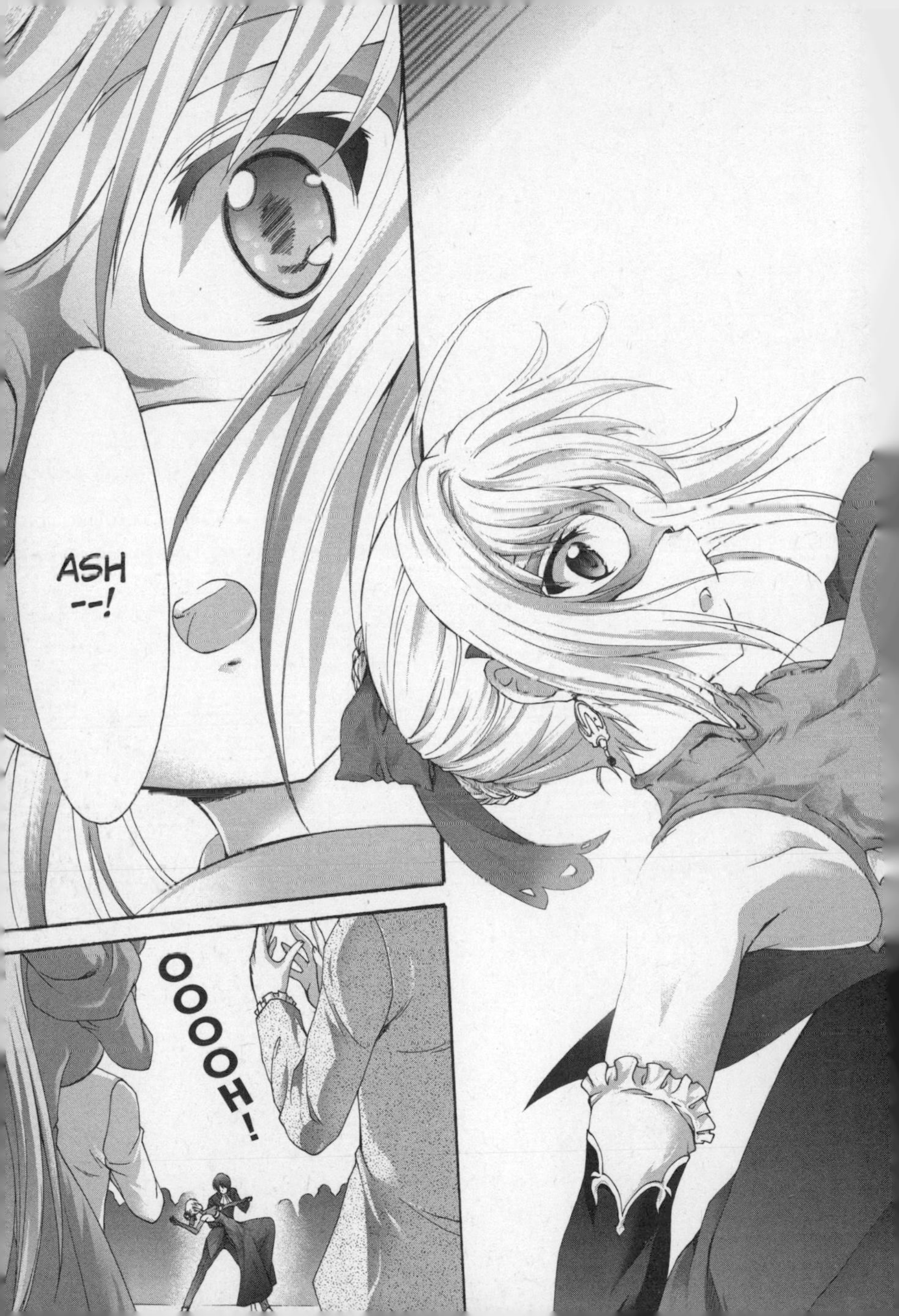
ASH --!
OOOOH!

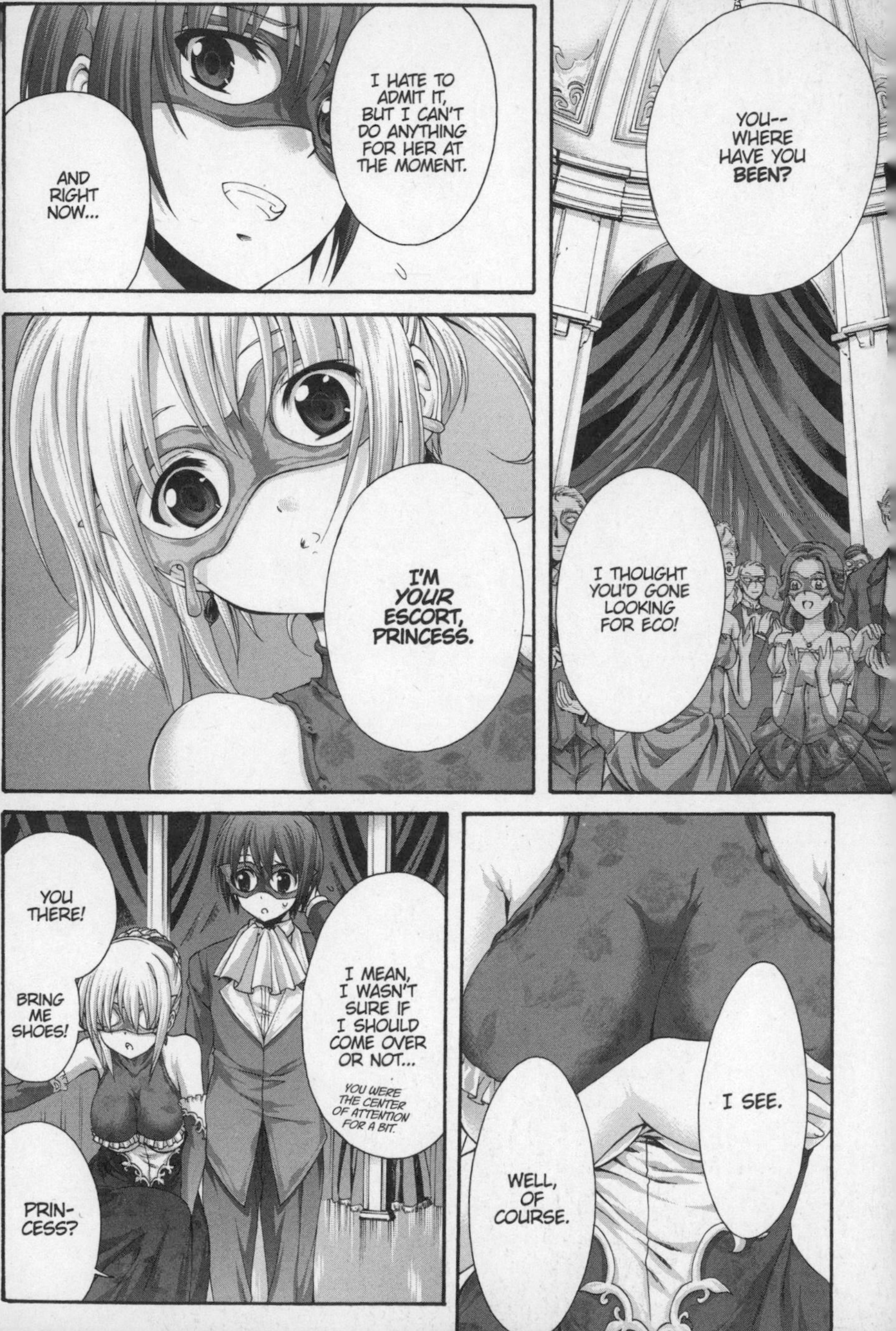
YOU-- WHERE HAVE YOU BEEN?
I THOUGHT YOU'D GONE LOOKING FOR ECO!
I HATE TO ADMIT IT, BUT I CAN'T DO ANYTHING FOR HER AT THE MOMENT.
AND RIGHT NOW...
I'M *YOUR* ESCORT, PRINCESS.
I SEE.
WELL, OF COURSE.
I MEAN, I WASN'T SURE IF I SHOULD COME OVER OR NOT...
YOU WERE THE CENTER OF ATTENTION FOR A BIT.
YOU THERE!
BRING ME SHOES!
PRIN-CESS?

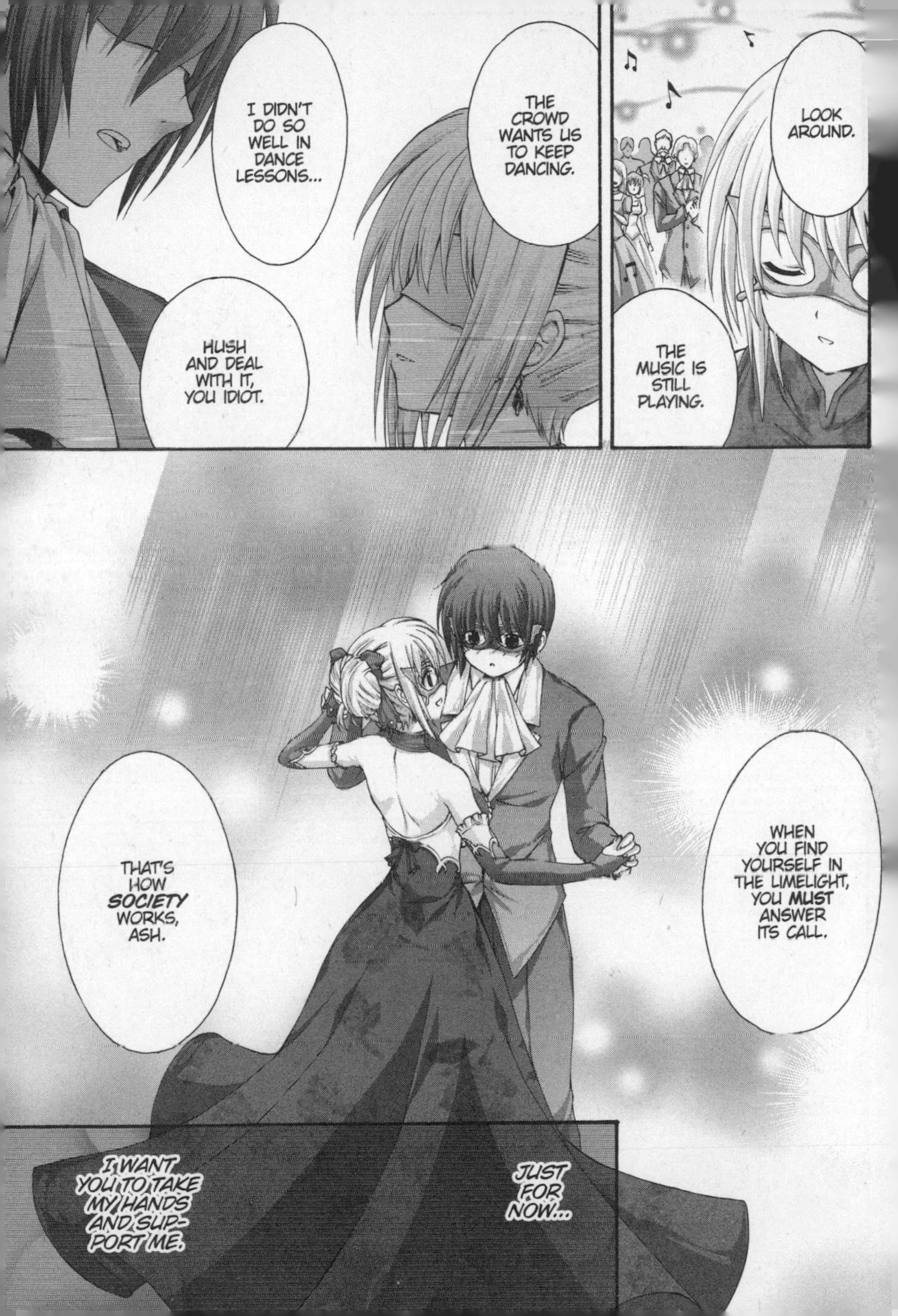
LOOK AROUND.
THE MUSIC IS STILL PLAYING.
THE CROWD WANTS US TO KEEP DANCING.
I DIDN'T DO SO WELL IN DANCE LESSONS...
HUSH AND DEAL WITH IT, YOU IDIOT.
WHEN YOU FIND YOURSELF IN THE LIMELIGHT, YOU MUST ANSWER ITS CALL.
THAT'S HOW SOCIETY WORKS, ASH.
JUST FOR NOW...
I WANT YOU TO TAKE MY HANDS AND SUP-PORT ME.

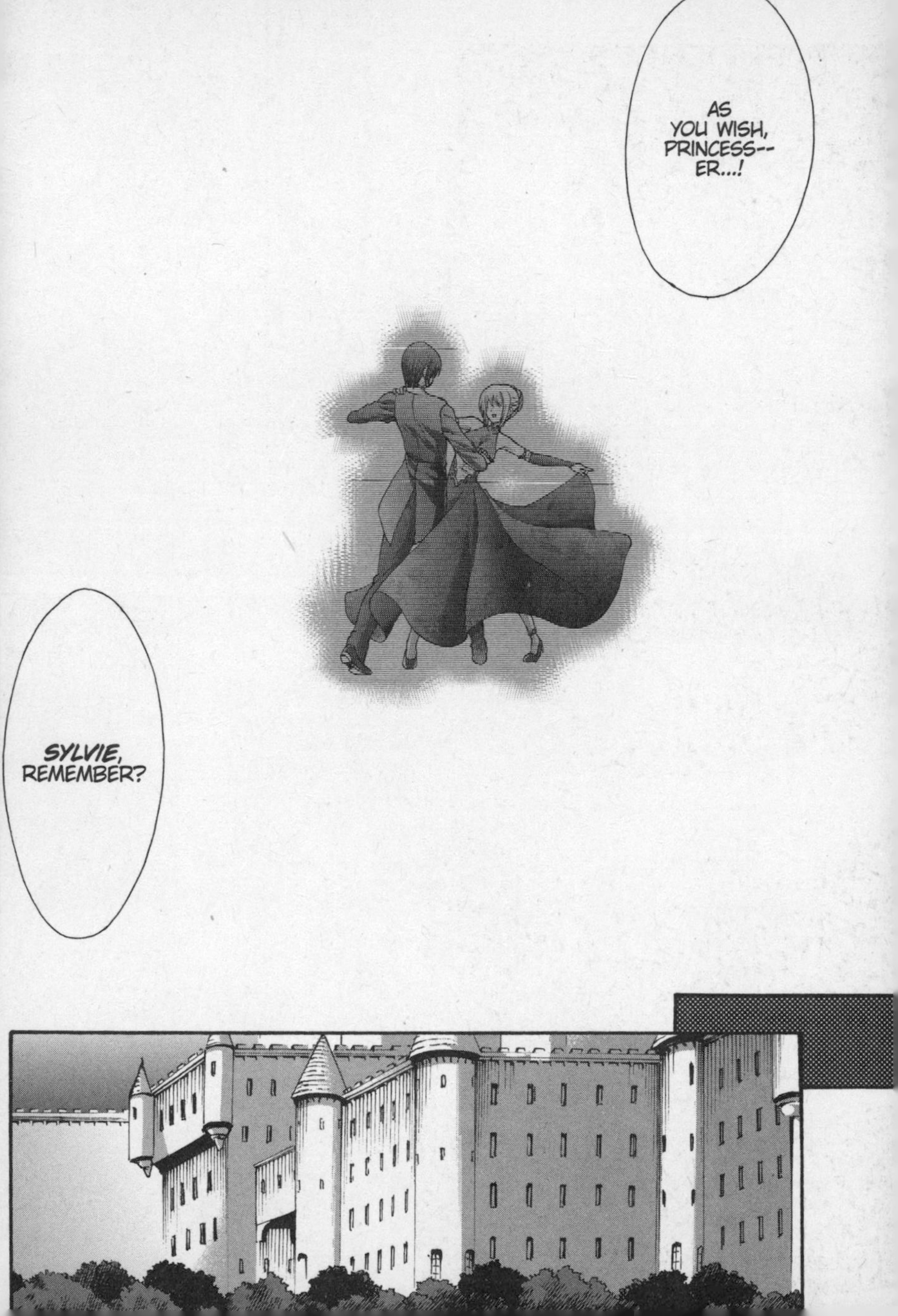
AS YOU WISH, PRINCESS-- ER...!
SYLVIE, REMEMBER?

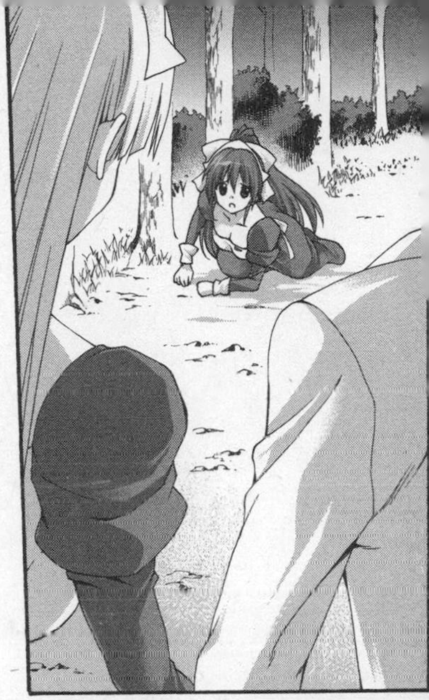

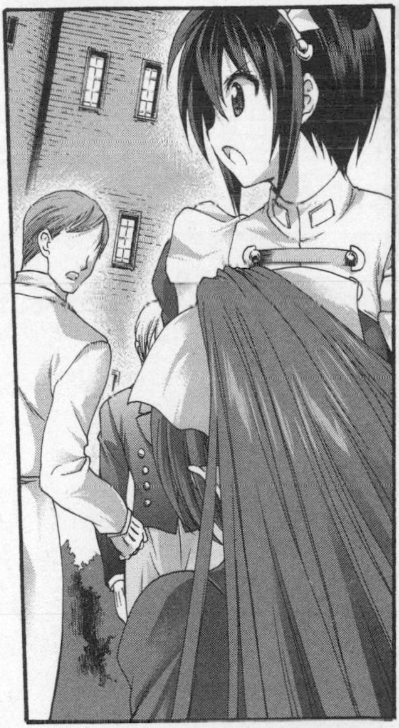

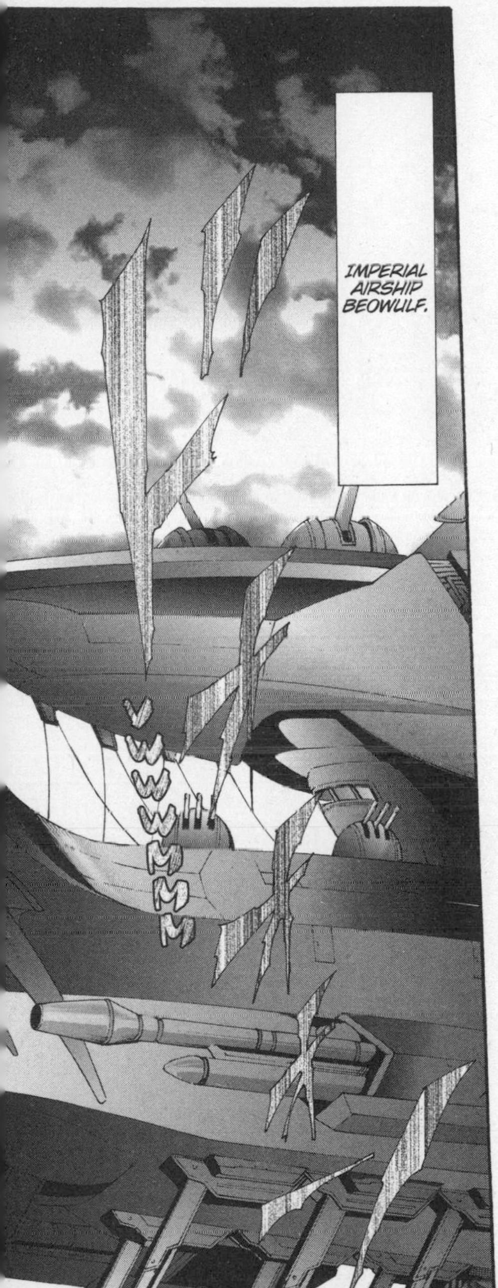
IMPERIAL AIRSHIP BEOWULF.
VWWWMMM

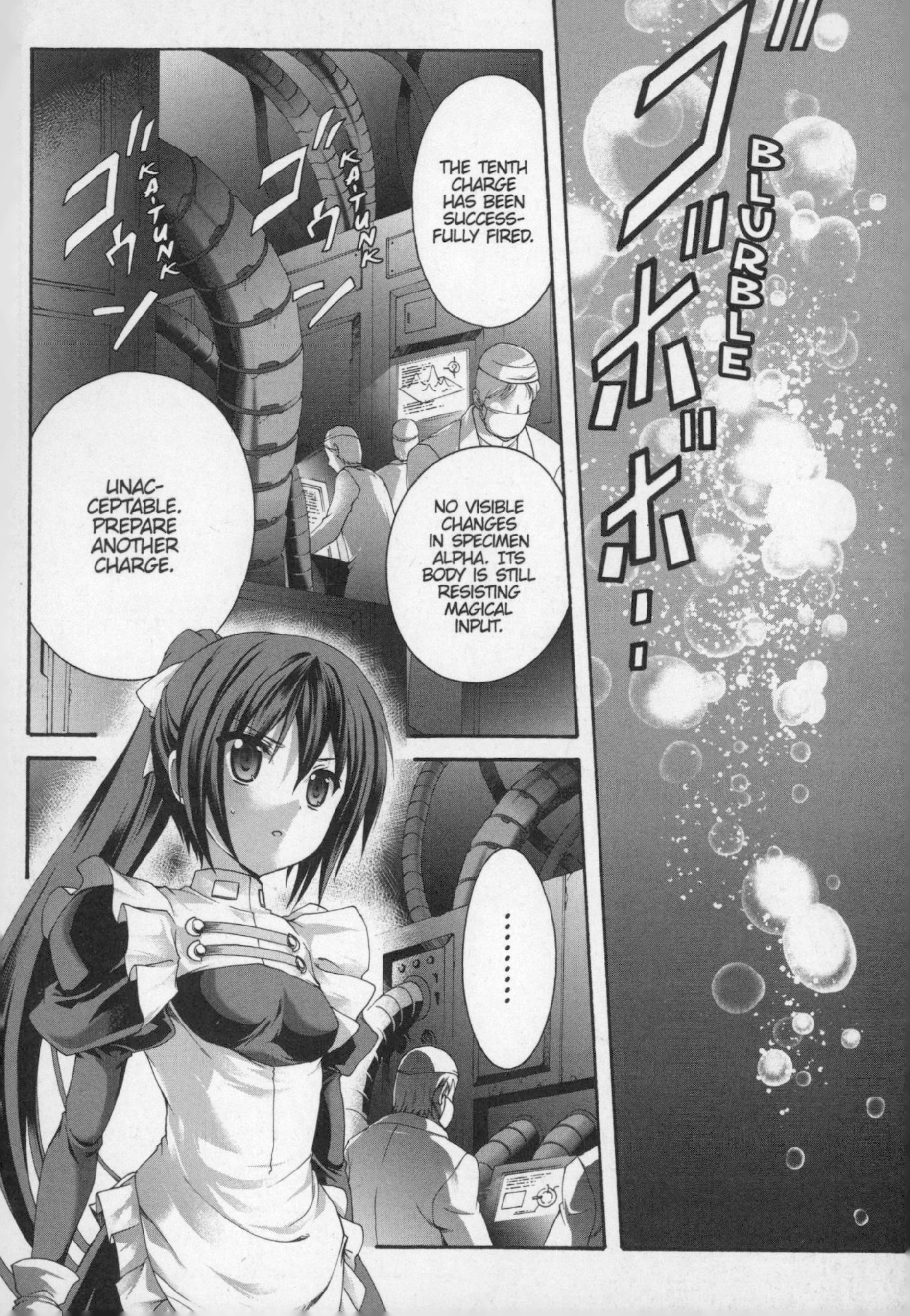
BLURBLE
THE TENTH CHARGE HAS BEEN SUCCESSFULLY FIRED.
KA-TUNK
KA-TUNK
NO VISIBLE CHANGES IN SPECIMEN ALPHA. ITS BODY IS STILL RESISTING MAGICAL INPUT.
UNACCEPTABLE. PREPARE ANOTHER CHARGE.
....

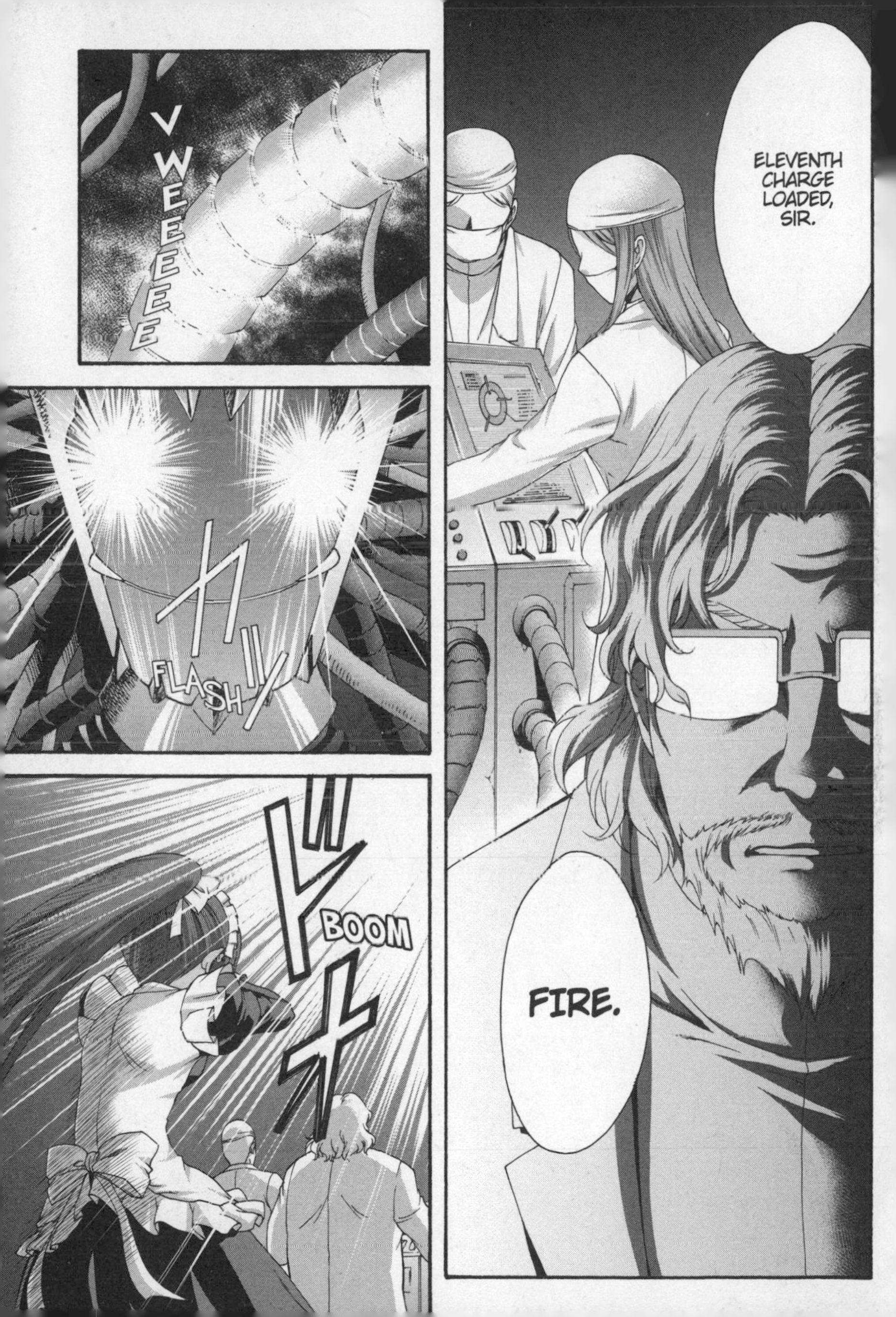
ELEVENTH CHARGE LOADED, SIR.
FIRE.
VWEEEEE
FLASH
BOOM

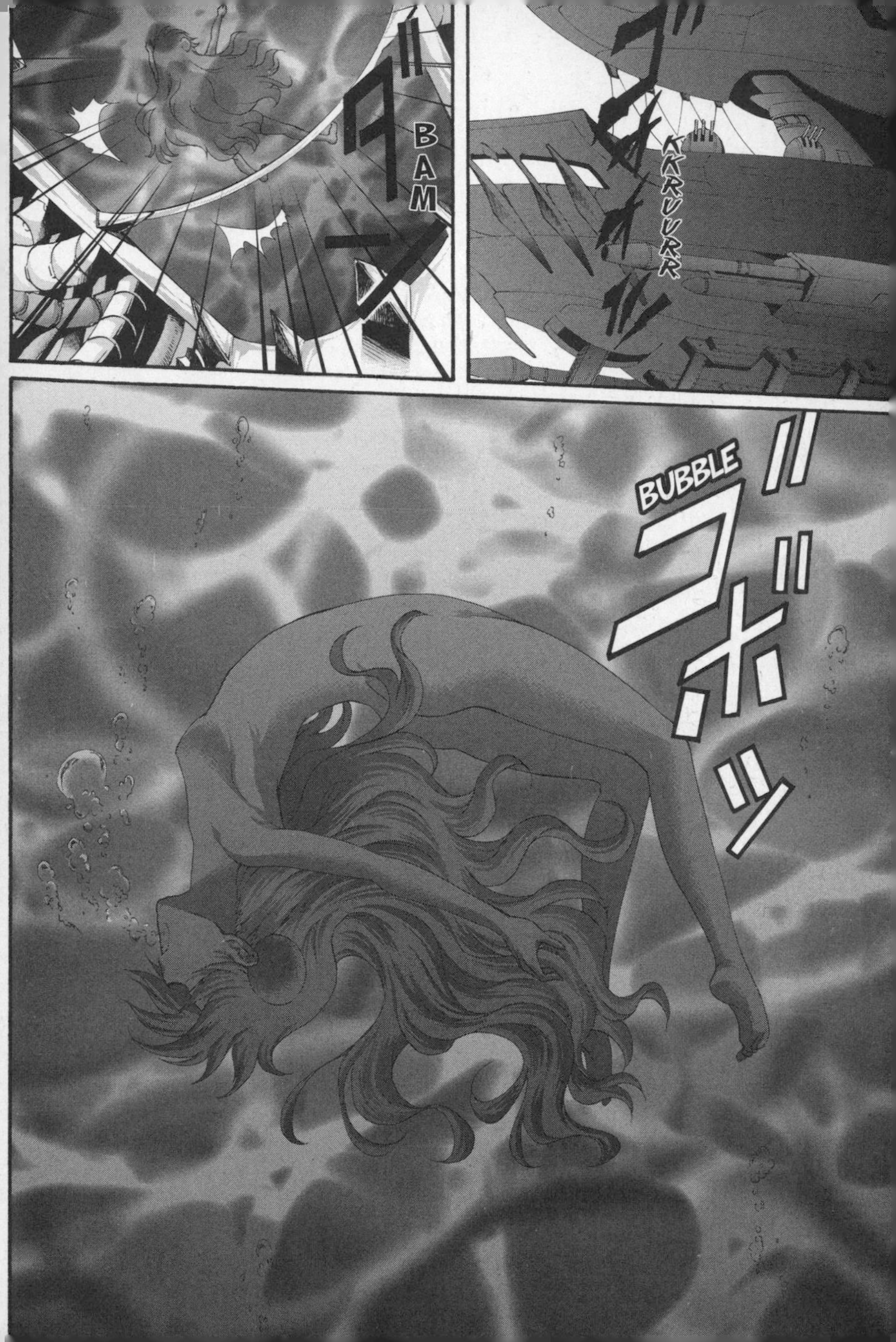
KKRUVURR
BAM
BUBBLE
ゴボッ

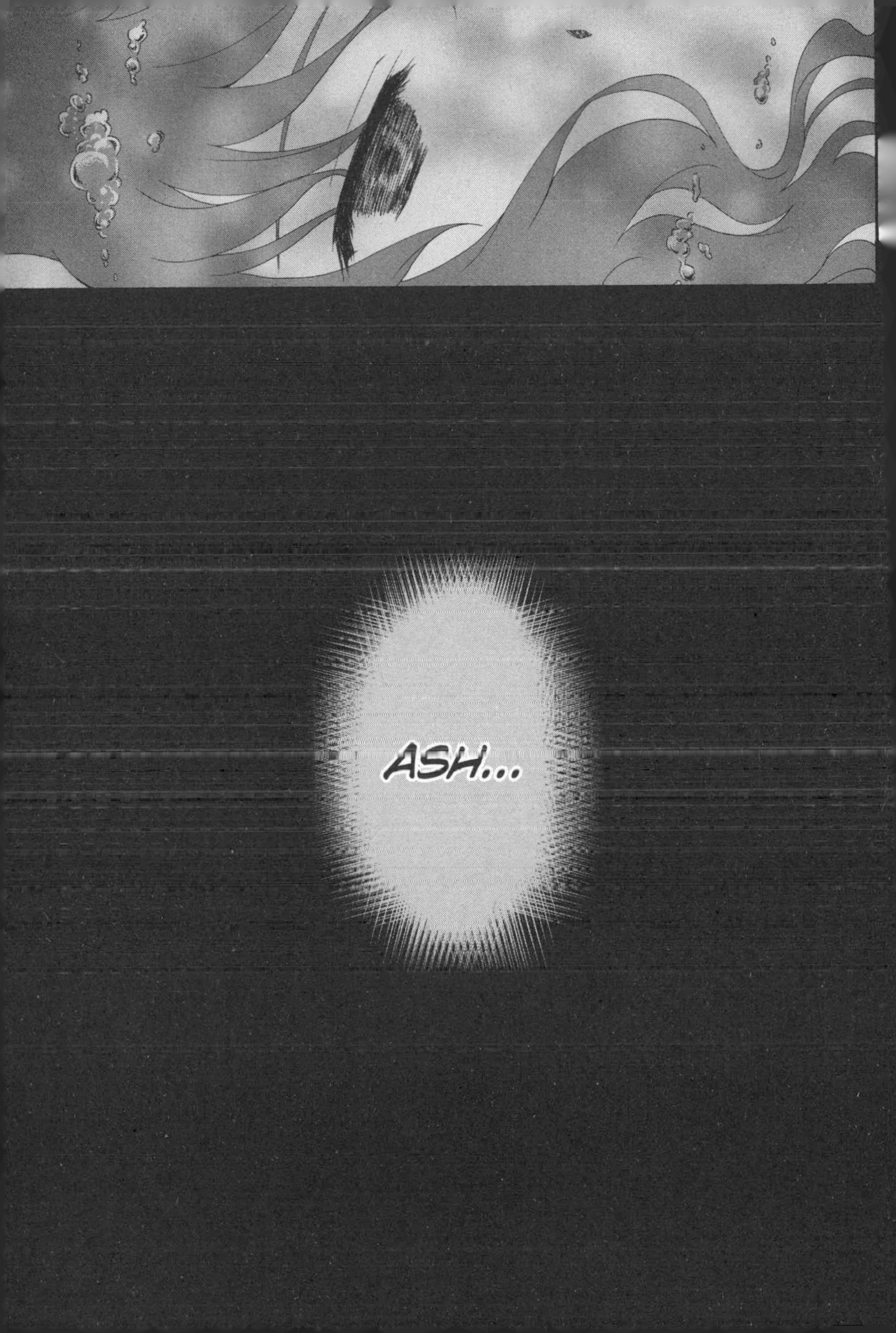
ASH...

星刻の竜騎士

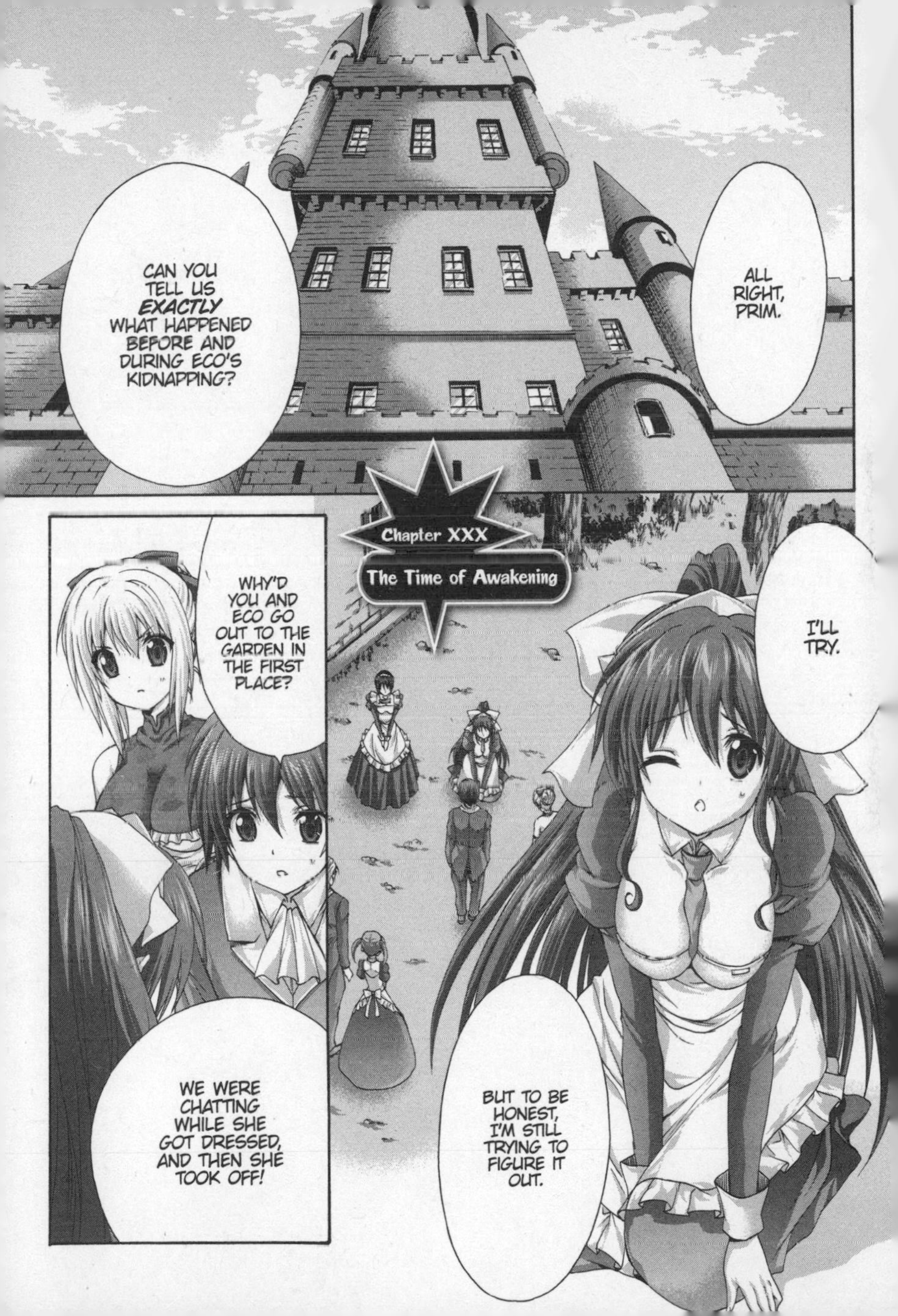
ALL RIGHT, PRIM.
CAN YOU TELL US *EXACTLY* WHAT HAPPENED BEFORE AND DURING ECO'S KIDNAPPING?
Chapter XXX
The Time of Awakening
I'LL TRY.
BUT TO BE HONEST, I'M STILL TRYING TO FIGURE IT OUT.
WHY'D YOU AND ECO GO OUT TO THE GARDEN IN THE FIRST PLACE?
WE WERE CHATTING WHILE SHE GOT DRESSED, AND THEN SHE TOOK OFF!

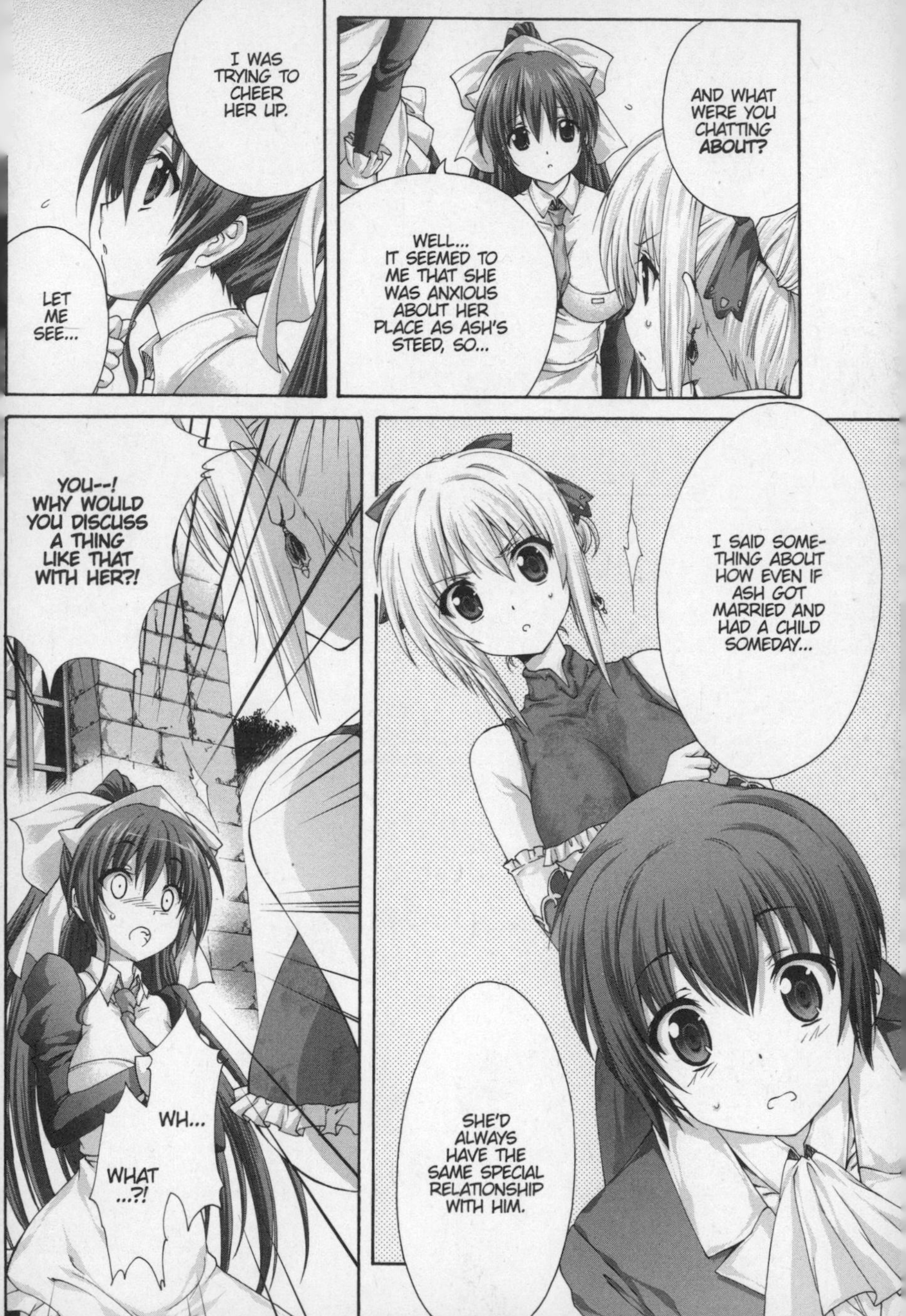
AND WHAT WERE YOU CHATTING ABOUT?
WELL... IT SEEMED TO ME THAT SHE WAS ANXIOUS ABOUT HER PLACE AS ASH'S STEED, SO...
I WAS TRYING TO CHEER HER UP.
LET ME SEE...
I SAID SOME-THING ABOUT HOW EVEN IF ASH GOT MARRIED AND HAD A CHILD SOMEDAY...
SHE'D ALWAYS HAVE THE SAME SPECIAL RELATIONSHIP WITH HIM.
YOU--! WHY WOULD YOU DISCUSS A THING LIKE THAT WITH HER?!
WH...
WHAT ...?!

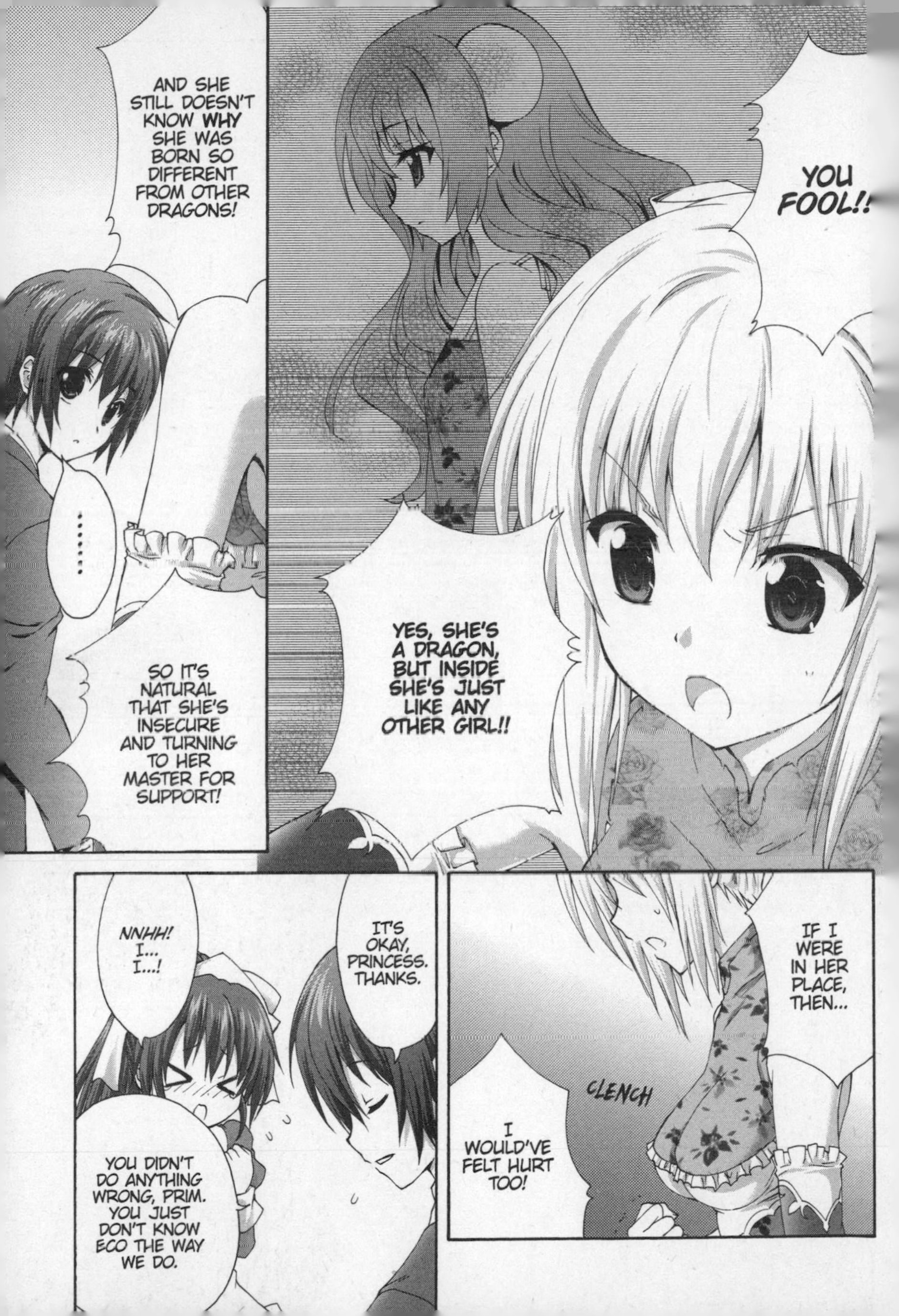
YOU FOOL!!
YES, SHE'S A DRAGON, BUT INSIDE SHE'S JUST LIKE ANY OTHER GIRL!!
AND SHE STILL DOESN'T KNOW WHY SHE WAS BORN SO DIFFERENT FROM OTHER DRAGONS!
......
SO IT'S NATURAL THAT SHE'S INSECURE AND TURNING TO HER MASTER FOR SUPPORT!
IF I WERE IN HER PLACE, THEN...
CLENCH
I WOULD'VE FELT HURT TOO!
IT'S OKAY, PRINCESS. THANKS.
NNHH! I... I...!
YOU DIDN'T DO ANYTHING WRONG, PRIM. YOU JUST DON'T KNOW ECO THE WAY WE DO.

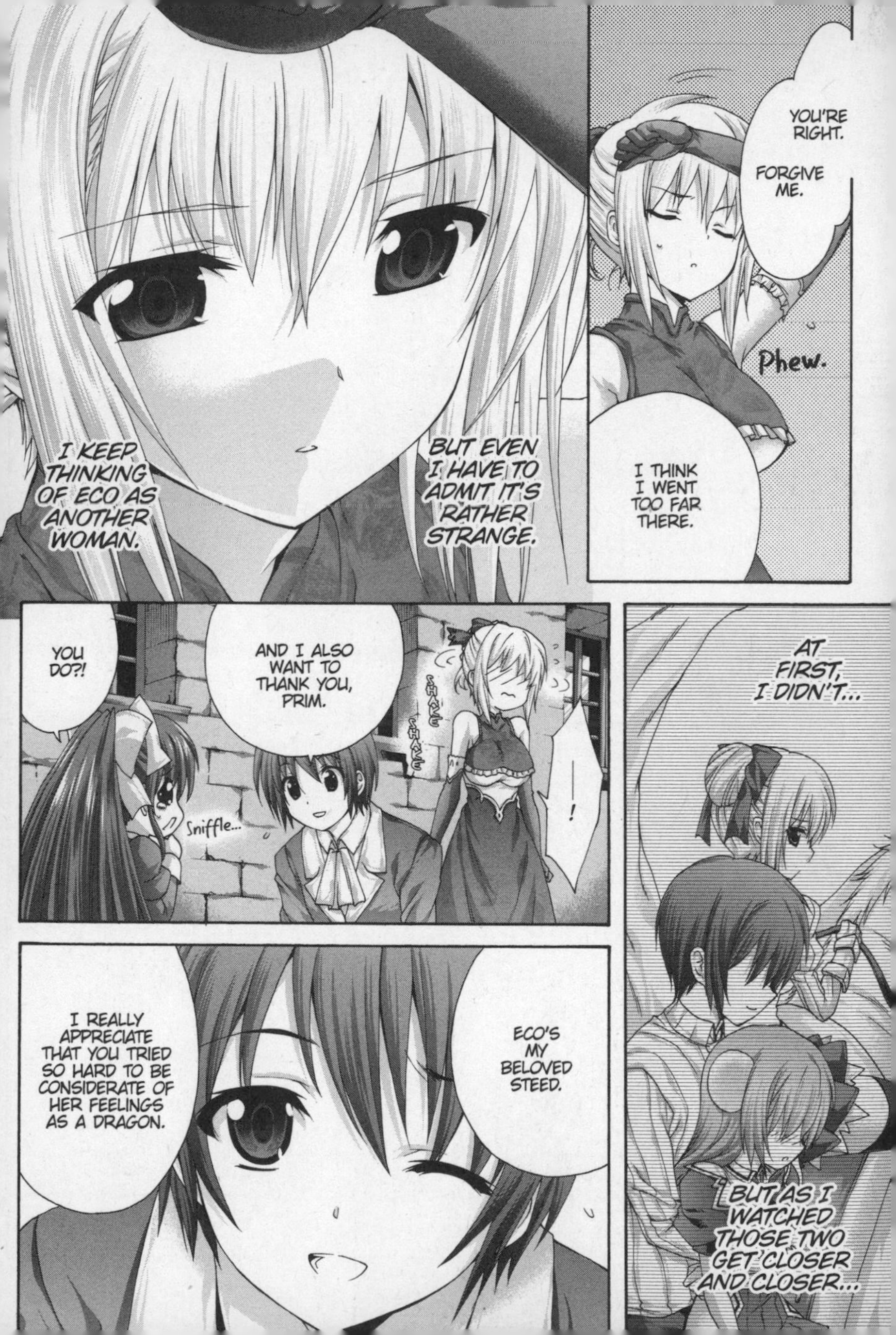
YOU'RE RIGHT.
FORGIVE ME.
Phew.
I THINK I WENT TOO FAR THERE.
BUT EVEN I HAVE TO ADMIT IT'S RATHER STRANGE.
I KEEP THINKING OF ECO AS ANOTHER WOMAN.
AT FIRST, I DIDN'T...
BUT AS I WATCHED THOSE TWO GET CLOSER AND CLOSER...
AND I ALSO WANT TO THANK YOU, PRIM.
YOU DO?!
SHAKE SHAKE
...!
Sniffle...
ECO'S MY BELOVED STEED.
I REALLY APPRECIATE THAT YOU TRIED SO HARD TO BE CONSIDERATE OF HER FEELINGS AS A DRAGON.

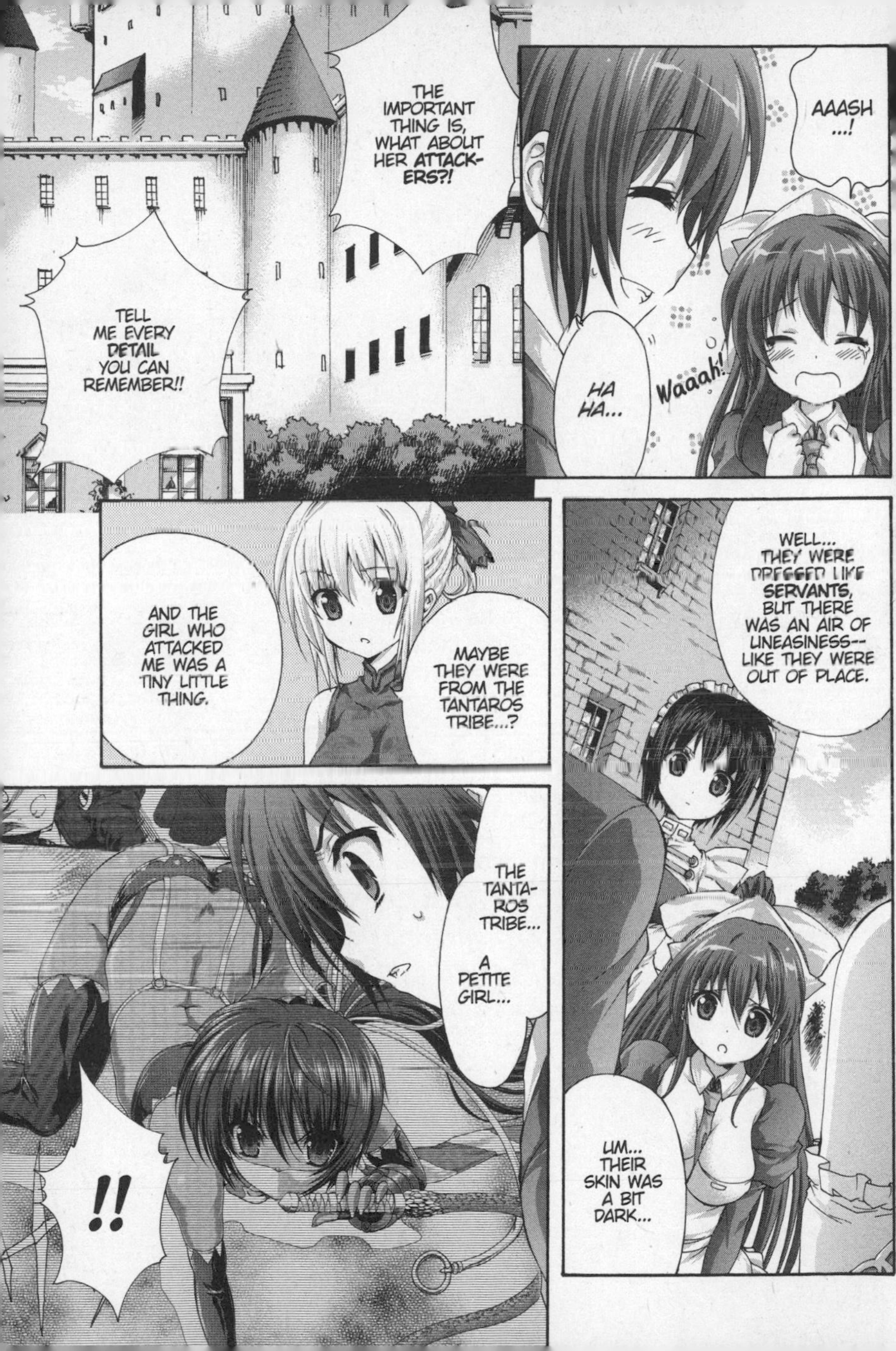
AAASH ...!
Waaah!
HA HA...
THE IMPORTANT THING IS, WHAT ABOUT HER ATTACKERS?!
TELL ME EVERY DETAIL YOU CAN REMEMBER!!
WELL... THEY WERE DRESSED LIKE SERVANTS, BUT THERE WAS AN AIR OF UNEASINESS-- LIKE THEY WERE OUT OF PLACE.
UM... THEIR SKIN WAS A BIT DARK...
MAYBE THEY WERE FROM THE TANTAROS TRIBE...?
AND THE GIRL WHO ATTACKED ME WAS A TINY LITTLE THING.
THE TANTA-ROS TRIBE...
A PETITE GIRL...
!!

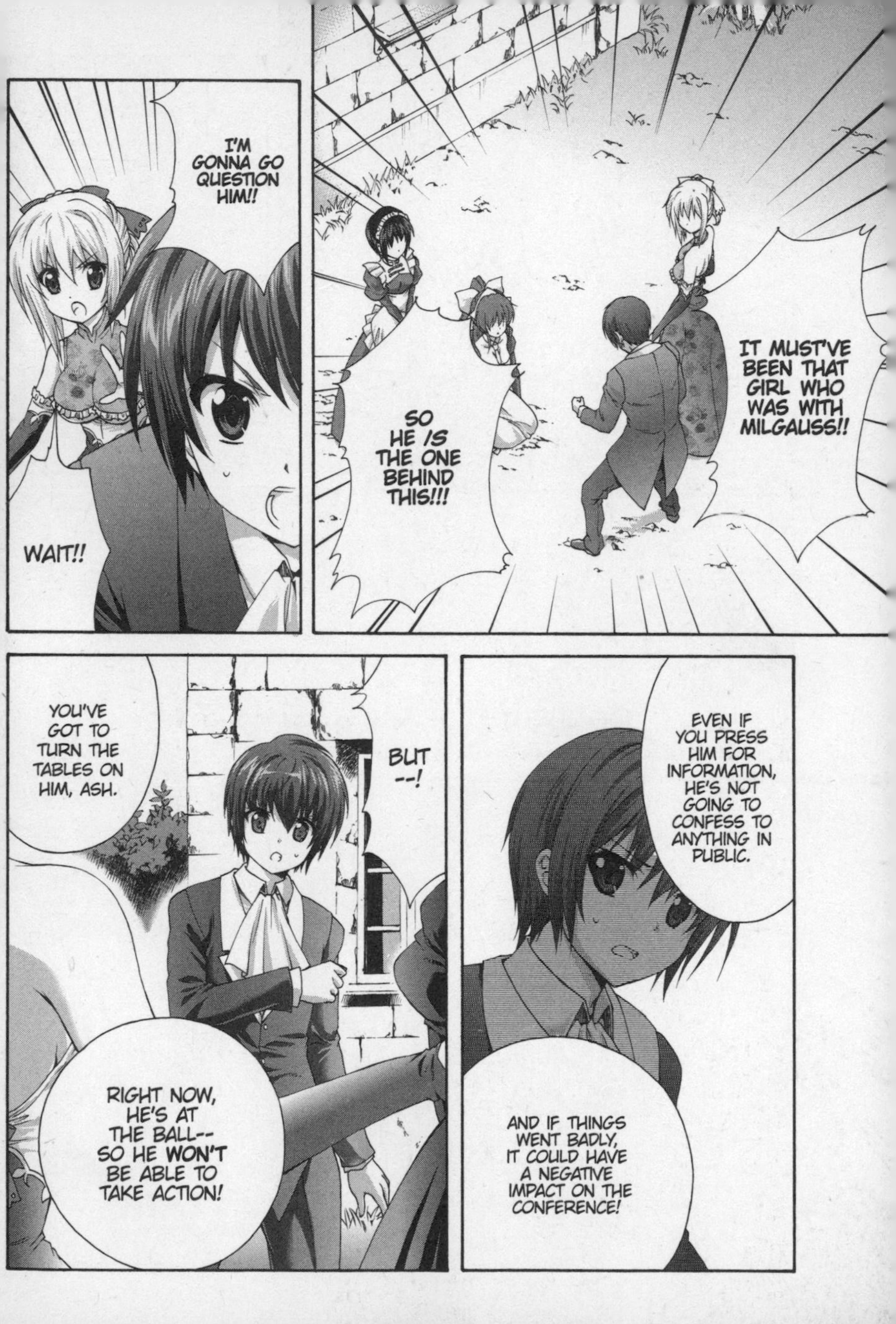
IT MUST'VE BEEN THAT GIRL WHO WAS WITH MILGAUSS!!
SO HE *IS* THE ONE BEHIND THIS!!!
I'M GONNA GO QUESTION HIM!!
WAIT!!
EVEN IF YOU PRESS HIM FOR INFORMATION, HE'S NOT GOING TO CONFESS TO ANYTHING IN PUBLIC.
AND IF THINGS WENT BADLY, IT COULD HAVE A NEGATIVE IMPACT ON THE CONFERENCE!
BUT--!
YOU'VE GOT TO TURN THE TABLES ON HIM, ASH.
RIGHT NOW, HE'S AT THE BALL--SO HE WON'T BE ABLE TO TAKE ACTION!

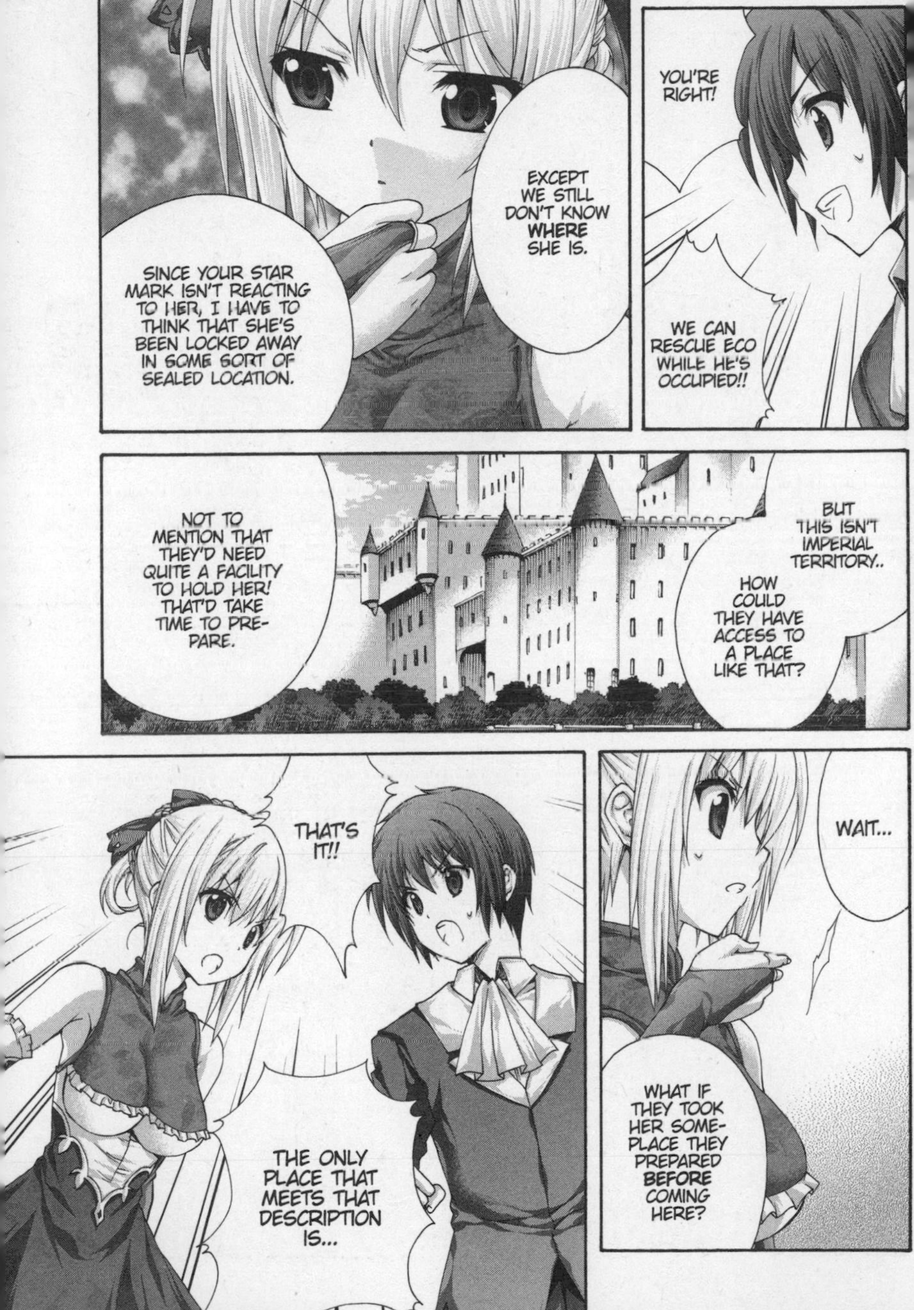
YOU'RE RIGHT!
WE CAN RESCUE ECO WHILE HE'S OCCUPIED!!
EXCEPT WE STILL DON'T KNOW WHERE SHE IS.
SINCE YOUR STAR MARK ISN'T REACTING TO HER, I HAVE TO THINK THAT SHE'S BEEN LOCKED AWAY IN SOME SORT OF SEALED LOCATION.
BUT THIS ISN'T IMPERIAL TERRITORY..
HOW COULD THEY HAVE ACCESS TO A PLACE LIKE THAT?
NOT TO MENTION THAT THEY'D NEED QUITE A FACILITY TO HOLD HER! THAT'D TAKE TIME TO PRE-PARE.
WAIT...
WHAT IF THEY TOOK HER SOME-PLACE THEY PREPARED BEFORE COMING HERE?
THAT'S IT!!
THE ONLY PLACE THAT MEETS THAT DESCRIPTION IS...

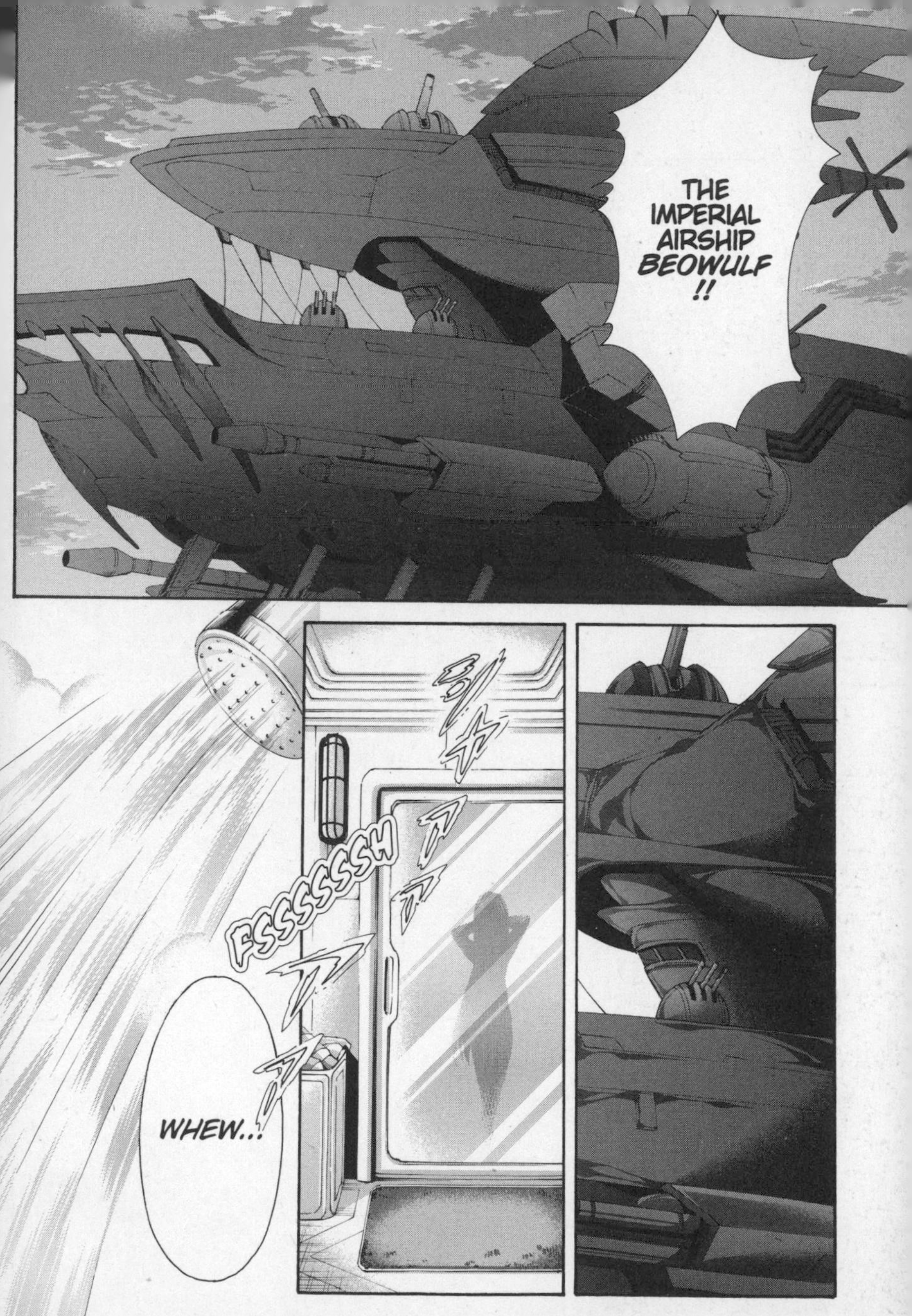
THE IMPERIAL AIRSHIP BEOWULF !!
FSSSSSSH
WHEW...

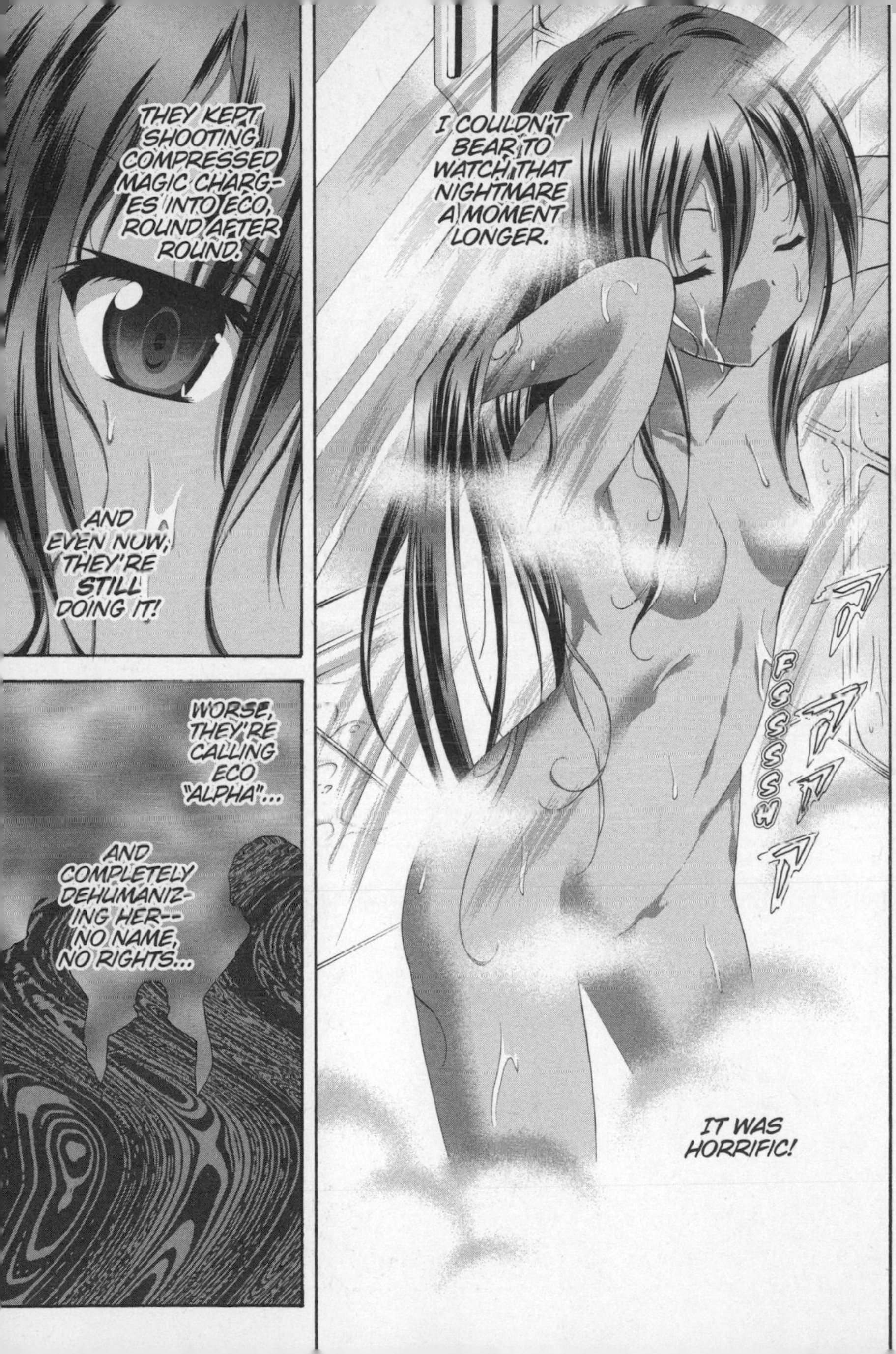

I COULDN'T BEAR TO WATCH THAT NIGHTMARE A MOMENT LONGER.
FSSSSH
IT WAS HORRIFIC!
THEY KEPT SHOOTING COMPRESSED MAGIC CHARG-ES INTO ECO, ROUND AFTER ROUND.
AND EVEN NOW, THEY'RE STILL DOING IT!
WORSE, THEY'RE CALLING ECO "ALPHA"...
AND COMPLETELY DEHUMANIZ-ING HER--NO NAME, NO RIGHTS...

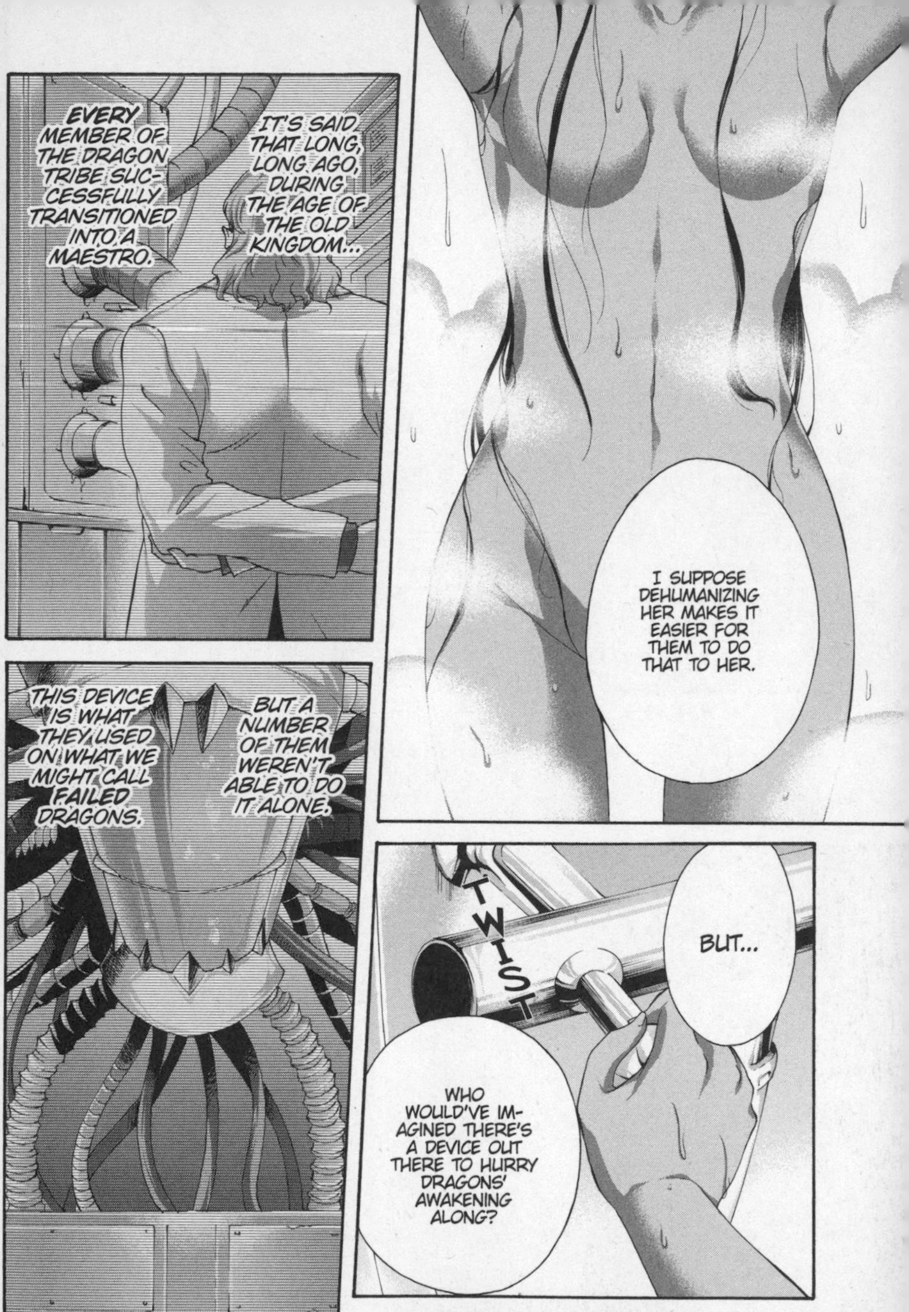
I SUPPOSE DEHUMANIZING HER MAKES IT EASIER FOR THEM TO DO THAT TO HER.
BUT...
TWIST
WHO WOULD'VE IM-AGINED THERE'S A DEVICE OUT THERE TO HURRY DRAGONS' AWAKENING ALONG?
IT'S SAID THAT LONG, LONG AGO, DURING THE AGE OF THE OLD KINGDOM...
EVERY MEMBER OF THE DRAGON TRIBE SUC-CESSFULLY TRANSITIONED INTO A MAESTRO.
BUT A NUMBER OF THEM WEREN'T ABLE TO DO IT ALONE.
THIS DEVICE IS WHAT THEY USED ON WHAT WE MIGHT CALL FAILED DRAGONS.

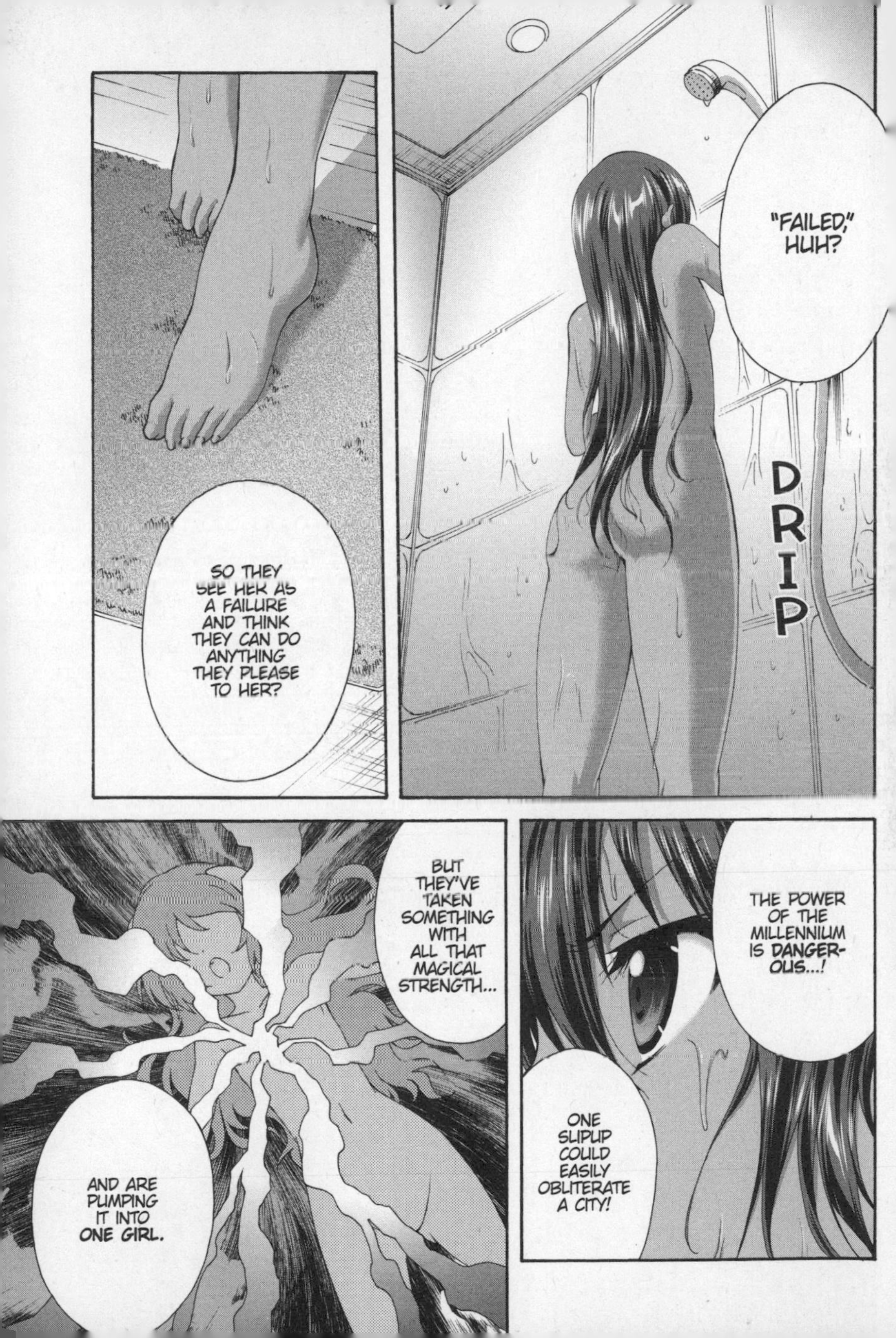
"FAILED," HUH?
DRIP
SO THEY SEE HER AS A FAILURE AND THINK THEY CAN DO ANYTHING THEY PLEASE TO HER?
THE POWER OF THE MILLENNIUM IS DANGER-OUS...!
ONE SLIPUP COULD EASILY OBLITERATE A CITY!
BUT THEY'VE TAKEN SOMETHING WITH ALL THAT MAGICAL STRENGTH...
AND ARE PUMPING IT INTO ONE GIRL.

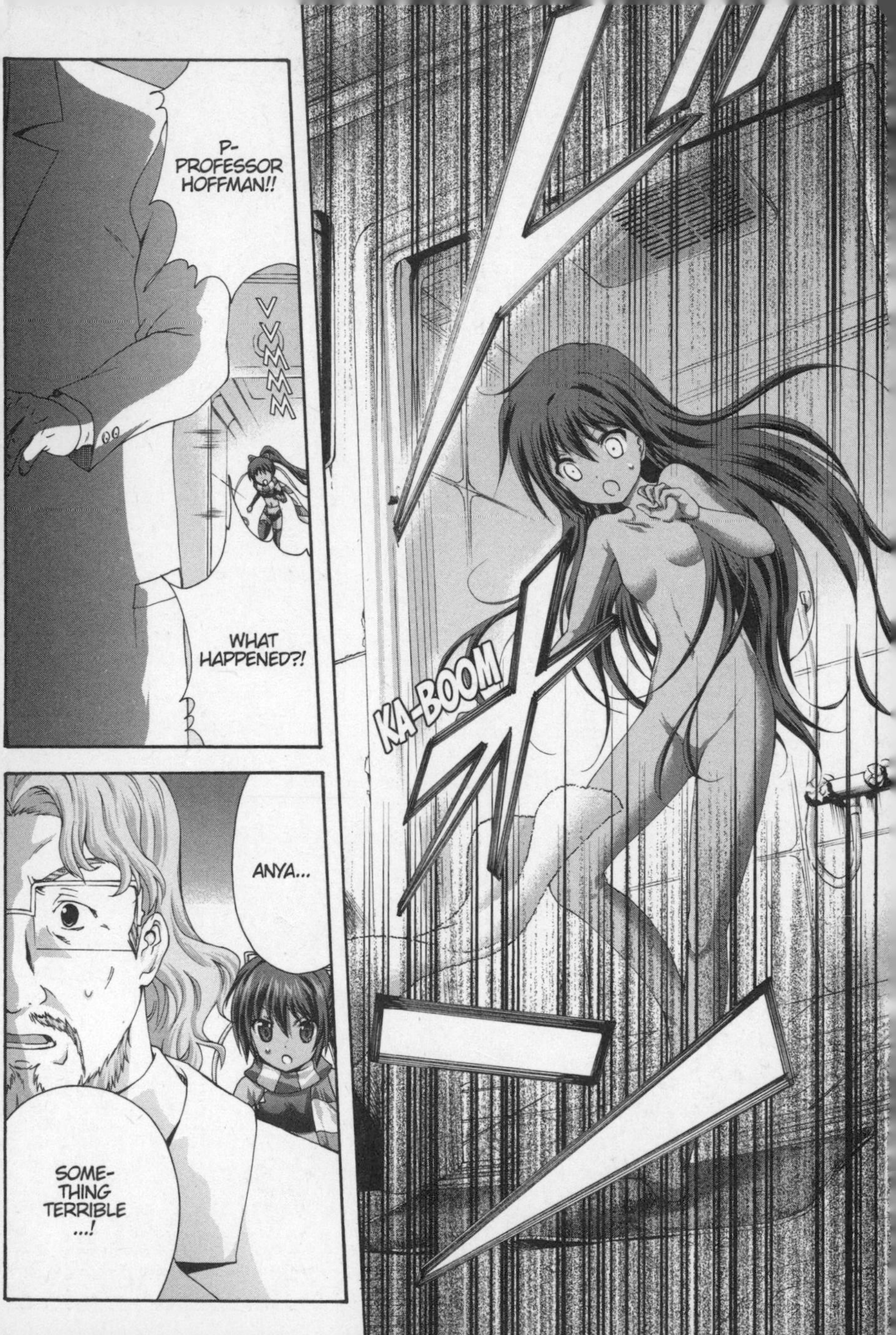
KA-BOOM
P-PROFESSOR HOFFMAN!!
VVMMMM
WHAT HAPPENED?!
ANYA...
SOME-THING TERRIBLE ...!

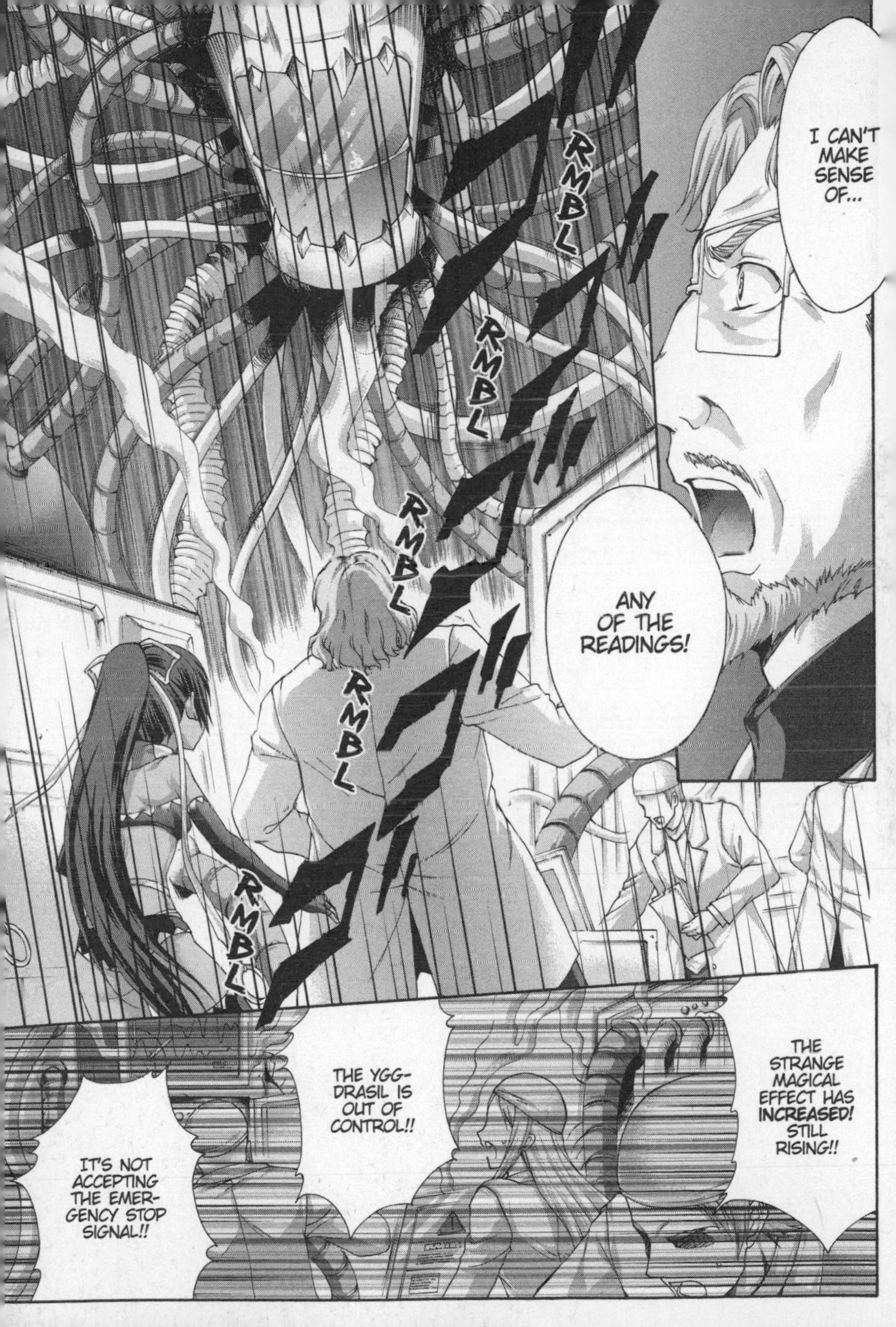
I CAN'T MAKE SENSE OF...
ANY OF THE READINGS!
RMBL
RMBL
RMBL
RMBL
RMBL
THE STRANGE MAGICAL EFFECT HAS INCREASED! STILL RISING!!
THE YGG-DRASIL IS OUT OF CONTROL!!
IT'S NOT ACCEPTING THE EMER-GENCY STOP SIGNAL!!

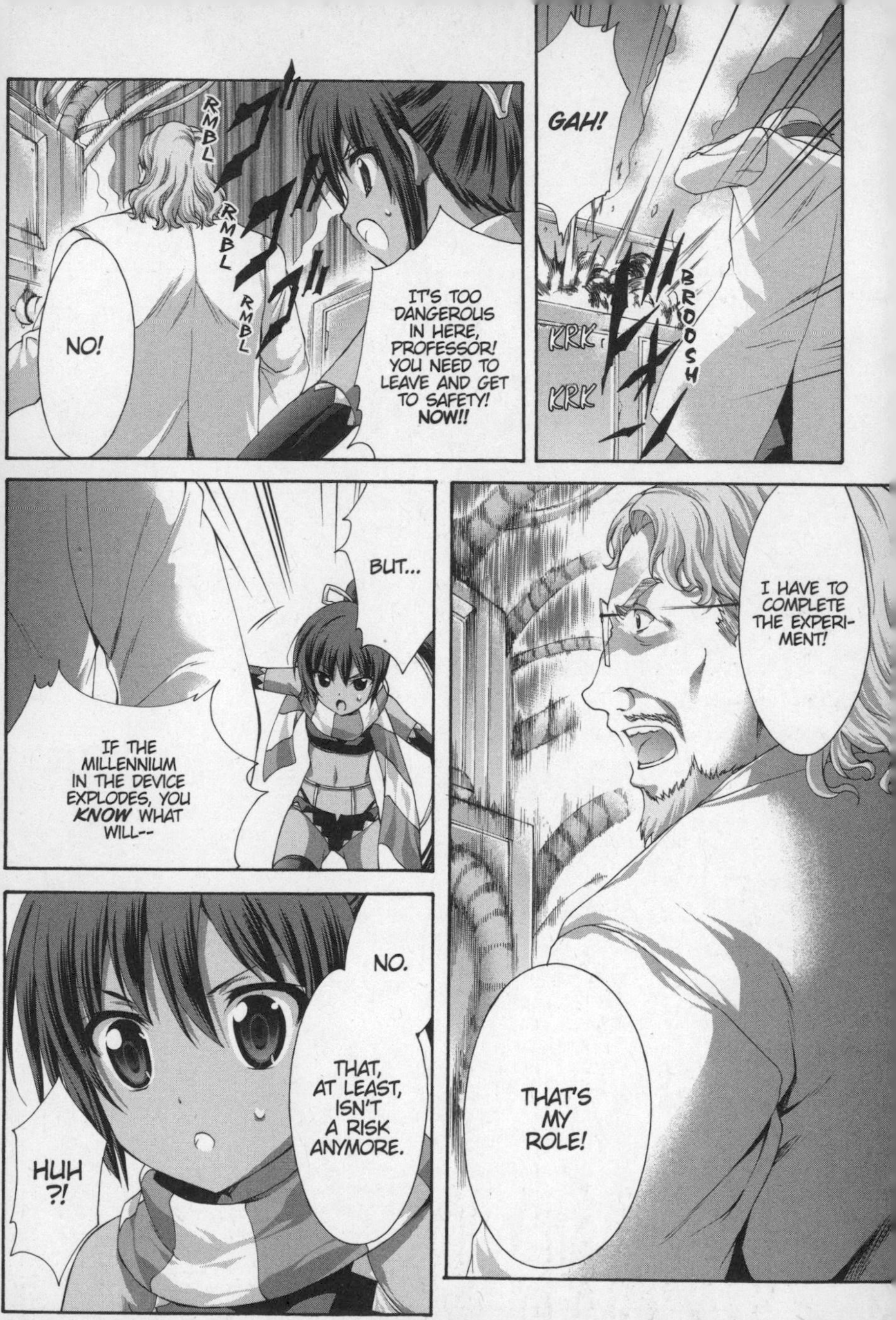
GAH!
BROOSH
KRK
KRK
RMBL
RMBL
RMBL
IT'S TOO DANGEROUS IN HERE, PROFESSOR! YOU NEED TO LEAVE AND GET TO SAFETY! NOW!!
NO!
I HAVE TO COMPLETE THE EXPERI-MENT!
THAT'S MY ROLE!
BUT...
IF THE MILLENNIUM IN THE DEVICE EXPLODES, YOU KNOW WHAT WILL--
NO.
THAT, AT LEAST, ISN'T A RISK ANYMORE.
HUH ?!

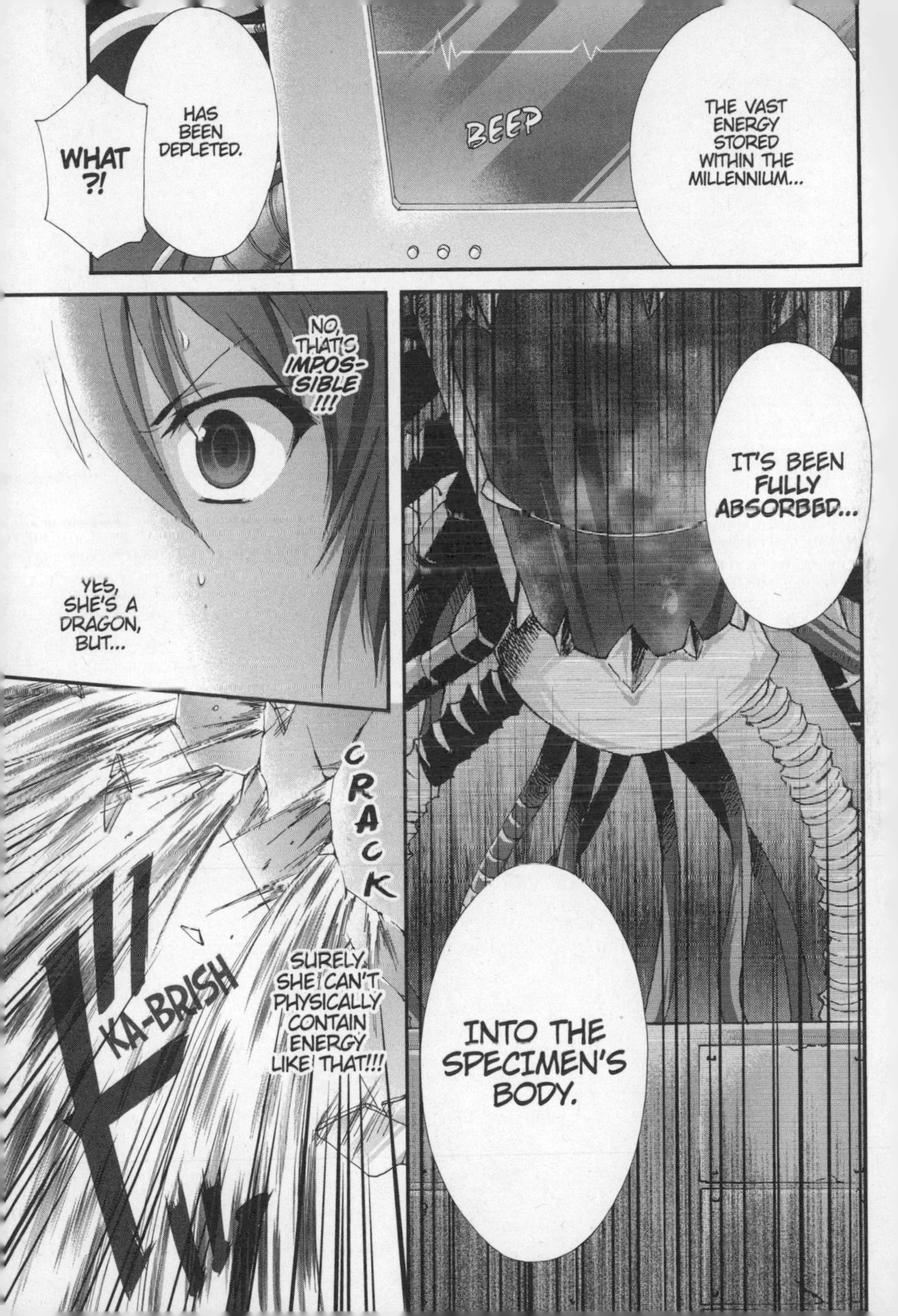
THE VAST ENERGY STORED WITHIN THE MILLENNIUM...
BEEP
HAS BEEN DEPLETED.
WHAT?!
IT'S BEEN FULLY ABSORBED...
INTO THE SPECIMEN'S BODY.
NO, THAT'S IMPOSSIBLE!!!
YES, SHE'S A DRAGON, BUT...
CRACK
SURELY, SHE CAN'T PHYSICALLY CONTAIN ENERGY LIKE THAT!!!
KA-BRISH

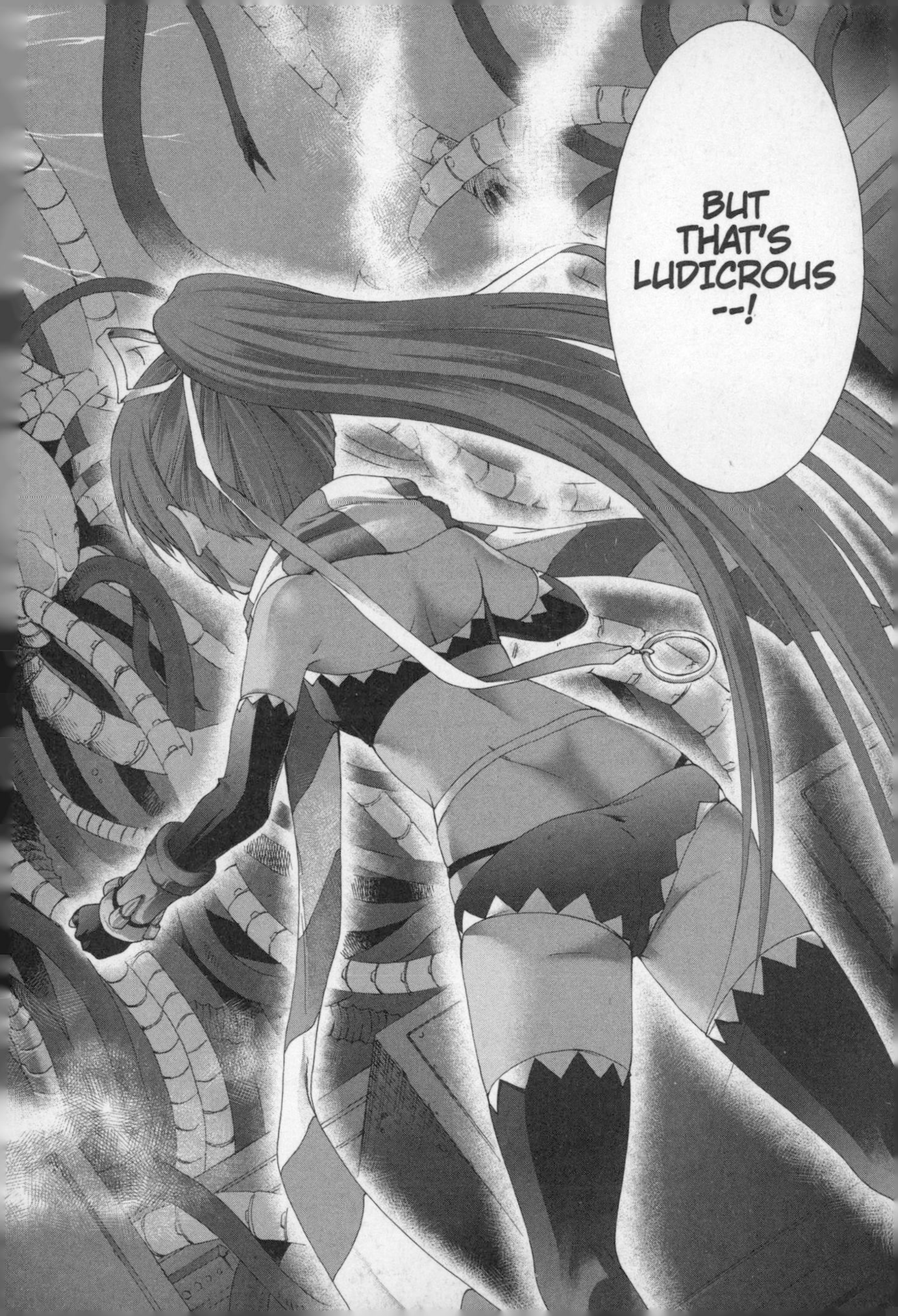
BUT THAT'S LUDICROUS --!

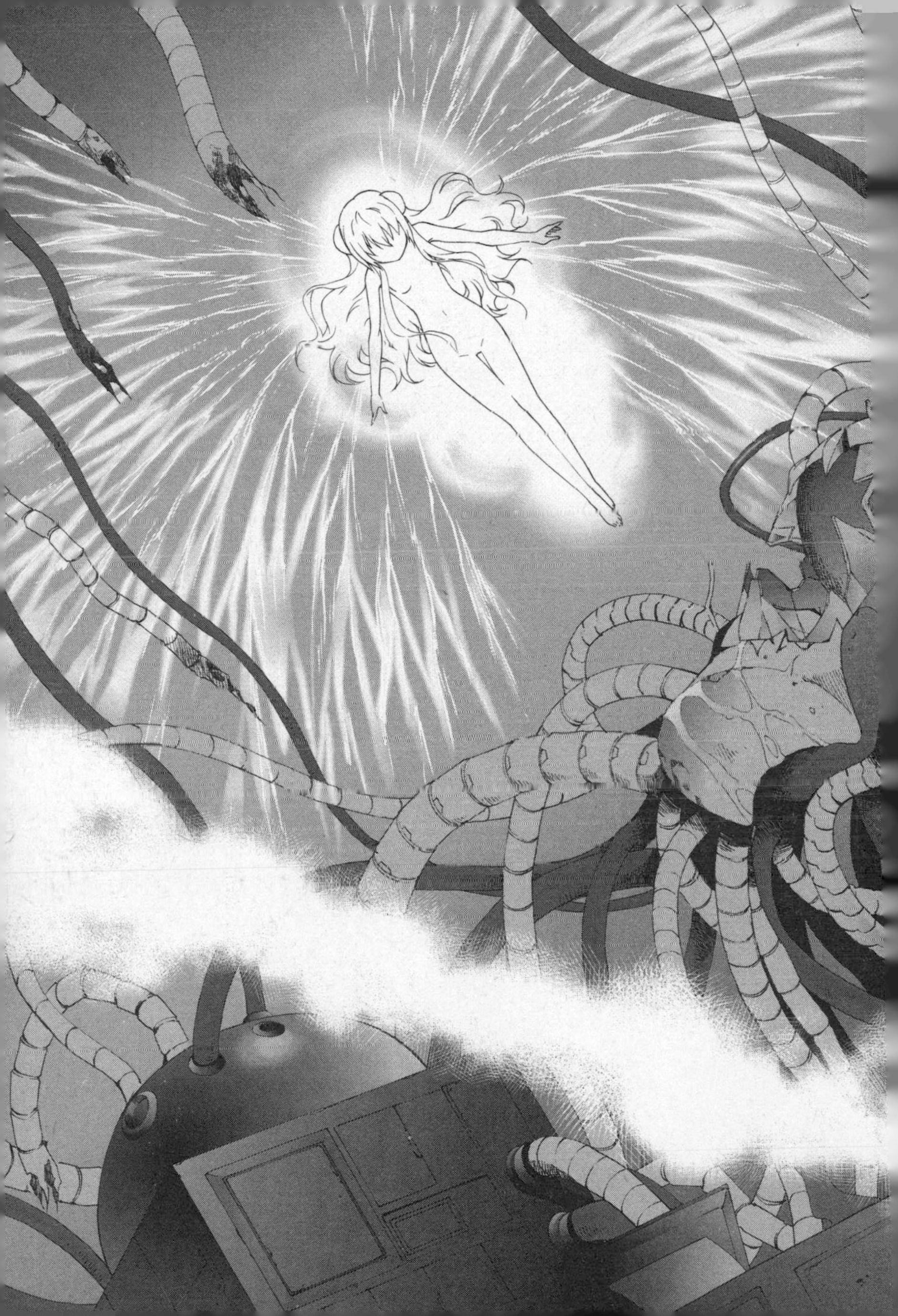

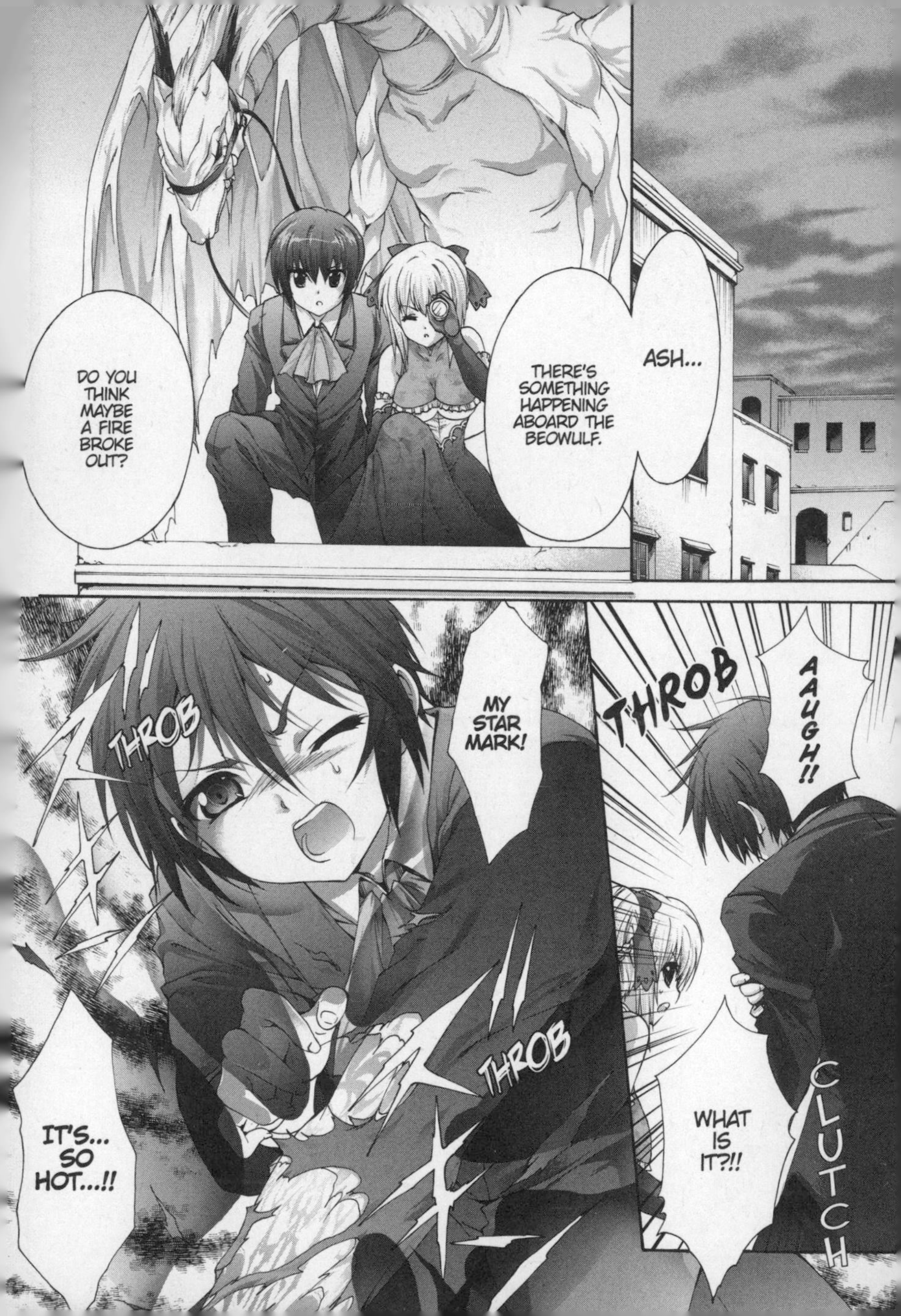
ASH...
THERE'S SOMETHING HAPPENING ABOARD THE BEOWULF.
DO YOU THINK MAYBE A FIRE BROKE OUT?
AAUGH!!
THROB
CLUTCH
WHAT IS IT?!!
MY STAR MARK!
THROB
THROB
IT'S... SO HOT...!!

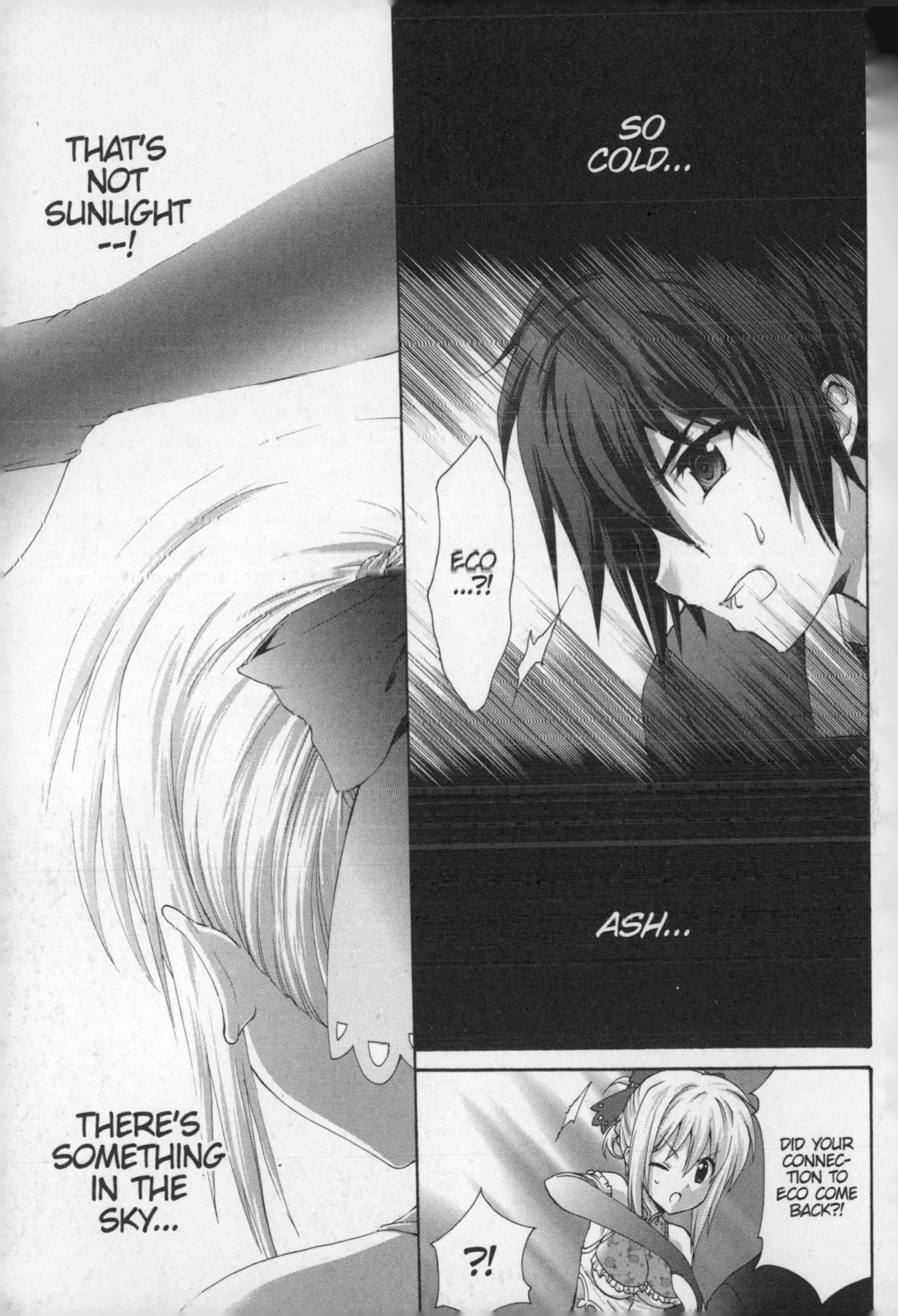
SO COLD...
ECO ...?!
ASH...
DID YOUR CONNECTION TO ECO COME BACK?!
?!
THAT'S NOT SUNLIGHT --!
THERE'S SOMETHING IN THE SKY...

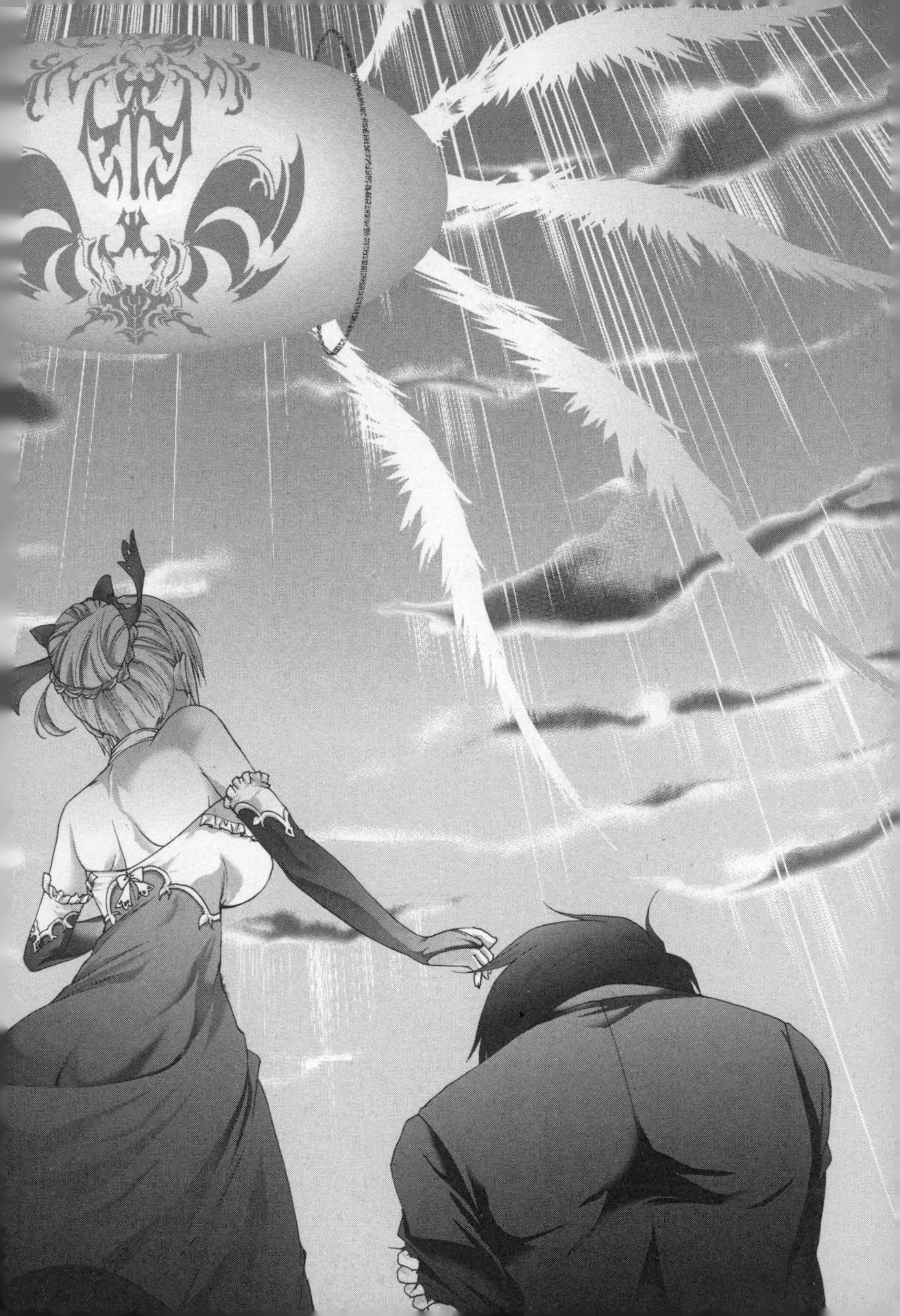

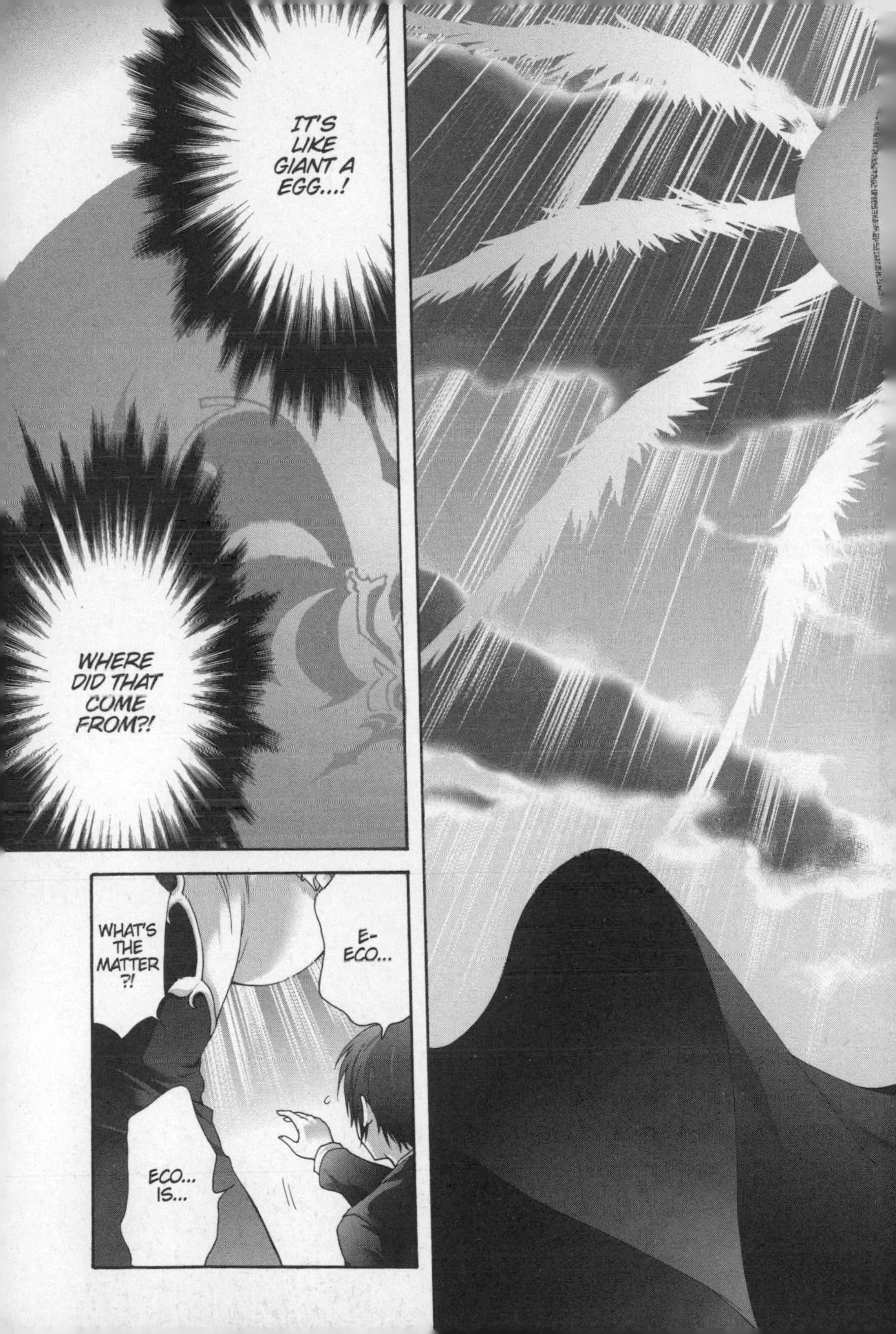
IT'S LIKE GIANT A EGG...!
WHERE DID THAT COME FROM?!
E- ECO...
WHAT'S THE MATTER ?!
ECO... IS...

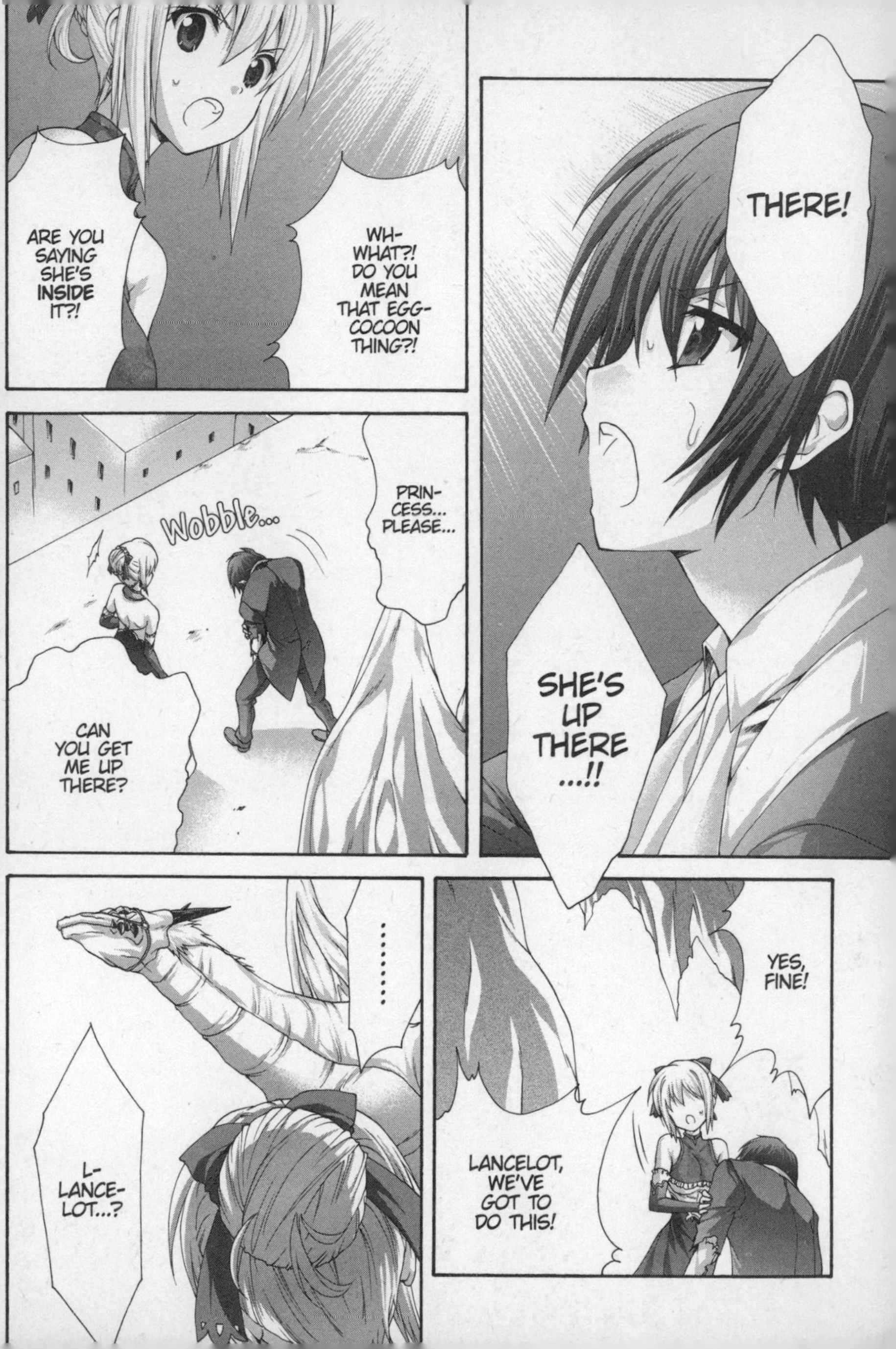
THERE!
SHE'S UP THERE ...!!
WH-WHAT?! DO YOU MEAN THAT EGG-COCOON THING?!
ARE YOU SAYING SHE'S INSIDE IT?!
PRIN-CESS... PLEASE...
Wobble...
CAN YOU GET ME UP THERE?
YES, FINE!
LANCELOT, WE'VE GOT TO DO THIS!
....
L-LANCE-LOT...?

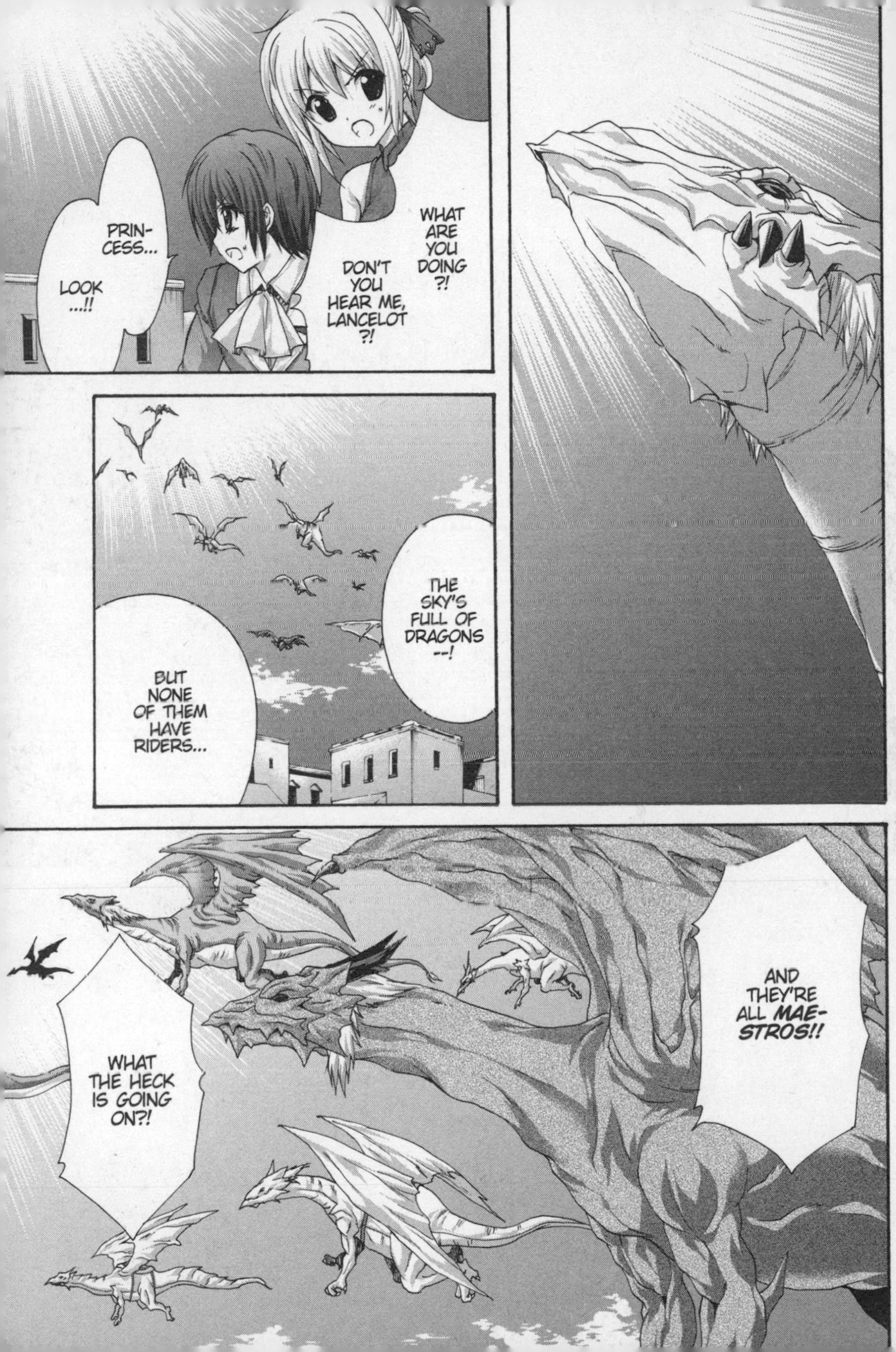
WHAT ARE YOU DOING?!
DON'T YOU HEAR ME, LANCELOT?!
PRINCESS...
LOOK...!!
THE SKY'S FULL OF DRAGONS--!
BUT NONE OF THEM HAVE RIDERS...
AND THEY'RE ALL *MAESTROS!!*
WHAT THE HECK IS GOING ON?!

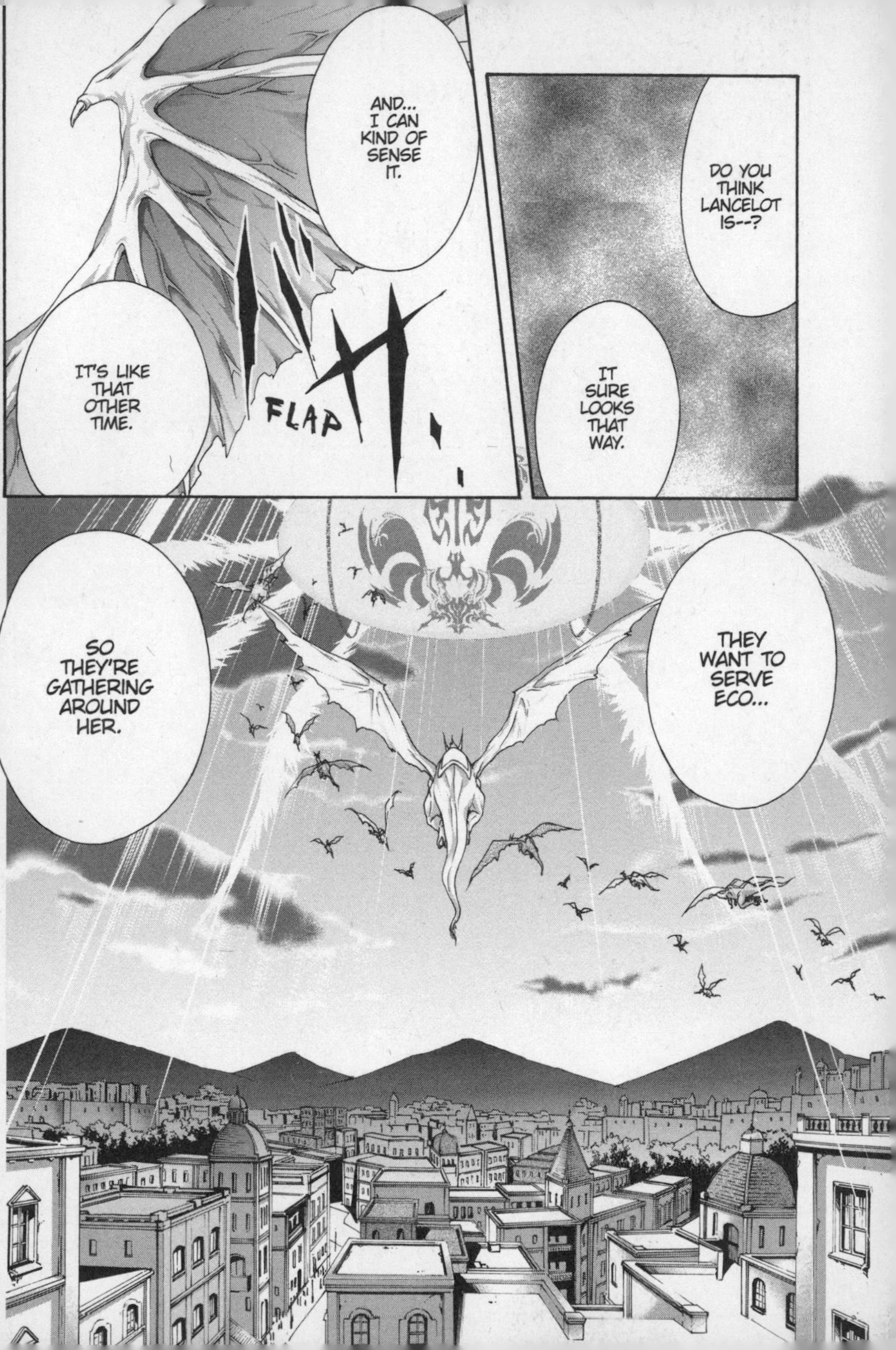
DO YOU THINK LANCELOT IS--?
IT SURE LOOKS THAT WAY.
AND... I CAN KIND OF SENSE IT.
FLAP
IT'S LIKE THAT OTHER TIME.
THEY WANT TO SERVE ECO...
SO THEY'RE GATHERING AROUND HER.

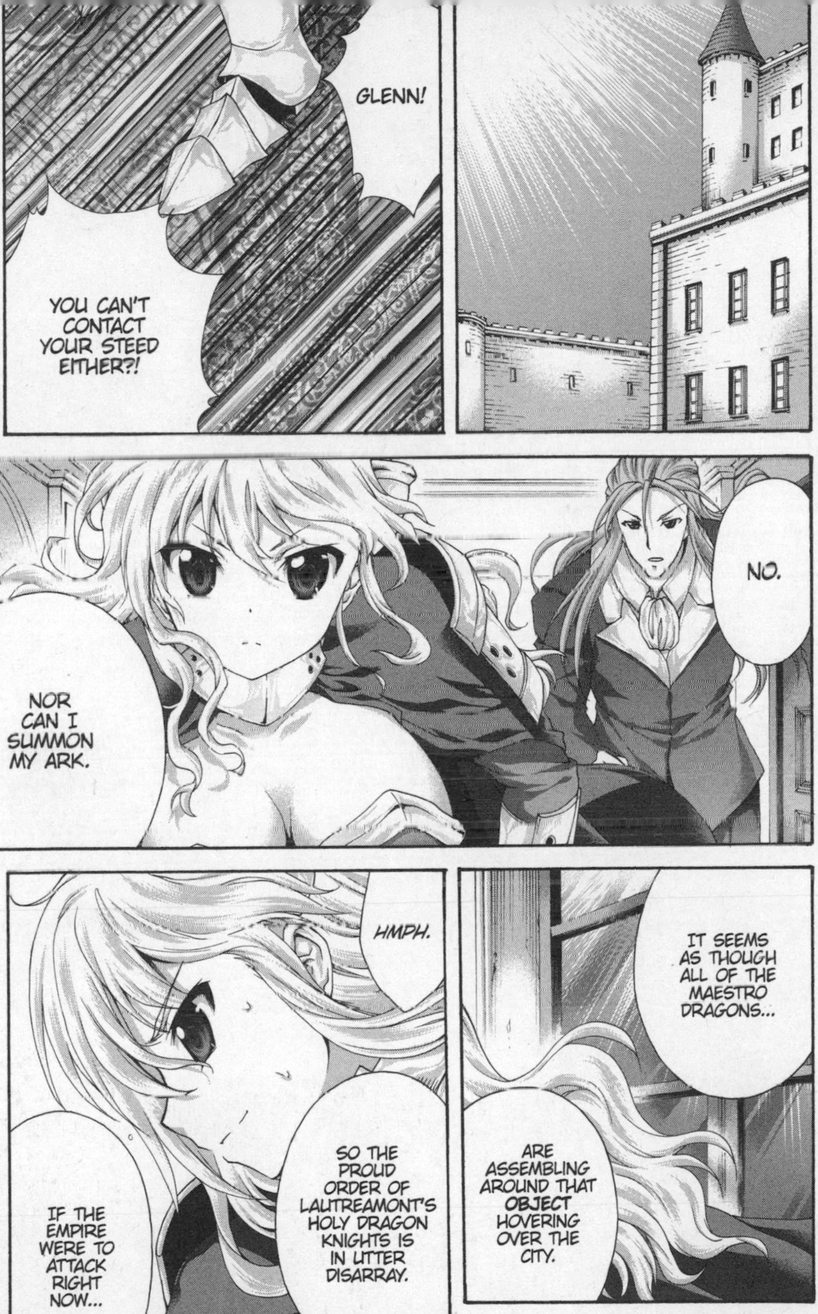
GLENN!
YOU CAN'T CONTACT YOUR STEED EITHER?!
NO.
NOR CAN I SUMMON MY ARK.
IT SEEMS AS THOUGH ALL OF THE MAESTRO DRAGONS...
ARE ASSEMBLING AROUND THAT OBJECT HOVERING OVER THE CITY.
HMPH.
SO THE PROUD ORDER OF LAUTREAMONT'S HOLY DRAGON KNIGHTS IS IN UTTER DISARRAY.
IF THE EMPIRE WERE TO ATTACK RIGHT NOW...

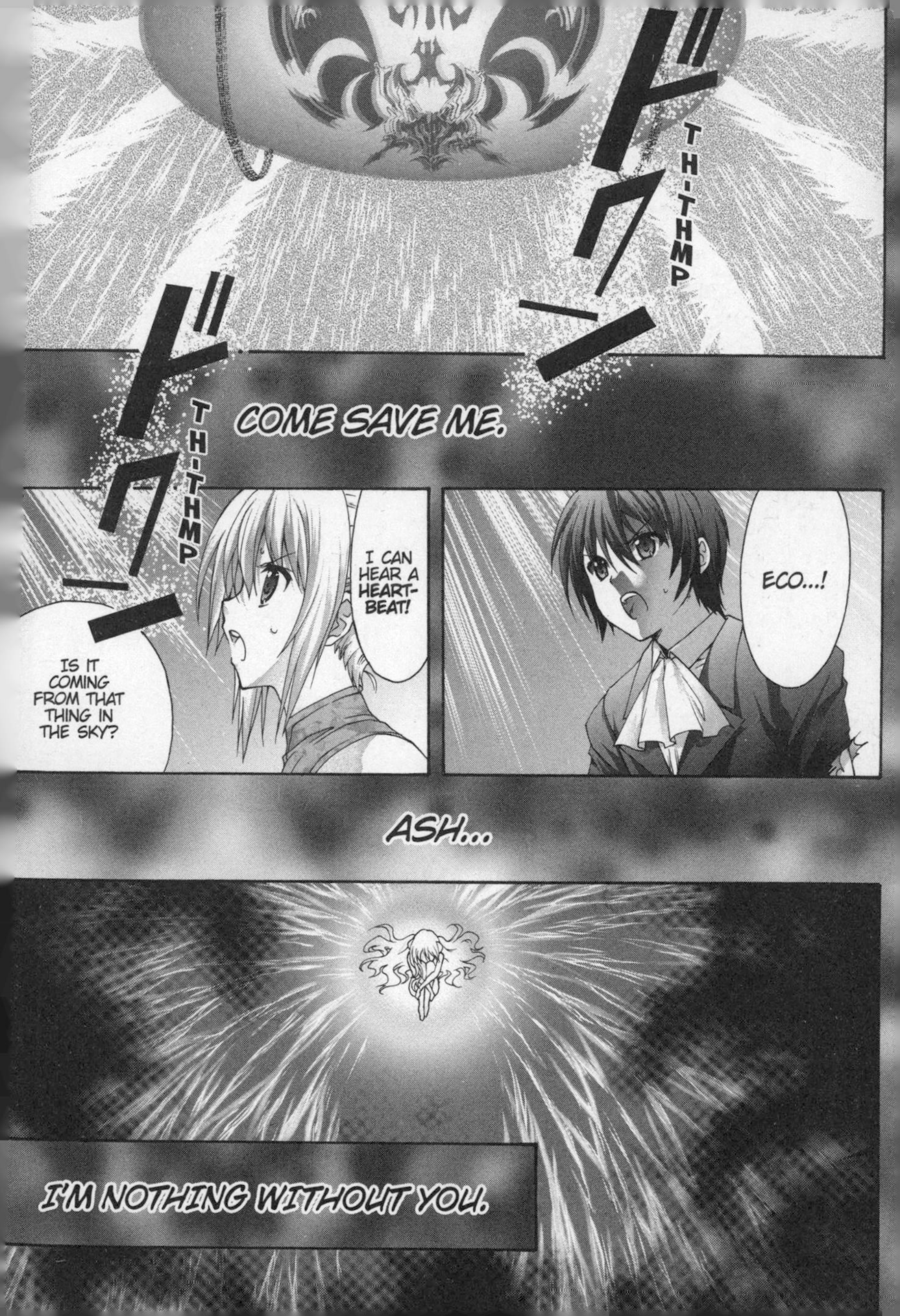
ドクン
TH-THMP
COME SAVE ME.
ドクン
TH-THMP
ECO...!
I CAN HEAR A HEART-BEAT!
IS IT COMING FROM THAT THING IN THE SKY?
ASH...
I'M NOTHING WITHOUT YOU.

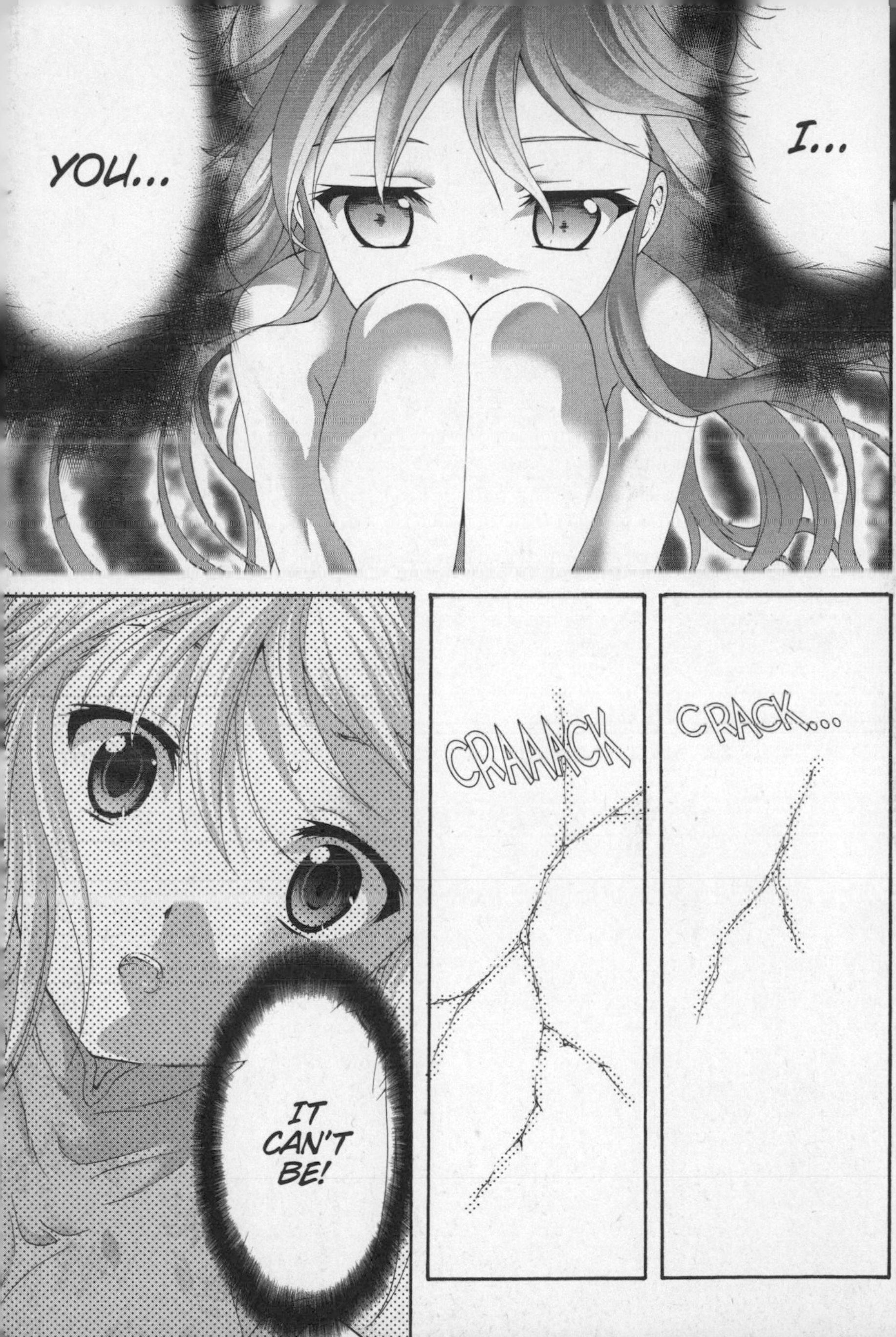
I...
YOU...
CRACK...
CRAAACK
IT CAN'T BE!

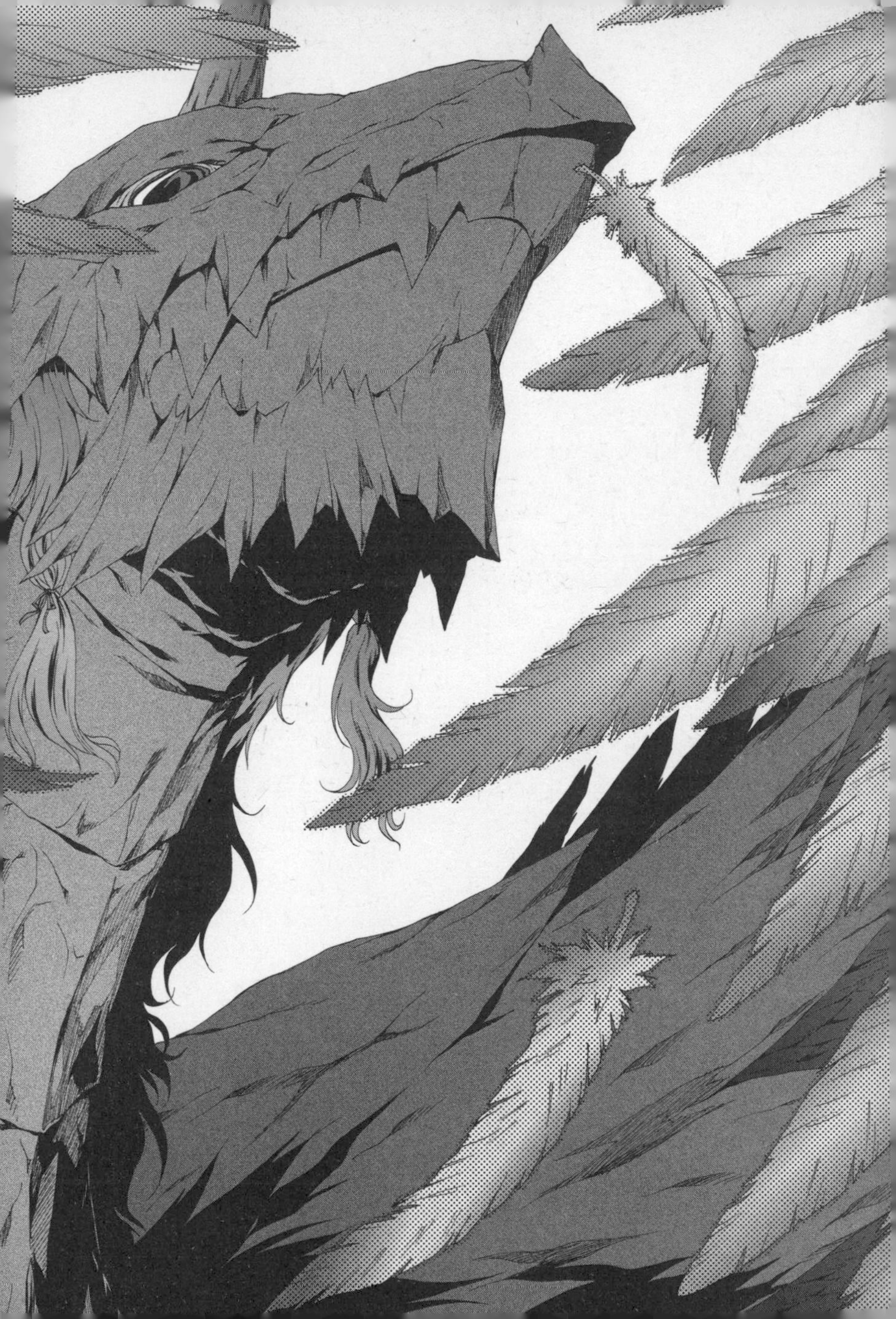

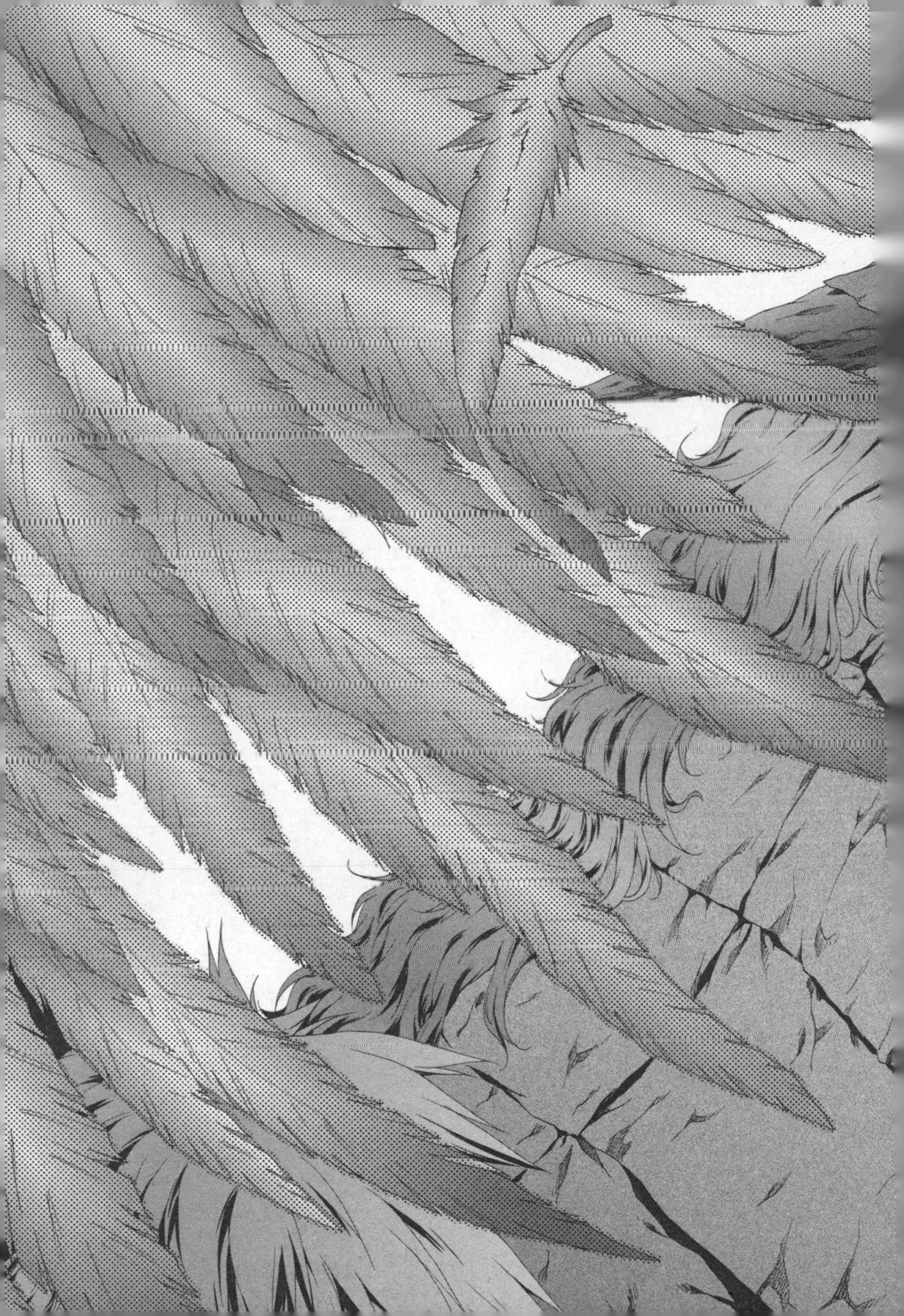

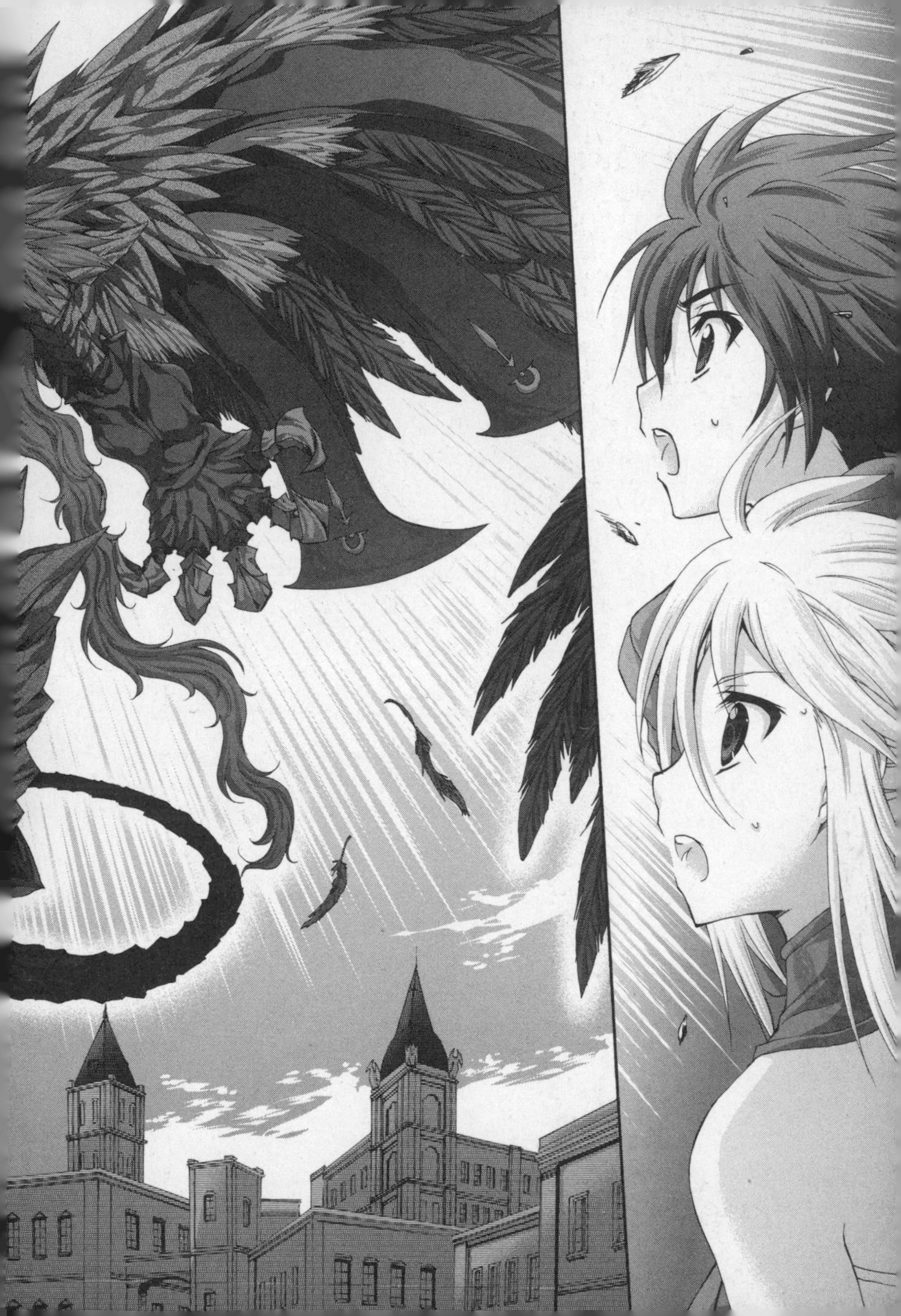

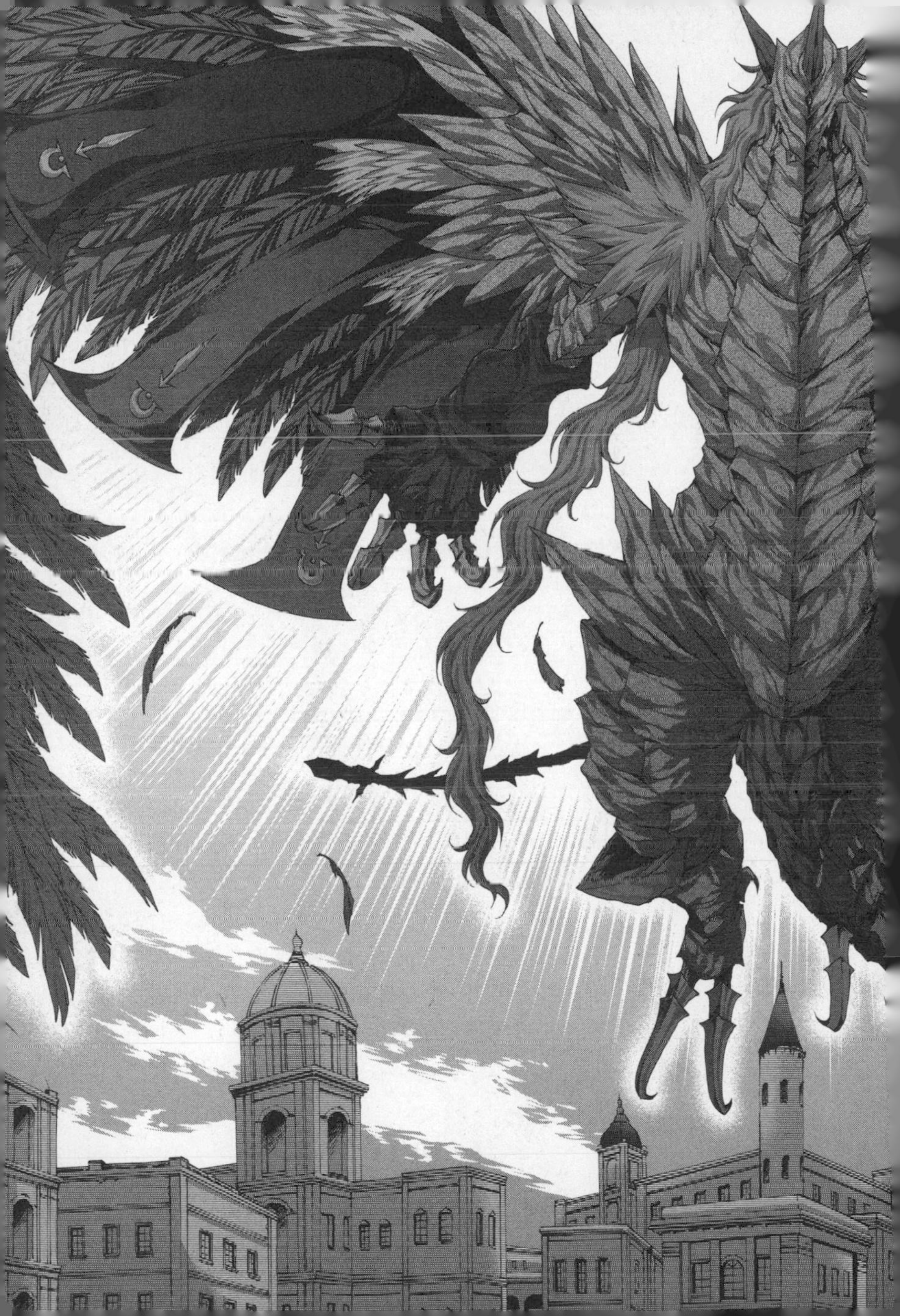

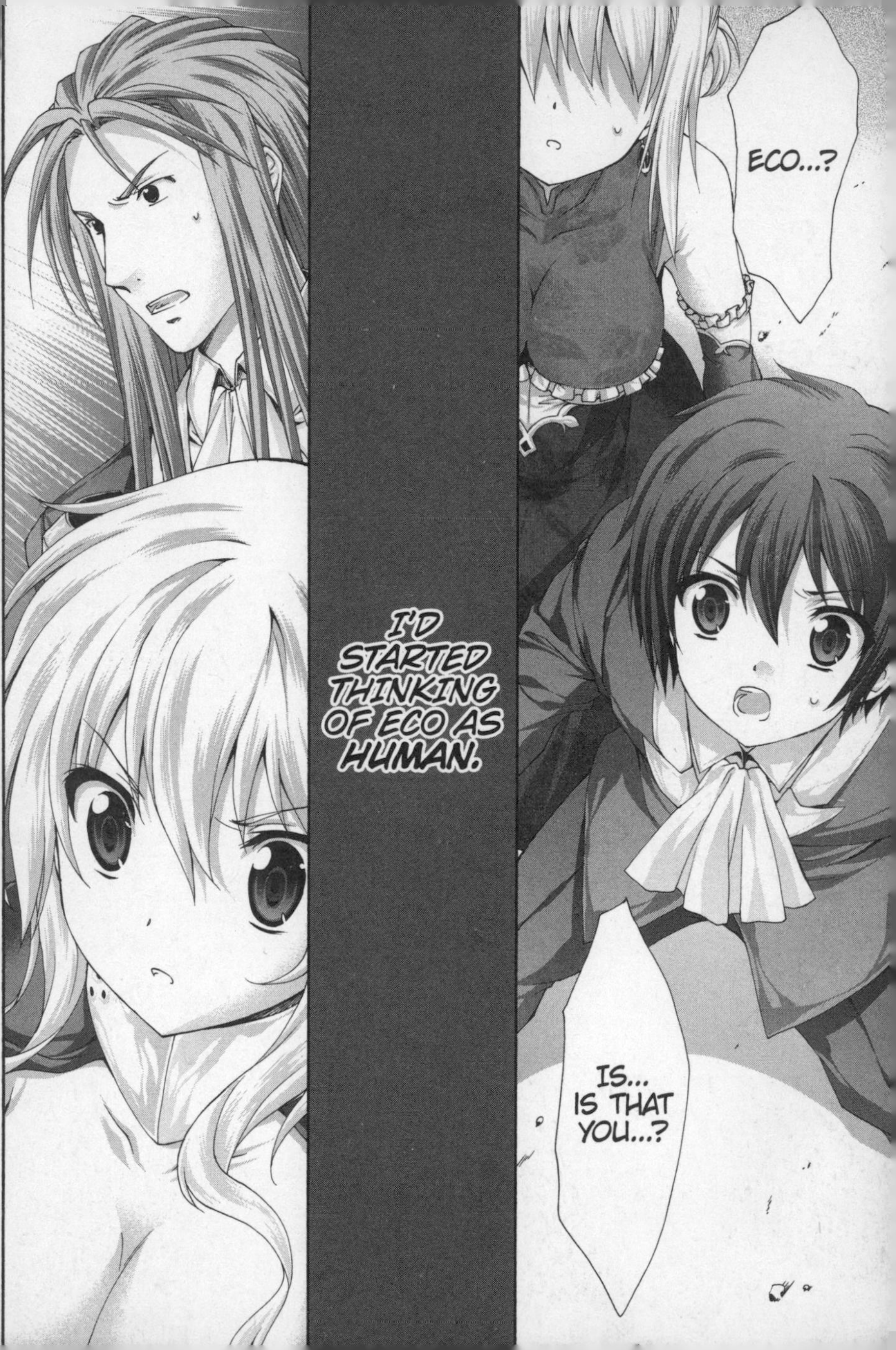
ECO...?
IS... IS THAT YOU...?
I'D STARTED THINKING OF ECO AS HUMAN.

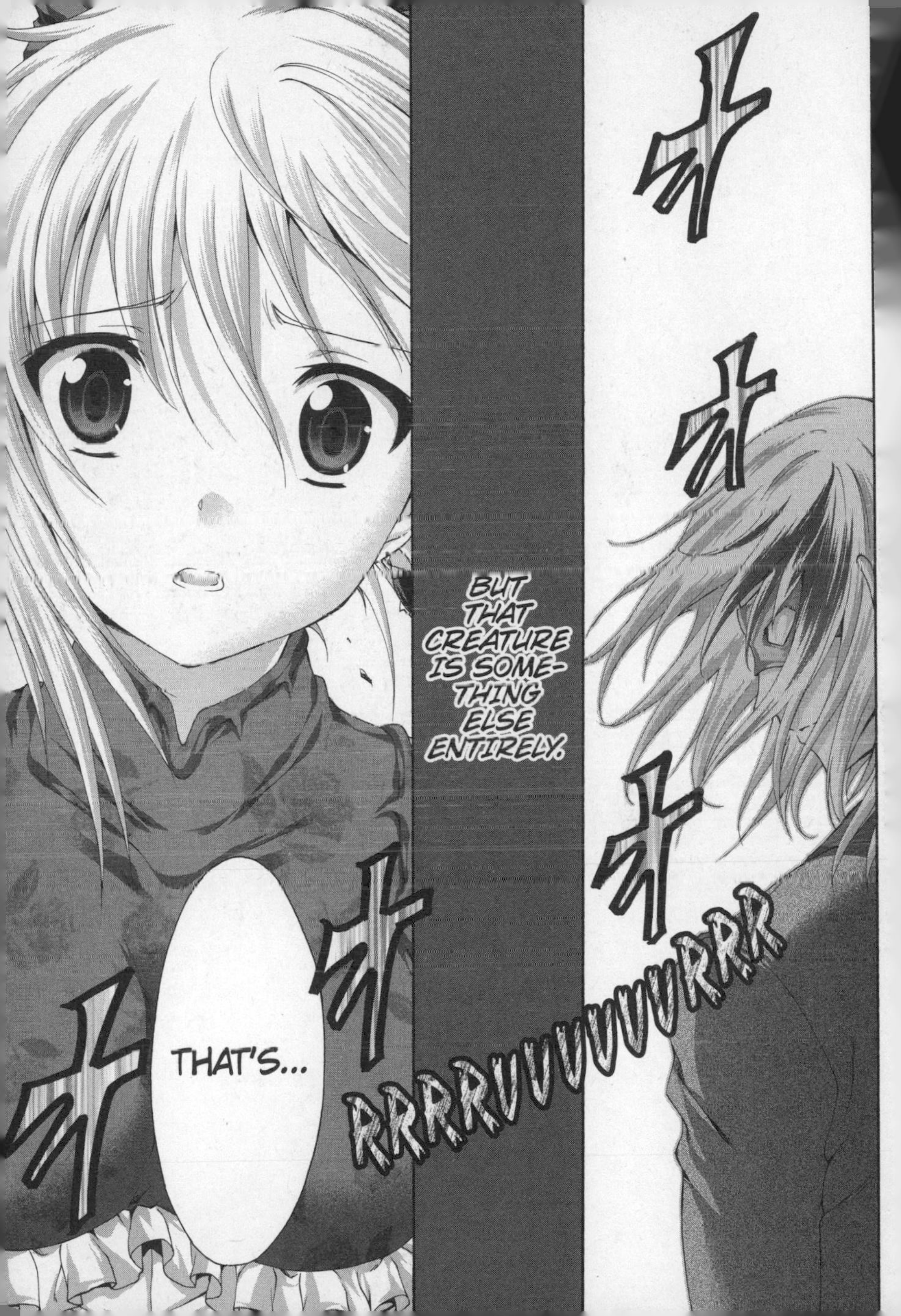
RRRRUUUUUURRR
BUT THAT CREATURE IS SOME-THING ELSE ENTIRELY.
THAT'S...

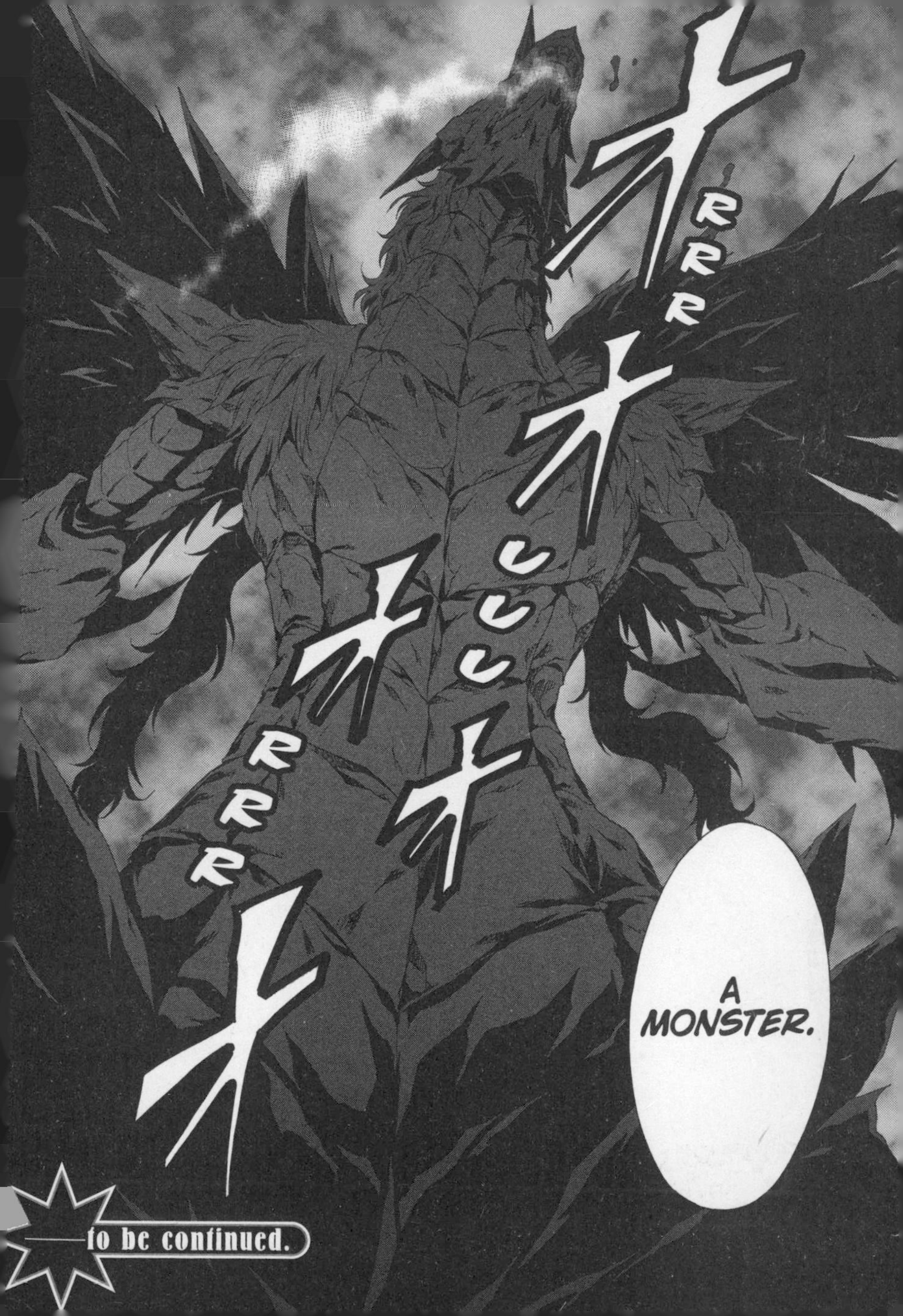
RRR
UUUU
RRR
A MONSTER.
—to be continued.

DRAGONAR
ACADEMY

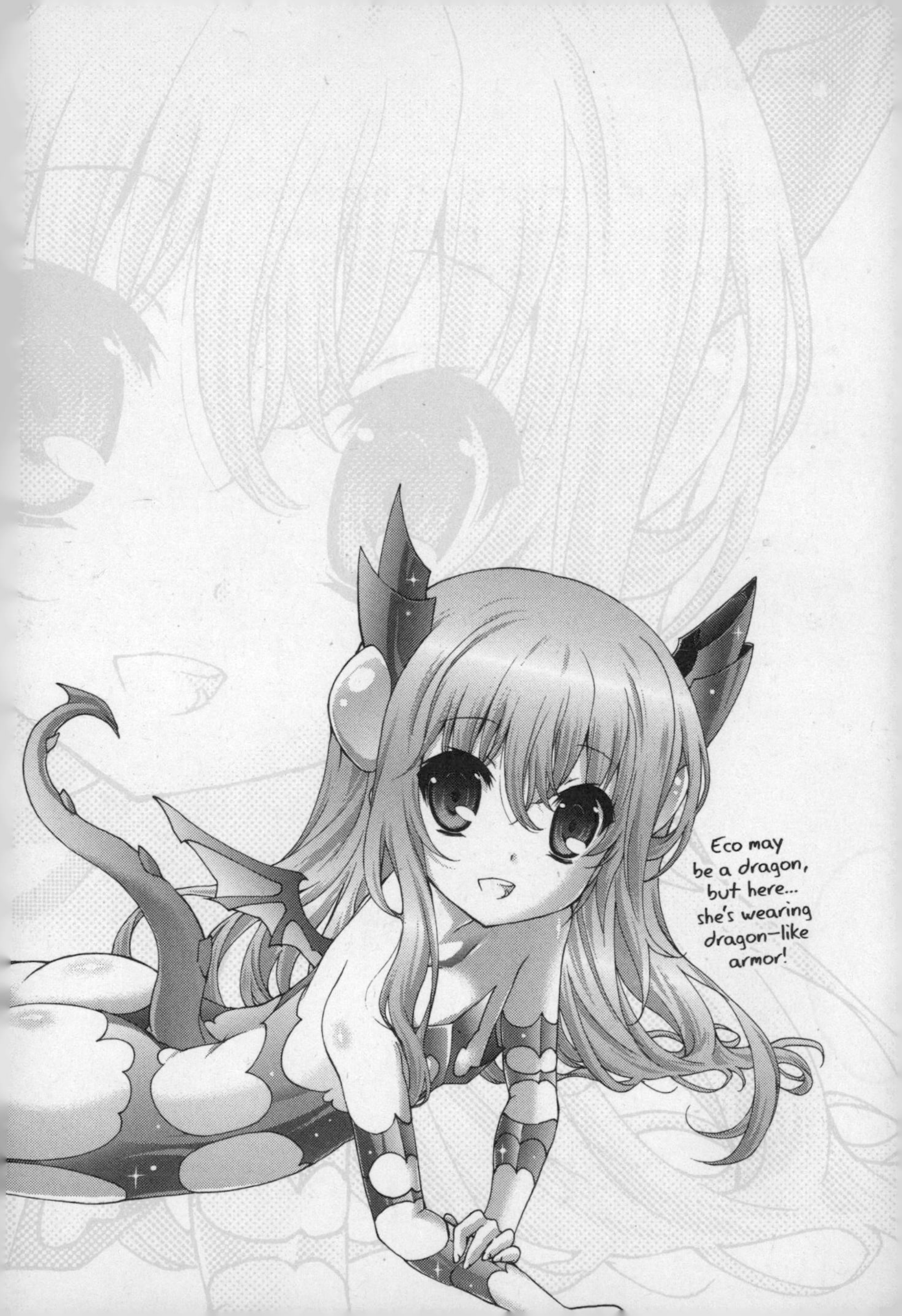
Eco may be a dragon, but here... she's wearing dragon-like armor!

AFTERWORD

It's me, RAN! Now that Eco's Awakening Arc has begun, we're approaching one of Dragonar's most exciting parts!

And we've got our first (brief!) look at Eco as a dragon, so from now on, drawing this manga will be a much bigger challenge for me. *laughs*

I promise I won't lose heart, and I'll keep doing my absolute best! It'd make me so happy if you all kept supporting and encouraging me.

See you in the next volume!

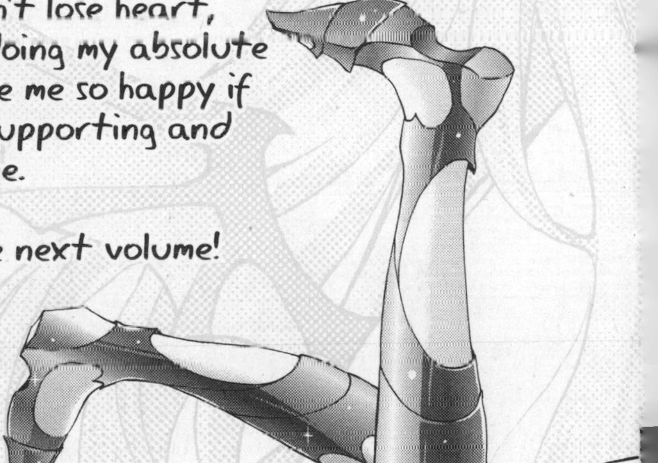

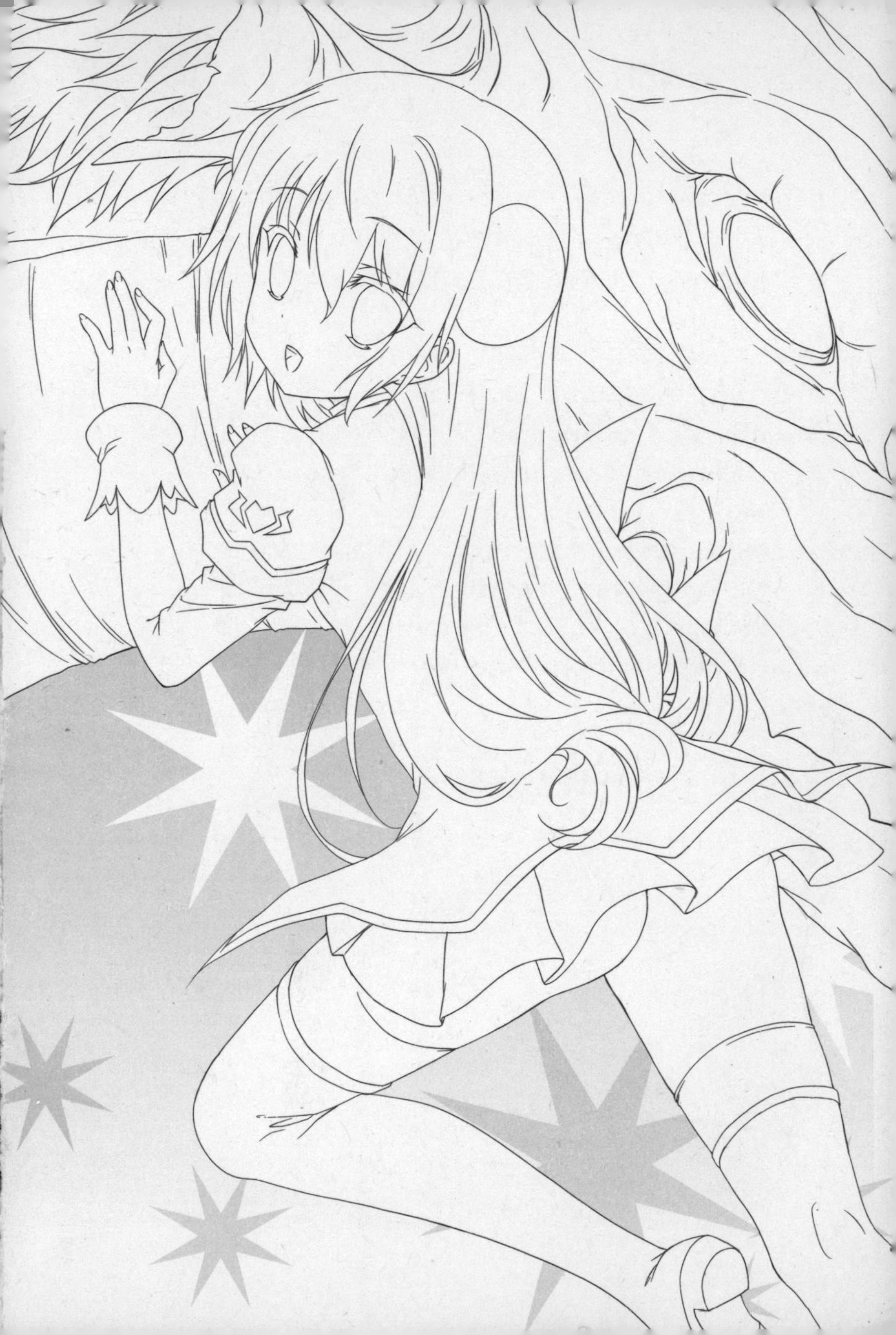